Privatization

PRIVATIZATION

A Theoretical Treatment

Dieter Bös

CLARENDON PRESS · OXFORD

1991

Oxford University Press, Walton Street, Oxford OX2 6DP
Oxford New York Toronto
Delhi Bombay Calcutta Madras Karachi
Petaling Jaya Singapore Hong Kong Tokyo
Nairobi Dar es Salaam Cape Town
Melbourne Auckland
and associated companies in
Berlin Ibadan

Oxford is a trade mark of Oxford University Press

Published in the United States
by Oxford University Press, New York

British Library Cataloguing in Publication Data
Data available
ISBN 0–19–828369–5

Library of Congress Cataloging in Publication Data
Data available
ISBN 0–19–828369–5

Printed in Great Britain by
Biddles Ltd
Guildford & King's Lynn

Preface

Privatization of public enterprises signals an advance of capitalistic thinking, as nationalization signalled an advance of socialistic thinking. It is the trust in the efficiency of markets, and the distrust in the efficiency of government, which explains the recent privatizations in many European states. The ideological background makes the topic fascinating for an economist, but also makes it necessary to proceed by means of a cool and neutral theoretical analysis to avoid any intermingling of personal value judgements and economic reasoning. This book employs the tools of the positive theory of industrial organization and the normative theory of public economics in order to build a concise framework for a theory of privatization.

The book is about privatization in Western-type economies. It concentrates on the sale of public assets in the environment of a capitalistic economy. Nevertheless, most of the theories developed or surveyed in the book should be of high interest for theoreticians and policy-makers in Eastern Europe, since privatization is one of the most important steps to be taken in the transition from a centrally-planned communist system to a decentralized market-oriented economy.

Many colleagues helped me in writing this book. It is a pleasure to thank them. First of all I would like to thank Andrew Schuller of Oxford University Press who initiated this book. Two anonymous referees of Oxford University Press helped improve the text. I am also grateful to the benevolent and critical participants in the many seminars on privatization I gave in Austria, Belgium, Germany, Israel, Japan, the Netherlands, Norway, the UK, and the USA. In Bonn, Lorenz Nett and Wolfgang Peters were discussion partners over many weeks of enjoyable joint research. Gábor Gyárfás, Elizabeth Harrison, Christian Keuschnigg, Kristina Kostial, Yew-Kwang Ng, Klaus Schmidt, Thomas Theisen, Friedrich Vogelbusch, and David Wildasin commented on an earlier draft of the book. I am also indebted to Lydia Danner and Heinz-Dieter Ecker for preparing the camera-ready manuscript and the Special Research Unit 303 at the University of Bonn for providing financial support.

Parts of this book have been published elsewhere, although they have been thoroughly revised and rewritten especially for this publication. This holds in particular for Part III ('Normative Theory'), in which various papers have been compiled into one coherent text. Nearly half of the book, however, is new text which has not appeared elsewhere, in particular the three extended surveys of theories on privatization in Part I ('Theoretical Background') and the chapters on efficiency, on regulation, and on partial privatization in Part II ('Positive Theory').

The publishers of the following papers gave permission to reproduce parts of my previous publications: Dieter Bös, 'A Theory of the Privatization of Public Enterprises', *Journal of Economics/Zeitschrift für Nationalökonomie*, Supplementum 5 (1986), 17–40; Dieter Bös, 'Privatization of Public Enterprises', *European Economic Review*, 31 (1987), 352–60; Dieter Bös, 'Welfare Effects of Privatizing Public Enterprises', in D. Bös, M. Rose, and Ch. Seidl (eds.), *Welfare and Efficiency in Public Economics* (Springer, Berlin–Heidelberg, 1988), 339–62; Dieter Bös and Wolfgang Peters, 'Privatization, Internal Control and Internal Regulation', *Journal of Public Economics*, 36 (1988), 231–58; Dieter Bös and Wolfgang Peters, 'Privatization, Efficiency and Market Structure', in B. Rudolph and J. Wilhelm (eds.), *Bankpolitik, finanzielle Unternehmensführung und die Theorie der Finanzmärkte: Festschrift für H. J. Krümmel* (Duncker & Humblot, Berlin, 1988), 367–92; Dieter Bös, 'Privatization of Public Firms: A Government–Trade Union–Private Shareholder Cooperative Game', in M. Neumann and K. W. Roskamp (eds.), *Public Finance and the Performance of Enterprises* (Wayne State University Press, Detroit, 1989), 343–63; Dieter Bös, 'Arguments on Privatization', in G. Fels and G. von Fürstenberg (eds.), *A Supply-Side Agenda for Germany?* (Springer, Berlin–Heidelberg, 1989), 217–45; Dieter Bös and Wolfgang Peters, 'A Principal–Agent Approach on Manager Effort and Control in Privatized and Public Firms', mimeo (University of Bonn, 1990); Dieter Bös and Lorenz Nett, 'Privatization, Price Regulation, and Market Entry: An Asymmetric Multistage Duopoly Model', *Journal of Economics/Zeitschrift für Nationalökonomie*, 51 (1990), 221–57.

Where passages of this book reproduce material of papers jointly written with Nett or with Peters, this is always explicitly mentioned at the beginning of the relevant passage; in the Normative Theory part of the book this is done on p. 223, n. 8.

Dieter Bös
Bonn, October 1990

Contents

Contents

1 Arguments on Privatization

Great Britain and France are the pioneers in the present wave of privatization in Western European economies. In Great Britain vital industries like telecommunications, gas, and electricity have been sold to the public. In France large industrial and financial conglomerates have constituted the main bulk of privatized enterprises. Other countries have been more hesitant to follow suit. West Germany, Italy, and the Netherlands have started to sell parts of the shares they hold in various industrial companies or banks.[1] In these countries nobody seriously considers privatizing large public utilities like telecommunications and postal services. If the public utilities are considered inefficient, programs of internal reorganization are launched instead of programs of privatization (as, for instance, with the telecommunications and postal services in West Germany and the Netherlands). Some other European countries, such as Belgium, the Scandinavian countries, and Austria, even lag behind Germany, Italy, or the Netherlands in privatization. Sweden and Denmark do not privatize because traditionally in these social democratic countries not too many firms have been nationalized. Austria hesitated in privatizing for a long time, in spite of its large sector of nationalized enterprises; meanwhile, however, major privatizations are being planned for the next years.

The recent peaceful revolutions in many Eastern European countries, moreover, launched privatization campaigns in these countries as a part of their move from a communistic to a capitalistic economic system. It is to be hoped that these countries will be able to learn from the Western privatization activities. However, it must not be overlooked that the first steps of privatization in a previously communistic state differ decisively from the sale of public enterprises in a predominantly capitalistic economy.[2] Typically there is no established stock market, the evaluation of the firms' value is very difficult, experienced managers are missing, the employees are always waiting for orders and without any self-

---

[1] DM9.4 billion is the total revenue which the West German Federal government raised by selling parts of its ownership rights between 1982 (when the Kohl government came into power) and 1989. British Gas alone raised £5.6 billion. For surveys of West German discussions on privatization see Knauss (1988a,b).

[2] See e.g. Frydman and Rapaczynski (1990), Hinds (1990), Kornai (1990), Lipton and Sachs (1990).

initiative, etc. In these states it will take time for the structures of
market economies to prevail in such a way as we usually presuppose
when constructing our (Western) models on industrial organization
and on public economics.

The word 'privatization' has many different meanings.[3] In
this book we concentrate on one particular concept only: the sale of
public assets. Other forms of privatization, like contracting out, de-
bureaucratization, promotion of competition by market processes,
'cold privatization', etc., are not considered.

Privatization is the partial or total transfer of an enterprise
from public to private ownership. As such, it is the precise reverse
of nationalization. Neither procedure is embarked upon primarily
for economic reasons, though there has often been an attempt to
include an economic rationale in the decision.[4] However, as this is
a book written by an economist, it deals with economic theories of
privatization. This does not mean that I am unaware of ideological, purely political, or other arguments in favor of privatization:
indeed, some short remarks on political and ideological reasons for
privatization will help start this chapter. Then, however, I will
turn quickly to the economic reasoning.

Needless to say, it is impossible to have a clear-cut dichotomization between political and ideological reasoning on the one hand
and economic reasoning on the other. Hence I label an argument
as 'political and ideological' if, in my opinion, the argument mainly
emphasizes the consequences of privatization in the political process and its ideological desirability from the point of view of some
party-political program. Therefore, I consider a reduction of trade
union power primarily as a shift in political power. This does not
mean, however, that one can ignore the serious economic, in particular distributional, consequences which may result from such a
political move.

1.1   Political and Ideological Reasoning

Large-scale privatization changes the *distribution of power* within a
society. Decisions on prices, investment, and technology are taken
out of the domain of public bureaucrats and policy-makers and
shifted to people who are responsible to private shareholders. Thus
large-scale privatization leads to a new distribution between private

[3] Thiemeyer (1986: 7–10) enumerates fifteen concepts of 'privatization'.
[4] For nationalization this argument can be found in Reid and Allen (1970).

and public economic power. Socialist ways of thinking are replaced by capitalist ones, as stressed for instance by Howell (1981).

Whether the reader welcomes all of the shifts of economic power which result from privatization depends on his political position. The trade union's influence, for instance, will typically be reduced by privatization. By way of an example, it has been argued that the privatization of the British electricity industry aims primarily at breaking the power of the miners' union because privatized electricity generation companies would import cheaper coal from abroad, thus reducing the size of the British coal industry and, consequently, reducing the importance of the miners' union.[5] Similarly, the first wave of privatization in West Germany 25 years ago was intended to reduce union power. The present strength of German trade unions, which are adamantly opposed to privatization and exert a strong influence on political parties, is a major impediment to any privatization in West Germany (von Loesch, 1983; Vogelsang, 1988). The German trade unions' opposition to privatization results mainly from the fear that employees in public firms might lose their privileges. These firms' employees may have to face wage reduction in case of privatization (Windisch, 1987: 23). Even worse problems would arise in the German railway and postal systems where many employees have civil servant status (Vogelsang, 1988).

The international distribution of power may also be influenced by privatization if too many shares of the privatized firm are bought by foreign investors. One should not forget that nationalization often has been conceived as a means of countering large-scale private enterprise, most of which is multinational in operation (Attali, 1978; Charzat, 1981; Holland, 1975, 1978). In Great Britain and France the government tends to keep a 'golden share', i.e. a veto right against undesirable takeovers and changes in control. (For details see Graham and Prosser, 1987: 36–8.)

Let us now turn to the most celebrated ideological argument: *democratization*. Conservatives regard privatization as a means of democratization because of the resulting more widespread ownership of shares. The 'man in the street' is given the opportunity

---

[5] It may be noted, however, that a high-percentage replacement of British coal by foreign coal would considerably increase the price of imported coal. Thus British coal could prove more competitive then than it does now on the basis of the present prices. Moreover, if a privatized electricity industry tried to replace British coal by foreign coal, the port unions could go on strike to help their miner colleagues.

to own parts of industries of national importance. Power in the economy is reallocated by replacing the government's sole ownership with broad-based private ownership. Moreover, distributional objectives may be attained by selling ownership rights to *many* private individuals, instead of only to a few institutional shareholders. Furthermore, a subsequent left-wing government cannot easily renationalize a firm if many shares are held by lower-income-earners and employees of the firm.

Therefore, the firms to be privatized are typically reorganized as joint-stock companies and the shares are sold to the public. Persons of modest means are attracted to these issues through appropriate government incentives. The typical incentive is the sale of shares at a price well below the attainable market price, as was done in Austria, Germany, and – more recently – Britain (Yarrow, 1986).

With respect to the practical success of a policy of 'people's capitalism', we face ambiguous evidence. Some early privatization activities in Great Britain faced the problem that the small investors sold their shares shortly after purchasing them in order to enjoy a quick profit. 'Within one month of flotation, the number of shareholders in Amersham had fallen from 62,000 to 10,000; within one year of flotation, the number had fallen from 150,000 to 26,000 in Cable and Wireless (first tranche) and from 158,000 to 27,000 in British Aerospace' (Yarrow, 1986: 357).[6] The resale in shares such as British Telecom, British Gas, and the Trustee Savings Bank has not occurred so quickly.[7] First, the government learned from its earlier mistakes. New shareholders were given loyalty bonuses (vouchers to set against phone or gas bills, one-for-ten bonuses) if they held on to their investment for some time, usually three years. Second, the early privatization activities reached sophisticated speculative shareholders whereas subsequent privatizations reached a broader public. Purchase of shares was made as easy as possible, whereas resale requires a broker.

It remains to be seen how successful the 'new' British policy will be in the long run. British Telecom in early 1989 still had 1.2 million 'small' shareholders out of 2.3 million who bought shares in 1984.[8] British Gas started with 4.5 million shareholders in De-

---

[6] See also Mayer and Meadowcroft (1985: 50–2).

[7] I am grateful to Kai-Uwe Kühn, Colin Mayer, John Vickers, and George Yarrow for informing me about finer details of the present British privatization activities.

[8] See the annual reports of British Telecom.

cember 1986 and had 2.5 million shareholders in April 1990.[9] In both cases nearly 50 percent of the shareholders sold their shares within a time span of 4–5 years. Only time can show how successful the policy will be — for instance after the bonuses have expired. The West German experience of the early 1960s showed that in the long run the small-income shareholders did not retain their shares; meanwhile the shares are held by 'groups and persons which in any case hold part of their wealth in the form of shares' (von Loesch, 1983: 20). Similar experiences have been made in Austria: 'It is easier to find shares for the people than people for the shares' (J. Bös, 1956: 1).

The French policy of people's shares was successful from the very beginning: 13 months after privatization 78 percent of the buyers were still holding their shares of St Gobain; 11 months after privatization 76 percent still had their shares of Paribas (Ministère de l'Economie, des Finances et de la Privatisation, 1988). The disturbance in the stock exchange in late 1987 led to a French discussion on how to insure lower-income shareholders against possible losses. One of the various possibilities mentioned was the interesting proposal to couple the sale of shares with a resale option.

It has fascinated me for a long time that conservatives want to promote democratization by privatization whereas socialists want to promote democratization by nationalization. The paradox is solved, of course, by noting the different meanings which have been given to democratization. Conservatives stress widespread ownership of shares; socialists emphasize democratic participation in the firm. Their keyword is 'self-government'; as Delors (1978) puts it, 'at the base of the pyramid, in the enterprise, the essential self-government function should be assigned to workers and management to extend the idea of community life'. However, the socialist arguments for self-government will not convince any committed adherent to privatization. He will not share the belief that nationalization might substitute co-operation for conflict and competition, a belief which has long been held in the socialist discussions of nationalization.[10] Even proponents of these ideas are aware of the difficulties in actually bringing about such fundamental changes in the functioning of firms and stress the danger of enterprises becoming politically oriented and bureaucratically dominated.[11]

---

[9] See Pint (1990) and the annual reports of British Gas.

[10] See for instance the survey of the history of the discussion of nationalization in the British Labour Party in Tivey (1966).

[11] Moreover, there are many alternative means of democratization within

Before concluding the treatment of political arguments on privatization, we should discuss the influence of the structure of government. In West Germany, for instance, many public enterprises are owned by states (Länder) and local communities. Needless to mention, social democratic state governments or social democratic mayors of large cities have no intention of privatizing. However, the conservative states in West Germany also typically stick to their public firms. The refusal of the then conservative government of Lower Saxony to sell its minority participation in the Volkswagenwerk and the well-known position of Franz Josef Strauss both exemplified a general hostility to privatization. Hence in West Germany there are constraints on a policy of privatization which do not exist in a country like the United Kingdom, where policy toward privatization is controlled entirely by the central government (Heald, 1988).

1.2   Economic Reasoning[12]

Let us begin with a provocative question: why don't we privatize national defense or the judiciary? The reason is a basic principal–agent problem which would arise between a government and some private military or jurisdictional units. Even if those units were carefully monitored and regulated by the government, we would fear private courts selling sentences in exchange for some sort of payment or private armies of mercenaries being interested in the promotion rather than the prevention of war. The military aspect also has a direct relevance for the present debate on privatization: public property of armament factories can be justified because it enhances the ability of the government to prevent illegal exports of armaments. This is a standard argument in Norway, although Norway has gone through the unwelcome experience of having its public Kongsberg Vapenfabrikk sell strategic technical equipment

privately owned enterprises, as the recent discussions on codetermination of employees and shareholders show. For further references see Backhaus (1979) and McCain (1980).

[12] A selection of literature on the economic arguments for privatization includes Beesley (1981), Brittan (1986), Hayek (1960: 253–8), Heald and Steel (1981, 1984), Kay, Mayer, and Thompson (1986), Kay and Thompson (1986), LeGrand and Robinson (1984), Olsen (1974: 327–31), Thiemeyer and Quaden (1986), Vickers and Yarrow (1985, 1988a,b), Walsh (1978), Windisch (1987), and the contributions in *Fiscal Studies* (1984, 1985).

to the Soviet Union. (Austria went through similar experiences when its public steel industry, VŒSt, sold arms to Libya and Iran.)

Turning to public utilities, here too we face principal–agent problems – at least when the government and the firm pursue different objectives. Ideally, therefore, privatization presupposes that the government is willing to accept the firm's objective, i.e. profit maximization. Other government objectives which a public firm might have been instructed to follow should then be pursued through taxation or subsidization policies, or given up completely. As we shall see in what follows, if public monopolies are privatized, the government often might not be willing to accept the results of profit maximization. However, similar problems could arise for firms in competitive industries, for instance if the government were to prefer those firms to charge lower prices to poor customers, or not to dismiss too many employees.

The examples of the preceding sentence illustrate that not only efficiency, but also redistribution of real incomes and stabilization impacts, are relevant to the decision to privatize public firms. Therefore in what follows we shall deal with economic arguments on efficiency, on distribution, and on stabilization.

1.2.1 Efficiency Arguments

Privatization can be justified on the grounds that it increases the *technological efficiency* of operations. Many empirical studies comparing private and public firms confirm that private enterprises are more efficient than public enterprises producing the same goods or very close substitutes, given the same or very similar technology, regulatory constraints, and financial capabilities. As could be expected, however, some counter-evidence also exists which shows exactly the opposite. Moreover, some further empirical studies report ambiguous results: the public firm is more efficient according to one indicator, whereas the private firm is more efficient according to another indicator. A survey of various empirical studies will be given in one of the next chapters.[13]

The main reason for increases in efficiency is the change in management behavior. There are several explanations for such a change.[14] First, privatization is accompanied by a reduction in

---

[13] See Sects. 3.2.1 and 3.2.2 below.

[14] I gratefully acknowledge an interesting discussion with Patrick Minford on this point.

government intervention. Second, the management of a privatized firm will look carefully at the market value of the shares arising from the discipline of the stock market. Third, the management has less power to influence government policy, because the close political connection between management and government will no longer exist. If the lower efficiency of a public firm is due to red tape, market forces should be welcomed for freeing the firm's management from some of the former bureaucratic constraints. If the lower efficiency of a public firm results from a socially desirable contribution to government objectives other than allocation, for instance income redistribution, then the government could think of regulating the firm even after total or partial privatization.[15]

Let us next turn to an argument which refers to *allocative efficiency*. A market structure argument has been used widely in the nationalization debates. It justifies public utilities on the basis that they are natural monopolies: it is cheaper for goods to be produced by a monopoly than by many firms, because the monopoly operates under economies of scale and scope. If there are sunk costs associated with market entry, the incumbent can sustain its monopoly position, and in such a case an unregulated private enterprise would exploit the market. Establishing a public enterprise should ensure economically or politically desired prices and at the same time guarantee the reliability of supply.

This can be a significant argument against privatization, or at least against complete deregulation. If a natural monopoly is privatized and if there are sunk entry costs, market forces will not prevent the monopoly from keeping its monopolistic position and exploiting this position in order to maximize profits. If the government is not willing to accept such a result, either it can refuse to privatize the monopoly, or it can regulate the privatized monopoly with respect to prices, quantities, rate of return, etc. Such regula-

---

[15] In recent studies on the performance of public firms, the empirical input–output figures of the most efficient public firms are taken as the basis of what is called a 'best practice function'. Recent papers are Färe and Grosskopf (1987), Perelman and Pestieau (1988), Tulkens (1986a,b). For a comparison of these three papers see Bös (1988a); for practical applications of these and related approaches to public transportation see Perelman and Thiry (1989). Such a procedure presupposes that there is at least one public firm in the sample which works efficiently in a practical sense. So there is always 'efficiency' in at least some public firms, although, most probably, the performance of even the best performing public firms would have been improved under private management. Hence, the concept of a 'best practice function' cannot be taken as a general justification of public ownership.

tory measures have been applied, for instance, to British Telecom and British Gas after their privatization.[16] These firms have been regulated according to a formula suggested by Littlechild (1983): a price index of monopolistically supplied services of the firm must not exceed the retail price index minus a politically chosen constant which intends to measure productivity increases. The constraint became known as '$RPI - X$' where RPI stands for retail price index and X is a politically chosen constant. The recent American discussion calls that a 'price cap regulation'.

However, any regulation of a privatized firm poses a dilemma for the government: if the government privatizes some enterprise, it wants to rely on the market and therefore should not engage in further regulation. How can the government then forestall unacceptable profit increases from monopolistic positions? One way would be for the government to attempt to promote competition, supporting private market entry so as to reduce the privatized firm's monopoly power. In the case of British Telecom, for instance, Mercury has been installed as a private competitor of the privatized firm.[17] However, practical experiences in this field have not always been satisfactory. In some cases there are not enough market entrants, or the privatized firm still holds special patents. In other cases there may be legal barriers which hinder entry by private firms. Even if new private firms enter the market, in most cases it is not perfect competition which results from promoting market entry, but either a market with a strong market leader and some adjusting followers, or an oligopolistic market where it is impossible to predict *a priori* whether high-profit collusion or low-profit competition will prevail.

It is interesting that the nationalization debate also has its market entry argument. As a case in point, the Labour Party Green Paper (1973) proposed the nationalization of 20–25 of the 100 leading manufacturing enterprises. This was to give the government an established position in the market using capitalistic market mechanisms to fight capitalistic (and foreign) market exploitation. Similar arguments influenced the French nationalization activities. In theory, public enterprises as market entrants are perceived to be centers of largely independent decision-making authority oriented toward welfare optimization instead of profit

---

[16] For details see Vickers and Yarrow (1985: 39–43), Vickers and Yarrow (1988*b*), and Beesley and Littlechild (1989).

[17] See Yarrow (1986). In a White Paper (1991) the UK government declared its firm intention to end the duopoly policy in telecommunications.

maximization. In practice, however, public firms which compete with private firms in oligopolistic markets typically behave like a private firm: British Petrol or British Airways, when they were still publicly owned, provide good examples.

To conclude the allocative argumentation, let me mention the problem of the *quality of public supply*. It has often been suggested that privatization or deregulation leads to a deterioration in quality. This case was put forward when the US airlines were deregulated. In the UK recently, similar accusations allude to the deterioration of telecommunications services. Privatization is likely to lead to quality deterioration whenever high quality is due to particular social obligations which a public firm is supposed to follow. Good examples seem to be the maintenance of public telephone booths, in particular in rural areas, or transportation services at off-peak hours, for instance at night.

I have dealt with this problem in a recent paper with Peters (Bös and Peters, 1988a). In that paper we assume that responsibilities in the privatized firm are shared between the board and the technological management, where the board makes the more strategic decisions about the firm's policy and the 'less important' decisions, like quality and the extent of firm-internal control, are left to the technological management. Within this management, privatization leads to partial or total displacement of public bureaucrats by private technocrats. Both groups are interested in producing high quality, but quality can be increased only if the expenses for control within the firm are increased. Public managers are inclined to accept more bureaucratic control within the firm if this brings about higher quality. Private managers are inclined to regard a high level of control as bureaucratic red tape, and thus to reduce over-bureaucratization at the expense of the quality of supply. Hence the reduction of quality can be found both in theory and in practice. In the theoretical model, it is simply the price for reducing the bureaucratic control in the firm.

1.2.2   Distributional Arguments

Privatization will increase private capital income in the economy, while nationalization will reduce it. Privatization does not simply transform government capital income into private income. Higher efficiency and profit orientation in the privatized firm will typically lead to higher profits than before and therefore the total sum of capital income will increase. The capital/labor income ratio could

also increase, and this effect might be accentuated by possible reductions of the trade unions' influence in the privatized firms.

However, we should not forget that the acquirer of new shares
has to pay the issue price. If the issue price equals the market
value of the share, then the income of the acquirer is not improved: rather, the discounted sum of dividend incomes (= value
of the share) simply replaces the money or other assets which have
been used to buy the share. Consider the case where only portfolio substitution is involved, with the private sector absorbing less
government debt and more assets of privatized enterprises than
without denationalization. The sum total of interest payments
and after-tax profits received by that sector will increase if the return on privately owned capital increases more than the interest on
government debt declines as a result of this alteration in portfolio
composition. The higher return on privately owned capital can, for
example, result from productivity increases owing to privatization
or from increasing share prices on the stock market. However, it
is sometimes claimed that persons of modest means and limited
access to capital markets can be induced to save more by the announcement of 'people's share issues' and the favorable conditions
with which such shares can be subscribed to by new investors. In
that case, if the additional private saving is not offset by increased
government deficits and if total productive investment rises, both
capital and labor incomes will go up. Hence the effect on the distribution of capital and labor incomes will differ from case to case
and will also depend on how far the issue price falls below the
market value of the shares.

As with the ideological and allocative arguments, once again a
similar, although reverse, argument holds for nationalization. We
hypothesized that nationalization reduces private capital incomes.
However, the government must pay compensation to the former
shareholders. In cases of 'full compensation', ideally the act of
nationalization itself would have no influence whatsoever on the
given distribution of incomes or wealth. The picture changes if the
compensation chosen is too high or too low. In the first case, the
former shareholders are the winners of the nationalization campaign. However, even in the second case they are not necessarily
the losers because what is 'too low' for a small investor may not be
'too low' for a large investor owning a block of stocks that would
be difficult to sell except at a substantial discount. Under such
circumstances large investors may be glad to be relieved of the
ownership of deficit or low-profit firms and to invest their compensation in fast-growing industries.

When dealing with the effects of privatization on the *personal* distribution of incomes, one should ask whether the intended widespread ownership of shares is a good policy for a redistribution of incomes. I do not believe so. Hence I dealt with 'people's capitalism' as a politically and ideologically grounded government instrument. Even if a broad public is enticed into buying shares, it will not be the poor, but the medium- and higher-income-earners who become shareholders. In the normative part of this book I shall show that in a welfare-economic framework it is not possible to argue that the poor should always be given more shares than the rich (see Section 14.3 below).

Distributional effects of privatization and nationalization are not restricted to the shift in ownership or to the problems of setting issue price or compensation. Contrary to private firms, public enterprises are often instructed to reduce the prices of goods which are demanded mainly by lower-income-earners, thereby influencing the personal distribution of *real* incomes. The extent of such distributional pricing policies will be reduced by privatization. Should this development be welcomed as an advantage of privatization, as many economists are wont to do? Should the implied reduction of internal cross-subsidization be considered as a favorable efficiency increase or as an undesired reduction of redistribution of real incomes? Let me present the arguments which favor the abolition of distributional pricing policies and afterwards make clear why I do not necessarily believe in these arguments.

(i)   First, *liberal economists* often oppose distributionally modified public pricing. They view progressive income taxation or income subsidies as the most effective instruments of income redistribution and wish to restrict public sector pricing to allocative objectives. ('Why do you want to favor poor people simply because they go by railway? If you regard them as poor give them money', as Alan A. Walters formulated it in a personal discussion with the author some years ago.)

The traditional liberals argue that income taxation distorts the labor–leisure decision only, whereas distributional public prices additionally distort relative prices throughout the economy. They contend that a rich man, reflecting upon his labor–leisure choice, considers not only the marginal income tax rate on additional income, but also that he has to pay more for certain goods than a poor man. By whatever means he is deprived of a dollar, the disincentive effect on his labor effort will be the same. Hence public pricing is an inferior instrument of redistribution. For any degree of redistribution it leads to the same welfare losses as an income tax, which arise from distorting labor–leisure choices, but also to additional welfare losses because of the distorted relative prices for goods (Ng, 1984).

However, in a second-best framework it can be shown that this conclusion is not valid. If we assume a social welfare function with the usual distributional weighting of individual incomes, and assume that income taxation and public pricing both are available policy instruments, then the level of social welfare which can be achieved must be greater than or at least the same as that which could be attained if an income tax were the only policy instrument. This result takes account of the disincentive effects of both progressive taxation and distributional pricing. There is, however, a special case where optimal prices equal marginal costs. This implies that pricing is restricted to allocation and redistribution is achieved through income taxation alone. The optimality of marginal-cost pricing, however, depends on very restrictive assumptions, namely, constant returns to scale and identical utility functions, which are weakly separable between labor and all goods together.[18] These assumptions are highly implausible. Normally, therefore, income taxation will not be the only, and hence universally superior, instrument of redistribution (Bös, 1984).[19]

(ii) *Social democrats*, on the other hand, oppose distributional public prices because they do not depend on the financial status of individuals, as does, for example, the income tax. The rich man in the second-class railway compartment offers a good example. Moreover, distributional price differentiation typically implies some quality differentiation which has often been criticized for ideological reasons. Objections have been based on the ideological appeal of uniform public supply of schooling, health, etc.

However, there are counter-arguments to these objections. Quality differentiation can be restricted to a few classes of different goods, or even totally avoided if it seems appropriate for distributional reasons. Moreover, distributional pricing can be tied to individual income by using an explicit means test: only income earners who pass a means test are eligible to buy at a lower price. There exist many examples of the practical relevance of such a

[18] This is the case if the marginal rate of substitution between any two commodities is independent of the labor supply. See, for instance, Atkinson and Stiglitz (1980: 435–7).

[19] Ng (1984) regards the use of a second-best policy, such as outlined in the text, as largely infeasible due to informational and administrative problems and political resistance.

pricing scheme, for instance cheaper basic fees of telephones, or reduced railway fares of low-income-earners.

It should be noted, finally, that the overall distributional consequences of privatization and nationalization need more explicit study.[20] Littlechild (1979: 29) concluded that 'nationalisation is a means of redistribution which is not conducive to informed debate, ... which inevitably leads to "unauthorised" redistributions, (and) is inferior to other, more explicit, methods of redistribution'. If this pessimistic conclusion is correct, then privatization need not necessarily imply a reduction of redistribution, but in any case a shift to a more explicit redistribution, which is to be welcomed. More detailed studies on the topic are still missing.

1.2.3   Stabilization Arguments

The long-standing planning tradition in some European economies, primarily France and the Netherlands, leads to heavy emphasis on the role of public enterprises in planning and stabilization. The French socialist author Attali (1978: 39) concluded that planning can be performed successfully only in case of 'control by the state of at least 50 percent of investment. That is the reason why in our Common Programme in France, we propose to nationalize nine of the main private enterprise groups ...'. Tinbergen (1967: 206) argued that 'the existence of a public sector of some size is a favourable basis for anti-cyclic policies in the field of investment'. It is well-known that the recent literature generally is very critical of the success chances of anti-cyclical policies. The political business cycle was only one model to damage the trust in the success of stabilization policies. The rational expectations approach also did its part to place stabilization policies in a bad light.

Moreover, anti-cyclical variation of public labor inputs and public prices has often been advocated. In long recessions, however, these policies can become counter-productive, maintaining economic structures instead of allowing the necessary changes. In the European steel industry, for example, there have been many situations since 1970 when these problems have arisen. This is exactly where the arguments in favor of privatization come in. Too much stabilization commitment in the long run cannot be combined with successful management of a firm. Unpopular measures,

---

[20] As Littlechild (1979: 29) observed, 'the pattern and cost of income redistribution consequent upon nationalisation is neither well known to, nor explicitly approved by, society as a whole'.

like the dismissal of employees, can best be performed by private firms which are not obligated to labor-market objectives. Like it or not, the long-run success of private capitalism is a decisive argument for privatization, even if Keynesian economists would argue that in the short-run nationalized enterprises are a good instrument of government planning.

1.3   The Influence on the Government Budget

1.3.1   Direct Effects

The government budget is influenced by the deficits and profits of those firms which are publicly owned in whole or in part. In privatization campaigns it is often claimed that the government is no longer obliged to finance those deficits which had been accepted in nationalized enterprises as the price for achieving income redistribution or stabilization objectives. Given the usual practice, government's expectations of financial gains from privatization should not be too high. Deficit enterprises tend to remain public. For those other enterprises that are privatized the government may lose future dividends, and the present value of this loss may well offset the non-recurring revenues from privatization (Heald and Steel, 1981: 359).

There is another direct budget effect of privatization: the government realizes revenues from selling assets. If share ownership is transferred, purchasers must pay some price. In privatization this is the issue or offer price which private acquirers are required to pay. In nationalization the price is the compensation which the acquiring government has to pay to the former private shareholders.[21] Both in privatization and in nationalization, it is customary to complain afterwards that the government has lost money. In the case of privatization it is usually argued that the offer price of the shares was set too low, because typically the value of the shares increases sharply in the first months after flotation. (For recent examples see Yarrow, 1986.) In the case of nationalization the argument is often heard that compensation was too high. For the recent French nationalization, Langohr and Viallet (1986) estimate that the former holders of the nationalized portfolios received a government-legislated takeover premium of about 20 percent over the value of the nationalized portfolio if it had not been nationalized.

---

[21] We exclude the case of 'confiscation', i.e. acquisition without payment.

1.3.2   Feedbacks on Public Expenditures, Tax Pressure, and Government Debt

Government revenues from privatization can be spent to finance public expenditures or to reduce the tax burden. To the extent that government expenditures and tax and non-tax receipts are not immediately affected by sales of government assets, the growth of government debt is reduced. The saving will be less if government asset sales, which economists view as a form of financing the deficit, reduce political pressures to reduce the fiscal deficit.

Increased welfare from higher public expenditures can be regarded as a rationale for a higher degree of privatization, as will be shown when dealing with the normative approach to privatization (see Section 15.1 below). The same holds if the tax pressure is reduced, because part of the government fiscal deficit can be financed by revenues from privatization. However, it can be shown in a general equilibrium model that the tax pressure is not necessarily reduced by privatization even if public expenditures and public debt remain unchanged (see Section 15.2.1 below). The reason why many people believe that privatization must reduce tax pressure seems to be that they count the cash receipt from selling the assets but not the reduction in the income which those assets would have generated. A general equilibrium model has the advantage that it includes the feedbacks which often are lost in the present discussion of privatization.

Part One

Theoretical Background

2 The Process of Privatization

When dealing with the process of privatization, we have to answer questions about how to move from public to private ownership: should the right to produce and sell particular goods be auctioned off to that private firm which offers the highest bid? Or should the public firm be transformed into a shareholding company and the shares be sold to the public? Should the government employ an underwriter? How should the government set the offer price of the shares? Should the offer price be fixed *a priori* and the potential investors be rationed by quantity (offer for sale), or should the potential investors be requested to bid for the shares and the shares be rationed by price (tender offer)? Should privatization be used to promote widespread share ownership of small investors to achieve a 'people's capitalism'? To what extent should the employees of the privatized firm be encouraged to buy shares?

2.1 The Fundamental Privatization Theorem

Two particularly well-known authors of the principal–agent literature[1] have presented a fundamental privatization theorem. This theorem 'provides conditions under which all of the government's objectives can be attained by an appropriately designed auction of the rights to produce a given product or service' (Sappington and Stiglitz, 1987: 568). It is a general theorem which shows under which conditions privatization is optimal. The conditions are rather strict, hence for practical purposes it is more important to discuss 'privatization failures', i.e. the reasons why the conditions of the fundamental theorem do not hold. When discussing these failures we learn a lot about the process of privatization.

Sappington and Stiglitz focus on the problem of transaction costs associated with intervention. Direct government intervention is cheaper under public provision than under private provision because the government has direct access to the information about the firm's production possibilities. However, according to the authors an ideal auction process can be applied which leads to welfare-optimal private provision without requiring government's knowledge of the production possibilities.

---

[1] As an introductory reference see Arrow (1986).

Sappington and Stiglitz's ideal setting is as follows. The government auctions the right to produce a given good or service.[2] Two or more risk-neutral private firms are willing to produce the good.[3] There is no collusion among the firms. They have symmetric beliefs about the state of technology. To simplify the analysis the authors assume increasing returns to scale, hence it is optimal to have one and only one firm. When contracting with the government, the chosen firm does not know the actual costs of production, but only a distribution of costs. Only afterwards, just prior to production, does the producing firm obtain precise information on costs.

The firms bid for the right to produce the quantity z and to obtain a particular compensation $\mathcal{P}(z)$ which is paid by the government. This compensation is equal to the government's social valuation of the produced quantity, $\mathcal{P}(z) = V(z)$. Hence this is an auction 'to become a regulated firm, where the payoffs to the firm are delineated by a predetermined valuation function' (Sappington and Stiglitz, 1987: 579). After the government has compensated the producer, it distributes the good to the consumers, either free of charge or at some adequate pricing procedure.

If we associate $V(z)$ with the sum of consumer surplus and revenue, the producing firm will maximize the sum of consumer and producer surplus which implies technological and allocative efficiency. Since the highest offer in the auction is identical to the expected profit of the firm, the expected monopoly profit goes to the government. Note that in this ideal setting the government does not need any information on the cost function.

However, in practice this ideal setting typically cannot be applied. Privatization failures, according to Sappington and Stiglitz, arise for the following reasons:

(i)   The rent acquisition by the government is imperfect if the contractor is risk-averse. In that case the bid does not depend on the expected cost alone but also on the variance of cost. The private firm must be paid a risk premium. Imperfect rent acquisi-

---

[2] The ideal setting assumes that output can be observed perfectly and costlessly.

[3] The extension of the theorem to a multiproduct firm is not straightforward because of the increasing informational requirements. However, as the authors explicitly mention, distributional objectives can be included in the government's objective function. Moreover, the government could also consider a dated vector of outputs to deal with the social valuation of all future quantities.

tion also occurs if the competition for the contract is limited and, therefore, the highest bid is not equal to the expected profit.

(ii)   The ideal setting can break down because the firm's liability is limited. Since the bid depends on expected profit, in practice the contracting firm may experience losses. If these losses are considered too high, the contractor may be allowed to renege on the contract, for instance if the losses are high enough to lead to the firm's bankruptcy. The ideal setting will also break down if the government cannot credibly commit itself not to cover the contractor's losses and not to tax away profits, even if they are extremely large. Given usual government practices, such commitments are not too credible.

(iii)   Information problems may become so serious that the ideal setting cannot be applied. The government may lack the precise information about its social valuation $V(z)$. The technology may be complex and subject to frequent change, so that a once and for all determination of a contract can not be considered optimal and permanent renegotiation is preferable.

(iv)   The ideal setting supposes that the firm is the single agent and that the government is the single principal. In practice, this setting breaks down because firm ownership and management are separated and managers may take their rent not in the form of profits, but in other ways. Likewise, the government as a single principal is a theoretical abstraction. In practice, hierarchical control leads to a much more complicated setting.

2.2   Franchising and Competitive Bidding

The previous subsection has illustrated why auctioning off public provision cannot be the general method of privatization to be applied in practice. Some less important public activities, however, can be privatized by franchising. This is true, for instance, of parts of the local transportation system (single bus lines), garbage collection, fire protection, and parts of health care.[4] Typically, a system of competitive tendering is chosen by the local privatizing communities. (Of course, this is not the theoretically perfect auction which is postulated in Sappington and Stiglitz's fundamental privatization theorem.)

Successful application of competitive tendering is possible only if the output required by the contractor can properly and precisely

[4] For UK evidence on 'contracting-out' see e.g. Thomas (1988).

be specified,[5] if the technology is relatively simple, if the future development of demand and costs is fairly predictable, and if no particular informational advantages of the incumbent or some particular bidder are expected. Additionally, entry costs must not be too high and handing over the firm's assets to the private franchisee must not pose too many problems.[6]

With respect to the more important publicly owned monopolies, however, franchising cannot serve as an adequate method of privatization. The prerequisites for successful franchising mentioned in the preceding paragraph[7] are not given. This prevents franchising of telecommunications, electricity, and gas. Typically, in these cases privatization proceeds by selling the ownership rights of the relevant enterprise to the public. We shall see how this is done in the following subsection.

2.3   The Flotation Process

The property rights of a government-owned firm can be sold to the public by an 'offer for sale' or by a 'tender offer'.

The more usual system is the *offer for sale*.[8] Here the government sets a price per share to be sold and invites applications. If the issue is oversubscribed, some form of quantity rationing is chosen. A common procedure entails a percentage reduction of all applications: if an issue is three times oversubscribed, every applicant gets a third of the shares for which he had applied. In the UK privatizations, however, a discrimination against institutional investors and in favor of small applicants took place. This is part of the 'people's capitalism' policy which will be treated in Section 2.4. If the issue is undersubscribed, the so-called underwriters take up the remaining shares at the fixed price. Underwriters are financial institutions which have agreed, in return for a fee, to buy any shares which are not bought by the public.[9] In the UK privatizations an underwriter was always employed, which seemed quite

[5] Some of the outputs can be precisely specified more easily than others. Garbage collection, for instance, is easier to specify than hospital cleaning. See Domberger (1988: 75).
[6] See Vickers and Yarrow (1988a, 112–13).
[7] See also Domberger (1988).
[8] It may be mentioned that most of the recent UK privatizations used this method in spite of its disadvantages.
[9] Moreover, underwriters operate as advisers, for instance with respect to the offer price, and as distributors of the issue: see below pp. 28–29.

meaningless given the usual oversubscriptions of the issues. However, the BP share offer in October 1987 unfortunately coincided with the great stock exchange crash. In this case the offer for sale was undersubscribed, the only case where this has occurred.[10]

The offer-for-sale flotation has serious disadvantages:

(i)   The shares typically are underpriced. When the offer price is fixed, neither the seller nor the underwriter knows the precise extent of demand for the shares. If a private company sells shares, risk aversion or information asymmetries may imply underpricing. If the government sells shares, the interest in wider share ownership leads to underpricing.

(ii)   Offers for sale induce strategic bidding. If the potential investors expect an oversubscription with subsequent quantity rationing, they will apply for more shares than they actually want. If the potential investors expect an undersubscription, they will not apply at all, in the hope of acquiring shares at some later stage at a lower price. Hence, expectations are self-reinforcing and the system is very unstable.[11]

In the case of a *tender offer*, the seller invites applications specifying both the quantity and price which the bidder is willing to pay. The price must exceed a minimum tender price which is fixed *a priori*. In the event of an oversubscription all applicants are ranked according to their willingness to pay. This makes it possible to calculate the 'striking price' at which demand equals supply. Shares then are allocated at the striking price to all bidders whose willingness to pay exceeds that price. In the event of undersubscription, the existing applications are satisfied at the minimum tender price, while the rest of the tranche is taken up by the underwriters.

Tender offers reveal an offer price reflecting market demand more accurately than offers for sale. Underpricing is low, sometimes negligible. A disadvantage of tender offers is their greater complexity. Bidders have to decide not only how many shares they want to buy at some fixed price, but also what price they are willing to pay. This may discourage inexperienced bidders.[12] Therefore,

---

[10]   Some underwriters asked the government to withdraw the issue. The government did not comply with this request. The Bank of England offered to repurchase shares at 50 percent below the offer price (Vickers and Yarrow, 1988a: 194). Finally most of the shares were bought by the Kuwait Investment Office (Bishop and Kay, 1988: 31).

[11]   See Bishop and Kay (1988: 28).

[12]   See Grimstone (1988: 110), Hyman (1988: 122).

tender offers are not the best procedure if wider share ownership is desired.

2.4   People's Capitalism and Underpricing

2.4.1   Empirical Evidence and Political Background

When in 1990 the twelve UK regional electricity distribution companies were privatized, at the end of the first trading day the shares displayed premia of between 42 and 66 percent on the issue prices. New issues of private firms face lower premia, the empirical estimates ranging from 10 to 19 percent.[13] Some further information on UK privatization offers for sale is given in Table 1.[14]

Table 1   UK Privatization Offers

Company	Gross proceeds from sale (£ million)	Offer price (pence)	Price at end of first trading day (pence)
British Telecom (1984)	3916	130	173 (+33%)
British Gas (1986)	5603	135	147.5 (+9%)
Trustee Savings Bank (1986)	1360	100	135.5 (+35.5%)
British Airports[a] (1987)	919	245	291 (+19%)
British Airways (1987)	900	125	169 (+35%)
Rolls Royce (1987)	1360	170	232 (+36%)

a Shares in British Airports (BAA) were sold by a combination of an offer for sale and a tender offer. In the case of the tender offer, the percentage rise in price relative to offer price was only 0.3.
Source: Vickers and Yarrow (1988a: 174).

Let us now turn to the political background. 'People's capitalism' is a conservative catchphrase which accentuates widespread ownership of shares, in particular by lower-income-earners. Maximizing the number of shareholders is an objective which often has

[13] See Rock (1986) and Buckland (1987), who also quote further literature on the topic.
[14] Following Vickers and Yarrow, we exclude the sale of the final tranche of the government's holding in BP in October 1987 which, unfortunately, coincided with the crash of the world equity market.

been followed by conservative governments when privatizing public enterprises. The underlying political concept is simple. Public
enterprises are owned by governments. From the point of view of
political philosophy (not of law, of course), this implies that public
enterprises are owned by the people. People's capitalism would
imply a shift from the philosophical, indirect, ownership to direct
legal ownership by the people.

People's capitalism is used to win political support for privatization. The typical Labour Party voter will not easily understand
that the government can sell people something which already be-
longs to them, at least indirectly. However, even Labour Party
voters will sooner accept a policy which sells a public firm to the
broad public than a policy which sells the firm to some big private
industry or cartel. The more international the cartel, the more
intensive the opposition.[15]

The search for political support for privatization is not just
a short-run problem. A conservative government is interested not
only in high voter acceptance at the moment it sells the shares
of a firm: it is also interested in preventing a subsequent left-wing
government from re-nationalizing the enterprise. Widespread ownership of shares makes re-nationalization more difficult. It would be
easier to re-nationalize Mr Rothschild's bank than a bank which
is owned by its employees and many lower-income-earners from
outside the bank. Hence the privatizing conservative government
is interested in maximizing both the number of shareholders who
buy shares and the number of those who retain their shares.

A policy of people's capitalism could easily fail because shares
are sold to lower-income-earners who are not prone to buy assets
such as shares. As already mentioned,[16] empirical evidence illustrates that there are two main problems which must be resolved.
First, the government has to supply the right incentives to induce lower-income-earners to buy the shares of a privatized firm.
Typically this is done by setting an offer price for the new shares
which is well below the price prevailing at the close of the first
trading day at the stock exchange. We call this the 'underpricing'
problem. Second, the government has to supply the right incentives to induce lower-income-earners to retain their shares. We call

[15] It is interesting to note that this argument restores the literal meaning of
nationalization as an instrument of making the economy 'national'. Both UK
and France have taken explicit precautions to prevent unwanted international
take-overs of privatized firms, for instance by withholding a 'golden share'.

[16] See pp. 3–5 above.

this the 'bonus' problem. Only the bonus problem is peculiar to
privatization and people's capitalism. Underpricing is a regular
phenomenon of public offerings of private firms, and well-founded
theoretical models on underpricing in the private-sector economy
have been constructed.[17] In the next subsection we will consider
these theories and discuss the possibility of applying them to the
case of privatization and people's capitalism.

2.4.2   Theories on Underpricing[18]

The relevant theories on underpricing in the private sector assume
different informational asymmetries between the firm, the underwriter, and the investors. In Rock (1986) some investors are better informed than the firm and the underwriter, whereas in Baron
(1982) the underwriter is better informed than the firm and implicitly sells this information to the firm. Both informational settings
may be correct in particular cases. Hence one cannot *a priori* re-

---

[17] However, underpricing may at least in part be caused by institutional
peculiarities of the stock exchange. Levis (1990) deals with an interest rate
effect in UK initial public offerings: applications for shares must be accompanied by payment for the full amount. If the issue is oversubscribed, so that
each applicant obtains only a portion of the shares for which he has applied,
it is some time before the applicant is refunded the difference between the
total value of subscription and the cost of the shares actually allocated to him.
Hence there are interest costs in terms of lost proceeds which constitute one
more reason for underpricing.

[18] In an interesting paper Myers and Majluf (1984) explain a reduction
in the issue price of shares of a private company for the case when the firm
announces it will issue common shares to meet the capital requirements for
undertaking an investment project. The fully informed management, which
acts in the interest of the old shareholders, issues shares if the project is a
bad project because in that case the old shareholders are favored over the
new shareholders. This inclination of the management is known to the stock
exchange. Hence the decision to issue shares is bad news and this negative
signal must be offset by a discount. Myers and Majluf's paper does not deal
with underpricing. In the Myers–Majluf model the issue price falls when the
issuing of new shares is *announced*, then it remains unchanged at the date of
issuing and at the first trading day (*ceteris paribus*, of course). Underpricing
means too low a price at the moment of *issuing* the shares with an increase
after issuing, typically measured by the price at the end of the first trading day.
In any case, the Myers–Majluf theory could not help us explain issue prices
in privatization cases. Privatization does not deal with a single investment
opportunity which is good or bad: rather, it deals with a total or partial sale
of a firm for political or ideological reasons. Issuing shares, therefore, never
signals a bad project.

ject one of these theories on grounds of an unrealistic assumption regarding informational asymmetry. However, we are interested in whether the above theories are good instruments for explaining the sale of assets in the case of privatization. I shall argue that, for different reasons, neither approach can be applied to the case of privatization. This is not meant as a criticism of these theories. They have not been formulated with privatization in mind, but with other phenomena in mind, for which they can well be considered as good explanations of empirical reality. It is only when these theories are transferred to another problem that they fail.[19] Let us consider this failure in more detail.

Rock (1986) postulates that there is a group of investors who are better informed than both the other investors and the firm issuing the new shares. The informed investors know the actual market value of the new issue. The uninformed investors only know the probability distribution of the values. Now consider the firm, wanting to sell at the expected value of the new shares. The informed investors know whether this is a good offer or a bad offer. In the first case they try to buy the whole issue, if possible. In the second case they do not buy any shares and the firm is left with the uninformed investors. These investors are as badly informed as the firm. If they are risk-neutral they buy shares if the offer price falls below the expected value of the shares. They buy more shares, the lower the offer price. The firm wants to attract a sufficient amount of uninformed investors to avoid the risk of being left without any investor. However, this requires selling the shares at a discount. This explains 'underpricing'. At the same time, underpricing increases the probability of the informed investors entering the market. Hence we obtain a paradoxical result: new issues are sold at a discount and, at the same time, the shares are rationed. According to Rock's theory, the uninformed investors are more likely to receive a full allocation of shares if the offering

---

[19] Some recent interesting papers interpret underpricing in the private economy as a signal from better informed firm owners to less informed investors. See for instance Allen and Faulhaber (1987), Grinblatt and Hwang (1989), and Welch (1989). However, in these models underpricing at an initial public offering is chosen to achieve higher proceeds for high-quality firms in future seasoned offerings. Hence these theories could explain underpricing only in the case of partial privatization. The list of UK privatizations, however, gives many examples of underpricing in cases of full privatization: see Vickers and Yarrow (1988a: 174) for a full list and Table 1 above for some examples. (In fact, there are only a few examples of partial privatization in the UK, the best known to be found in telecommunications and in power generation.)

is overpriced and a rationed allocation if it is underpriced. This is the well-known winner's curse.

Is it possible to transfer Rock's theory to the case of privatization? I doubt it. We would have to assume that the government, the underwriter, and most investors are badly informed and, simultaneously, that some institutional investors have private inside information. Rock explains such an informational setting as follows. The issuing firm and the underwriter lose any informational advantage because they pass over to the consumer-investors all the information they have. In the case of privatization, the 'man in the street' typically will have less information than the government and the underwriter even if the issue prospectus contains all relevant information that the government and underwriter possess. After all, the broad public does not consist of skilled investors (where 'skilled' does not mean 'insider knowledge' but only refers to the investor's ability to learn details about a new issue of shares). Moreover, in a privatized industry undesired takeovers can be prohibited by some 'golden share' or similar precautions. There should, therefore, be fewer rumors and less possibility of inside information than in the private economy. Last but not least, the government wants to attract the broad public for ideological reasons and not for fear of being left without any investors. It has to consider its reputation, and this reputation could be at risk if too high an offer price is chosen. Hence the government follows a rationale which differs decisively from Rock's assumptions.

Is Baron (1982) more applicable to our case? In this model a firm offers a delegation contract to an underwriter who sets the offer price and distributes the shares. The number of shares to be issued is assumed to be fixed. Both the firm and the underwriter are risk-neutral. Thus risk sharing is not the reason for delegating the issuing of shares to an underwriter. The underwriter's functions are restricted to advising the firm and distributing the shares. It is less costly to distribute shares if they are offered at a lower price. The underwriter wants to maximize his own profit, i.e. the difference between the compensation paid by the firm and the costs of the distribution. The compensation depends on the offer price, the proceeds from the issue,[20] and the report on the relevant capital market information which is the internal knowledge of the underwriter. Therefore, we face a 'principal–agent'

---

[20] Baron (1982: 958) hints at banking practices which involve 'rebates' in the form of overtrading and soft-dollar designations, in which case the proceeds are neither globally nor locally a linear function of the offer price.

problem. The firm wants to maximize the net proceeds of the issue, i.e. proceeds minus compensation to the underwriter. However, it can only maximize the expected net proceeds because it lacks the precise information about the capital market. The compensation must be set in such a way that, in maximizing his own profit, the underwriter implicitly maximizes the net proceeds of the issue. This implies that the underwriter's compensation contains some payment for information about the capital market. In Baron's model the optimal offer price is a decreasing function of the issuer's uncertainty about the market demand for the shares. Hence the uncertainty of the issuer explains the underpricing.

The informational setting of Baron's model is quite realistic. Moreover, the UK government used an underwriter for privatization. The discussion of underpricing in the UK often came to the conclusion that 'underpricing is ... greatly to the benefit of City institutions' (Vickers and Yarrow, 1988a: 178). There is yet another assumption in Baron's paper which fits the UK privatizations. Typically, underwriting is chosen if an issuer is more risk-averse than the underwriter. Given, however, that a government's ability to bear risk is greater than that of any City institution,[21] it suffices that Baron excludes the risk component of a delegation contract and deals with the underwriter's function as an adviser and distributor. In spite of this, I still do not think Baron's model is an adequate explanation of underpricing in the case of privatization. The underwriter in Baron's model is needed by the firm for distribution and information purposes. The government, in the case of public utilities, could use its own distribution apparatus for the sale of shares, for instance by selling shares of a telecommunications utility at post offices. Moreover, in the UK examples the government did not employ the underwriter for information purposes: rather, it fixed too low an issue price for political reasons.

A theory of people's capitalism, which includes a theory of underpricing, requires modelling of the *political background* of privatization:

(i)   The government wants to attract many small investors who will buy and retain the shares. Hence, underpricing can be explained without resorting to informational asymmetries among issuer, underwriter, and various investors: underpricing may simply be the catalyst for increasing the demand for stock from people who would not have thought of buying shares in the first place.

---

[21] See Vickers and Yarrow (1988a: 183).

The only remaining information asymmetry is the government's incomplete knowledge about the investors' individual characteristics.

(ii)   The models of private issuers assume the issuer wants to maximize the proceeds of the issue. The government may not be totally unaware of the nice side-effects of privatization which result from the cash revenue from selling shares. However, high cash revenue implies a high offer price which must be traded off against the low offer price the government needs to attract many shareholders.

(iii)   The government may appreciate increased dividends from its remaining shares in the privatized firm if privatization leads to higher profits because of efficiency increases. However, the government will feel responsible for protecting the firm's customers from too high prices if the firm is a monopoly. Hence the government, instead of maximizing its cash revenue, will regulate the privatized firm, thereby reducing its own cash revenues from dividends.

(iv)   The government does not necessarily need an underwriter (see, for example, Vickers and Yarrow, 1988a: 183).

To date, unfortunately, theories achieving all of these objectives have not been constructed and this will remain an important area for research.

2.5   Employee Share Ownership

People's shares, as treated in the previous subsection, are only one of the policies whereby privatizing governments aim at socio-political objectives. Employee shares are another policy of that type. In most of the recent UK privatization cases more than 90 percent of the firms' employees bought shares in their own firms.[22] The number of employee shareholders increased drastically, although the overall proportion of shares owned by employees is still small because the typical employee shareholder owns only a few shares.

In a recent paper Grout (1988) concludes that overall the employees do not gain from share ownership. The sale of employee shares, according to Grout, is only in the interest of the non-employee shareholders and, in the case of privatization, in the revenue interest of the government. Let us first present Grout's reasoning. His unexpected result is rooted in the outcome of the

---

[22]   For detailed data see Grout (1987).

wage negotiations. The owners and the employees share the aggregate revenue of the firm according to a Nash bargaining solution.[23]
When sharing a given revenue, it does not matter whether the employees receive money as wage-earners or as dividend-recipients.
The bargaining only determines a particular sum of money which
the employees receive. If they have more employee shares, the
higher dividends will reduce their wage bill. The sum of wage income plus dividend income, both net of taxes, remains constant
for any amount of employee shares. In contrast to wage incomes,
however, dividend incomes require the acquisition of shares and
therefore the payment of some issue price. Hence the employees
should opt for wage incomes only, as they receive the same amount
of money and have no additional costs. The more employee shares
they buy, the higher the expenses for this portfolio without getting
any penny more.

This conclusion is superficial, however, as shown in Bös and
Nett (1989). Grout's argument is valid for the constant revenue
case, but issuing employee shares changes the firm's revenue. Unfortunately, Grout ignores this effect. Let me briefly illustrate
how this effect works. Let us assume, as Grout does, that non-
employees are the majority shareholders, and hence they determine the level of investment activity of the firm. In doing so they
also consider employee wages which will be negotiated at a later
stage. The non-employee shareholders are long-run oriented and
maximize the value of the firm, i.e. the discounted sum of future
profits. Investment is an increasing function of the percentage of
employee shares, because wages to be paid per unit of revenue decrease if employees hold more shares: the employees contribute
to costs proportionate to their share ownership. Furthermore, if
the tax rate on dividends is significantly lower than the tax rate
on wage incomes, the investment decision is likely to lead to an

---

[23] Grout (1988) describes the negotiations as a Rubinstein (1982) game,
whose subgame-perfect solution can be shown to be equal to the one determined by the Nash bargaining solution as shown by Binmore, Rubinstein, and
Wolinsky (1986). A simple explanation of the term 'subgame-perfect solution'
is as follows. Consider a game which can be split up into subgames. The
behavior in any subgame depends only on the subgame itself. Each player
first calculates the equilibria of the 'last' subgames, i.e. those subgames which
cannot be partitioned into other subgames. Then he proceeds to the 'last-but-
one' subgames and calculates their equilibria, thereby anticipating what will
happen in the last subgames. This backward induction is carried on until the
total game is solved. The resulting equilibrium is called subgame perfect. For
a precise definition see Selten (1975).

overinvestment in the sense that the marginal revenue product of capital is lower than the marginal costs at the optimum. Therefore, total revenue, which is negotiated by the firm and the employees at a later stage, increases with employee shares.

Any employee pondering about his investment in shares perfectly anticipates the consequences of his purchase. He knows that an increase in employee shares will increase revenue. On the other hand, the employees have to pay a price for their shares, although per unit of revenue they receive a constant income from wages and dividends. Since the two effects countervail, employees may either gain or lose from their share purchase. Grout neglects the possibility that the increase in revenue can be high enough to sufficiently compensate employees. A counterexample is given in Bös and Nett (1989). This example shows that the positive effect on revenue can outweigh the negative effect on income net of the issue price to such an extent that the employees gain from the introduction of employee shares.

If this is not the case, then employees are never interested in buying shares at their market price unless they have an additional incentive. A low tax rate on dividend incomes serves as such an incentive if an employee already owns assets with returns taxed according to the income tax rate. In that case the employee can change the composition of his portfolio, from assets with highly taxed returns to employee shares with lower taxed dividends. In my opinion it is unrealistic to assume that this is the usual case. The employees of privatized firms who bought the shares typically were *new* shareholders and not speculators who changed the composition of their portfolios.

In this book, the problem of employee shares will be taken up in one of the Positive Theory chapters.[24] Like Grout, we build a model on the interplay between the government, the shareholders, and a trade union. Beyond Grout, however, we also include the government's adjustment of the anticipated policy of the firm.

---

[24] See Sect. 9.1 below.

3 Incentives and Efficiency in Public and Privatized Firms

The productive results of any firm are due to the interaction of various economic actors which can be modelled in a three-tier setting. In a public enterprise the first tier consists of the government. In a fully privatized firm the first tier consists of the private shareholders. In the next tier of a public enterprise we typically have a planning board, which makes general decisions on prices, wages, and output and input quantities. In a fully private firm these decisions are ordinarily made by senior management personnel. The third tier contains lower-level 'technological' management personnel who decide on 'how efficiently' the output is produced. (In a simple Leibenstein view of the world, this is expressed as how near the actual production comes to the frontier.)

If we concentrate on the privatization of public utilities, then privatization is a change in the objectives of the owners, from welfare to profit maximization. Furthermore, it is a change in the information available to the owners: private shareholders typically are better informed about demand or cost conditions than public bureaucrats. It is also a change in the character of members of the senior and the technological management: market-oriented technocrats replace red-tape public bureaucrats.

The changes in objectives, information, and character lead to differences in incentives and efficiency in public and privatized firms. In the following survey we deal first with some theoretical approaches regarding incentives. We begin with a simple benchmark model and then proceed to more sophisticated principal–agent approaches which relate owners, senior management (board), and technological management. Second, this survey concentrates on the empirical investigations of efficiency differences among public enterprises, private firms, and firms in mixed public–private ownership.

3.1 Objectives and Incentives

3.1.1 A Benchmark Model on Ownership and Efficiency

In their benchmark model on ownership and economic efficiency, Vickers and Yarrow (1988a: 35–9) deal with the trade-off between allocative and productive efficiency which results from total privatization of an unregulated monopoly. The objective of the firm changes from welfare maximization to profit maximization, which implies a tendency toward higher prices as we move from marginal-cost pricing to monopoly prices. In terms of allocative efficiency, this is a step in the wrong direction. On the other hand, managerial incentives to reduce costs are strengthened. It is also easier to monitor cost-reducing activities. Hence the unit costs will be reduced by privatization. In terms of productive efficiency, this is a move for the better.

Vickers and Yarrow present a very simple benchmark model to show the basic structure of the trade-off. Their model[1] assumes a one-product firm which produces under constant marginal costs. However, the firm can control these costs by making outlays for such activities as R&D or through additional managerial effort. Let $R(c)$ denote the outlay that is required to achieve a marginal cost of production equal to c. ($R(c)$ also includes the monetary evaluation of the manager's disutility from effort expanded on cost reduction.) Lower marginal costs correspond to higher $R(c)$ and therefore the first derivative is negative: $R_c < 0$.

The ideal objective of the manager of the private firm is to maximize profit,

$$(p - c)z(p) - R(c), \qquad (3.1)$$

where $z(p)$ is the demand function. However, for some exogenous reasons the manager is not given the right incentives and his objective function reveals a distorted trade-off between the costs of effort and the benefit of greater profit. Accordingly, the manager of the private firm maximizes

$$(p - c)z(p) - aR(c) \qquad a > 1. \qquad (3.2)$$

The more imperfect the managerial incentives, the higher is a. More intensive monitoring reduces a.

In a similar fashion, the ideal objective of the manager of a public firm is to maximize the sum of consumer and producer surplus:

$$S(p) + (p - c)z(p) - R(c). \qquad (3.3)$$

As is usual in first-best theory, we ignore the financing of the firm's deficit which arises if the above objective function is maximized with respect to p and c. (Since price is equated to marginal costs, the deficit equals $R(c) > 0$.) Once again, the manager is not

---

[1] This model is similar to Shleifer's (1985) model on yardstick regulation. See below Sect. 4.3.2.

given the right incentives and incorporates a wrong trade-off in his objective function, namely

$$S(p) + (p - c)z(p) - bR(c) \qquad b > 1. \tag{3.4}$$

The more imperfect the managerial incentives, the higher is b. More intensive monitoring reduces b.

Privatization is a move from maximizing (3.4) to maximizing (3.2). If the public firm gives the more correct incentives, $a \geq b$, the public firm is both allocatively and productively more efficient. Public ownership guarantees higher welfare. Typically, however, we expect less perfect monitoring in the public firm, so that $a < b$. It follows from considerations of continuity that the public firm will be welfare-superior if a is only slightly less than b. The private incentive system must be significantly better to lead to higher welfare under private ownership. This holds in particular if the private manager faces a situation which induces him (i) to a high deviation from allocative efficiency (low price elasticity of demand) and (ii) to only small improvements in productive efficiency (low elasticity of costs with respect to cost-reducing investments). For welfare to be higher under private ownership in such an environment, monitoring in the private firm must be particularly accurate. In other words, a/b must be particularly small.

Vickers and Yarrow (1988a: 37–9) illustrate these connections by calculating a numerical example with isoelastic demand and isoelastic cost-reduction investments. Their model neatly reveals the trade-off between public and private ownership. Its advantage is its simple structure. Needless to say, nobody can expect such a model to be more than a starting point for a discussion of the trade-off between allocative and productive efficiency in the course of privatization. Further modelling will have to make endogenous the incentive structures in the principal–agent relations in the public and the private firm.

3.1.2 The Principal–Agent Relation between the Owner and the Firm[2]

The price and production decisions of any firm result from the interaction between owners and management. In a public firm the government operates as the principal whereas in a private firm the

---

[2] This subsection is based on Bös and Peters (1990).

shareholders take the lead. In both cases the management can be treated as the agent. Principal–agent approaches are characterized by asymmetric information. When attempting to achieve his goals, the principal is handicapped by lack of certain information which only the management knows precisely. For example, there may be particular parameters affecting efficiency which only the managers know, the principal's knowledge being restricted to the distribution of the parameters. Managerial effort may be unobservable and therefore impossible to monitor. Since the principal cannot directly observe the activities of the management, he cannot directly control the behavior of the manager. The management has its own objectives, hence it may choose an effort level which is not efficient. This particular situation must be taken into account by the principal when he defines the reward structure of the management.

This difficult problem has been dealt with in many papers. Classics on the general theory of the principal–agent approach are the papers by Grossman and Hart (1983), and by Guesnerie and Laffont (1984).[3] More specialized papers have concentrated on the regulation of public utilities.

In these papers, the regulating principal's lack of information refers either to production or to demand characteristics. Baron and Myerson (1982) model regulation with unknown total costs. Freixas and Laffont (1985) and Laffont and Tirole (1986, 1990a) model principal–agent relations where total costs are observable but managerial effort and some random efficiency parameter are unobservable. Lewis and Sappington (1988) consider the regulation of a monopolist with unknown demand.

These papers, however, have not been written with privatization in mind. Rather, they refer to privately owned monopolies which are regulated by the government. Of course their basic ideas also hold for regulated public enterprises. However, previous studies have not investigated the change in the principal–agent relationship that results from privatization.

Bös and Peters (1990) apply the Laffont–Tirole (1986) approach to a comparison between public and private monopoly.[4] They compare the behavior of a price-setting firm which is initially public and then is completely privatized. The public and the

---

[3] For a recent survey see Caillaud, *et al.* (1988).

[4] As an alternative see Roemer and Silvestre (1989) who apply the Baron–Myerson (1982) approach. For another recent paper on the subject see De Fraja (1990b).

privatized firms are assumed to face the same economic environment, viz. the same demand function and the same technology. The private owners are assumed, however, to be clever investors whose informational status compares favorably with that of the bureaucrats who are supposed to audit the public enterprise. Privatization, therefore, means that the management faces a better informed principal than before.

Privatization also changes the objectives of the firm, typically from multiple goals to a one-dimensional objective, i.e. from a weighted sum of consumer and producer surplus to profit. Hence the authors specify the following objective functions:

public firm: $W = \lambda S(p) + (1 - \lambda)\Pi$ with $\lambda \in [0; 1/2]$,
privatized firm: Π.

Here $S(p)$ is consumer surplus and Π is the deficit or profit of the firm. S and Π are two objectives which are combined by the weights λ and $(1 - \lambda)$, where $\lambda = 1/2$ implies the usual government objective of the sum of consumer and producer surplus and $\lambda < 1/2$ means a stronger emphasis on the distortionary effects of financing a possible deficit. However, $\lambda < 1/2$ could also mean that the government is interested less in consumer welfare and more in getting some profit from the firm. To define welfare as a weighted sum of consumer surplus and profit is the simplest possible description of a government with multiple objectives.

Moreover, privatization changes the extent of control. Bös and Peters define control as activities which reduce marginal costs. These activities can be carried out by the principal or by the agent. In the first case the authors speak of external control; the second is called internal control. Examples of external control include

• in the case of a private firm: activities of consulting firms like McKinsey if required by the owners or by special members of the board appointed at the request of particular private owners;

• in the case of a public firm: examinations by special government commissions or by government representatives which have been appointed to check the performance of the public management.

Internal control includes those managerial activities which aim at reducing marginal costs. This internal control is part of the overall activities of the management. In Bös and Peters (1990) it is considered to be that part of the manager's effort which reduces the marginal costs.

Now consider a one-product enterprise which covers demand z at price p. Common knowledge of both principal and agent are the market demand function $z(p)$ and the cost structure

$$C = (k - \vartheta d - e)z + t + h(d). \qquad (3.5)$$

The marginal costs c consist of some basic costs k which can be reduced by the principal's external control d and the agent's effort e. The principal's control d is effective up to an efficiency parameter ϑ. As both principal and agent know, this efficiency parameter is a random variable which is uniformly distributed between the lowest value, $\underline{\vartheta}$, and the highest value, $\overline{\vartheta}$. Overhead costs arise for two reasons. First, the manager is paid a reward t which is a remuneration for his effort e. Second, costs of $h(d)$ must be spent in order to finance the external control d.

Total costs are observable and this information can be used by the principal to calculate the marginal costs c. The principal of the public firm is assumed *not to know the actual value* of the parameter ϑ, whereas the principal of the private firm does know ϑ. Accordingly, the public principal cannot further disaggregate the marginal costs: he observes c, but not e and not the actual value of ϑ. The private principal knows ϑ and uses his information on c to calculate the agent's effort e.

Therefore the principal of the *privatized firm* stipulates a contract with the manager:

$$T = \begin{cases} t & \text{if} \quad e = e^* \\ 0 & \text{otherwise.} \end{cases} \qquad (3.6)$$

The private principal is fully informed. However, he needs the manager for production and sale. Hence the participation of the manager must be guaranteed. Accordingly, the private principal cannot dictate any arbitrarily high effort. The manager will stay in the firm only if his utility does not fall below his reservation utility $\overline{U}$, which is the critical value where the manager starts to look for another job. Therefore, the principal has to consider the manager's participation constraint,

$$U(t, e) \geq \overline{U} > U(0, 0), \qquad (3.7)$$

where t is the manager's reward and e is his effort. The manager's utility is increasing in income, decreasing in effort; and we assume that work pays.

Since the private principal knows the actual value of ϑ, he can maximize the profit for this particular value, taking account of the manager's participation constraint. This approach of the privatized firm implies monopoly prices,[5] efficient external control, efficient effort, and a binding participation constraint. The reward is chosen in such a way that the manager only gets his reservation utility. The principal in the privatized firm is powerful enough to depress the manager's reward and to fully monitor his effort to guarantee an optimum at the manager's reservation utility.

In the *public firm* the principal is only imperfectly informed and therefore cannot condition the manager's reward on effort. Rather, he has to enter into the following contract with the manager: for any ϑ, as signalled by the agent, the principal is willing to engage in control $d(\vartheta)$ and to pay the following reward:[6]

$$T = \begin{cases} t & \text{if } c = c(\vartheta) \text{ and } p = p(\vartheta) \\ 0 & \text{otherwise.} \end{cases} \tag{3.8}$$

The manager realizes that he will get an income depending on the announced $\hat{\vartheta}$ if the *ex post* marginal costs correspond to a value $c(\hat{\vartheta})$ as stipulated in the contract. He will try to earn this income by exerting as little effort as possible. Hence the manager is interested in announcing too low a value of ϑ. However, the manager cannot announce any arbitrarily low ϑ whatsoever. He is restricted by the principal's ability to observe the correct value of the marginal costs. When announcing a particular value $\hat{\vartheta}$, the manager knows that the principal realizes that an identical value of marginal costs can be attained in a twofold way, namely by a false or a true announcement:[7]

$$c = \begin{cases} k - \vartheta d(\hat{\vartheta}) - e(\vartheta, \hat{\vartheta}) & \text{for } \hat{\vartheta} \neq \vartheta \\ k - \hat{\vartheta} d(\hat{\vartheta}) - e(\hat{\vartheta}) & \text{for } \hat{\vartheta} = \vartheta. \end{cases} \tag{3.9}$$

Since the principal can observe only the numerical value of c — and not ϑ and e — he cannot detect whether the management has lied. A consistent lie of the management, therefore, consists in

---

[5] Price regulation could easily be introduced into the model.

[6] When contracting, the principal does not know the actual value of ϑ. Therefore he is unable to set the desired price $p(\vartheta)$, and this task must be shifted to the manager. Hence the reward must also be conditioned on $p(\vartheta)$.

[7] Note that $\hat{\vartheta}$ is announced to the principal, hence $\hat{\vartheta}$ in the two equations (3.9) is the same, whereas ϑ is not, owing to the principal's lack of perfect information.

choosing $e(\vartheta, \hat{\vartheta})$ in such a way that equations (3.9) are fulfilled for the announced $\hat{\vartheta}$ and c is the same in both equations. This means

$$e(\vartheta, \hat{\vartheta}) = e(\hat{\vartheta}) + (\hat{\vartheta} - \vartheta)d(\hat{\vartheta}). \qquad (3.10)$$

According to this formula the manager may reduce his effort by announcing too low a value of ϑ. In such a case the principal will wrongly believe that the manager worked harder than he actually did, in order to cope with the bad state of the world which would correspond to the low ϑ. To avoid such strategic behavior of the manager, the reward scheme in (3.8) must be chosen in such a way that the management has an incentive to announce the correct value of ϑ. This is achieved if the management's utility is maximized by announcing $\hat{\vartheta} = \vartheta$: the best 'lie' is the truth. The mathematical derivation of such an incentive-compatible reward scheme is complicated. Avoiding any mathematical details, let us only mention the result: if the manager shall be impelled to announce the correct information, which the principal cannot observe, then his utility must be strictly increasing in the actual value of the parameter ϑ. The explicit consideration of this condition guarantees incentive compatibility.[8]

The public principal takes account of the incentive compatibility and the participation constraint and maximizes the weighted sum of consumer surplus and producer surplus, $\lambda S(\vartheta) + (1-\lambda)\Pi(\vartheta)$, integrated over all possible states of the world. In this optimization approach d, t, and p are control variables and the manager's utility is the state variable. The results of this optimization lead to the following conclusions (Bös and Peters, 1990):

(i)   The public firm sets prices according to an inverse elasticity rule, where the chosen price–cost margin depends on the particular mix of the multiple goals. Marginal-cost pricing is chosen only if the simple sum of consumer and producer surplus is maximized. Privatization implies a move to monopoly pricing.

(ii)   Typically, the government's control of a public firm is less than efficient;[9] the control of private owners is efficient.

---

[8] The second-order condition is not explicitly included by the authors to make the model more tractable.

[9] 'Less than efficient' always refers to a benchmark minimum of costs where the produced quantity and the manager's utility are equal to the results of the contract which results from maximizing the weighted sum of consumer and producer surplus given the incentive compatibility and the participation constraint.

(iii)   Typically, the manager of a public firm engages in less effort than is efficient; in a privatized firm the manager's effort is chosen efficiently.

(iv)   There is one exceptional case where control and effort of a public firm are efficiently chosen: the case of the best of all possible worlds ($\vartheta = \overline{\vartheta}$). The reason is a sort of external effect. Since the manager's utility must increase in ϑ, any decision on the manager's reward and effort at some level influences the decisions on reward and effort at all higher levels of ϑ. These external effects can be seen as a sort of 'costs of incentive compatibility' which make it worthwhile to choose inefficiently low control and effort. Only at the top, $\overline{\vartheta}$, do the external effects vanish and efficiency prevail.

(v)   The reward to the manager of a public firm varies more across states of nature than would be efficient. In an unfavorable economic environment the reward is less than efficiency requires, whereas the opposite is true in a favorable environment. On the other hand, the manager in a privatized firm is always rewarded efficiently.

(vi)   It is irrelevant whether the public manager is incompletely informed about the particular mix of the government's multiple objectives as long as the government chooses an incentive-compatible reward to the manager.

The Bös–Peters approach is *general* because it does not *a priori* specify the manager's reward function and therefore copes with incentive compatibility in a satisfying way. On the other hand, the approach is rather *special* because it assumes the observability of total costs and also assumes a very specific cost function. Later sections[10] present principal–agent models where precisely the opposite assumptions are used. There either costs or demand are assumed to be unobservable and the cost and demand functions are not subject to restrictive specification. This generality, however, does require a particular *special* assumption: we shall restrict the analysis to linear reward schemes of the manager.

Another possible limitation of Bös and Peters (1990) is the information setting underlying their approach. It seems to be acceptable to assume that owners of privatized firms are better informed about the firm's technology than the bureaucrats who monitor a public enterprise. Bös and Peters overstate that point by assuming the privatized firm knows the actual value of ϑ and, therefore, after some simple calculations, has full knowledge. In

---

[10]   Chs. 6 and 8 below.

practice, the privatized firm will also face some lack of information, albeit we expect private capitalists to have better knowledge of economic parameters than bureaucrats do. Hence, in the models to be presented in later sections dealing with positive theory, we shall present full-information benchmark models for both a public and a privatized firm and then proceed to incompletely informed principals in both privatized and public firms.

3.1.3 Principal–Agent Relations between Government and Firm

Even if a firm is fully privatized, principal–agent relations between the government and the firm may not be completely eliminated. If the government dislikes some of the consequences of privatization, it may decide to regulate the firm with respect to prices, investment, or employment. This directly leads to the following question: why is privatization desirable if the desired optimum requires maintenance of government regulation? In an extreme case, the same management runs the firm before and after privatization and the same government officials control the firm before and after privatization. Hence, why should privatization improve productive efficiency? If the government objectives remain the same and sophisticated regulation is applied: why should privatization deteriorate allocative efficiency?

To answer the above questions, the incentive structures of the two types of organization have to be compared.[11] Privatization implies the introduction of one more principal, namely the private shareholders. The government representative cannot deal with the managers of the privatized firm directly, as in the case of a public firm. Instead, he has to bargain with the private owners who, in turn, control the managers. The government representative is either called 'government' or 'bureaucrat' depending on the respective objective function attributed to him in the literature. Furthermore, there is an institution which decides whether privatization coupled with regulation is preferable to public ownership.[12] In theoretical papers this institution is often simply called 'govern-

----

[11] A related paper which appeared too late to be included in this survey is Pint (1991).

[12] The particular choice of this institution depends on the relevant country's constitution. It may alternatively be the parliament, the government, some ministry or some special institution like the German 'Treuhandanstalt' ('fiduciary company') which is in charge of the privatization of East German nationalized enterprises.

ment', however, it is better to coin a special term like 'privatization body'[13] or 'framer'.[14] Figure 1 illustrates this institutional setting.

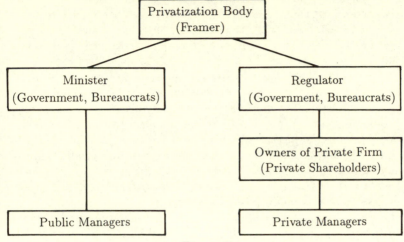

Figure 1

Source: simplified version of a figure of Shapiro and Willig (1990: 60).

The introduction of private shareholders as an additional principal means that privatization is characterized by the deliberate introduction of an informational barrier. To simplify the analysis, let us assume that not only the manager but also the owner of a firm is perfectly informed about costs and demand. This assumption is found in each of the papers treated in this subsection. Hence the minister in charge of the public firm is perfectly informed about costs and demand, however, the regulator of a privatized firm is not perfectly informed. It is the private shareholders who have this perfect information. In this way privatization changes the allocation of information. At the same time privatization changes the allocation of residual rights of control, which is important if the relationship between manager and owner is governed by an incomplete contract. Moreover, privatization makes it more difficult for government-bureaucrats to control managers by incentive rewards because these require explicit or implicit side payments to the private shareholders.

Since there are so many additional difficulties which arise from the inclusion of private shareholders in the relevant principal–

---

[13] This term is used in various papers by Bös or Bös and Peters.
[14] This term is coined by Shapiro and Willig (1990).

agent approaches, different models highlight different features of the problem. In each of the papers considered here the efficiency consequences depend decisively on the particular choice of incentive and information structures. Typically the authors derive special trade-offs, concluding that there is no general answer to the question of whether privatization is preferable to nationalization, but that it depends on the parameters of the particular case.

Schmidt (1990) concentrates on the trade-off between productive and allocative efficiency. Productive efficiency can be increased by an uncontractable effort of the manager which reduces expected production costs. However, the public manager has no incentive to do so because he faces a soft budget constraint. The government cannot credibly commit to punish him by reducing production or shutting down the firm since it is *ex post* optimal to 'forgive' high costs. In the privatized firm, however, the government deliberately decides to be less well-informed about costs because it is no longer the owner. This makes it optimal for the regulating government to distort production in high-cost states by shutting down the firm earlier than under nationalization. This punishment, which now is a credible threat, gives better incentives to the managers who will increase productive efficiency in order to reduce the probability of incurring higher costs. Allocative efficiency is also distorted by privatization since production is distorted in high-cost states.

For anyone not acquainted with information economics, the result of 'more effort in the privatized firm' is quite plausible and not unexpected. However, it is by no means the typical result of models of this branch of literature, such as those of Laffont and Tirole (1990*b*)[15] or Shapiro and Willig (1990). In their models privatization *reduces* effort. In the regulated firm private owners earn an information rent. In contrast to the regulator, they are perfectly informed about cost and demand and, since regulation must guarantee positive expected profits, this asymmetric information at least indirectly leads to remuneration of the private owners. More explicitly, in the regulated firm private shareholders require a rental contract r. If z is the incentive reward paid by the government, the manager obtains an income of only $z - r$. Hence, the existence of shareholders makes it 'more costly to elicit the same effort level as in the public firm and the regulator settles for a lower level of effort' (Laffont and Tirole, 1990*b*: 20).

---

[15] It may be in the interest of the reader to learn that Laffont and Tirole's 1990*b* paper is based on the authors 1986 paper on regulation with observable total costs which we mentioned in the preceding subsection.

The reduction of effort is the bad news of these models. However, there is also good news. In Shapiro and Willig (1990), privatization reduces the possibility of government-bureaucrats pursuing their own agenda. The public minister has better opportunities to pursue his own agenda because he is perfectly informed about costs and demand, whereas the regulator is restricted by his lack of perfect information with respect to these variables. Therefore, by deliberately introducing an information barrier between government-bureaucrats and private managers, privatization restrains bureaucrats when they pursue their private agenda. This is a decisive advantage of privatization.[16]

Laffont and Tirole (1990b) describe another trade-off: privatization reduces effort on the part of managers; however, it also increases investments. In their model, investments have two alternative uses. First, they can be used to yield internal benefits to the managers, in which case 'outsiders' like the government or the shareholders do not benefit. Second, they can be used to yield external benefits to outsiders, leaving nothing for the managers. The investments and the benefits from investments are not verifiable. However, once investments in public firms are sunk, the government which has the residual rights of control over the public firm can 'expropriate' the managers by using the investments for purposes not originally intended. It may, for instance, tell the public managers to use the returns from their investments to keep excess labor. Anticipating such government behavior, public managers refrain from investing. In the private regulated firm, however, private shareholders have no incentive to reallocate the benefits of investments and the government cannot do so because it no longer has the residual rights of control. Hence private managers will invest.

3.1.4 Principal–Agent Relations Within the Firm: Board versus Technological Management[17]

It is not only the principal–agent relation between the owner and the firm which changes as a result of privatization: the decision process within the firm will also change. In Bös and Peters (1988a) the

---

[16] This advantage holds both (i) if government-bureaucrats are given a free hand (discretionary policy) and (ii) if bureaucrats have to operate under special restrictions mandated by the framer (nondiscretionary policy).

[17] This subsection is taken from Bös and Peters (1988a).

responsibilities in the privatized firm are shared between the board and the technological management. As 'the board' we denote those managers who decide on prices, outputs, and production inputs. The technological management decides on control inputs (*internal control*) and informs the board of the production possibilities which result from the chosen control inputs. Only the technological management is fully informed about the technology of the firm. The board lacks this information. However, the technological management informs the board about how the control inputs depend on outputs, on production inputs, and on the extent of privatization. This information is used by the board when planning production.

Changes in the technology are due to the decisions of the technological management of the privatized firm. This management knows the exact relationship between all inputs and outputs,

$$g(z_+, z_-, d) = 0, \tag{3.11}$$

where z_+ is a vector of outputs, z_- a vector of production inputs, and d a vector of control inputs. Applying a netput concept, we have $z_+ > 0$; $z_- < 0$; $d < 0$. The control inputs are used in the administration of that firm which the government is going to privatize. For ease of explanation they are fully separated from production inputs, although some production inputs may be of similar type to control inputs. For instance, we have administrative labor inputs which cannot be used for productive purposes. We assume decreasing returns to control, but allow for all sorts of returns with respect to both z_+ and z_-.[18] The reasons for these assumptions will become clear when we deal with the optimal decision-making of the technological management.

Privatization leads to the replacement of a bureaucratic staff by a market-oriented technological management. Both public and private managers try their best to be efficient. For any set of inputs z_-, a manager will reach the production possibility frontier by maximizing chosen output bundles along a ray $s\bar{z}_+$ where $s > 0$ denotes a scaling factor. In production theory s is well-known as a Farrell measure of output efficiency (Färe, 1988). However, any choice of s requires costs of control $p_d d$ corresponding to the technology $g(s\bar{z}_+, z_-, d)$. p_d is the vector of control-input prices.

The subjective importance of technical efficiency and of the costs of control differs between the two groups of managers. This

---

[18] The assumption of decreasing returns to control could be replaced by assuming $g(\cdot)$ is quasi-concave in d; i.e. the scale-elasticity may be greater than one but each control input has an elasticity of production less than one.

is captured by the utility functions

$$U = U(s\bar{z}_+, p_d d); \quad V = V(s\bar{z}_+, p_d d), \tag{3.12}$$

where U refers to the public managers and V to the private managers. The utility functions are assumed to be strictly increasing in the arguments $U_1 := \partial U/\partial(s\bar{z}_+) > 0$ and $U_2 := \partial U/\partial(p_d d) > 0$, and analogously for V.[19] Moreover, they are quasi-concave in the scale factor and in control costs.

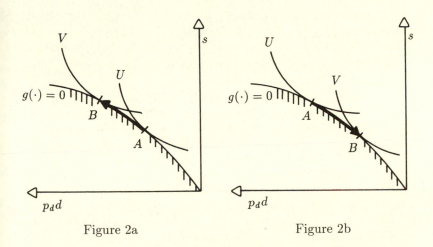

Figure 2a   Figure 2b

In Figure 2a the market-oriented private technocrats concentrate on increases in s and are willing to accept the higher costs of control. In a public firm the public managers' optimization leads to point A; a full transition to private technological management implies a movement towards point B. This is a case where X-inefficiency[20] is reduced at the expense of higher control costs. Note that this follows the Stigler approach of X-inefficiency rather

---

[19] For the positive sign of U_2 and V_2, recall the netput concept, $d < 0$.

[20] There are many different ways to define X-inefficiency. In one of his papers Leibenstein (1969: 600) expressed it as follows: 'I have referred to the degree to which actual output is less than maximum output (for given inputs) as the degree of X-inefficiency, and increases in output with the same inputs as increases in X-efficiency.' However, to understand the basic philosophy of Leibenstein's general X-efficiency theory, the reader should read Leibenstein's 1976 book or at least his short 1978 paper on the topic.

than the Leibenstein approach.[21]   The firm always produces an 'efficient' input–output combination, but the efficient combination is shifted if the control costs change.

In Figure 2b the opposite happens. The public technocrats are insensitive to control costs. They are accustomed to the hierarchical structure of the firm, to red tape and other expensive procedures of internal control. The private technocrats prefer less hierarchy and less expensive control, even if that implies a reduction in the scale of outputs. Here control costs are reduced at the expense of a reduced scale of output.

In the case of full privatization, all public technocrats are replaced by private managers. In the case of partial privatization, more bureaucrats are replaced the higher is the degree of privatization. This degree can be measured by the percentage of shares of the firm which are owned by private shareholders, Θ. Throughout this book it will be convenient to speak of Θ percent, but to define Θ as a figure between zero and one.

Now let $\lambda(\Theta)$ denote the percentage of private managers in the technological management. In a public firm we have no private managers, so $\lambda(0) = 0$. On the other hand, all public technocrats are replaced if the firm is fully privatized and, therefore, $\lambda(1) = 1$. For all cases in between, the percentage of private managers is higher, the higher is the extent of privatization. This shall be captured by assuming an increasing function $\lambda(\Theta)$.

Let the two groups of technocrats enter into negotiations. A special case of such negotiations would be as follows. Define $\overline{U}(\Theta)$ and $\overline{V}(\Theta)$ as the security levels of the two groups of technological managers for any degree of privatization which is exogenously given to the technological management. Consider now a symmetric Nash bargaining solution with a continuum of agents. We aggregate identical agents, namely the $\lambda(\Theta)$ percent of private technocrats and the $(1 - \lambda(\Theta))$ percent of public technocrats. Then the bargaining solution can be written as[22]

$$\max_{d,s} \mathcal{B} = (U - \overline{U})^{1-\lambda(\Theta)}(V - \overline{V})^{\lambda(\Theta)}$$

$$\text{subject to} \quad g(s\overline{z}_+, z_-, d) = 0. \tag{3.13}$$

The game is played cooperatively as long as the utilities U^* and V^* which result from the cooperative solution exceed the respective

[21]   See Leibenstein (1976, 1978), Stigler (1976).
[22]   See for instance Roth (1979: 15–17). For an alternative concept to justify an objective function like (3.13) see Holler (1985: 249–58).

security levels $\overline{U}$ and $\overline{V}$. It should be noted in passing that in the limiting cases, $\Theta = 0$ and $\Theta = 1$, the optimization is also well-defined, although there is no bargaining as only one group of representatives decides on d and s.

The optimal $s^*(z, \Theta)$ determines the output quantities which the firm will choose when combining outputs, control, and production inputs. Hence we have

$$s^*\overline{z}_+ = z_+ \tag{3.14}$$

for any bundle $\overline{z}_+$. Moreover, we have the optimal control inputs

$$d^* = d^*(z, \Theta). \tag{3.15}$$

A maximum in s can be obtained only if, at the optimum, the curvature of the indifference curve $\mathcal{B}$ is greater than the curvature of the production function, as follows from the respective second-order condition.[23] Otherwise the indifference curve and the production function would intersect. Excluding such an intersection is a weaker condition than excluding increasing returns. Only scale effects that are 'too large' are excluded from the analysis.

Choosing the optimal control inputs always implies the minimization of control costs. More information about the process of control can be obtained from the first- and second-order conditions for an optimum. The second-order condition shows that an interior maximum is achieved if the technology exhibits decreasing returns to control. Note that the optimal control inputs d^* depend on the production netputs and on the exogenously given degree of privatization.

One interesting question remains to be answered. In Figures 2a and 2b we distinguish two types of technological managers. Does privatization correspond to Figure 2a or to Figure 2b; i.e., does privatization imply an increase in the scale of output which is made possible by an increase in control costs (Figure 2a), or does privatization imply a reduction of control costs coupled with a reduction of the scale of output (Figure 2b)? Bös and Peters (1988a: 246–7) arrived at the result that only Figure 2b describes what happens in the case of privatization. If there are no possible reductions of control costs from selling any shares, the firm remains in public ownership. Too little output is not taken as the reason for starting to privatize. Therefore, 'inefficient' public firms may remain

---

[23] Formally, $\partial^2 s/\partial d^2|_\mathcal{B} < \partial^2 s/\partial d^2|_g$.

public, because the low output level could only be cured by an unwanted increase in control costs. In the case of partial and total privatization, the changes in the personal composition of both the management and the board of the firm do not only lead to a reduction of control costs, but also to an increase in profits. Undesirable profit increases are traded off against desirable further control cost reductions. Shares will be sold as long as, in the government's opinion, the control cost reductions are large enough to outweigh unwanted profit increases.

Before concluding this subsection, let me mention some criticism which could be raised against the Bös–Peters (1988a) approach. The transition in technology is due to a change in utility functions. The private managers are characterized by a different type of utility function from that of the public bureaucrats. It is the difference in personality types which drives the technology changes. Private technocrats, for example, may have been educated differently from public bureaucrats whose individual judgments are formed by a sort of civil servant ethos. The private technocrats, possibly Yuppy-types, start from different personal attitudes with respect to economic activities.

In modern theory there is a strong bias against such assumptions.[24] Many modern theorists feel better if they assume that individuals have identical utility functions but operate under different incentive schemes. In this book I shall apply the latter approach when dealing with principal–agent problems in public *vis-à-vis* fully privatized firms. However, I do not believe this principal–agent approach is the only correct way to model the world. The reader should be aware that the problem at stake is quite fundamental. It is the old problem of whether it is the personality that is decisive, as reflected in one's utility function, or the economic environment, as reflected in the incentive schemes. In Bös and Peters (1988a) we have chosen a model of personality choices. In the present book (Chapters 6 and 8) I have chosen a model of incentive structures.

3.2   Comparing Efficiency: Empirical Evidence

3.2.1   *Efficiency Comparisons Between Private and Public Firms*

Here it is not necessary to deal with all of the various case studies.[25] Rather it is sufficient to survey the surveys of empirical studies on

---

[24] See for instance Roemer and Silvestre (1989).

[25] Some recent studies include Atkinson and Halvorsen (1986), Chaffai

efficiency comparisons between private and public firms. Some early surveys enthusiastically reported that the evidence was in favor of the private-sector performance, as found for instance in De Alessi (1980). In one of their papers, Bennett and Johnson (1980) even wrote: 'Without exception, the empirical findings indicate that the same level of output could be provided at substantially lower costs if output were produced by the private rather than the public sector.' Some later surveys became a little more cautious.

In their widely quoted 1982 survey, Borcherding, Pommerehne and Schneider concluded:

The literature seems to indicate that (a) private production is cheaper than production in publicly owned and managed firms, and (b) given sufficient competition between public and private producers (and no discriminative regulations and subsidies), the differences in unit cost turn out to be insignificant. From this we may conclude that it is not so much the difference in the transferability of ownership but the lack of competition which leads to the often observed less efficient production in public firms.

I believe this is a fair statement on the basis of the empirical comparisons between public and private firms prior to 1982. However, we should not ignore that at the same time another widely quoted survey on the topic, written by Millward and Parker (1983), arrived at the conclusion that

there is no systematic evidence that public enterprises are less cost effective than private firms. The poorer performance, in this respect, exhibited in the studies of refuse collection and water supply ... has to be balanced against the absence of any significant difference in Canadian railways and Australian airlines and the superior performance in US electric power.[26]

In Boyd's (1986) survey the relevant literature is also summarized with the conclusion that there is no systematic difference between performance under public and private ownership.

Recently, however, Boardman and Vining (1989) presented a survey which once again suggested

an edge for the private sector, but the results vary considerably across sectors ... Evidence of the greater efficiency of private companies appears

(1989), Côté (1989), Färe, Grosskopf, and Logan (1985), Feigenbaum and Teeples (1983), Foreman-Peck and Waterson (1985), Lawarree (1986), Leray (1983), McGuire and Ohsfeldt (1986), and Pryke (1982).

[26] A similar conclusion can be found in Parker (1985).

to be in the delivery of services where governments' subcontracts to the private sector and their monitoring costs – for example, for refuse collection, fire protection and nonrail transit – are relatively low. The health-related literature also suggests greater efficiency for the private sector, but because few of the studies control for service quality differences ... they are not wholly convincing ... In sectors where there is some evidence of superior public efficiency (electricity and water[27]), there is limited competition or the private firms are highly regulated.

It is interesting to note that Boardman and Vining's conclusion with respect to the effects of a lack of competition is exactly the opposite of Borcherding, Pommerehne and Schneider's (1982) *raisonnement*.

Furthermore, to cope with the separation of efficiency differences which result from ownership and from other sources, like competition, Boardman and Vining (1989) compared the efficiency of 409 private companies, 57 public enterprises, and 23 enterprises in mixed public–private ownership, all of which were contained in the list of the 500 largest manufacturing and mining corporations in the world outside the USA, as compiled by *Fortune* magazine in 1983. They obtained 'robust evidence that state enterprises and mixed enterprises are less profitable and less efficient than private corporations'.

3.2.2   The Efficiency of Firms in Mixed Private and Public Ownership

With the sole exception of the USA, firms with mixed private and public ownership are not rare exceptions, but are a very common form of partnership between private and public sectors. The recent papers by Boardman, Eckel and Vining (1986) and by Boardman and Vining (1988) abound with empirical examples, including developed countries like *Canada*[28] (Domtar[29], Canadian Pacific Ltd., Telesat Canada), *France* (Elf Aquitaine, Compagnie Française des

---

[27]   Boardman and Vining surveyed 21 papers which compared the efficiency of public and private electricity and water utilities. Of these, 6 studies came up with higher efficiency of the public corporations, 6 studies reported no difference or ambiguous results, and 9 studies led to the conclusion that the private companies are more efficient.

[28]   See the survey by Mintz (1980), who lists 76 companies in mixed private and public ownership (if one counts the subsidiaries of the various holding companies as separate enterprises).

[29]   See the case study by Boardman, Freedman and Eckel (1986).

Petroles – CFP), *Germany*[30] (Volkswagen, Lufthansa), and *Japan* (Japan Airlines, where until recently the government held 50 percent of the company, Electric Power Development Co). In the UK only 50.2 percent of British Telecom shares were sold in 1984 and the two main power generation companies were partially privatized in early 1991. Mixed enterprises also are important in developing countries, often as joint ventures of the developing country with Western venture capitalists. Western private firms joined ventures with Eastern Europe's communist countries even before the more recent political change in these countries.

There are many reasons why mixed enterprises may emerge. In this book we are interested in those reasons which relate to privatization, i.e. where mixed private and public ownership results from the government selling part of its shares in a formerly public enterprise. Therefore, I mention only in passing that the reverse can happen as well: the government may purchase parts of private firms as a bail-out, or enter a joint venture with private capital owners who would not set up a fully private enterprise because the venture is too risky or because the government engagement in the development of particular regions or key industries makes business in those areas more profitable. (The latter means that the probability of receiving subsidies or relief from particular legal requirements increases with the extent of government ownership.)

In the course of privatization, mixed enterprises may be the result of *financial problems*. They may be the consequence of the government needing money and, accordingly, divesting itself of part of its property – enough to receive a sufficient amount of money but not enough to lose full control of the firms involved. A good example is the recent Austrian 'privatizations', where the government always retained at least 51 percent of the shares. Another financial impetus for the emergence of mixed enterprises, at least as a transitory phenomenon, may result from the government's wish to maximize the revenues from selling a public firm. Although capital markets seem to be able to swallow the 100 percent sale of large public utilities like British Gas, it may be better to sell in

---

[30] For a detailed catalogue see the annual publication of the German Federal Minister of Finance on the Federal government's participation in mixed enterprises (*Die Beteiligungen des Bundes*). The direct and indirect participations of the Federal government (including 'special properties' like rail and mail) were reduced from 958 on December 31, 1982 to 487 on December 31, 1983 – by selling shares of VEBA whose indirect participations were quite numerous – and then in smaller steps to 337 on December 31, 1989. Of course, the German unification led to a major increase of this figure in October 1990.

tranches. This is particularly applicable if the privatization is performed not as a tender offer but as an offer for sale, as is common in the UK. In the case of an offer for sale, the offer price is fixed prior to selling the shares, which reduces the government's ability to skim off potential rents from the buyers of shares. If shares are sold in more than one tranche, the government can renegotiate the offer price. Accordingly, by learning the behavior of the stock market, the government should be able to raise more revenue from its sales.[31] This is particularly relevant if the stock market does not have enough knowledge of how shares of public utilities like gas or electricity should be evaluated: both underwriters and institutional investors will be quite cautious in such a case. However, when the second tranche is to be handled, they will know better. Finally, the people's capitalism movement often leads to mixed enterprises.[32] Since the government has to choose a low issue price of the shares and often gives bonuses to obtain widespread distribution of shares for a longer time, people's capitalism is a costly matter. Accordingly, the government is often unwilling to sell 100 percent of some public firm as 'people's shares'.

Partial privatization which leads to mixed enterprises may also result from the government's desire to retain its power in the firm in order to curtail profit-maximizing behavior, which may be detrimental to particular *public policy goals*.[33] Public utilities with monopolistic market positions provide good examples of instances where the government fears that a profit-maximizing firm would exploit its market position. As an alternative to regulation, the government can retain the ownership of a part of the firm. Its remaining ownership rights enable the government to influence the firm's decisions. Government representatives on the board and government protégés in the technological management may advocate a compromise between profit and welfare maximization. The government representatives and protégés provide the government with inside information – as a sort of 'spies' in the firm – which is an important advantage of internal control and internal regulation. The use of partial privatization as a means to cope with the trade-

---

[31] Compare Vickers and Yarrow (1988a: 184).

[32] Good examples are the Austrian and German people's capitalism activities in the 1950s and early 1960s.

[33] In Germany a conservative member of parliament recently proposed to give up the government's majority ownership in Lufthansa, but to retain 26 percent of the shares in order to guarantee government control over certain important decisions.

off between profit and welfare maximization is the heart of the normative theory in this book. However, it should be mentioned that, in case of informational asymmetries between the board and the technological management, partial privatization may lead to wrong management incentives. The informational advantages and the incentive disadvantages of partial privatization will be treated explicitly when dealing with positive theories of privatization.[34]

Table 2:   Control and the Behavior of Mixed Enterprises

Government Proportion of Total Shares	Private Share Distribution	
	Concentrated	Dispersed
Low	High private owner control, strong profit-maximizing pressure.	Low owner control high management discretion. Disproportionate government control.
Medium	Indeterminate control. Joint owner control if consensus on objectives; if not, management may exhibit cognitive dissonance.	Intermediate government owner control, with some management discretion. Private owners relatively weak.
High	High government owner control. Little control by private owners. Pressure to fulfil the rationale of public owner.	High government owner control. Strong pressure to meet government objectives. Minimal control by private owners.

Source: Boardman and Vining (1988: 29).

After considering the reasons for mixed enterprises to emerge in the course of privatization, we now turn to a short treatment of the *behavior of firms in mixed private and public ownership*. In one of their recent papers, Boardman and Vining (1988) develop a typology of the behavior of mixed enterprises by distinguishing them according to the government proportion of total shares and the private share distribution as shown in Table 2. The authors give many institutional examples for their six categories of mixed

[34] See Ch. 8 below.

enterprises. They argue that government control increases with the proportion of shares, whereas private control increases with concentration. The latter part of their hypothesis is of particular interest for privatization because people's capitalism is precisely a policy which aims at dispersed private share distribution. Does this imply that the government chooses partial privatization by people's capitalism in order to retain its power over the firm? I think this is incorrect. The assumption of weak control in the case of dispersed private ownership is unappealing. Rather, I would argue that it is the *capital market* which is controlling, even if there is dispersed ownership. If the firm strongly deviates from profit maximization, as the weak position of the dispersed private shareholders might suggest, then the dividends and hence the market value of the firm would be reduced. Obviously, potential share buyers would soon learn that 'people's capitalism' issues are a bad buy and should not be bought in the first place. Actual shareholders would try to get rid of their shares in due course.

Let me deal with another interesting point in the Boardman–Vining (1988) theory. They argue that ownership conflicts in mixed enterprises are less probable if the firm is originally established with joint public and private participation. If the mixed ownership is instead created by a government buy-in, the conflict potential is higher. This is of interest for privatization because here the mixed ownership does not arise *ab initio*. Hence, according to the Boardman–Vining approach, partially privatized firms face a high conflict potential. It is expected to be particularly high if the government objectives are vague and changing. If they are clear and stable, the authors expect 'limited conflict, often on distribution of profits rather than goals'.

However, in my opinion, these hypotheses are not fully convincing. Whether conflict potential increases with a buy-in or, in the case of privatization, with a buy-out depends very much on the way ownership is transferred. If we face a sort of hostile government buy-in, as in the Boardman, Freedman, and Eckel's (1986) case study on the Domtar takeover, then of course the conflict potential is high. However, if a government buy-in rescues the firm from bankruptcy, I would not expect a high conflict potential. In the case of privatization, where the ownership transferral always is friendly and voluntary, I would not expect too much conflict. Perhaps, in some cases, the emergence of a mixed enterprise as the result of privatization could even be regarded as joint public–private establishment of a new firm. What about the increase in the conflict potential arising from government objectives being vague and changing? There is certainly a point in that. However, it is also easy to imagine intense conflict on the basis of a unique, clear, and stable government objective and some easy compromise in the case of vague multiple objectives, the management satisfying the government with respect to one objective while trading off some other objectives.

Finally, we must have a look at the *empirical evidence* on the profitability and efficiency of mixed enterprises compared with that of both private and public enterprises. Mintz (1980) finds a sample of Canadian mixed enterprises to be 'less profitable than other non-financial firms, but not significantly less profitable than the highly-competitive retail trade and highly-regulated transportation industries'.[35] Viallet (1982) finds that the returns on mixed firms' shares do not differ from the returns of those of private firms. Boardman and Vining (1989), in their study of 409 private, 23 mixed, and 57 state-owned enterprises[36] (as part of the 500 largest mining and manufacturing corporations in the world outside the USA), find that, 'with respect to profitability, mixed enterprises perform about the same or worse than state-owned enterprises while in terms of efficiency, mixed enterprises perform about the same or slightly better than state-owned enterprises'. The Boardman–Vining (1989) study illustrates that in many cases the mixed public and private ownership structure obviously puts the firm in a category similar to public enterprises. Conflicts between private and public shareholders may emerge over multiple and unclear government objectives, leaving a wide scope for discretionary management behavior. This is the result of too little theoretical thinking about the proper role of mixed enterprises. Boardman, Eckel, and Vining (1986: 235–6) mention that mixed enterprises *may* be more efficient than public enterprises because (i) they may be a cost-minimizing way for government to reconcile profitability and social goals, (ii) they give inside information to the government in a simple and cheap way, and (iii) they avoid costly accounting procedures and other government restrictions and controls which prevail in public enterprises. In the normative theory part of this book we justify partial privatization exactly along the lines of the Boardman–Eckel–Vining (1986) paper. Only if the theoretical role of mixed ownership is

---

[35] This conclusion has been reached on the basis of three measures of profit rates: the after-tax rate of return to shareholders' equity, before-tax rate of return to equity, and after-tax rate of return to equity and debt.

[36] Examples of mixed enterprises in that sample are British Petroleum, Canada Development Corporation, and Volkswagen.

clearly understood can inefficiency-increasing conflicts be avoided and the mixed enterprise be used as an instrument to reconcile the conflicting objectives of profit and welfare maximization.

3.2.3 Efficiency and Takeover Threats

Recently, I asked a prominent US economist why privatization might increase efficiency. His spontaneous answer was: takeover threats. Public enterprises do not face them, privatized enterprises do. This, in his opinion, was the decisive difference in the incentives of the management. The takeover threat leads to higher efficiency in the privatized firm. Is this 'Chicago view' correct?

Most empirical studies on takeovers of private firms have concentrated on changes in market values of the companies involved and have shown huge increases in the values of the acquired firms but, on average, small positive or negative changes in the value of the acquiring firm.[37] If the capital market is assumed to be perfect, this result reflects increases in the profitability of the acquired firm which, in turn, must result from increases in productive efficiency. However, this argument is superficial. Scherer (1988) rejects the hypothesis of the always-perfect capital market and concludes that 'operating performance [of the acquired firms] neither improved nor deteriorated significantly following takeover' (p. 76). This persuasive argument is in line with papers by Cowling *et al.* (1980), Malatesta (1983), Newbould (1970), and Singh (1971, 1975).

If efficiency increases are not the main consequence of takeovers, it is more appropriate to focus on the transfer of rents which results from takeovers (Shleifer and Vishny, 1988). According to this theory, takeovers mean a transfer of wealth from managers and employees to the shareholders of the acquired firm. This transfer often has been justified by the free-cash-flow theory (see, for instance, Jensen, 1988), which postulates the residual property right of the shareholders: managers and employees have the right to receive only that compensation which has explicitly been contracted: remaining cash flows must be directed to the shareholders. However, in practice managers often use the remaining cash flow for non-value-maximizing objectives. The takeover, according to that

---

[37] Franks and Harris (1986a,b), Mandelker (1974), Asquith (1983), Jarrell, Brickley, and Netter (1988). The losses seem to be more important in the longer run. See the empirical studies by Jensen and Ruback (1983) and Magenheim and Mueller (1987).

theory, gives the shareholders what had been withheld by the management. However, even if that might be correct, a benefit–cost analysis of a takeover should aggregate all gains and losses: the gains of shareholders of the acquired company, possible losses of shareholders of the acquiring company, and losses in income and jobs of managers and employees compared to their incomes from new positions.

Even if a takeover itself does not influence efficiency, takeover *threats* might do so. Perhaps one could argue that takeovers have no impact on efficiency because, prior to the takeover itself, takeover threats have already led to efficient production. However, the evidence on this hypothesis is inconclusive. Some recent studies even argue that efficiency losses may result from the threat of takeover: managers facing takeover threats engage in short-run profit maximization activities to reduce the probability of becoming a takeover target.[38] According to Vickers and Yarrow (1988a: 19–21) there are ambiguous consequences of an increase in the takeover probability which stem from an exogenous change in the market for corporate control. First, the incumbent manager has an interest in increasing his personal utility by reducing his personal effort while he is still in control of the firm. Second, he also realizes that his shirking increases the probability of takeover. This gives him an incentive to increase his personal effort.

In light of this recent literature, it is not difficult to reject the hypothesis that takeover threats are the main reason why privatization may lead to higher efficiency. Let us distinguish between privatized firms which operate in competitive markets and fully behave like private firms, and privatized firms which operate in a monopolistic position and are regulated by the government. Firms in the first group face all the usual takeover threats. However, we have seen the ambivalent evidence on the efficiency effects of takeovers threats. Hence we cannot unambiguously conclude that efficiency is increased when firms are exposed to takeover threats after privatization. Firms in the second group are regulated and the raider knows that he too will be regulated after executing a successful takeover. Therefore the regulated firms are not attractive candidates for a takeover. Profits will be low even after takeover, while divestiture typically will be legally forbidden. Since the privatized utility knows it is not a good target for potential raiders, there is no takeover threat at all and consequently no influence

---

[38] For a recent theoretical study see Stein (1988).

on productivity.[39] If in addition a 'golden share' had been stipulated, the privatized utility would be 200 percent protected against
takeovers.[40]

[39] Vickers and Yarrow (1988a: 22) mention only one argument which pro-
tects public utilities against takeovers, namely their considerable size. I believe
this is an incorrect argument, given the many takeovers of huge firms which
have taken place since the invention of junk bonds. For recent US experiences
see, for instance, Varian (1988: 3), Jensen (1988: 22, 25).

[40] See Graham and Prosser (1988: 84–5).

4 Market Allocation in the Transition from Public to Private Firms

Full privatization means that the government withdraws from the direct economic engagement involved in public ownership. This may imply a transition to an indirect engagement via regulation or even to the complete renunciation of the government's engagement in the firm's activities. The government's complete withdrawal is appropriate if unregulated markets bring about socially desirable results.

For public utilities, *regulated private ownership* is an intermediate step in the move from government power to the governance of markets. Price regulation typically means that the government wants to assure low prices of goods whose consumption is of particular importance for a large portion of the population. However, price regulation of a fully privatized firm is different in spirit from price regulation of a public enterprise. In the public firm, the price constraint is directly relevant for the government budget. It determines the government's revenue from the firm or the deficit which must be covered by taxes or by public debt. Hence the revenue-cost constraint relates to the opportunity costs of the activities of the public firm. Compared with alternative uses of financial means, the magnitude of the activities of the public enterprise is restricted by the revenue-cost constraint. This refers to the reconciliation between the public firm and other public projects and the private sector from which the money must come to finance a public utility's deficit. In the case of regulated private ownership, the price constraint refers only to the consumers. They shall be protected against monopolistic exploitation. There is no connection between the price constraint and the government budget.[1] This makes it possible to define the constraint of a privatized firm only in terms of prices. $RPI - X$ precisely reflects this change in the spirit of price constraints. Although information about the revenues and costs of the privatized firm has to be considered if the

---

[1] Only indirectly could a price constraint of a privatized firm be relevant for the government's budget: when setting the issue price of the shares in the case of privatization, a lower issue price must be chosen if regulation of the privatized firm has been announced. This reduces the government's revenues in the process of privatization. Later on, however, no connection between the price constraint and the government's budget exists.

regulator wants to keep the firm profitable,[2] this is only a participation constraint without relation to the opportunity costs of government money versus private money.

Full *reliance on markets* is the final step in the move from government power to the governance of markets. The market position of fully privatized firms differs decisively from the market position of public enterprises, in particular in the case of public utilities. If publicly owned, these utilities are sheltered from aggressive market forces. Privatization implies that this protection is relinquished. The theoretical treatment of the market position of privatized firms, therefore, has more in common with private than with public enterprise theory. For instance, entry into privatized utilities markets must be explicitly taken into account. We also should deal with the question of how the privatizing government might encourage market entrance if private initiatives are too weak.

Policies of privatization, moreover, can be used in a challenging way to build up desirable market structures. In a duopolistic market with two public enterprises, it is possible to privatize one enterprise, leaving the other one in public ownership. The result is a 'mixed' duopoly, where the welfare-oriented public enterprise sets limits on the profit-oriented pricing policy of the privatized firm, whereas the privatized firm exerts pressure on the productive efficiency of the public enterprise. It is also possible to split up a public enterprise into several companies and to privatize only some of them. In this case we also obtain a 'mixed' market structure. Divesting a public utility in the process of privatization, moreover, can be used to introduce direct or indirect (yardstick) competition where prior to privatization no competition existed. Vertical separation of upstream and downstream production could also be imposed if there are several successor companies of a single public enterprise. The recent privatization of electricity in the UK is the best practical example of privatization coupled with a separation of production units.

In the following survey we treat both intermediate and final steps of the move from government power to the governance of markets. Accordingly, we always begin with a short treatment of public firm theories, then proceed to theories of regulated privatized firms, and, in conclusion, treat theories of privatized firms without government regulation.

---

[2] See Schmalensee (1989). The problem will be treated in more detail in the following section.

4.1 Monopolistic Markets

4.1.1 The Public Monopoly

The economic theory of public monopolies can be divided into two parts: positive theory and normative theory. The positive theory describes how a public firm actually behaves. The normative theory prescribes how a public firm should behave.

The *normative theory* refers to higher-order value judgments typically measured by some sort of social welfare function which combines the individual consumer utilities and a policy-maker's valuation of these utilities. There have been several waves of discussion on the normative theory of public-sector pricing. The first wave began with Hotelling (1938), who advocated marginal-cost pricing on welfare grounds, even if increasing returns to scale lead to a deficit of the public enterprise. The second wave was the second-best movement. One example in Lipsey and Lancaster's (1956/57) seminal paper referred to a public enterprise which adjusts to monopolistic price–cost margins in the private economy. In that case it is not welfare-optimal if the public enterprise sticks to marginal-cost pricing. In adjusting to the private monopolistic prices, public prices must be increased if privately and publicly priced goods are substitutes, and decreased if they are complements.[3] The third wave started with the revival of the Ramsey rule by Baumol and Bradford (1970): public-sector pricing under a revenue-cost constraint leads to an inverse-elasticity rule, at least if cross-price elasticities are low. Accordingly, the public monopoly must choose higher price–cost margins for price-elastic goods. The undesired distributional consequences of Ramsey prices can be eliminated by applying Feldstein prices,[4] which result from the maximization of a distributionally weighted social welfare function.

In the late seventies and early eighties peak-load pricing was the central concern of the literature on public utilities. Because of the concentration on the practical problems of peak loads, dogmatic aspects of the normative theory of public-sector pricing receded into the background. Even Drèze's (1984) paper on public pricing in the presence of rationed labor markets did not lead to

---

[3] Note that the Lipsey–Lancaster paper, and the stream of literature following it, does not deal with the strategic aspects of oligopoly theory, but with monopolistic competition. For further details and references see Bös (1986a: 225–30).

[4] See Feldstein (1972a,b,c).

a new wave of normative theory about public monopolies. It was not until informational asymmetries became central in theories of regulation that new impacts were made on the theory of public-sector pricing. It must be noted, however, that principal–agent approaches to public monopolies can consist of both normative and positive theories, depending on the government's objective function.

Let us now turn to the *positive theories* of public monopolies, which, in contrast to the normative theory, have a comparatively short history. The construction of positive theories began in the late seventies and early eighties when an increasing number of papers was devoted to public firms' non-welfare-maximization objectives. Niskanen's (1971) 'mixed bureau' can be seen as a precursor of this development: the mixed bureau is a public enterprise which wants to maximize a budget composed of government grants and revenues from selling output to customers.[5]

The positive theory of public enterprises starts from those managerial or political objectives which are applied in practice. Typically, profit maximization is excluded from the analysis. Consequently other objectives are of relevance. The managers are prone to maximize output or revenue because these figures have been rising impressively during recent decades and therefore are good candidates for indicating managerial success. A good example was London Transport's policy of passenger miles maximization as applied in the late seventies.[6] Sometimes, managers are instructed to apply objectives which represent the 'political fashion of the day'. Energy-saving policies in the mid-seventies are good examples of this, as is the minimization of the cost-of-living index by public pricing.[7] The latter policy was explicitly applied by the UK government under Edward Heath.

Sometimes 'positive theory' refers to political intentions in the narrow sense of the word. Then public firms must operate so as to maximize votes.[8] The zero tariffs of local public transportation, which often are used as a means to attract voters in local elections, provide a good example of this. Whereas public-sector pricing affects the whole constituency of voters, the decisions of employment and investment affect only a small proportion of the constituency. Public-firm workers typically are well organized,

---

[5] See Bös, Tillmann and Zimmermann (1984).
[6] See Glaister and Collings (1978) and Bös (1978b).
[7] For an extensive treatment of these problems see Bös (1978a).
[8] See Bös and Zimmermann (1987).

however, and the powerful trade unions which operate in public firms over-accentuate labor interests, most likely with the result of output inefficiency and of cost inefficiency.[9]

More recently, the positive theory of public firms has begun to deal with the incentives of the firm's management, given imperfect information on the part of the government or some other regulating authority.[10] Instead of only recognizing inefficiencies as the price for the achievement of some public policy goal, the manager's reward can be made contingent on the public goal. This would inspire more efficiency without giving up the goal. A good example is Chamley, Marchand, and Pestieau's (1989) proposal to link management's incomes in public firms to labor hired in the firm.[11]

4.1.2 The Regulated Privatized Monopoly

If a privatized firm retains monopolistic power in the supply of at least some of its products, unconstrained profit maximization will lead to high prices which are undesired by the privatizing government. Like any other privately owned public utility, such a firm will be subject to regulation to avoid consumer exploitation by too high prices. The rate-of-return regulation which has been applied in many countries for many years has been criticized:

(i)   for its lack of incentives toward cost reduction and innovation in technology, because increasing capital inputs imply an increase in the allowed profit;

(ii)   for its capital-distorting effects: since the allowed rate of return is defined as a percentage of the capital inputs, profit can be increased by producing too capital-intensively – the so-called Averch–Johnson effect;

(iii)   because of its high information requirements for the regulatory authority: since the profit allowed is defined as a percentage of the capital inputs, the regulator has to determine what depreciation policy is appropriate, and how joint capital costs are allocated between regulated and unregulated services, and between the various regulated services.[12]

---

[9] See Gravelle (1984) and Rees (1984b).
[10] Rees's (1984a) 'public enterprise game' is a particularly well-known example. See also Rees (1988).
[11] The authors suggest manager incomes which depend on welfare and on labor hired in the firm, where the income schedule is linear.
[12] See, e.g., Littlechild (1988: 55), and Braeutigam and Panzar (1989).

The US Federal Communications Commission, FCC (1987, 1988), proposed replacing rate-of-return regulation with 'price-cap' regulation in the market for local and long-distance telephone service. Meanwhile, many US states have adopted price-cap regulation of intrastate telephone services provided by AT&T, and the FCC has recently begun to apply price caps on AT&T's prices for interstate services.[13] Price caps typically refer to prices for monopolistically supplied goods. Regulators rely on markets to prevent excessive prices for any other goods which are supplied by the regulated firm. A separate price cap can be defined for every single good in monopolistic supply. If the index m denotes monopolistically supplied goods, the firm faces constraints $p_m \leq \bar{p}_m$, where the price ceilings $\bar{p}_m$ are set by the regulator and the firm can choose any price p_m up to the limit $\bar{p}_m$. However, the flexibility of the regulated firm can greatly be enhanced if a joint price ceiling is defined for a basket of services supplied by the firm. The best-known example of such a joint ceiling is the $RPI - X$ regulation: an average price of some bundle of the firm's products must not exceed the retail price index minus an exogenously fixed constant X. This form of price regulation has been proposed by Littlechild (1983) and is the basis of the regulation of, *inter alia*, British Telecom, British Gas, and the UK public electricity suppliers (i.e. the twelve area companies responsible for the local distribution of electricity).

In static full-information models, using price caps of the type $p_m \leq \bar{p}_m$ is superior to other types of regulation because, like competitive markets, they only impose price ceilings without further distorting inputs or outputs. However, the more uncertain the costs of the firm, the higher the price ceilings must be set in order to keep the regulated firm profitable. At high levels of uncertainty, cost-plus regulation will be preferred to price-cap regulation, in particular if the regulator's objective is to maximize consumer surplus; if the objective is to maximize total welfare, which includes the firm's profits, cost-plus may be less preferred than price caps because the higher price limits are less damaging to the objective (Schmalensee, 1989). Since asymmetric information is intrinsic to price regulation, it may be a good idea to let the firm choose between various forms of regulation so as to exploit its private knowledge about its capabilities and cost-reducing activities. In Lewis

---

[13] Mathios and Rogers (1989) present an empirical investigation comparing AT&T's prices for intrastate, direct dial, long-distance telephone services in states that apply price-cap regulation with those services in states which continue to use rate-of-return regulation.

and Sappington (1989) the firm chooses between a modified rate-of-return regulation and a modified price-cap regulation. Firms with a potential for large productivity improvements self-select for price caps.

Let us now turn to some important practical implementation issues which shall be treated at the example of $RPI - X$ regulation.

(i)   The $RPI - X$ constraint refers to an average price. Averaging requires weighting of the single prices and the regulator must decide which weights to choose. Natural choices of weights would be the product quantities, either of the present period or of the period before. In the UK, however, the chosen weights are the share of the previous period's total revenue that the respective service earns.[14] A detailed analysis of the possible distortions caused by various weighting schemes will be given in Chapter 7.

Moreover, constraining an average price allows the regulated firm to rebalance the prices of the various services it supplies. British Telecom, for instance, used the $RPI - X$ regulation to increase rental charges and local calls, but to reduce prices of particular long-distance calls.[15]

(ii)   Price-cap regulation is applied in both monopolistic and oligopolistic markets. British Telecom's price regulation, for instance, includes both local calls and national long-distance calls, where the latter are exposed to competition by Mercury. The inclusion of long-distance calls actually weakens price regulation of local calls. Technological advance and competitive pressure are greatest with respect to long-distance calls. Hence their prices should in any case fall sharply. The inclusion of these services in the price-cap formula allows higher increases in the price of local calls without violating $RPI - X$ on average.[16]

(iii)   Prices are capped with reference to the retail price index. No forecast problems arise if the index of the previous period is

---

[14] This implies a similarity between the $RPI-X$ regulation and the well-known Vogelsang–Finsinger (1979) mechanism. Vogelsang (1988b) therefore extends this mechanism by combining it with price capping. His improved regulatory formula converges to Ramsey pricing if a steady state is achieved. Neu (1988) criticizes Vogelsang's steady-state assumption and suggests weights for the prices which include estimates of the growth rates of the various products. If the growth rates have been estimated correctly, then Ramsey prices result. A related paper is by Brennan (1989).

[15] For details see Vickers and Yarrow (1988a: 224–5).

[16] See Vickers and Yarrow (1988a: 213). See also White Paper (1991: 33–5) for the inclusion of international services within the cap, accompanied by an increase of British Telecom's X from 4.5 to 6.25 percent.

used.[17] However, if the rate of inflation changes, the regulated firm may be constrained too much or too little. This may become a serious problem if inflation changes rapidly. Alternatively, an estimate of the present-period RPI may be taken, coupled with a correction term to avoid strategic overestimation and windfall gains. Some special provision may be taken for increases in costs which fluctuate considerably and are beyond the firm's control, like North Sea gas in the case of British Gas. Then we have an $RPI - X + Y$ regulation.[18]

The use of RPI has been criticized because the basket of items used in the retail price index contains many goods which are irrelevant to this particular regulation like food or mortgage costs. In addition, it also contains goods which are already an element of the regulatory formula like Y-factor fuel costs in the regulatory formula which is applied to British Gas. Helm (1988a) proposes replacing the RPI with either an industry-based index or a cost-of-inputs index.

(iv)   Most crucial, of course, is the determination of X. Cynics argue that for privatized firms X typically has been chosen too low to give the firm higher profits, which increases the government's revenue from the sale of shares.[19] 'X can in fact be chosen on the basis of a whole range of criteria. Though nominally a price rule, it is these criteria which determine what sort of animal $RPI - X$ actually is' (Helm, 1988a: 113).

In principle, X should be determined according to the firm's potential for price reduction. This would imply setting X on the basis of an index of expected productivity increases, taking into account the combined effects of demand increases and economies of scale.[20] In practice, setting and revising X seems to be contingent on regulators' assessment of what a fair rate of return is for the firm.[21] Then $RPI - X$ may be close to rate-of-return regulation.

The $RPI - X$ regulation must provide for revising X when necessary. One of the main advantages of price caps over rate-of-return

---

[17] As in the case of British Telecom.

[18] For details see Helm (1988a) and Letwin (1988: 130–41).

[19] See Helm (1988a: 113). More recently Green (1990: 13) presented the same idea with respect to the '$RPI+X$' regulation of the UK public electricity suppliers: '...X between zero and 2.5 %, to finance future investment which would otherwise depress the companies' issue prices.'

[20] For details see Vickers and Yarrow (1988a: 214–15).

[21] When resetting X for British Telecom in 1989, the regulator indicated that rate of return was the most important criterion, but not the only one. See Beesley and Littlechild (1989: 460), or Cave and Trotter (1990: 59–61, 73).

regulation is that it gives an incentive to cut costs. In a theoretical model where X is set for ever, this incentive is preserved. However, if the firm knows that X is going to be revised, for instance if the rate of return is too high, the firm will start to behave strategically, not cutting the costs as much as desirable.[22]

Increasing X increases the incentives for cost reduction. A higher X leads to lower prices and higher quantities. The higher the quantity, the higher the returns on cost reduction.[23] Of course, there is a limit to this effect. If X becomes too high, the firm will require a revision of the regulatory formula in order to at least recover its costs.

4.1.3 The Private Monopoly

In the late seventies and early eighties, the role of potential competition was accentuated: private monopolies were said to be effectively controlled by potential competition.[24] Accordingly, in a sort of Chicago School view of the world, private monopolies were often said to be harmless: they could not exploit their market position because they had to face the threat of market entry. Even a firm which produced under specific economies of scale and scope[25] could not choose monopoly prices in the Cournot sense. If this view were correct, privatizing governments would not have to bother about price regulation of privatized monopolies. The threat of entry would prevent any consumer exploitation.

However, recent literature has shown that private monopolies must be seen in a more pessimistic way. First, entry-deterring prices are always possible as long as there are sunk costs associated with market entry. If entry costs are high, the incumbent prices will also be high. The over-accentuation of the contestability of monopolies, as presented in many papers in the late seventies and early eighties, has only resulted from the assumption of zero sunk costs of market entry.

[22] Littlechild (1988: 59).
[23] For a detailed discussion see Cabral and Riordan (1989: 95–6).
[24] A comprehensive treatment of the approach is Baumol, Panzar, and Willig (1982).
[25] Baumol, Panzar, and Willig (1982) carefully define the specific cost advantages of such monopolies. The sustainability of a monopoly requires decreasing ray average costs and transray convex costs. These modern concepts correspond to economies of scale and scope, respectively.

Second, the theory of contestability in the late seventies and early eighties assumed that incumbents and potential entrants have the same access to the most recent technical development and therefore can operate under identical cost functions. By the same token, full information of both incumbent and entrant was assumed. This is clearly unrealistic. We will find that an incumbent, in contrast to an unexperienced newcomer, often has an informational advantage based on past production experience.

Recent theories which explicitly consider sunk entry costs, strategic entry deterrence, and asymmetric information are typically game-theoretic. They highlight the strategic interactions, giving many more weapons to both incumbent and entrant than the theory of contestable markets, which dealt with market entry as if the incumbent's production possibility frontier were the only relevant problem.

4.2 Oligopolistic Markets

4.2.1 Public Oligopoly

Let us begin the treatment of oligopolistic markets by dealing with the case of an oligopoly in which several public enterprises compete with each other. Such oligopolies can be found in markets for energy, where customers can choose between publicly supplied gas and publicly supplied electricity. They also can be found in public transportation if a public bus company and a public rail (underground) company compete or if a public railway company has to cope with competition from a public airline. Competition between several publicly owned banks has been a common phenomenon in many countries.

In a *normative treatment* of the problem, ideally the oligopoly problem is reduced to a monopoly problem where various publicly owned factories are perfectly coordinated to achieve a social optimum. Consider a fully informed benevolent planner who wants to maximize welfare by supplying one or more goods publicly. If there are diseconomies of scale and scope, maximizing welfare requires that production be split up into various units. The planner sets the welfare-optimal number of production units and then instructs these units to set those prices which he has calculated to be welfare-optimal. Since the behavior of the various production units is fully coordinated by the planner, there is no intrinsic oligopoly problem left. We are back to monopoly theory.

If the planner's welfare orientation is not impeded by any exogenous constraints, marginal-cost pricing will be chosen. Since, at the optimum, some production units may realize increasing returns to scale and others decreasing returns, some of the production units may incur a deficit (Vogelsang, 1990: 34). Let us now consider the imposition of exogenous constraints, taking as an example revenue-cost constraints. We will not obtain a 'real' theory of oligopoly if the planner applies one objective function (welfare) and one revenue-cost constraint for various production units, implying full coordination of their policies. Baumol, Panzar, and Willig (1982: 334–6) call this a *viable-industry* Ramsey solution, which implies minimization of production costs in the industry and, typically, deficits for at least one firm. By way of illustration, consider an energy ministry which runs the two production units of electricity and gas and faces a parliamentary decision which specifies that its overall deficit should not exceed some fixed amount.

It is difficult to find institutional justifications as to why various public production units should follow a policy which is characterized by *one* welfare function but *separate* profit constraints for each unit (the *viable-firm* Ramsey solution according to Baumol, Panzar, and Willig, 1982: 337–43). There is no welfare justification for such a splitting-up of profit constraints. If political institutions like the parliament are hostile to internal transfers between publicly owned firms, why should they accept general welfare maximization as an objective of the various production units, but oppose welfare-optimal internal transfers?[26]

As an alternative policy, one could think of policy-makers who want to apply an 'arm's length approach' to public firms by decentralizing the planning units: each firm should maximize its own contribution to welfare, given its own revenue-cost constraint (called an *autarkic* Ramsey solution according to Baumol, Panzar, and Willig, 1982: 343–5). However, this is a suboptimal policy in a theoretical framework which considers the maximization of welfare by a benevolent, fully informed planner. If an arm's length approach is to be applied to improve the incentives of managers of public firms, it is better to give up the normative approach and turn to *positive theories* which accept asymmetric information and conflicting objectives of the government and management. (Both

---

[26] The only possible explanation of the various profit constraints could be given by the entry costs of potential market entrants. However, this is not dealt with in the present subsection where we assume that there was no market entry. For the case of market entry see the following subsection on mixed markets.

government and management may be interested in objectives which differ from welfare!) Unfortunately, to my knowledge there are no positive theories of public oligopoly to be found in the literature. This is regrettable since one can think of many theories which could be constructed to deal with the phenomenon.

In the first step of such positive theorizing, non-cooperative behavior of the public firms should be dealt with, for the moment leaving the government aside. In a public duopoly, for instance, the budget-maximizing managers of two public firms may compete and each may have incomplete information about the cost function of its competitor. As a second step, a sequential game could be modelled. In the first stage of this game the government, as owner, announces incentive-pay schedules for the managers of the duopolistic firms. In the second stage, the managers simultaneously set the prices of the supplied goods. The sequential game could then be extended to include capacity decisions which need not be taken simultaneously by the public duopolists.

4.2.2 Mixed Markets

In this subsection we deal with oligopolistic markets where at least one public firm and at least one private firm compete with each other. Such a 'mixed' public–private market can be the result of privatization, of nationalization, or of market entry. In the first case some but not all public firms of an oligopolistic market have been privatized in order to increase productive efficiency. In the second case some but not all private firms have been nationalized in order to improve welfare. In the third case either a public firm enters the market of a private incumbent or vice versa.

Some recent models on mixed markets deal with a duopoly consisting of one private and one public enterprise. The private firm maximizes profit, the public firm maximizes welfare. Both participants in the market are perfectly informed. Then the welfare properties of the various duopoly solutions are compared. If the public firm takes the Stackelberg leader position, welfare is improved over the Nash solution (Bös, 1986a: 236; Vickers and Yarrow, 1988a: 51–2). In special cases, however, the Stackelberg follower position can be welfare-superior to the leader position (Beato and MasColell, 1984). A similar problem arises if the number of firms is greater than two. De Fraja and Delbono (1989) present an interesting special case where the public firm cannot obtain the welfare-desirable Stackelberg leader position. The authors show that higher welfare can be obtained if the public firm maximizes profit instead of welfare. The public firm produces less than it would under its welfare objective, but induces a welfare-enhancing expansion in the output of the private firms.

A priori, these models have nothing to do with privatization. However, they can easily be interpreted as the result of privatization if the private firm in any such model is considered to be the result of a privatization process. By way of an example, we could compare (i) a model with two public firms, both maximizing welfare, with (ii) a model of one public and one private firm, where the private firm is perceived as the privatized equivalent of the second public firm in model (i). Let us apply this sort of interpretation to the Beato–MasColell (1984) model. We have a public and a private firm, both producing the same homogeneous good. The private firm was publicly owned, but has now been privatized. We learn from Beato and MasColell that after privatization a Stackelberg-follower position for the remaining public firm may be welfare-optimal. This contradicts the usual second-best paradigm. The Stackelberg-follower position of a welfare-maximizing public firm implies marginal-cost pricing, although there is a market distortion caused by the privatized firm's profit maximization.

Even more interesting is a recent paper by Cremer, Marchand, and Thisse (1989).[27] They consider an economy with n firms producing a homogeneous good. m of the n firms are publicly owned and choose welfare-maximizing break-even quantities. The other firms are privately owned and maximize profit. The analysis is restricted to Cournot–Nash equilibria. If the cost functions were identical, the welfare maximum would be attained in an economy with public firms only.[28] However, the authors introduce an asymmetry in the cost functions: in public firms the employees are paid a premium over the market wages prevailing in the private firms.[29]

---

[27] See also De Fraja (1991).

[28] As, for instance, in Merrill and Schneider (1966: 409–10).

[29] Some critics feel uneasy about the authors' treatment of the wage premium. This premium does not enter the consumer surplus which the firm wants to maximize. However, it is taken into account in the break-even constraints of the individual public firms. This specification implies that the wage premium is treated as a pure transfer. The public firm has an objective function which consists of the sum of consumer and producer surplus where, at the optimum, the producer surplus including the wage premium is equal to zero. Hence, in writing down the objective function, the producer surplus including the wage premium can be omitted and only consumer surplus is maximized. Obviously, the optimal quantities depend on the wage premium.

Let us now start with an economy comprised exclusively of private firms and attempt to determine how many firms should be publicly owned in order to achieve a welfare maximum. It is welfare-improving to nationalize one firm: the behavior of the public firm leads to higher aggregate output which is sold at lower market price. Now consider the nationalization of further enterprises. At the non-cooperative solution of the game the nationalized firms behave as if they cooperated; i.e., they behave like one institution. Hence it is welfare-superior to have only one public break-even firm rather than two or more, because each public firm has to finance the same amount of sunk costs. Therefore it is welfare-optimal to nationalize only one firm. This result is similar in spirit to the results in the normative theory part of this book, where a single *firm* is partially privatized to achieve the optimum trade-off between a higher productive efficiency and a lower welfare orientation.[30]

In Cremer, Marchand, and Thisse, inefficiency of public firms is exogenously introduced by assuming a premium over the market wages prevailing in private firms. However, the theory of mixed markets can also be used for an endogenous explanation of higher public-sector pay. De Fraja (1990a) deals with a two-stage game: in the first stage a public and a private enterprise simultaneously and independently bargain with a trade union to determine wages. The public firm maximizes welfare, the private firm maximizes profits. The bargaining solution is of the Nash type. In the second stage the two firms are engaged in a non-cooperative Cournot competition on the output market. The outcome of the second stage is perfectly anticipated in the first stage. As a result of the two-stage game the public firm chooses higher wages.

The public-wage premium is due to asymmetric firm responses to wage increases of the other duopolist. Higher wage always implies a higher price and, hence, a lower quantity sold. However, an increase in the private wage leads to a significantly higher level of output by the welfare-maximizing public firm and, in turn, to a significant reduction of the residual demand left for the private firm. An increase in the public wage, on the other hand, implies much less increase in output by the profit-maximizing private firm and, consequently, has less influence on the residual demand left for the public firm. Therefore, the public firm loses relatively less by wage increases. This is then exploited by the trade union in wage negotiations.

----

[30] The basic features of this approach are presented in Ch. 13 below, see in particular Sect. 13.2.

De Fraja (1990a) further investigates the effects of privatization by examining the transition from the original mixed market to a duopoly of two profit-maximizing firms. Surprisingly, 'the wage in the privatized firm remains approximately the same as it was before, but the wage in the other firm increases considerably'. The reason for this result is as follows: the privatized firm changes from high-output strategies to low-output strategies. Hence, a higher residual demand is left for the other firm. This increases the monopoly rent which can be divided between the other firm and the trade union.

A mixed market also arises if a private firm enters into the market of a public enterprise as modelled in Ware's (1986) two-stage game. There is one public incumbent and one potential entrant. In stage one of the game the incumbent chooses his capacity, i.e. the maximum quantity he can produce in the second stage of the game. This is the strategic advantage of the incumbent: in stage two his capacity costs are sunk costs, whereas an entrant must commit new capacity prior to entry.

At the beginning of stage two the potential entrant faces the decision of whether or not to enter the market. If he enters, incumbent and entrant play Cournot–Nash, where the Cournot–Nash solution depends on the capacity chosen by the incumbent because this capacity determines the incumbent's reaction function. Hence, depending on the capacity of the incumbent, the potential entrant may enter or stay out of the market. By choosing a high capacity in stage one, the incumbent can reduce the entrant's profits. There may even exist investment policies which totally deter entry.

Consider a 'natural monopoly' situation. According to Ware, a monopoly is natural if supply by one firm leads to maximal welfare. This is not the usual definition of a natural monopoly because it explicitly takes account of both cost- and demand-side properties of the market. In the one-input, one-output case subadditive costs are a sufficient but not a necessary condition to have a natural monopoly in Ware's sense. Hence his definition is less stringent than the usual one which is found, for instance, in Sharkey (1982). In a 'natural monopoly' situation, according to Ware, a public incumbent always deters private entry by offering the welfare-maximizing output.

Now assume a U-shaped average cost function and consider an increase in demand. At some point it becomes welfare-optimal to have the relevant good supplied by two firms and we have a 'natural duopoly'. However, given Ware's specifications, at that point an entrant would accrue a deficit, hence no private firm would enter, although supply by two firms would be welfare-optimal. The market is stuck in an 'unnatural monopoly'. The welfare orientation of the public firm makes market entry unprofitable, because too high a capacity is chosen and too high a quantity is supplied by the incumbent to induce entry by a profit-seeking private firm. The point of an 'unnatural monopoly' seems interesting. However, if it is welfare-optimal to have two firms, why doesn't the government simply establish a second public firm in the case of an 'unnatural monopoly'? Why does it wait for a private entrant? The straightforward move seems to be the establishment of a public firm which may be privatized afterwards as soon as the conditions of profitable private entry are met.

For yet another reason, Ware's paper is interesting with respect to the theory of privatization. Privatization of the incumbent firm could be seen as a possible way to induce an efficient two-firm market structure and to escape from the 'unnatural monopoly'. However, Ware (1986: 651–2) argues that the welfare-oriented public firm will have chosen so high a capacity in stage one of the game that privatization at the end of stage one comes too late. Given the capacity inherited from the public firm, the privatized firm still produces too much and therefore entry is unprofitable. An interesting feature of Ware's model is the accentuation of how far privatized firms can be affected by the heritage of their public past. Unfortunately, however, Ware's proposition on privatization is based on a solution which is not subgame-perfect. The public firm starts with a capacity which is built up under the assumption of the firm's remaining public. Then, unexpectedly, privatization occurs at the beginning of stage two and the privatized firm makes the best of the given capacity. Ware's proposition may break down if the public firm correctly anticipates its being privatized at the beginning of stage two and sets capacity so as to guarantee maximum welfare (i.e. entry) in stage two.

4.2.3   Regulated Oligopolistic Markets

In this subsection we deal with oligopolistic markets where only one firm is privatized and regulated. The other firms in the market are private and unregulated.

This type of market can first occur in the case of '*internal regulation*' of a privatized firm, i.e. if the firm is only partially privatized. Here the government wants to promote its welfare interest directly by placing its own representatives on the firm's board of directors. The partially privatized firm in the oligopolistic market is characterized by an objective function which results from some compromise between profit and welfare. Fershtman (1990) deals with a duopoly consisting of such a partially privatized firm and a private firm. Since the reaction functions of the duopolists depend on the objective functions, the partial privatization of one firm changes the Cournot–Nash equilibrium, with unexpected results: if there are two identical firms, one private and one partially privatized, at the Cournot–Nash equilibrium the privatized firm earns the higher profit and the private firm's profits are below the regular Cournot profits. In addition, potential market entry will be influenced by the ownership of the incumbent, since the profitability of market entry depends on the incumbent's reaction function, which is shifted if the incumbent is partially privatized. Hence, it is possible that a firm is not a natural monopoly while being private, but becomes a natural monopoly as the consequence of partial privatization.

Let us now turn to another case of a regulated oligopolistic market. If a public utility is privatized, the government often tends to *regulate the enterprise with respect to its prices (external regulation)*. The lower prices of the privatized firm make market entry less profitable, but not impossible. There is not much special literature on entry into regulated markets;[31] in fact, Chapter 10 in the positive theory part of this book is one of the few contributions. Another interesting contribution to the topic is due to Estrin and de Meza (1988). They deal with an incumbent who chooses average-cost pricing and an entrant who wants to maximize his profits. In the first stage the incumbent monopoly produces a single good under increasing returns to scale. At the beginning of the second stage the other firm enters if entry is profitable. If entry occurs, in the second stage the duopoly game is one of either Bertrand or Cournot competition. The entrant produces a single good which may be a close or a distant substitute[32] of the incumbent's good. The entrant's costs may be higher or lower than those of the incumbent. Both players are fully informed about each other's demand and cost functions and about the strategies to be chosen.

---

[31] The problem is briefly addressed in Cave and Trotter (1990: 74–82).

[32] The authors define a substitute to be distant if, for a demand function $p_i = \alpha - \beta z_i + \gamma z_e$, the absolute value of β is significantly different from γ. In the demand function the index i denotes the incumbent, the index e refers to the entrant.

Let us first deal with the authors' results in the case of *Cournot competition*. When both firms sell an identical good and there are economies of scale throughout, entry will not occur if the incumbent is at least as efficient as any potential entrant. Moreover, the authors show that entry typically leaves the consumer worse off. The only exception is a case where the incumbent is expelled from the market and the entrant 'has a truly enormous cost advantage' (Estrin and de Meza, 1988: 72). Simulation analyses for linear demand functions and quadratic cost functions are performed by the authors to evaluate more complicated settings. The quantitative results show that entry is more likely to occur if the firms compete with distant substitutes and if the entrant has considerable cost advantages.

Since *Bertrand competition* is more aggressive, in many cases the incumbent does not survive. The flavor of the simulations seems to be as follows: while there are some cases of profitable entry which are socially undesirable, on the whole profitability and increases in social welfare go hand in hand. The reason is that cost advantages for the entrant have to be huge to allow entry, while product differentiation is a new positive feature of successful entry. The latter tends to raise welfare, measured by consumer surplus, as well as to dissipate scale economies.

There are many more possible cases of regulated oligopolistic markets, depending on the various types of regulation. A privatized telecommunications or electricity distribution firm may be obliged to connect other licensed firms to its public network or grid. A privatized railway company may be obliged to allow the common use of its tracks and signalling facilities. Many further case studies will be necessary to understand the strategic behavior in such regulated oligopolistic markets.

4.2.4   *Private Unregulated Oligopolies*

In this subsection we deal with oligopolistic markets where all firms are private and unregulated. One firm, however, is a privatized firm and has particular characteristics from its past when it was a public enterprise. These characteristics influence its strategic behavior.

In Chapter 10 below, which is based on Bös and Nett (1990), the privatized firm has inherited excess capacity. This gives the privatized firm a strategic advantage: it is able to choose an optimal capacity without any capacity installation costs. Any private competitor, however, has to pay for capacity installation. This cost asymmetry is one of the driving forces of the market-entry model considered later in this book.

In a similar way, a golden share will influence the behavior of a privatized firm because, in contrast to its private competitors, it does not have to fear takeovers.

Inheritance from its public past is not always an advantage for the privatized firm. Traditionally, high trade-union influence, inherited overpayment of workers, and inherited red tape may reduce the privatized firm's strategic potential. Last but not least, the public may expect a formerly public firm not to behave too capitalistically, but to recall at least some of the welfare obligations of its past.

The theoretical endpoint of our treatment of oligopolistic markets is a situation where the privatized firm cannot be distinguished from any other private firm. Then, of course, the usual theories of oligopolistic private firms are to be applied. It is not the purpose of this subsection to survey these theories. Best known are the paper by Dixit (1980) on the role of investment in entry deterrence and the paper by Milgrom and Roberts (1982) which deals with a signalling game between an incumbent and a potential market entrant: a highly productive incumbent may choose low prices as signals of his productivity and thereby deter entry.

4.3 Integration or Separation of Production

4.3.1 Public Production Units

It is a political decision whether public production units are integrated or separated. Excessive integration can be caused by historical reasons, by socialist parties' interest in large units of production (with high trade-union influence), or by the government's interest in cross-subsidization. For example, there is no inherent economic reason why postal services, telecommunications services, and bank services should be provided by only one enterprise. However, this was the classical PTT system which only recently has been abolished in countries like West Germany and the Netherlands. The trade unions in West Germany opposed this divestiture of the PTT system as a form of 'privatization', where the word privatization did not mean the sale of assets but referred to the government's intention to bring about a firm structure which corresponds with a private economy's market forces. Another example of excessive integration was London Transport, which combined the production of bus and underground services and was split into two separate production units in 1984 (see Bös, 1986a: 345–8).

The political decision on integration or separation can also be influenced by the size of the governmental unit (Spann, 1977: 74–5). The optimum scale of production for government-produced goods may be smaller than the size of the governmental unit. However, for political reasons there may be, for instance, only one school district for each local community, only one local public enterprise for garbage collection, etc. Privatization of public enterprises provides a chance of achieving the optimum firm size, in particular if market entry is allowed.

4.3.2   Yardstick Regulation

Yardstick regulation can be applied if two or more regulated firms operate in a similar economic environment. The yardstick which is used for the regulation of any firm does not depend on the firm's own decision, but on the other firms' decisions. Therefore, there is no incentive for strategic behavior of the regulated firm. If, for example, the regulator requires information on the costs of a firm, the management will reveal the correct costs because this revelation does not influence its own regulated profit maximum.

In the case of privatization, yardstick regulation is possible if some public firm is split into two or more privatized firms, for instance if a centralized electricity generation or distribution company is split into two or more smaller companies or if decentralized water supply companies are established.[33] Such a splitting is meaningful if the privatized industry faces decreasing or constant returns to scale or if increasing returns to scale are not too important. In the latter case the efficiency gains from yardstick regulation must be high enough to offset the efficiency losses from divesting the public monopoly.

The concept of yardstick regulation was presented first by Shleifer (1985).[34] Consider an economy with many identical one-product firms.[35] Each firm faces the same downward-sloping de-

---

[33] Yardstick regulation has been proposed in the Littlechild Report (1986) on regulation of the UK water authorities. See Vickers and Yarrow (1988a: 115, 415–19).

[34] And by Yarrow (1985).

[35] The model we treat in the text is presented in Shleifer (1985: 323–4). Recall the Vickers–Yarrow (1988a: 35–9) benchmark model which has similar features.

mand function in a separate market.[36] The manager of each firm wants to maximize profit. The firms operate under constant marginal costs. These marginal costs, however, can be reduced by cost-saving investments, for instance in R&D.

Let us deal with a government which is restricted to price regulation. (It cannot directly regulate profits by lump-sum taxes or transfers.)[37] The regulator wants to achieve a second-best welfare optimum where each firm covers its costs, which include both the variable production costs and the R&D costs. If the regulator knew how R&D could reduce the firm's marginal costs, he would instruct the firm to operate welfare-optimally by imposing a price which equals average costs at the welfare-optimal level of R&D. However, because of incomplete information the regulator cannot calculate this price. He cannot observe the R&D technology, but only the actual marginal costs and the actual R&D expenditures after production has taken place. The manager has no incentive to inform the regulator about the true R&D technology because such truth-telling would result in zero profits. Hence the regulator needs a mechanism which induces truth-telling. Yardstick regulation is such a mechanism.

The first step in yardstick regulation is that each firm informs the regulator about the marginal-cost level and the R&D expenditures at which it will operate. Then the regulator determines the regulated price for each firm. The price regulation of each firm is independent of the firm's own declarations. It is only based on the averages of the costs and the averages of R&D expenditures of the other firms. Knowing the demand function, the regulator calculates the price constraint for each firm in such a way that the firm's profit is zero with respect to these averages. Afterwards the firms have to produce at the declared costs and R&D expenditures and to sell the product at the regulated price. It can be shown that there exists a Nash equilibrium where each firm operates at

[36] The model can be extended to market-specific demand curves. However, complications arise if the regulator does not know the various demand curves.

[37] Shleifer (1985: 322–3) and Vickers and Yarrow (1988a: 116–17) concentrated on a basic model where lump-sum taxes can be collected from consumers and be distributed to the firms without loss of welfare. While I believe it is fair to assume lump-sum transfers in a benchmark model, I dislike the assumption that money can be taken away from consumers without their recognizing it. However, if consumer surplus in the basic Shleifer model is specified as $S(p,T)$, where T is the lump-sum transfer, the results of the basic model break down; marginal-cost pricing is no longer optimal. Therefore, in my text I prefer to present the simpler average-pricing model.

the second-best level of marginal costs and of cost-saving R&D investments.[38]

It is fascinating to see how this approach overcomes the regulator's difficulties in obtaining information. He announces the regulatory rules without having any information on costs. Then the firms give him correct information on costs, because giving this information does not affect their profits. On the basis of his correct information the regulator sets the price. The firm has incentives to minimize costs because any cost reduction is in the firm's own best interests; the advantages accruing to the firm are not taken away by regulation. A firm which operates more efficiently than the other firms has a clear advantage because of its better performance, hence each firm has an incentive to operate efficiently.

Unfortunately, the fascinating clarity and straightforwardness of yardstick regulation is flawed if the actual application is considered. The main counterarguments are as follows:

(i) The model loses much of its elegance if firms do not have uniform characteristics. Shleifer[39] proposes a 'reduced-form regulation' which uses predicted costs on the basis of a regression analysis linking marginal costs and exogenous characteristics of all firms. The reduced-form regulation is exact if the regression explains 100 percent of the variance of costs among the firms. Typically, however, this will not be the case. Moreover, regulation leads to undesired consequences if one or more of the exogenous characteristics can be strategically influenced by the firms.

(ii) The analysis excludes information asymmetries with respect to demand. However, the government may lack precise information about demand functions, in particular if the firms are not identical.

(iii) The regulator must commit himself not to help the firms if inefficient production leads to difficulties or even leads to bankruptcy.[40] It is difficult to understand how a regulator of a privatized firm can commit himself in such a way. It would not be credible if the government threatened to let some privatized water authorities go bankrupt.

(iv) Collusion among the firms leads to a break-down of the model. In the case of privatization, the contacts between the various new firms will be very close, therefore collusion could occur

[38] For a proof see Shleifer (1985: 322, 324). For the equilibrium, which is treated in our text, uniqueness has not been proved by Shleifer.

[39] Shleifer (1985: 324–5).

[40] Shleifer (1985: 323).

easily. There may also be a problem of parallel inefficient behavior, without explicit collusion, following those rules of thumb which had been applied in the public firm prior to privatization.

4.3.3 Network Problems

When privatizing telecommunications, electricity, or gas, the following network problem arises.[41] The final product often is produced by means of at least two intermediate goods. Long-distance telephone calls consist of a trunk link and local links; supply of electricity requires generation and distribution. Typically, one of the intermediate goods can be supplied competitively, like interurban telephone links, generation of electricity, and production of gas. The other intermediate good, however, is supplied monopolistically, either because a natural monopoly actually exists, or because the producer has a statutory monopoly. Good examples of monopolistically supplied intermediate goods are the national grids of electricity and gas and the local telephone networks.[42]

If the supplier of the monopolistic good is allowed to enter the market for the competitive good, he will typically try to thwart competition in order to maximize profits. This can be avoided by vertical separation or by regulation of a vertically integrated firm. The policy of separation does not allow the monopolist to enter the other market; this was the American way of breaking up AT&T. British Telecom, however, serves as an example of a regulated, vertically integrated firm. Which policy should be chosen depends on the advantages and disadvantages of vertical integration as discussed in many recent papers. The interested reader may be referred to the handbook paper by Perry (1989).

First, there has always been the neoclassical focus on *market imperfections* which favor vertical integration. Consider a final good which is produced by a combination of two intermediate goods: one is supplied by a monopoly, the other in an *imperfectly* competitive market. If the monopoly is allowed to expand into the competitive sector, it can better deter entry,[43] it can apply price discrimination within the competitive market, and it can extract

---

[41] See Vickers and Yarrow (1988a: 69–76).

[42] Technical progress can destroy natural monopolies. If wireless phoning became available by a reliable and cheap technology, local telephone calls could be a very competitive market.

[43] See Perry (1989: 197).

rents from the competitive market.[44] The extraction of rents consists in the internalization of the gains which resulted from the non-marginal-cost pricing in the imperfectly competitive market. Vertical integration thus eliminates successive mark-ups which prevail in cases of vertical separation.[45]

Second, vertical integration can be advantageous because *technological economies* are utilized, for instance with respect to compatibility standards and technical linkages.[46] Economies of sequence[47] are given if an integrated technology is more productive than its separated counterpart. Spulber and Sengupta (1989) show that the economies of sequence are vital for the sustainability of integration under free entry, comparable to the role of economies of scope in a multiproduct firm.

A third group of arguments in favor of vertical integration refers to the presence *of uncertainty and of private information*. Upstream firms want to assure their market for outputs, given their incomplete information about the demand for the final goods. Downstream firms want to assure their supply of input, given their incomplete information about the investments of the input-producing firm(s). Vertical integration allows the acquisition of valuable private information, although it is not always ensured that there is no remaining principal–agent problem within the integrated firm.

Finally, *transactional economies* can be enacted by vertical integration, since internal exchange will be cheaper than contractual exchange. The keyword here is 'asset specificity' (Williamson, 1975). The specificity of investments gives the relevant firm the opportunity to extract quasi-rents, at least in an uncertain and complex environment. The transaction costs of negotiating and enforcing contracts make it too costly to write long-term contracts which effectively rule out opportunistic behavior by the firm which has engaged in the specific assets. Vertical integration may be a superior way to avoid this opportunistic behavior. The literature

---

[44] In cases like telecommunications, gas, and electricity the competitive and the monopoly input, which are necessary to produce the final good, typically are combined in *fixed* proportions. Hence the competitive producers cannot substitute away from the monopoly input toward the competitive inputs. Since fixed proportions eliminate a source of inefficiency of vertical separation, the elimination of these inefficiencies cannot be used as argument in favor of vertical integration in telecommunications, gas, or electricity.

[45] For a good treatment of these problems see Waterson (1984: ch. 5).

[46] See Berg and Tschirhart (1988: 465–6).

[47] This term was coined by Spulber (1989).

on *incomplete contracts* deals with a similar problem, however, without reference to transaction costs. If it is too costly to specify performance obligations for all states of nature or even to specify performance itself, a contract fails to reduce opportunistic behavior and vertical integration may be preferable to external exchange.

In the preceding paragraphs advantages from vertical integration meant advantages for the integrated firm. This does not necessarily imply an increase in welfare. If the profit maximization of the vertically integrated firm leads to undesirably high profits, regulation becomes necessary. If the vertically integrated firm is regulated with respect to its rate of return, it may inflate internally charged input prices. The higher costs are then passed on to the consumer.[48] This problem can be cured either by setting a price-cap constraint which depends only on the output prices, or by directly regulating the internal input-supply prices.[49] The latter alternative causes greater information problems.

---

[48] See Berg and Tschirhart (1988: 467–8).

[49] The optimal prices of intermediate goods can be found by applying the normative or positive theory models on public-sector pricing which are extensively treated in Bös (1986a). These models specify all goods as netputs which may be bought by both consumers and producers. Hence pricing of intermediate goods is always included in the models. Sometimes, however, special models which concentrate on some particular institutional setting may be of interest, as for instance Ebrill and Slutsky (1988).

Part Two
Positive Theory

5   What is Positive Theory?

Positive theories describe how a firm actually behaves. There are two benchmarks: positive theories of private firms and positive theories of public firms. Depending on the case in question, the behavior of a privatized firm can be explained either by directly applying the theories of private firms or by combining particular elements of the theories which deal with private and public firms, respectively.

Competitive industrial firms or commercial banks are privatized with the intention of leaving the firm to the market and the market to the firm. The privatized firm faces the same government regulations as any other firm in a comparable position. It behaves like a private firm: it maximizes profits; it pays incentive-based incomes to the managers which depend on profit; and its management operates with that degree of bureaucratic red tape which is usual in the private economy. In such a case, any positive theory of private firms can be applied directly to the privatized firm. The result of privatization can then be modelled by comparing private (= privatized) and public enterprises: analytical approaches refer to the differences in incentive structures, whereas empirical studies deal with various measures of productivity in private and public firms.

If public utilities are privatized, however, arguments which previously led to nationalization often remain of some importance for the privatized firms. Economies of scale and scope may still be prevalent after privatization. The government may expect the privatized firm not to exploit monopolistic market power because the services of the firm are of special importance to the population and lower-income-earners cannot do without them. It may be difficult to promote market entry, at least in the short run. The trade unions' influence may still be strong after privatization, as the old labor force may still hold their jobs. The institutional structures still may be too bureaucratic; the vertical and horizontal integration too excessive.

The similarity in problems facing publicly owned and privatized utilities leads to similarities in the positive theories. Therefore, it is possible to adopt parts of the positive theories which have been developed for public enterprises, for instance, when modelling profit or price constraints, cover-all-demand requirements, overcapacities, and overmanning caused by trade unions. Step by step, however, elements of the private-economy decision processes can

be integrated into models originating from the positive theories of
public enterprises:

- changing the firm's objective from welfare to profit maximization (however, in the case of partial privatization, it may suffice to
consider a partial move from welfare to profit maximization);
- changing the firm's production possibilities, for instance by
assuming an institutional resetting of the relations between senior
management ('board') and technological management;
- changing the informational setting, by assuming better information of owners and managers in privatized firms.

In principle, positive theory means the rejection of a welfare-
based theory. The application of a welfare function of the usual
type can be challenged for various reasons. Welfare functions imply far-reaching assumptions on individual utility, namely cardi-
nal utilities which can be compared interpersonally. Hence, from
the theoretical basis, welfare as the objective of a firm is more
debatable than profit. Moreover, welfare is an abstract concept
which often fails to motivate managers and employees of a firm.
Positive theory objectives seem to be more successful in stimulat-
ing performance than normative theory objectives. For example,
the management of a public transportation enterprise may find it
rather tedious to be theoretically 'correct' and follow a marginal-
cost pricing rule – and then be faced with the consequential deficit.
In practice, the incentives for higher performance are much better
if profit, output, or revenue can be taken as objectives of the firm.

However, some welfare arguments can be found in positive
theories. First, governments often actually are interested in welfare. They regulate the prices of monopolized privatized firms in
order to avoid consumer exploitation. They do not want privatized
public utilities to realize 'excess' profits. Behind those policies are
welfare arguments, although it may not be adequate to model them
by means of a welfare function. A positive theory, which considers
the objective functions of governments such as described above,
requires some welfare arguments although the analysis will refrain
from saying the government 'should behave like this'. Instead we
say: the government chooses a particular regulation of prices or
profit. The basis of this regulation is the government's belief that
consumers should not be exploited. This belief can be called a
welfare interest, because economists tend to think of low prices as
correlated with high consumer surplus. This argument is correct
even if the basis of the government interest in low prices is its interest in attracting votes. If voters are attracted by what economists

call higher welfare, the Buchanan-type politician is interested in welfare.

Second, welfare arguments can be perceived as benchmarks. It may be appropriate, for instance, to consider the way in which the efficiency of a privatized, profit-maximizing firm deviates from the benchmark model of a public firm which maximizes the sum of consumer and producer surpluses. The benchmark model itself is part of the normative theory which is taken as the basis of comparison for the positive theory of the privatized firm.

Part II of this book begins with principal–agent approaches to illustrate the way in which the transition in ownership changes objectives and incentives in the firm (Chapter 6). If in a public firm the government is imperfectly informed about costs or demand, typically it fails to achieve X-efficiency and allocative efficiency. Even sophisticated incentive-pay schedules will be shown to fail in achieving efficiency. In a private firm with imperfectly informed private shareholders, the concept of incentive pay can be shown to be successful in achieving X-efficiency, although it fails with respect to allocative efficiency: incentive-pay schedules typically link manager pay to profit which leads to profit-maximizing prices. If the privatized firm is a public utility, profit maximization implies monopoly prices, which are undesired. This eminent market failure is the basis of the government's regulation of privatized utilities, which we treat in Chapter 7. Since the recent UK practice has applied that particular price constraint, we consider alternative variants of '$RPI - X$'. As an alternative to price regulation of a fully privatized firm, some countries prefer partial privatization where the government's interests are realized through compromises between the government's and the private shareholders' representatives on the board of the firm. Chapter 8 evaluates the pros and cons of partial privatization versus regulated private ownership. We show the differences in the principal–agent setting of the two alternatives which imply an informational advantage but an incentive disadvantage of partial privatization.

In Chapter 9 we deal with the interplay between the government, the shareholders of the firm, and a representative trade union. This chapter shows how a dominant trade union prevents the private shareholders of a privatized firm from receiving any net income from dividends and confines the government to that minimum revenue requirement which is necessary to induce the government to privatize. All profits which exceed the government minimum revenue requirement go to the employees by a plan of employee shares or are used to keep inefficient jobs in the firm.

Yet another way to control a privatized firm is the encouragement of market entry; therefore, in Chapter 10 we deal with special problems of market entry into regulated markets. This is a special problem of privatized utilities. Immediately after privatization there is not enough market entry to warrant forgoing regulation. However, this regulation impedes further market entry. We will show this feedback mechanism in detail.

6 Efficiency and Privatization

6.1 Two Benchmark Models

Let us consider an enterprise which undergoes a shift from 100 percent public ownership to 100 percent private ownership. The enterprise operates in a monopolistic environment: it is not necessarily a monopoly in the strict sense, but the market is not fully competitive either. When publicly owned, the enterprise does not exploit its monopolistic market position. However, will the management be given the right incentives to work X-efficiently? On the other hand, when privately owned, the enterprise exploits its monopolistic position, because in this chapter we exclude any regulation of the privatized firm. However, profit maximization should imply the best incentives for X-efficient operations.

Efficiency changes are brought about by privatization because of (i) changes in the owners' objectives and (ii) changes in the managers' incentives. In our analyses we employ approaches found in the literature on principal–agent theory. The owner of the firm is the principal; the management of the firm is the agent. In the case of a public firm the government is the owner; in the privatized firm the private shareholders act as owners. The management is assumed to be equally capable in both a public and a private firm. Lack of efficiency in a public firm is caused not by an unable bureaucratic staff, but by wrong incentive structures. Give the bureaucrats the right incentives and they will behave as any management of a private firm.

Admittedly, this is a strong, maybe even one-sided, position. It may happen that in some cases of privatization an improvement in efficiency results from a management personnel replacement, where red-tape-minded public bureaucrats are replaced with private managers with a Schumpeterian spirit. In fact, in some of my earlier papers (Bös and Peters, 1988a,b) I take precisely the latter position. However, this is not the approach applied in this chapter. Here I start from the other extreme of equally capable managers in both public and privatized firms. The analysis of this chapter implies, for instance, that hiring managers from the private sector and letting them work in a public enterprise with wrong incentive structures will not *per se* improve the efficiency of a public firm.

Before turning to the detailed principal–agent approaches, we want to develop two benchmark models, one for a public firm, one for a private firm. They are both full-information models. The principal fully observes all relevant variables. He calculates those prices, manager effort, and manager income which maximize the value of his own objective. The manager is instructed to put into practice the optimal amounts of the variables mentioned above. The principal is fully able to monitor the agent's behavior, and therefore he can fire a manager whose effort falls below the pre-scribed level. Hence, direct prescription of effort is an efficient way of dealing with the manager.[1] The manager, on the other hand, is in a weaker position. He cannot maximize his own objective unless this objective happens to coincide with the principal's. The only way out of his frustration is to leave the job. He will do so if his on-the-job utility falls below his reservation utility, which is the utility he could realize at another job. Hence the principal is not fully free in choosing the effort and income of the agent: he must consider the agent's participation constraint.

In the following analyses we deal with a one-good monopolistic firm (not necessarily a full monopoly, but not a fully competitive firm either). The firm faces a demand function expressed as

$$z = z(p); \qquad z_p < 0, \qquad (6.1)$$

where z is the quantity and p is the price. We assume market-clearing behavior, hence z also serves as the symbol of the supplied quantity. The production of z involves costs expressed as

$$C = C(z, e); \qquad C_z > 0, \ C_e < 0, C_{ee} > 0, \qquad (6.2)$$

where e is the effort of the manager.

The manager has a concave utility function which is positively related to his income I and negatively to his effort e. In the benchmark models I is directly fixed by the principal and is functionally independent of the agent's effort. The manager is willing to work for the principal as long as his utility does not fall below his reservation utility $\overline{V}$. This is captured by the participation constraint

$$V(I, e) \geq \overline{V}; \qquad V_I > 0, V_e < 0. \qquad (6.3)$$

After these notational details we are ready to describe the benchmark models of the public and of the privatized firm, respectively.

---

[1] In the next subsection we shall see that this is tantamount to saying that no incentive compatibility constraint is needed in the model.

6.1.1   The Benchmark Model of a Public Firm

In the public firm the government is the principal. It maximizes a social benefit–cost difference measured by the sum of consumer surplus,

$$S = S(p); \qquad \partial S/\partial p = -z(p), \qquad (6.4)$$

and producer surplus,

$$\Pi := pz(p) - C(z, e) - I. \qquad (6.5)$$

In the above definitions we assume the population is large so that the manager's income can be neglected in the consumer surplus. However, the manager's income is a relevant factor of the firm's profits (or deficits).

The social benefit–cost difference is maximized with respect to the principal's instruments p, I, and e and subject to the agent's participation constraint. This constraint is always binding: as long as the agent's utility V exceeds the reservation utility level, it is always possible to increase the social benefit–cost difference by reducing income I or increasing prescribed effort e until V is exactly equal to $\overline{V}$. We associate the shadow price β with the participation constraint and describe the government's optimization problem by the following Lagrangean function:

$$\mathcal{L} = S(p) + pz(p) - C(z, e) - I - \beta \left[V(I, e) - \overline{V} \right]. \qquad (6.6)$$

Differentiating with respect to p yields the marginal-cost pricing rule which implies *allocative efficiency*:

$$(p - C_z)z_p = 0. \qquad (6.7)$$

Differentiating with respect to e and I gives[2]

$$-C_e - \beta V_e = 0, \qquad (6.8)$$

$$-1 - \beta V_I = 0. \qquad (6.9)$$

Taken together, these conditions yield

$$V_e/V_I = C_e. \qquad (6.10)$$

---

[2] Here and in the following we assume an interior solution for $\underline{e} < e < \overline{e}$.

Following Gravelle (1982) we call this the *X-efficiency* rule.[3] To interpret this rule, we define $-V_e/V_I =: \mathrm{MRS}(e, I)$ as the manager's marginal rate of substitution between income and effort. This rate of substitution is increasing in effort: the higher the manager's effort, the more income he must be given to allow him to remain at the same utility level. The marginal rate of substitution is compared with a marginal rate of transformation, as defined along the cost function, $-C_e/C_I =: \mathrm{MRT}(e, I)$.[4] This rate of transformation is decreasing in effort. X-efficiency implies equality of the rate of substitution and of transformation. X-inefficiency is found whenever this equality does not hold. Typically, in economic practice we expect $\mathrm{MRS} < \mathrm{MRT}$; i.e., the effort exerted is too low for X-efficient production (the costs are greater than those required for X-efficiency). From the theoretical point of view, X-inefficiency could also occur as a result of too much managerial effort. In practice, however, this case can safely be excluded.

It might help us to understand our definition if we start from the usual neoclassical type of cost function $C(z)$. Effort is not explicitly included as an input. Since the costs of effort accrue in utility terms rather than monetary terms, effort also is not included in the monetary value of input costs captured in C. Changing the level of effort shifts the cost function and, correspondingly, the production possibility frontier. Optimizing with respect to effort, therefore, implies the choice of a particular cost function. Equation (6.10) can be understood as the choice of such an optimal effort and the corresponding cost function. Effort which is lower implies higher costs and can therefore be called X-inefficient.[5]

6.1.2   The Benchmark Model of a Privatized Firm

The shareholders of the firm are interested in the market value of the firm, which in the simplest one-period benchmark model is identical to the firm's profit. The shareholders are fully informed; therefore, the private manager is in the same weak condition as the public manager in our preceding model. The shareholders unanimously maximize the following Lagrangean function with respect

---

[3] Note that this defines X-efficiency according to a cost function instead of the production possibility frontier.

[4] We define $C_I := 1$.

[5] Once again, this is similar to Stigler's (1976) approach to X-efficiency, not Leibenstein's (1976, 1978).

to p, e, I:

$$\Pi - \beta(V - \overline{V}). \tag{6.11}$$

This leads to the monopoly-pricing rule

$$\frac{p - C_z}{p} = -\frac{1}{\epsilon}, \tag{6.12}$$

where ϵ is the price elasticity of demand. Hence the private firm does not operate at the allocative optimum since this requires marginal-cost pricing. The effort of the manager is fixed according to

$$V_e/V_I = C_e, \tag{6.13}$$

which is the condition for X-efficiency.

In the benchmark models, therefore, the public firm is superior to the privatized firm. The public firm guarantees both allocative and X-efficiency, whereas the privatized firm violates the postulate of allocative efficiency. We shall see how this superiority is lost if more realistic principal–agent approaches are analyzed.[6]

6.2   Linear Incentive Schemes

The principal–agent approaches cope with the information asymmetry between the principal and the agent. There are particular variables which can be observed only by the agent. The principal only knows the distribution of the variables. Now assume principal and agent follow different objectives. The principal's inability to observe some variables makes it impossible to monitor the agent perfectly and directly. Hence it is meaningless if the principal explicitly instructs the agent to maximize the principal's objective. Instead, the principal must choose an indirect way to monitor the agent. The compensation which he pays as reward of the agent's effort must embody an incentive for the agent to maximize the principal's objective.

Throughout this chapter we assume that the principal is risk-neutral. The agent, however, will alternatively be risk-neutral or

---

[6] Rees in a different framework obtains a result which is of the same spirit as ours: X-efficiency of a public enterprise is achieved in the full-information world (Rees, 1984b: 183), but X-inefficiency can result if there is uncertainty of both management and government about demand and cost (Rees, 1984b: 188).

risk-averse. The inclusion of risk-averse managers seems of particular importance if public firms are to be considered, because public firms often attract risk-averse managers.[7]

Consider some variable ϑ which influences profit or welfare. When the principal and the agent negotiate the compensation of the agent, both know only the distribution of ϑ, which is described by the probability density function $f(\vartheta)$. Hence at this moment both can plan only in terms of the expected profit or welfare. Therefore, when the manager decides to work for the principal, his decision is based on $f(\vartheta)$. Only after entering the employment can the manager observe the actual value of ϑ. He then sets the price of the product and his own effort level according to ϑ and thereby maximizes his personal utility. After production begins, the principal is able to observe price, output, and effort and to compensate the manager according to the previously negotiated contract.

Both unknown demand and unknown costs can be captured as special cases of the general approach mentioned above. Asymmetric information of the demand function is at stake if the difference $\mathcal{D}$ between revenue and costs is specified according to

$$\mathcal{D}(p,e,\vartheta) := pz(p,\vartheta) - C(z(p,\vartheta),e). \qquad (6.14)$$

On the other hand, the modelling of unknown costs requires

$$\mathcal{D}(p,e,\vartheta) := pz(p) - C(z(p),e,\vartheta). \qquad (6.15)$$

To avoid clumsy notation, we will not handle the case of both unknown costs and unknown demand; however, this extension is fairly straightforward and is left to the reader.

The principal has to solve the following problem. He wants to maximize the expected value of his *objective function* $\mathcal{O}(p,e,\vartheta)$. This value may be expressed in terms of welfare, for instance, or perhaps profits. We assume $\mathcal{O}$ is measured in monetary units, hence social utility is measured in terms of consumer surplus. The principal has to choose the compensation $I(p,e,\vartheta)$ which he pays to

---

[7] Sometimes it has been argued that managers in public firms may be willing to take more risks than managers in private firms, because it is not their money which is at stake. However, this argument refers to the firm whose managers are paid a fixed salary and therefore do not bear any personal risk. The principal–agent problem we are dealing with refers to the question as to why public managers receive this fixed salary. It is here that the risk-averse attitudes of the managers matter.

the agent. The dependence on p, e, and ϑ is easily explained if one thinks of a compensation as a percentage of profit or welfare. When maximizing his objective (minus the compensation), the principal must make sure that the contract is incentive-compatible and that the agent is willing to accept the job.

Incentive compatibility is given only if the price and the effort level maximize the agent's utility $V(I, e)$. This is because the principal cannot directly observe the variable ϑ and therefore cannot fully monitor the agent's behavior. Hence the principal must accept the agent's utility maximization as a constraint of his, the principal's, optimization. This is the only way to reach a consistent plan. Any other plan is inconsistent, because the agent would not behave according to such a plan and the uninformed principal has no weapon to directly enforce some behavior of the agent. The only thing he can do is to rely on the selfishness of the agent and to take account of his utility maximization.

The *participation constraint* is similar to that of our benchmark models: the agent must at least expect to reach his reservation utility, otherwise he will not accept the job. A special problem of the agent's participation refers to the danger of ruin. To avoid this problem, we assume that any incentive schedule is fixed in such a way that the manager's income is never negative. This allows us to avoid the clumsiness of adding an explicit no-ruin constraint to the optimization problem.[8]

In this chapter, we employ the Chamley–Marchand–Pestieau (1989) linear incentive schemes.[9] If the manager's income depends on two variables, for instance on profit Π and total labor inputs L, the incentive-pay schedule is as follows:

$$I = k + a\Pi + bL. \qquad (6.16)$$

In case of such a linear compensation, the incentive compatibility can be taken into account by substituting the agent's reaction functions into the principal's objective function and also into

---

[8] For a non-linear incentive scheme such a constraint would not cause many problems. For a linear scheme, however, the matter could be more tedious, because a binding no-ruin constraint would shift the whole linear scheme upwards. For some mathematical details of how to define a no-ruin constraint see footnote 11 below.

[9] The possible superiority of linear incentive schemes (over non-linear ones) can be explained by the presence of stochastic disturbances. See Holmstrom and Milgrom (1987).

the relevant constraints.[10] The agent's reaction functions are expressed as $p(a,b,k,\vartheta)$; $e(a,b,k,\vartheta)$. These functions result from the agent's utility maximization, given a linear incentive scheme with parameters a,b,k.[11]

Since the principal can observe the actual values of p and e *ex post*, he can then compute the actual value of ϑ if the reaction functions are monotone in ϑ. However, this *ex post* information is useless, because the managerial compensation scheme was previously determined in a binding contract signed by the principal and the manager (Chamley, Marchand, and Pestieau, 1989).

6.3 Efficiency of the Privatized Firm

Empirical investigations of the managerial remuneration in private firms have shown that the firm's profits and the firm's sales are decisive determinants of managers' salaries.[12] Therefore we expect the salaries in the privatized firm to follow this pattern, whereas the salaries in the public firm are fixed independently of profit or sales. It is this difference in the incentive structure that leads to the changes in efficiency which result in the event of privatization.

For the simplest description of the principal–agent relation in a privatized firm we choose a linear compensation function which depends on the difference between revenue and costs,[13]

$$I = k + a\mathcal{D}(p,e,\vartheta). \tag{6.17}$$

On the basis of this incentive scheme, the manager maximizes his utility:

$$\max_{p,e} \; V(I,e). \tag{6.18}$$

---

[10] The reader might think of the similar procedure which holds for Sheshinski's (1972) linear income tax compared with Mirrlees' (1971) first-order approach to the general problem where the functional form of the income tax is not specified *a priori*.

[11] A no-ruin constraint in the case of a linear incentive scheme could be defined as follows. Assume $\vartheta \in [\underline{\vartheta}, \overline{\vartheta}]$. The utility-maximizing income of the manager equals $I[a,b,k,\vartheta]$. Assume that ϑ is ordered in such a way that $I_\vartheta > 0$. Then a no-ruin constraint would be $I(\underline{\vartheta}) \geq 0$. As already mentioned, we do not explicitly add this constraint to avoid clumsiness.

[12] See, for instance, Murphy (1985).

[13] The compensation does not depend on profit, because profit itself depends on the compensation: $\Pi = \mathcal{D} - I$. This circularity is avoided by choosing compensation according to (6.17).

As in the benchmark model of the private firm, the manager violates the condition of allocative efficiency by setting the monopoly price. Moreover, he may also violate the condition of X-efficiency since he behaves according to

$$V_e/V_I = a\, C_e. \tag{6.19}$$

As long as $0 < a < 1$, the manager ignores part of the cost savings which result from increases in his effort. Hence he chooses too low an effort level and the allocation is X-inefficient. Only if $a = 1$ will X-efficiency result. To obtain X-efficiency, the whole revenue-cost difference must be given to the manager; the principal will, however, negotiate a fixed amount $k < 0$ which is paid to him by the manager.

Let us next deal with the principal's optimization. Once again we assume that shareholders unanimously want to maximize profit, given the manager's participation constraint. Therefore we have the following optimization approach:

$$\max_{a,k}\ (1-a)E\mathcal{D}(\cdot) - k$$

$$\text{subject to } EV(k + a\mathcal{D}(\cdot), e(\cdot)) \geq \overline{V}, \tag{6.20}$$

where $(\cdot)$ is a shorthand notation for (a, k, ϑ) and E is the expectation operator with respect to ϑ. We have substituted the agent's reaction functions $p(\cdot)$ and $e(\cdot)$; they are also included in $\mathcal{D}(\cdot)$. To solve the optimization problem we formulate the Lagrangean function

$$\mathcal{L} = (1-a)E\mathcal{D}(\cdot) - k - \beta[EV(k + a\mathcal{D}(\cdot), e(\cdot)) - \overline{V}]. \tag{6.21}$$

With respect to the *participation constraint*, the Kuhn–Tucker conditions are as follows:

$$\beta(EV - \overline{V}) = 0; \quad \beta \leq 0. \tag{6.22}$$

The conflict of interests between the principal and the manager implies that, starting from the optimum, an exogenous increase of the reservation utility $\overline{V}$ reduces the principal's objective. Hence $\beta < 0$,[14] which implies that the participation constraint is always

---

[14] For this sort of interpretation of Lagrangean parameters see Panik (1976: 225).

binding: when entering into the contract with the principal, the manager's expected utility is always depressed to his reservation utility. Unfortunately, this implies that *ex post* some manager may have to fulfill a contract which gives him less than his reservation utility. This is the result of formulating the participation constraint in expected utility. If the manager had known the precise value of ϑ at the moment of contracting, the principal would have had to guarantee participation for any possible value of ϑ, not only with respect to some expected value. In that case the manager would have had a stronger position when signing the contract. Assume that ϑ is ordered in such a way that $\mathcal{D}_\vartheta > 0$. Then, in models where the agent knows ϑ when entering into the contract, his utility is an increasing function of ϑ; the participation constraint is binding only for the lowest possible value of ϑ.[15]

Let us next deal with the *optimal compensation* which is paid to the manager. At an optimum with positive a and k the following marginal conditions hold:[16]

$$(1-a)E\mathcal{D}_a - E\mathcal{D} - \beta\ EV_I(\mathcal{D} + a\ \mathcal{D}_a) - \beta\ EV_e e_a = 0, \quad (6.23)$$

$$(1-a)E\mathcal{D}_k - 1 - \beta\ EV_I(1 + a\ \mathcal{D}_k) - \beta\ EV_e e_k = 0. \quad (6.24)$$

Using the properties of the manager's optimum, we find the following helpful relations:

$$\mathcal{D}_a = [z + (p - C_z)z_p]p_a - C_e e_a = -C_e e_a, \quad (6.25)$$

$$EV_e e_a \overset{(19)}{=} EV_I a\ C_e e_a \overset{(25)}{=} - EV_I a\ \mathcal{D}_a. \quad (6.26')$$

Analogously, we can derive

$$EV_e e_k = -EV_I a\mathcal{D}_k. \quad (6.26'')$$

Substituting the conditions (6.26) into (6.23) and (6.24), we obtain

$$(1-a)E\mathcal{D}_a - E\mathcal{D} - \beta\ E(V_I\ \mathcal{D}) = 0, \quad (6.27)$$

$$(1-a)E\mathcal{D}_k - 1 - \beta\ EV_I = 0. \quad (6.28)$$

Taken together, these conditions describe the principal's choice of a and k as follows:

$$(1-a)\left[E\mathcal{D}_a - \frac{E(V_I\mathcal{D})}{EV_I}E\mathcal{D}_k\right] = E\mathcal{D} - \frac{E(V_I\mathcal{D})}{EV_I}. \quad (6.29)$$

---

[15] See, for instance, Bös and Peters (1990).
[16] Cf. Chamley, Marchand, and Pestieau (1989).

If the manager is risk-neutral,[17] we have $E\mathcal{D} = E(V_I\mathcal{D})/EV_I$ and the principal chooses $a = 1$.[18] In this case the entire revenue-cost difference is forwarded to the manager, who consequently bears all the risk. The shareholders will receive a constant payment of the amount k, which has been negotiated *ex ante*. From our analysis of the manager's optimization we know that, for $a = 1$, X-efficiency is realized; however, allocative efficiency is not.

It is important to note that $a = 1$ is not necessarily optimal if the manager is risk-averse or risk-loving.[19] If the manager is risk-averse, $a > 1$ cannot be optimal. This is very plausible because it implies that the risk-averse manager never bears more risk than the risk-neutral manager. The proof follows the Rothschild–Stiglitz (1970), Stiglitz (1974) line. We compare three contracts:

(i) a contract with arbitrary k_1 and $a_1 > 1$;

(ii) a contract with $k_2 = k_1 + (a_1 - 1)E\mathcal{D}(p, e, \vartheta)$, however with $a_2 = 1$, where the agent promises to take precisely the same contingent actions as in contract (i);

(iii) a contract with the same k and a, and with the same amount of compensation, as contract (ii); however, the agent now is free to choose his actions.

The expected value of the agent's compensation is equal for the first and for the second contract:

(i) $EI_1 = k_1 + a_1 E\mathcal{D}, \quad a_1 > 1,$

(ii) $EI_2 = k_2 + E\mathcal{D} = k_1 + (a_1 - 1)E\mathcal{D}(p, e, \vartheta) + E\mathcal{D} = k_1 + a_1 E\mathcal{D}.$

However, the probability distribution of the second contract has a lower variance, because weight is shifted from the tails of the distribution to the center. Hence the risk-averse agent strictly prefers the second contract to the first, because it implies a mean-preserving decrease in risk. The principal is risk-neutral, therefore only considers the expected value of the compensation, and is indifferent between the first and the second contract. Therefore contract (ii) dominates contract (i) although contract (ii) is not feasible because it is not incentive-compatible. If negotiations

---

[17] For the following interpretation, see Chamley, Marchand, and Pestieau (1989).

[18] Assuming that the second expression on the left-hand side is not zero.

[19] The manager signs the contract if $EV(\cdot) \geq \overline{V}$. He decides according to his expected utility; the variance of utilities is not relevant for his participation constraint. The manager's attitudes toward risk are expressed only by the properties (concavity) of his utility function.

on the choice between (i) and (ii) were to occur, the second contract would be chosen, although in practice this contract would
not work.

Next we compare the second and the third contracts. The
agent prefers the third contract to the second because he feels that
he cannot be worse off if he is free to choose. The principal, once
again, is indifferent because by definition the compensation is identical in contracts (ii) and (iii). Therefore contract (iii) dominates
contract (ii). Moreover, contract (iii) would work in practice, in
contrast to contract (ii), which was introduced only for the sake
of the argument. By transitivity, the third contract dominates the
first and therefore $a > 1$ can never be optimal. Therefore $a \leq 1$
must be chosen.

Let us summarize the result of this subsection. Given the linear compensation (6.17), the risk-neutral management should be
awarded the entire revenue-cost difference, whereas the shareholders should obtain an *a priori* fixed lump sum. If the management
is risk-averse, the risk may be shared between owners and management. In that case the revenue-cost difference is split up: part of
it goes to the manager, part of it goes to the shareholders.

Next we will deal with the simplest principal–agent approaches
of a public firm to elaborate as clearly as possible the basic effects
of privatization.

6.4   Efficiency of the Public Firm

6.4.1   *Fixed Manager Income and Low Manager Effort*

Let us begin with a rather extreme case of manager pay, the case of
an *a priori* fixed income k, which is independent of profit, sales, or
effort. Public firms may come close to this extreme case of manager
pay

(i)   if guidelines for civil servants' pay are applied in public
firms. For instance, many employees of the German railway and
postal systems are, in fact, civil servants! Then the centralized
setting of guidelines for civil servants' incomes makes it impossible
to adjust incomes to managerial success. As Millward and Parker
(1983: 222) formulated: 'paradoxically, public enterprises, and especially those closely integrated with government, sometimes lay
down strict operating guidelines for pecuniary income when the
productivity of management is less easy to judge in terms of profitability. If pecuniary income is so constrained...';

(ii)   if the management of the firm itself turns out to be content with a fixed salary and not to be interested in an incentive scheme of reward. As Reder (1975: 34) formulated: 'since public employers tend to avoid activities that involve payment by results, workers who prefer to be employed in situations where they can increase their earnings per time period by expending extra effort or by using unusual skill will tend to avoid such employment';

(iii)   if the bargaining between the government and the respective trade unions has led to a general tendency against any form of incentive payment. For many examples of such a tendency in the history of UK nationalized industries, see Pryke (1981).

Our first principal–agent approach to analyzing a public firm, therefore, is very simple. We assume that the agent gets an *a priori* fixed income k. His utility V depends on this fixed income, on effort, and on some variable (ϕ), the precise value of which is unknown to both principal and agent at the moment of contracting. $V(k, e)$ instead of $V(k, e, \phi)$ would imply the principal's precise *a priori* knowledge of the agent's optimization, which would bring us back to the benchmark model. As we shall see, it is not difficult in this context to include two variables, ϕ and ϑ, which are unknown to both principal and agent when entering the contract.

After the contract has been agreed upon, the manager observes the precise value of ϕ and accordingly maximizes

$$\max_{\underline{e} \leq e \leq \overline{e}} V(k, e, \phi). \tag{6.30}$$

This agent will be as lazy as possible: the Kuhn–Tucker approach (6.30) yields

$$V_e \leq 0 \quad \text{if } e = \underline{e} \tag{6.31'}$$

or

$$V_e = 0 \quad \text{if } \underline{e} < e < \overline{e}. \tag{6.31''}$$

If we follow the typical assumption $V_e < 0$, the manager in the public firm will exert minimal effort.

As is easily seen, it is meaningless to instruct such a manager to set the price p: his utility does not depend on p and therefore he is indifferent with respect to the price. Hence the price p and the manager's income k are set by the principal, which in this case is the government.

The government maximizes a social benefit–cost difference subject to the manager's participation constraint. The manager's choice of e, namely $\underline{e}$, is directly substituted into the government's optimization approach. Thus incentive compatibility is guaranteed. The government is only imperfectly informed about the cost function, and therefore about the revenue-cost difference $\mathcal{D}(p, \underline{e}, \vartheta)$. The government's optimization is described by the following Lagrangean approach:[20]

$$\max_{k,p} \; E_\vartheta[S(p) + \mathcal{D}(p, \underline{e}, \vartheta) - k] - \beta[E_\phi V(k, \underline{e}, \phi) - \overline{V}]. \qquad (6.32)$$

The compensation k is set according to

$$-1 - \beta E_\phi V_k = 0. \qquad (6.33)$$

This condition is similar to equation (6.9) above. However, the lack of information makes it impossible to set the socially optimal k: when contracting, neither agent nor principal knows the precise value of ϕ. Moreover, the expectation $E_\phi V_k$ is calculated for the lowest possible effort of the manager.

The comparison with the benchmark equilibrium of a public firm clearly shows how X-efficiency is violated. Instead of an explicit marginal condition with respect to effort (6.8), we have the degenerate result that $e = \underline{e}$. Hence the cost-saving effect of effort C_e is totally neglected in this first principal–agent model of a public firm.

Let us now turn to the government's pricing rule. The price is equated to the expected marginal costs,

$$p = E_\vartheta C_z(z, \underline{e}, \vartheta). \qquad (6.34)$$

This is not optimal, however, for the following reasons:

(i)   We have *ex ante* marginal-cost prices only, because the price is equated to the *expected* marginal costs; *ex post* the price may significantly deviate from the *realized* marginal costs.

(ii)   The expected marginal costs are too high, because the effort level $\underline{e}$ is suboptimally low.

The degenerate results of the present approach show the consequences of an *a priori* fixed manager income. The results could not have been found in models which postulate that both principal and agent have complete information and which therefore assume that the agent can be directly instructed to operate at a certain effort level.

---

[20] If ϑ refers to the demand function, we have $S(p,\vartheta)$ instead of $S(p)$.

One could argue that the above principal–agent model is a caricature of the relation between the government and a public firm. Unfortunately, I fear it is a very good caricature which clearly illustrates that the simple introduction of asymmetric information and selfish managers is enough to fully explain the low efficiency of a public management which is paid according to a fixed income schedule.

6.4.2   Profit Constraint

It is very usual in economic practice to instruct the public management to set prices which are cost-covering, or which lead to a minimum profit, or to a maximum deficit, as expressed in

$$E_\vartheta \Pi(p, e, \vartheta) \geq \Pi^o. \tag{6.35}$$

Can the imposition of a profit constraint solve the principal–agent dilemma presented in the preceding subsection? For any given income k, the manager optimizes $V(k, e, \phi)$ and, as a result, sticks to the minimum effort $\underline{e}$. If the manager is required to determine the price p, he can use the revenue-cost constraint to find the price $p(k, \underline{e}, \vartheta)$.[21] To consider the government's policy, we could substitute the manager's reaction functions $e = \underline{e}$ and $p = p(k, \underline{e}, \vartheta)$ into the government's objective function and into the profit constraint. However, this is a tedious way to show that the manager's income is set inefficiently. Therefore, we once again assume that the price is set by the government, which then faces the following optimization problem:

$$\max_{k,p} E_\vartheta[S(p) + \mathcal{D}(p, \underline{e}, \vartheta) - k] - \beta[E_\phi V(k, \underline{e}, \phi) - \overline{V}]$$

$$- \gamma[E_\vartheta \mathcal{D}(p, \underline{e}, \vartheta) - k - \Pi^o]. \tag{6.36}$$

It follows that the compensation k is set inefficiently: as in the previous subsection, k is based on expectations instead of true values and on an inefficient effort $\underline{e}$. Moreover, there is an additional distortion from the profit constraint. Hence the simple imposition of a profit constraint does not solve the problem of the inefficiency of the public firm.

---

[21] Note that Π in (6.35) equals $\mathcal{D} - k$. Hence the price varies in k.

6.4.3   The Public Manager who is Interested in the Firm

Until now we dealt with public managers whose sole interest was achieving high income with little effort. Under a fixed-income scheme the manager exerts as little effort as possible (low e). Fortunately, in many cases this pessimistic view of public management is not a realistic description of economic practice. Public managers care for the firm because they want to identify themselves with the firm and want to be successful in their job. However, they are not allowed to maximize profits. Hence they do not take profits as indicators of their success.

The best-known alternative indicator of public manager's success is the *size of the budget*. The Niskanen public bureaucrat is interested not only in income and effort, but also in his personal prestige and power. His prestige and his power increase if he has many subordinates, if he is responsible for managing large amounts of money – in short, if his budget is as large as possible. His own self-interest drives the bureaucratic manager to consider the firm's budget explicitly when choosing his optimal effort.

For a typical public firm, budget revenues accrue from two sources: from customer service revenues and from a grant $\mathcal{G}$.[22] The public manager faces both a market demand $z(p)$ and a 'sponsor demand' $\mathcal{G}(z)$, similar to Niskanen's 'mixed bureau' (1971: 87–105). However, there is a great difference between these 'demand' functions: the sponsor does not consume any quantity of good z, but only pays for it. Hence we shall characterize $\mathcal{G}$ as a political valuation function rather than as a demand function; thus we refer to 'grant $\mathcal{G}$'.

The mixed bureau can be interpreted as a public enterprise which sells its goods or services at prices which do not cover costs and expects some ministry to cover its deficit. The most interesting economic feature of such a bureau is the particular demand–cost balance. In extreme situations the mixed bureau may be constrained by demand only: customers and sponsor are willing to grant a budget that altogether exceeds the underlying costs. (Assume that a unique optimum exists in such a case because of the satiation properties of customers' and sponsor's demands.) Usually, however, we expect the mixed bureau to be constrained by the deficit limit (or profit prescription) Π^o, such that

$$pz + \mathcal{G}(z) - C(z, e) - k = \Pi^o. \tag{6.37}$$

<hr>

[22] For an extensive discussion of the following see Bös (1986a: 293–6).

This revenue-cost constraint implies an interesting twofold political influence on the bureau. On the one hand, the sponsor is willing to appropriate a grant $\mathcal{G}$, depending on the quantities produced. On the other hand, the bureau is expected to break even, to avoid excessive deficits, or to achieve a profit ($\Pi^o \gtreqless 0$ respectively).

The Niskanen bureaucrat as manager of a public firm can therefore be described as maximizing utility,

$$V(k, e, pz + \mathcal{G}(z)); \qquad V_k > 0, V_e < 0, V_B > 0, \qquad (6.38)$$

subject to the revenue-cost constraint (6.37), where V_B is the derivative with respect to the budget.

In practice, budget maximization is not the only objective in his own interest that a public manager may follow. Proving managerial success with reference to sales or output data is also of particular interest for public enterprises. Let us briefly characterize these objectives.[23]

Sales are a somewhat superficial indicator of economic success. Management is often inclined to use such an objective mainly because in the recent rapid-growth past these figures grew impressively. Attempting to show managerial success with reference to sales data is also of interest in private enterprises. Baumol (1959: 47–8) pointed out that in practical business any 'program which explicitly proposes any cut in sales volume, whatever the profit considerations, is likely to meet a cold reception'. The public manager, who is interested in the sales of his firm, can be described as maximizing

$$V(k, e, pz); \qquad V_k > 0, V_e < 0, V_{sal} > 0, \qquad (6.39)$$

where V_{sal} is the derivative with respect to sales. Of course, the government has to impose a revenue-cost constraint of the usual type,[24] otherwise the manager would fully ignore production costs and choose his lowest possible effort position.

Output maximization also can often be found in practice. For example, some ten years ago London Transport explicitly followed a policy of passenger miles maximization.[25] In this case the public manager optimizes

$$V(k, e, z); \qquad V_k > 0, V_e < 0, V_z > 0, \qquad (6.40)$$

---

[23] The following paragraph is taken from Bös (1986a: 298).
[24] *Not* the mixed-bureau constraint of equation (6.37) above.
[25] See Glaister and Collings (1978), Bös (1978b).

where V_z is the derivative with respect to the quantity of output. The manager would choose zero prices unless restricted by a revenue-cost constraint. Notice that this is precisely the pricing which maximizes consumer surplus in the absence of a revenue-cost constraint.

There are certainly many other indicators of success in which a public manager might be interested. However, the basic problems which arise in the cases of managers who draw direct satisfaction from the success of their firm can be shown by way of one adequately chosen example. For didactical reasons we choose the simplest example, namely the maximization of output.

Let us assume that demand is unknown to both principal and agent at the moment they enter into a contract. They only know that demand $z(p, \vartheta)$ depends on the variable ϑ whose probability density is known. As in the previous subsections, the manager gets a fixed income k. His utility depends on this income, on his effort, and on the output of the firm.

When the manager decides on price and effort, he knows ϑ and can therefore solve the deterministic optimization

$$\max_{p, \underline{e} \le e \le \overline{e}} V(k, e, z(p, \vartheta)) - \lambda[pz(p, \vartheta) - C(z(p, \vartheta), e) - k - \Pi^o]. \quad (6.41)$$

His *effort* will be determined according to

$$V_e \le -\lambda C_e \qquad \text{if } e = \underline{e} \qquad (6.42)$$

or

$$V_e = -\lambda C_e \qquad \text{if } e > \underline{e}. \qquad (6.43)$$

Although the corner solution may occur, interior solutions are also possible. To compare such an interior solution with the benchmark model, we divide (6.43) by V_k to obtain

$$\frac{V_e}{V_k} = -\frac{\lambda}{V_k} C_e = -\frac{\partial V^*/\partial \Pi^o}{\partial V^*/\partial k} C_e = \text{MRS}(\Pi^o, k) C_e, \qquad (6.44)$$

where V^* is the optimum value of the manager's utility. The intensity of the manager's effort depends on the manager's marginal rate of substitution between his income and the prescribed profit, which, in turn, influences demand and hence output. This marginal rate of substitution is positive because $V_e < 0$ and $C_e < 0$ require $\lambda < 0$: otherwise (6.43) could not hold. Hence the manager's utility falls if the profit target Π^o is increased. This is very plausible given the manager's interest in a low price.

The benchmark model requires effort according to $V_e/V_I = C_e$ (6.10). In the present case, however, too low an effort level is chosen if $\mathrm{MRS}(\Pi^o, k) < 1$. This is plausible: $\mathrm{MRS} < 1$ describes a manager who is interested more in his income than in output. Hence he chooses a low effort level. On the other hand, $\mathrm{MRS} > 1$ characterizes an output-oriented bureaucrat who is less interested in income. Accordingly, he chooses too high an effort level.

Let us next turn to the pricing decision of the output maximizer. The respective marginal condition can be written as

$$\left[p - \left(C_z + \frac{V_z}{\lambda}\right)\right] z_p = -z. \qquad (6.45)$$

The easiest way to interpret this pricing rule is as a direct comparison with the pricing rule of a profit-maximizing monopolist,

$$(p - C_z)z_p = -z. \qquad (6.46)$$

From this comparison we can conclude that the output-maximizing manager behaves as if he were a monopolist but underestimates marginal costs. (Instead of C_z, he calculates 'marginal costs' of $C_z + V_z/\lambda < C_z$.)

The manager's choice of effort and price is explicitly taken into account when the principal determines the manager income k. We impute to the principal an objective function ES. Given the profit constraint $E\Pi = \Pi^o$, the optimization of ES is equivalent to the optimization of $E(S + \Pi)$. The principal maximizes the following Lagrangean function with respect to k:

$$\mathcal{L} = ES(p(\cdot)) - \beta\{EV[k, e(\cdot), z(p(\cdot))] - \overline{V}\}$$
$$- \gamma[ED(p(\cdot), e(\cdot), \vartheta) - k - \Pi^o]. \qquad (6.47)$$

To avoid clumsy notation, $(\cdot)$ stands for (k, ϑ).

The optimal managerial income, accordingly, is determined by

$$ES_k - \beta EV_k - \gamma(ED_k - 1) = 0, \qquad (6.48)$$

where ED_k consists of the various derivatives resulting from the agent's choice of price and effort. In EV_k, additionally, the direct utility response of managerial income matters.

Since the profit constraint holds for each and any income k, we can differentiate the constraint with respect to k. The resulting equation

$$ED_k = 1 \qquad (6.49)$$

can be used to simplify the condition of the optimal manager income. Substituting (6.49) into (6.48) yields

$$-E(zp_k) - \beta EV_k = 0. \tag{6.50}$$

The resulting manager income shall be interpreted by comparing it with a hypothetical benchmark income. This hypothetical income results from

$$-1 - \beta EV_k = 0, \tag{6.51}$$

which is the expectational equivalent to the first-best condition of the deterministic benchmark model of a public firm.[26] Note that $\beta \leq 0$ is held constant for the comparison between the hypothetical benchmark income resulting from (6.51) and the actual income resulting from (6.50). We do not conduct a comparative-static analysis[27] of changing k, but make a hypothetical comparison of a reference income (6.51) and an actual income (6.50) using a single optimization approach.[28]

The comparison focuses on $E(zp_k)$. As can be seen directly from equation (6.50), the sign of this term is linked to the sign of $EV_k = EV_I + EV_e e_k + EV_z z_p p_k$. Increasing income influences the manager's utility in a threefold way:

(i)   First, there is a direct utility increase from an increase in income, $EV_I > 0$.

(ii)   Second, the increasing income changes the manager's effort. Let us assume that $e_k > 0$, which means that higher income increases manager's effort.[29] Then the increasing income implies a disutility which results from the higher manager's effort, $EV_e e_k < 0$.

(iii)   Third, the increasing income implies a change in price and hence in output. If higher income leads to a higher price of the product, then the manager's utility is reduced, because the higher price reduces output.

At the benchmark optimum the direct utility effect dominates and EV_k is positive, otherwise equation (6.51) could not hold. Let

---

[26] In this model we obtained $-1-\beta V_k=0$, as shown in (6.9) above.

[27] For such an analysis in a simpler framework see Chamley, Marchand, and Pestieau (1989).

[28] In a comparative-static analysis we would obtain β_k, the sign of which is indeterminate.

[29] In their simpler approach, Chamley, Marchand, and Pestieau (1989) prove that $\bar{e}_k > 0$, where $\bar{e}$ is the compensated effort.

us assume that EV_k is also positive at the actual optimum (6.50). Then $p_k \geq 0$: higher managerial income always leads to a higher price.

A comparison between the benchmark income and the distorted actual income requires a statement about $E(zp_k) \gtrless 1$. For this purpose we recall the differentiation of the revenue-cost constraint. Equation (6.49) can be written as follows:

$$E(zp_k) = 1 + E(C_e e_k) - E[(p - C_z)z_p p_k]. \qquad (6.52)$$

The effort-related term on the right-hand side is negative since we assume $e_k > 0$. The output-related term, however, is positive unless the price falls below marginal costs. Therefore $E(zp_k)$ becomes less than unity if the effort-related term dominates, and exceeds unity if the output-related term dominates. Figure 3 illustrates the comparison between benchmark income and actual income for an arbitrary functional shape of $E(zp_k)$.

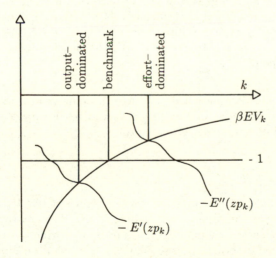

Figure 3

Let us first treat the *effort-dominated case* where $E(zp_k) < 1$ at the optimum. Here managerial effort responds very intensively to increasing income and higher effort implies considerable cost savings. Hence $E(C_e e_k)$ has a large absolute value and dominates the output-related term. As Figure 3 illustrates, in this case the manager's income exceeds the benchmark income.

In the *output-dominated case*, on the other hand, the actual income falls below the benchmark income. Higher income does not lead to too great an increase in effort. The output effect dominates. The manager recognizes that his higher income implies higher prices and reduces consumer demand for the product. Hence he is willing to accept a lower income because he draws enough satisfaction from the resulting increase in output.

6.4.4   A Welfare-Oriented Incentive Scheme for a Public Manager

The appropriate incentive scheme for a manager of a private firm is based on his participation in profit. Consequently, an appropriate incentive scheme for a public manager should be based on his participation in welfare. Loeb and Magat (1979) are best known for the development of an incentive mechanism where the regulator gives the consumer surplus to the manager. In that case the manager maximizes the sum of consumer and producer surplus which is welfare-optimal. The same basic idea can be found in one of Finsinger and Vogelsang's (1981) incentive mechanisms and in Chamley, Marchand, and Pestieau (1989)[30] In our framework, the introduction of such a welfare-oriented incentive scheme proceeds as follows. If we denote $S + \mathcal{D} =: W$, the public manager should earn an income[31]

$$I = k + aW. \tag{6.53}$$

Let us briefly deal with this incentive scheme before mentioning our main criticism. The manager maximizes utility $V(I, e)$ and chooses effort and price according to

$$p = C_z, \tag{6.54}$$

$$V_e/V_I = aC_e. \tag{6.55}$$

The marginal-cost pricing is allocatively efficient (we have not assumed a profit constraint to be imposed). X-efficiency results only if $a = 1$. Whether this happens depends on the principal's decision, which can be described by the following optimization approach:

$$\max_{a,k} (1 - a)EW(\cdot) - k - \beta[EV(k + aW(\cdot), e(\cdot)) - \overline{V}] \tag{6.56}$$

---

[30] Additionally, in their model the manager income linearly depends on labor employed by the public enterprise.

[31] For didactical purposes, in the income schedule (6.53) we use the same symbol a as in (6.17) although it describes another economic dependency. For the dependency of income on $\mathcal{D}$ recall footnote 13 above.

where $(\cdot)$ stands for (a, k, ϑ). The formal treatment of this approach is fully equivalent to the private manager's incentive mechanism we dealt with previously in Section 6.3. The principal's decision can be characterized by

$$(1-a)\left[EW_a - \frac{E(V_I W)}{EV_I}EW_k\right] = EW - \frac{E(V_I W)}{EV_I} \qquad (6.57)$$

which is precisely equation (6.29) for W instead of $\mathcal{D}$. For a risk-neutral agent, $a = 1^{32}$ and the agent receives the whole sum of consumer plus producer surplus in exchange for a fixed payment k, which goes to the principal. For a risk-averse agent we obtain $a \leq 1$ by analogously applying the proof of Section 6.3. The risk-neutral agent, therefore, will operate both allocatively efficiently and X-efficiently.

We now come to our criticism of this approach. The criticism is simple. Profit is something monetary which is earned by the firm. Hence it seems only too natural to give at least part of the profit to the manager whose job it is to work for this profit. Consumer surplus, however, does not exist as a stream of money: it is utility which is measured in monetary terms. Consequently, a real problem arises if the sum of consumer and producer surplus shall be paid to the public manager, because there is no flow of money which expresses consumer surplus and can be given to the manager. In practice, a clearing system would result, which most voters would never understand and never accept. Recall our implicit assumption that $I > 0$. Hence we expect a result where the management gets a percentage of a monetarily expressed welfare and pays a fixed amount k to the government, where $a(S + \mathcal{D}) > |k|$. Now think of an annual report of a railway company, where the interested voter finds the following statement: 'Compensation for the management consists of $39 billion of consumer surplus minus $5 billion deficit. On the basis of this gross compensation of $34 billion the management has to pay to the government a previously agreed lump-sum payment of $33.5 billion.' We think that voters' first impression would be that this is a ridiculous statement. Then they would try to understand what the concept of consumer surplus actually means and – at least in the case of a multiproduct firm – get terribly confused.

Matters might become even worse: the optimal managerial income may imply small k and large a, for instance $k = 0$ and

---

[32] Assuming the square bracket on the left-hand side is not zero.

$a = 1$. Then tax funds or public debt must be used to finance managers' incomes, which are determined by a purely theoretical utility measure. Would the public understand and accept such managerial compensation? I think not.

Therefore, in my opinion the Chamley–Marchand–Pestieau incentive scheme could be applied in practice.[33] I do not recall any annual report of a public firm which has ever published calculations of consumer surplus.

6.4.5 Performance-Related Manager Pay in Public Enterprises

After recognizing that welfare-related managerial pay cannot be applied in practice, what can the government do to achieve X-efficiency in a public enterprise? Several suggestions have been put forward and we shall discuss them in what follows.

First, the government could think of mimicking private firms' incentives by offering profit-related pay to the public manager. Unfortunately this is no way out of the dilemma. The manager will maximize $V(k + a\mathcal{D}; e)$. This implies X-inefficient effort. As in the privatized firm, we have

$$V_e/V_I = a\, C_e. \tag{6.19}$$

However, the government is interested in maximizing the sum of consumer and producer surpluses. The manager's income depends on producer surplus only. Therefore, equation (6.57) is replaced by

$$ES_a + (1-a)\left[E\mathcal{D}_a - \frac{E(V_I\Pi)}{EV_I}E\mathcal{D}_k\right] - \frac{E(V_I\mathcal{D})}{EV_I}ES_k$$
$$= E\mathcal{D} - \frac{E(V_I\mathcal{D})}{EV_I}. \tag{6.58}$$

Even if the manager is risk-neutral, a is not necessarily equated to unity. Therefore, profit-related managerial pay will always lead

---

[33] Restricting the manager's income to the amount which is earned by the firm is no solution of the dilemma. Consider the following restrictions: $0 \leq k + aE(S+\mathcal{D}) \leq E\mathcal{D}$. The right-hand constraint may or may not be binding. If it is not binding, it is without interest. If it is binding, the expected managerial income is equal to the expected difference between revenue and costs and the manager will maximize profits – we shall see in the next subsection that X-inefficiency results in such a case.

to X-inefficient behavior. Moreover, monopoly pricing will result, thus implying allocative inefficiency.

Performance-related managerial pay seems to be a better way to cope with the efficiency of a public firm. It seems to imply a trend toward X-efficiency without implying a trend toward monopoly pricing. Hence pay schedules which are tied to performance could be thought of as an adequate policy for improving the efficiency of a public firm and, therefore, as an attractive alternative to privatization. In the following, I shall show that, unfortunately, the alternative to privatization is not as attractive as it originally appeared.

Consider a government which links managerial pay to the percentage reduction of unit costs,[34]

$$I = k + a \left(\frac{C_o/z_o - C/z}{C_o/z_o} \right). \tag{6.59}$$

The index 'o' refers to that base period which is taken as reference.[35] We assume that costs are specified according to

$$C = C(z(p), e, \vartheta). \tag{6.60}$$

Linking manager's pay to the reduction of unit costs constitutes a non-linear income schedule. However, since the schedule is well specified, we can proceed in the same way as we did in the case of a linear income scheme: we let the manager maximize his utility and explicitly consider the resulting price and effort in the government's optimization approach. Formally, $p(k, a, \vartheta)$ and $e(k, a, \vartheta)$ are substituted into the government's objective function and into the relevant constraints.

Let us first deal with the public manager's optimization. He will maximize his utility:

$$\max_{p,e} V \left[k + a \left(1 - \frac{C/z}{C_o/z_o} \right); e \right]. \tag{6.61}$$

The manager will choose *effort* according to

$$\frac{V_e}{V_I} = \frac{a}{z(C_o/z_o)} C_e, \tag{6.62}$$

---

[34] It should be noted that unit costs are actually used as a performance indicator in economic practice. See, for instance, the recent annual reports of the British Post Office, which publish unit-cost reductions as one of the various targets set for the post office by the government.

[35] Once again, to avoid clumsy notation, we use the parameter 'a' instead of any other special parameter, say $a_{C/z}$.

which is X-inefficient unless $a = z(C_o/z_o)$. Here the regulating government faces an insurmountable task. If the pay schedule has to be contracted *ex ante*, i.e. before even the manager knows ϑ, it is impossible to set the parameter a in such a way that *ex post* $a = z(C_o/z_o)$ will be realized. The quantity produced is $z(p)$ and the manager's optimization leads to a dependence of price on ϑ, namely $p = p(k, a, \vartheta)$. The best the government can do *ex ante* is to set $a = Ez(C_o/z_o)$, but this does not necessarily imply X-efficient production *ex post*. The government could, of course, stipulate that it is willing to pay *ex post* according to $a = z(C_o/z_o)$, but this implies a switch from a performance-related pay schedule to a cost-related pay scheme, $I = k + a - C$.[36]

The *price* which will be set by the manager follows from the following condition:

$$-\frac{V_I}{z^2(C_o/z_o)}(zaC_z z_p - aC z_p) = 0. \qquad (6.63)$$

Consider first the case of decreasing returns to scale. There is an interior solution for $V_I, z > 0$, leading to

$$C_z = C/z. \qquad (6.64)$$

This rule implies minimal unit costs, which is allocatively optimal, at least in the long run. However, if the firm operates under increasing returns to scale,[37] there is no interior solution to (6.63) because $C_z < C/z$ for all z. The management will apply the corner solution with $z = \infty$. Hence it will apply zero prices, extending production to infinity which, in the model, is the best way to minimize unit costs. Needless to say, this is not a meaningful policy to be applied in practice. To avoid such a degeneration the government would have to add a revenue-cost constraint.

Therefore, let us next deal with the performance-related pay of public managers in the presence of a revenue-cost constraint. The manager has to consider

$$\Pi = pz(p) - C(z(p), e, \vartheta) - k - a\left(1 - \frac{C/z}{C_o/z_o}\right) \geq \Pi^o. \qquad (6.65)$$

---

[36] However, if the government is interested in maximizing welfare or profit, this incentive scheme will lead to neither X-efficiency nor allocative efficiency.

[37] If constant returns to scale are given, we have $C_z = C/z$; in that case the result is determined by demand.

Accordingly, he sets effort according to

$$-V_I \frac{a}{z(C_o/z_o)} C_e + V_e + \lambda C_e - \lambda \frac{a}{z(C_o/z_o)} C_e \leq 0, \qquad (6.66)$$

where λ is the Lagrangean multiplier associated with the manager's constraint $\Pi \geq \Pi^o$. An interior solution $e > \underline{e}$ is quite likely and in this case X-efficiency is attained if, at the optimum, the parameter a happens to be equal to $z(C_o/z_o)$. However, as already mentioned, such a parameter cannot be contracted *ex ante* if a performance-related pay schedule instead of a cost-related is desired.

The price is set according to a difficult formula which is definitely allocatively inefficient and, moreover, hard to interpret. Hence the precise formula may be skipped.

Let us next turn to the behavior of the principal. The government may be assumed to maximize expected consumer surplus subject to the manager's participation constraint and the expected profit constraint. It takes account of the manager's choice of effort and price, $e(a, k, \vartheta)$ and $p(a, k, \vartheta)$. The relevant Lagrangean function is

$$ES(p(\cdot))$$

$$-\beta \left\{ EV \left[k + a \left(1 - \frac{C[z(p(\cdot)), e(\cdot), \vartheta]/z(p(\cdot))}{C_o/z_o} \right); e(\cdot) \right] - \overline{V} \right\}$$

$$-\gamma \left[E\mathcal{D}[p(\cdot), e(\cdot), \vartheta] - k - a \left(1 - \frac{E(C(\cdot)/z(\cdot))}{C_o/z_o} \right) - \Pi^o \right]. \qquad (6.67)$$

Since the profit constraint holds for each and any a and k, we substitute $(E\Pi)_a = 0$ and $(E\Pi)_k = 0$ into the first-order conditions of the government's optimization and obtain

$$ES_k - \beta EV_k = 0, \qquad (6.68')$$

$$ES_a - \beta EV_a = 0. \qquad (6.68'')$$

The optimal income schedule shall be interpreted by comparing it to a hypothetical benchmark schedule. This hypothetical manager's income is determined as follows. Consider a fully informed government which chooses the parameters k and a according to

$$\max_{k,a} \ S(p) + pz(p) - C(z, e) - k - a \left(1 - \frac{C/z}{C_o/z_o} \right)$$

$$\text{subject to } V \left[k + a \left(1 - \frac{C/z}{C_o/z_o} \right); e \right] \geq \overline{V}, \qquad (\beta), \ (6.69)$$

where β is the Lagrangean parameter associated with the manager's participation constraint. The relevant marginal conditions are

$$-1 - \beta V_k = 0, \tag{6.70'}$$

$$\frac{C}{z(C_o/z_o)} - \beta V_a = 0. \tag{6.70''}$$

The benchmark income schedule is then determined by the expectational equivalents of these government's conditions, namely

$$-1 = \beta E V_k, \tag{6.71'}$$

$$E\left(\frac{C}{z(C_o/z_o)}\right) = \beta E V_a. \tag{6.71''}$$

For the comparison with the benchmark schedule we transform the government's optimum conditions (6.68). We differentiate the profit constraint $E\Pi = \Pi^o$ with respect to a and k. On the basis of this differentiation we obtain expressions for $E(zp_i) = -ES_i$; $i = a, k$, which can be substituted into the conditions (6.68). Then the government's optimum conditions read as follows:

$$-1 + E[(p - C_z)z_p p_k] - E(C_e e_k) = \beta E V_k, \tag{6.72'}$$

$$E\left[\frac{C}{z(C_o/z_o)}\right] + E\left\{\frac{a z_p p_a}{z(C_o/z_o)}\left(C_z - \frac{C}{z}\right)\right\} + E\left[(p - C_z)z_p p_a\right]$$
$$- E\left[C_e e_a\left(1 - \frac{a}{z(C_o/z_o)}\right)\right] = \beta E V_a. \tag{6.72''}$$

Let us now compare the benchmark income schedule (6.71) with that schedule which is actually chosen by the government and determined by (6.72). Note that we do not perform a comparative-static analysis of the government's optimum. Such an analysis is too complicated and does not lead to economic results, whereas particular qualitative properties of the optimal income schedule can be clarified by comparing the government's optimum to the benchmark optimum.

As a first simple case of interpretation, consider a government's optimum where $C_z = C/z$. This means either cost minimization, in case of decreasing returns to scale, or constant returns to scale. In this case, equation (6.72'') is simplified by the vanishing of the cost-related term $E\{\cdot\}$. Then the government's optimum conditions differ from the benchmark conditions by the inclusion of (i) effort-related terms, which depend on $C_e e_i$, $i = a, k$, and (ii) price-related terms, which depend on $(p - C_z)z_p p_i$, $i = a, k$. We assume that the budget constraint has been chosen so high that the price exceeds the marginal costs.

In both equations (6.72) the interplay between the effort- and price-terms is similar to the case of the output-oriented manager which we treated in Section 6.4.3 and illustrated in Figure 3. Of course, there is no output-oriented manager in this subsection, hence a high price is not particularly disliked by the manager, but only by the welfare-oriented government. Moreover, we have a system of two equations which must be considered simultaneously. However, the basic structure of the problem is similar to the one-dimensional problem of the output-oriented manager. According to the most plausible interpretation, there is a trade-off between effort- and price-effects: higher a or k increase effort, which is desirable, but also increase the price, which is undesirable.

We assume $e_a, e_k > 0$; hence domination of effort-terms will imply a tendency toward values of a and k in excess of the benchmark values. However, there is an interesting asymmetry. In (6.72''), the effort-related term would be equal to zero if the firm worked X-efficiently, whence $a = z(C_o/z_o)$: a parameter a which leads to X-efficiency does not distort the benchmark pay schedule. In such a case, any deviation of a from its benchmark equivalent is caused only indirectly, via the influence of k on effort.

We can also assume $p_a, p_k > 0$, whence an increase in the manager income increases the price of the product.[38] Therefore, domination of price terms will imply a tendency toward values of a and k which fall below the benchmark values.

Let us finally give up the assumption of $C_z = C/z$. In particular, we want to include the possibility of increasing returns to scale. It is evident that the performance-related pay has a stronger hold on a firm which operates under increasing returns to scale because there are better opportunities to reduce unit costs by expansion. The instrument which sets this effect in motion, is the performance parameter a; a cost-related term enters (6.72'') only: no equivalent can be found in (6.72'). Hence, if increasing returns are particularly relevant, the performance parameter a will tend to exceed the

---

[38] Consider equations (6.68) and recall $\beta \leq 0$. At the benchmark optimum (6.71) both EV_a and EV_k are positive. Hence we assume that they are also positive at the actual optimum (6.68). Then $p_a, p_k > 0$ directly follows from (6.68), since $ES_i = -E(zp_i)$, $i = a, k$.

corresponding benchmark value, whereas the lump-sum income k can be expected to be low.

6.5   Conclusion

In this chapter we have seen that, in a privatized firm where the manager's income depends on profit, the manager has an incentive to produce X-efficiently if he is risk-neutral. The price, however, will be set according to monopoly pricing, which is allocatively inefficient. We need explicit regulation of the privatized firm to cope with allocative efficiency. We will deal with this regulation in the next chapter of the book.

In this chapter we have also seen why a typical public manager with a fixed salary has an incentive to work as effortlessly as possible. Only if he himself is interested in the success of the firm, for instance in its output, will he exert more effort. We then considered a fine theoretical concept of a welfare-oriented incentive scheme for a public manager. Unfortunately, I argue that this scheme is not applicable in practice. Therefore, we investigated performance-related managerial pay schedules in public firms. However, the results were disappointing. Hence privatization and subsequent regulation of the privatized firm seems to be an appropriate choice to improve the efficiency of a firm.

6.6   Appendix: Multi-Objective Schemes

In private firms managerial salaries can often be explained by their depending on both profit and sales (see for instance Murphy, 1985):

$$I = k + a_\Pi \Pi + b_S pz, \qquad (6.76)$$

where a_Π and b_S are appropriately chosen weights.

In public firms the government often wants the firm to consider multiple objectives and, correspondingly, we would expect a managerial incentive scheme which depends on welfare and some other target. A good example is Chamley, Marchand, and Pestieau's (1989) managerial income, which depends on both welfare W and labor input L such that

$$I = k + a_W W + b_L L. \qquad (6.77)$$

How do the multiple objectives influence the efficiency of the firm? There is a simple rule which guarantees X-efficiency, although not allocative efficiency. If the principal's objective is $\mathcal{O}(p, e, \vartheta)$, a linear incentive scheme implies X-efficiency if

$$I = k + a_{\mathcal{O}}\mathcal{O} \qquad (6.78)$$

and the agent is risk-neutral. This holds if $\mathcal{O}$ is a unique objective or any weighted multiple objective. The trick is the identity of the principal's and the agent's objective. Maximizing $V(I, e)$, the agent is interested in maximizing the principal's objective and this leads to X-efficiency.

Obviously, the above incentive scheme rule will seldom hold in practice. As soon as the principal gives other weights to the various objectives, typically there will be neither X-efficiency nor allocative efficiency, even if the agent is risk-neutral. This holds in particular if the principal's objective differs from the variables which are relevant in the incentive scheme. In practice, the most relevant case for private firms is a principal who wants to maximize the value of the firm or the profit and a manager whose income can best be explained by reference to profit and sales. In public firms we could think of a principal who aims at maximum welfare but defines an incentive scheme which linearly depends on welfare and labor input. In these cases general results on the parameters of the relevant incentive schemes cannot be found and even particular special results are hard to obtain.

7 Regulation of a Privatized Firm

Recently price-cap regulation has been applied to privatized utilities in the UK, in particular for telecommunications, gas, and electricity pricing. The regulation of these public utilities has been introduced to cope with the trade-off between efficiency increases and price increases which are both expected to result from privatization.

According to the British regulation, price increases of monopolistically supplied goods must not be higher than the increase of the retail price index (RPI) minus a politically chosen constant X. Accordingly, in the UK the constraint became known as $RPI - X$.

This regulation, proposed by Littlechild (1983), intentionally avoids tying regulation to the rate of return on capital. In the present chapter I shall deal with $RPI - X$ in precisely this spirit. Hence I shall not argue that regulatory reviews will endogenize X on the basis of rate-of-return arguments, because such an interpretation transforms $RPI - X$ into a sort of rate-of-return regulation, which is not the original intention of the Littlechild formula. I shall explicitly show that X must remain a political constant to obtain desirable economic results. Note that choosing X as a political constant does not preclude linking it to *expected* productivity increases (Beesley and Littlechild, 1989: 461).

This chapter concentrates on a static aspect of price-cap regulation which has not been dealt with in recent publications on the topic. Dynamic aspects, as mentioned, for instance, in Vickers and Yarrow (1988a: 86–8, 214–16), are not examined.

7.1 Four Cases of Price-Cap Regulation

Our analysis concerns a public utility which maximizes profit

$$\Pi = pz, \tag{7.1}$$

where $p = (p_1, \ldots, p_n)$ is a vector of prices, $z = (z^+, z^-) = (z_1, \ldots, z_r, z_{r+1}, \ldots, z_n)$ is a vector of netputs. The usual convention on the sign of netputs holds: positive quantities denote outputs, negative quantities denote inputs $(z^+ > 0, z^- < 0)$.

Inputs and outputs are combined according to a technology:

$$g(z) = 0. \tag{7.2}$$

As we deal with a public utility, all sorts of returns to scale are allowed.

The utility has been instructed to cover all demand for its outputs:

$$z^+ = x(p) \tag{7.3}$$

where the vector x denotes aggregate consumer demand. Some of the outputs are sold on competitive markets, others on monopolistic markets. 'Monopolistic' simply means that the utility is a price-setter, whereas prices on competitive markets are exogenously given to the utility. We define three subsets of prices,

$$p = (p_c, p_{mon}, p_{inp}), \tag{7.4}$$

where p_c indicates the prices of competitive outputs, p_{mon} the prices of monopolistic outputs, and p_{inp} the prices of inputs. The elements of the vector p_{mon} are denoted p_m.

The utility's instruments are:

(i) the prices of monopolistically supplied goods p_m. The prices of competitively supplied goods and the prices of inputs are exogenously given. The firm has to take these prices as given by the market;

(ii) the inputs of the firm z^-. Note that the outputs $z^+ = x(p)$ are determined via market demand. Hence they are influenced by the utility setting p_{mon}, and also depend on the other, exogenously given, prices.

When maximizing profit, the utility has to consider any existing price-cap regulation. A price index of the monopolistically supplied goods, PI_{mon}, must not exceed the retail price index RPI minus some constant X,

$$PI_{mon} \leq RPI - X. \tag{7.5}$$

There is no government restriction with respect to prices of competitively supplied goods. Here the government relies on market forces to keep these prices low. Note, however, that the retail price index also depends on the prices of those goods which the privatized firm supplies for sale in competitive markets.

For a detailed analysis of price-cap regulation we must precisely define the price index PI_{mon} and the 'X' percent to be deducted from the retail price index.

Ideally, the price index of the monopolistically supplied goods would be a subindex of the retail price index. The weights of this index would be the percentages of consumed quantities of an adequately chosen base period. Hence we would have

$$PI_{mon} = \frac{\sum p_m x_m^o}{\sum p_m^o x_m^o},\qquad(7.6)$$

where x_m^o is the quantity of good m in the commodity basket of the retail price index. The superscript o refers to the base period.

Unfortunately, in practice another procedure is applied. Oftel[1] (1986: 10) states: 'The average is to be calculated by using as weights the revenues that British Telecom reasonably believes to have been received from each relevant class of business.' Let us formalize this statement by defining the following measure of the average price increase of monopolistically supplied goods (note that this is no longer a price index of any of the usual types):

$$PI_{mon} = \sum_m \frac{p_m x_m}{\sum_k p_k x_k}\frac{p_m}{p_m^o}.\qquad(7.7)$$

In this index revenues depend on prices and hence a complicated feedback of regulation on prices is implied. We shall come to that problem at a later stage of the analysis.

There is another problem in setting the price-cap constraint, namely that of setting X. Ideally X should be chosen as an estimate of the firm's increase in productivity,[2]

$$X_t = \frac{\sum_{i=1}^n p_i^{t-1}(z_i^t - z_i^{t-1})}{\sum_{i=1}^n p_i^{t-1} z_i^{t-1}} = \frac{\sum_{i=1}^n p_i^{t-1} z_i^t}{\sum_{i=1}^n p_i^{t-1} z_i^{t-1}} - 1,\qquad(7.8)$$

where $t, t-1$ are indices of time. The reader should recall that in our model outputs are measured by positive quantities, inputs by negative quantities. Hence formula (7.8) is a sum of adequately weighted output increases minus a sum of adequately weighted input increases.

Increasing productivity leads to a tighter price-cap constraint. Hence the firm facing price-cap regulation with endogenous productivity component will trade off profit increases and productivity increases, which will lead to lower productivity increases than would otherwise be possible. Therefore it seems less distorting to

[1] Oftel – Office of Telecommunications – is the regulatory authority for British Telecom.
[2] This convenient definition can be found in Vogelsang (1989: 34).

choose X as an exogenous variable which cannot be manipulated by the firm. This is done in practice if X is a politically fixed percentage.[3] Such a political determination can be considered in our model if X is treated as an exogenous variable.

The above specifications allow four different cases of price-cap regulation as described in Table 3.

Table 3   Price-Cap Regulation: Four Cases

PI_{mon}	X	
	Productivity, endogenous	Political influence, exogenous
Price index weights, exogenous	Productivity-distorted regulation	Political regulation
Revenue weights, endogenous	Twice-distorted regulation	Revenue-distorted regulation

7.2   The Effects of Regulation

The decision of the public utility can be captured by the following optimization approach:

$$\max_{p_m, z^-} \quad pz$$
$$\text{subject to } z^+ = x(p),$$
$$g(z) = 0,$$
$$PI_{mon} \leq RPI - X. \tag{7.9}$$

It is convenient to substitute the cover-all-demand constraints into the objective function and the other constraints. Hence we describe the firm's optimization by the following Lagrangean function:

$$\mathcal{L} = \sum_{i=1}^{r} p_i x_i(p) + \sum_{i=r+1}^{n} p_i z_i^-$$
$$- \beta g(x(p), z^-) - \chi(RPI - X - PI_{mon}), \tag{7.10}$$

---

[3] For institutional details of the UK experience, in particular with respect to British Gas and British Telecom, see Sect. 4.1.2 above.

where β and χ are Lagrangean multipliers. The effects on pricing and on inputs differ according to the four cases of regulation we treat in this chapter.

7.2.1   Political Regulation

We start with the simplest case of a price-cap regulation where the firm cannot manipulate the constraint because in the constraint all variables other than prices are exogenously given. The constraint on prices is:

$$\frac{\sum_m p_m x_m^o}{\sum_m p_m^o x_m^o} \leq \frac{\sum_{i=1}^r p_i x_i^o}{\sum_{i=1}^r p_i^o x_i^o} - X. \qquad (7.11)$$

The regulated firm applies the following marginal conditions (where we have abbreviated $I^o := \sum_{i=1}^r p_i^o x_i^o$ and $M^o := \sum_m p_m^o x_m^o$):

$$\mathcal{L}_{p_m} : \sum_{i=1}^{r} \left(p_i - \beta \frac{\partial g}{\partial x_i} \right) \frac{\partial x_i}{\partial p_m} =$$

$$- x_m \left[1 - \chi \left(\frac{x_m^o / x_m}{I^o} - \frac{x_m^o / x_m}{M^o} \right) \right] \qquad (7.12)$$

$$\mathcal{L}_{z_i^-} : p_i = \beta \frac{\partial g}{\partial z_i^-} \qquad\qquad i = r+1, \ldots, n. \qquad (7.13)$$

Let us now interpret the marginal conditions $\mathcal{L}_{p_m}$: what is the structure of the prices of monopolistically supplied goods? We normalize the wage rate $p_n = 1$ and therefore obtain as the nth condition in (7.13)

$$1 = \beta \frac{\partial g}{\partial z_n^-}. \qquad (7.14)$$

Hence we can define

$$c_i := \frac{\partial g}{\partial z_i^+} \bigg/ \frac{\partial g}{\partial z_n^-} = \beta \frac{\partial g}{\partial z_i^+}, \qquad (7.15)$$

where c_i is a shadow price which measures the marginal costs of labor of producing output z_i^+. For convenience we denote c_i as 'marginal costs'.[4]

---

[4] For details of this convention see Bös (1986a: 81–3).

Now recall the market-clearing conditions $x = z^+$ and substitute the shadow prices c_i into $\mathcal{L}_{p_m}$ to obtain the following price structure:

$$\sum_{i=1}^{r} (p_i - c_i) \frac{\partial z_i^+}{\partial p_m} = -z_m^+(1 - R_m). \qquad (7.16)$$

The correction term R_m is defined as

$$R_m = \chi \frac{x_m^o / x_m (M^o - I^o)}{I^o M^o} \geq 0, \qquad (7.17)$$

where R_m is non-negative because we have $\chi \leq 0$ (Kuhn–Tucker) and $M^o < I^o$. (The sum M^o contains fewer outputs than I^o.)

This pricing structure can be interpreted by a comparison with public-sector pricing according to Feldstein (1972a,b,c). For this purpose consider the following Lagrangean function which describes a problem that is dual to Feldstein's:

$$\mathcal{L} = \sum p_i x_i(p) - \sum p_i z_i^- - \beta g(x(p)) - \gamma(W - W^o), \qquad (7.18)$$

where W is a Bergsonian welfare function and W^o is some desired level of welfare. Differentiation with respect to any price p_m yields

$$\sum_i (p_i - c_i) \frac{\partial z_i^+}{\partial p_m} = -z_m^+(1 - F_m). \qquad (7.19)$$

Once again, we have a correction term, namely F_m, which is defined as[5]

$$F_m = -\gamma \sum_h \frac{\partial W}{\partial v_h} \frac{\partial v_h}{\partial \kappa_h} \frac{x_{mh}}{x_m} \geq 0. \qquad (7.20)$$

Here v_h are the indirect utility functions, κ_h the individual non-labor incomes, and x_{mh} the individual consumption of consumer h. Aggregation yields $\sum_h x_{mh} = x_m$. The sign of the Lagrangean multiplier $\gamma \leq 0$ follows from the Kuhn–Tucker conditions.

F_m represents distributional characteristics, in other words, the individual consumption shares of good m weighted by the social marginal evaluation of the individual incomes of the respective consumers. If some good is a necessity, the social weights are high for the individuals with high consumption shares and F_m is high.

---

[5] We have applied Roy's identity to obtain (7.20).

If a good is a luxury, the social weights are low for the individuals with high consumption shares and F_m is low.

As monopoly prices require that

$$\sum_i (p_i - c_i)\frac{\partial z_i^+}{\partial p_m} = -z_m^+, \qquad (7.21)$$

we can argue: the Feldstein firm behaves as if it were a monopolist who inflates each price elasticity of demand by $1/(1 - F_m)$.[6]

The operation of this procedure can be illustrated most easily if we neglect cross-price effects. Then, for a price above marginal costs the inflating factor $1/(1 - F_m)$ will be positive and will increase with increasing F_m. The price elasticity of demand must therefore be overestimated and the degree of overestimation increases with increasing social valuation of individual consumption as reflected in F_m. Above all, the demand elasticity of necessities must be overestimated because monopolistic pricing always implies greater care in the pricing of goods with higher demand elasticities. This implies relatively lower prices of necessities.

Let us now turn to those prices which result from the $RPI - X$ regulation. We see explicitly that the pricing structures (7.16) and (7.19) are formally identical after replacing F_m with R_m. Hence $RPI - X$ pricing follows the Feldstein rule if R_m has the same qualities as F_m, i.e. if it is higher for necessities than for luxuries. Can we prove such a property of R_m? Consider x_m^o/x_m. The periodical revisions of price indices in developed countries have shown a shifting of consumption from necessities toward luxuries. Hence x_m^o/x_m is higher for necessities and lower for luxuries; therefore, we have exactly the same sort of weighting as in Feldstein's distributionally modified prices. This might be surprising: qualitatively, maximizing profits under a price-cap constraint has the same distributional effects as maximizing a welfare function with distributional aims! This result is due to the fact that, when choosing Laspeyres indices, the constraint takes account of the weights of the base period in which necessities bought by lower-income groups are given higher weights than those which would correspond to present consumption. This is a desirable distributional consequence of the 'politician's error', i.e. of acting on the basis of past consumption patterns.

---

[6] Divide (7.19) by $(1 - F_m)$ and define $(\partial z_i^+/\partial p_m)/(1 - F_m) = (\partial z_i^+/\partial p_m)^{infl.}$. Elasticities can then be obtained easily by multiplying each partial derivative with the corresponding price/quantity ratio p_m/z_i^+.

Furthermore, we have to bear in mind that with a constant basket of commodities the distributionally desirable effects increase quantitatively with the passage of time because deviations of actual consumption from the corresponding proportions of the basket in the base period increase with time. Therefore, after some years price-cap regulation may imply not only qualitatively equal, but also quantitatively similar, results as the explicit consideration of distributional welfare weights.

From the theoretical point of view this result is not too surprising. It has been well-known since Bös (1978a) that minimizing a Laspeyres price index under a profit constraint leads to distributionally positive results of the Feldstein type. Profit maximization under price-cap regulation is exactly the dual problem: therefore, the results should be the same.

Finally, a short remark on the input policy of the privatized firm.[7] The inputs are chosen so as to equate the ratios of marginal productivities to the price ratios. We call this an undistorted input policy. As we shall see in following subsections, for other price-cap regulation specifications, the input policy is distorted.

Summarizing, I favor the political regulation approach: the monopolistically supplied goods are priced in a distributionally positive manner and the input policy is undistorted.

7.2.2 Revenue-Distorted Regulation

Let us now turn to a form of price-cap regulation where the price index of the monopolistically supplied goods is calculated by using the revenues of the relevant goods as weights. The variable X is still politically determined and therefore exogenous. Hence the firm faces the following constraint on prices:

$$\sum_m \frac{p_m x_m}{\sum_k p_k x_k} \frac{p_m}{p_m^o} \le \frac{\sum_{i=1}^r p_i x_i^o}{\sum_{i=1}^r p_i^o x_i^o} - X. \qquad (7.23)$$

This constraint requires low price increases of goods with high revenue shares. However, it cannot be said what this means in general. The relevant marginal conditions are:

$$\mathcal{L}_{p_m} : \sum_{i=1}^r (p_i - c_i)\frac{\partial z_i^+}{\partial p_m} = -z_m^+\left[1 - \chi\left(\frac{x_m^o/x_m}{I^o} - DR_m\right)\right] (7.24)$$

---

[7] This interpretation is based on the $\mathcal{L}_{z_i^-}$ conditions (7.13).

$$\mathcal{L}_{z_i^-} : \quad p_i = \beta \frac{\partial g}{\partial z_i^-}; \qquad\qquad i = r+1,\ldots,n. \qquad (7.25)$$

The distorted revenue effects DR_m are quite complicated expressions with indeterminate signs. Hence there is no reason to write them down explicitly. We cannot learn anything from their formal structure. Therefore, the only positive message is that the input structure remains undistorted.

Before concluding this subsection, let us think of possible improvements of a revenue-weighted price-cap regulation. In fact, there is a very simple method for such an improvement: let the firm choose the revenue weights of the base period. Such a regulation has informational advantages because weights from the past are well-known figures both to the firm and to the regulator. Simple algebraic manipulation yields the following result:

$$\sum_m \frac{p_m^o x_m^o}{\sum_k p_k^o x_k^o} \frac{p_m}{p_m^o} = \frac{\sum_m p_m x_m^o}{\sum_k p_k^o x_k^o} = \frac{\sum_m p_m x_m^o}{\sum_m p_m^o x_m^o}. \qquad (7.26)$$

Base-period revenue weights change the revenue-weighted average of price increases into a usual Laspeyres-type price index. All results of the preceding subsection hold. Obviously, the use of revenue weights of the year before $(t-1)$ has a similar effect. Quantitatively, however, the distributional effects of such pricing will be much less pronounced than when weights from a more remote base period are employed.

7.2.3   Productivity-Distorted Regulation

Next we investigate a variant of price-cap regulation which endogenizes X. We assume that X is a measure of the firm's productivity, as defined in (7.8). In our static analysis all prices p_i^{t-1} and quantities z_i^{t-1} are assumed to be exogenously given. We do not deal with dynamic or steady-state price paths. We consider a privatized firm facing the following price regulation:

$$\frac{\sum_m p_m x_m^o}{\sum_m p_m^o x_m^o} \le \frac{\sum_{i=1}^r p_i x_i^o}{\sum_{i=1}^r p_i^o x_i^o} - \frac{\sum_{i=1}^n p_i^{t-1} z_i^t}{\sum_{i=1}^n p_i^{t-1} z_i^{t-1}} + 1, \qquad (7.27)$$

where variables without time index refer to the present period.

The marginal conditions $\mathcal{L}_{p_m} = 0$ are the same as in Section 7.2.1 on political regulation, because the productivity index does not depend on any present prices. Hence the distributionally positive price structure of monopolistically supplied goods holds; however, the conditions $\mathcal{L}_{z_i^-} = 0$ are distorted. We obtain

$$p_i + \chi \frac{p_i^{t-1}}{I^{t-1}} = \beta \frac{\partial g}{\partial z_i^-}; \qquad i = r+1, \ldots, n, \qquad (7.28)$$

where $I^{t-1} := \sum_1^n p_i^{t-1} z_i^{t-1}$. Note $\chi \leq 0$ from the Kuhn–Tucker conditions.

For the following interpretation let us rewrite the marginal condition as follows:

$$\widetilde{p}_i = \beta \frac{\partial g}{\partial z_i^-} \quad \text{where} \quad \widetilde{p}_i = p_i + \chi \frac{p_i^{t-1}}{I^{t-1}} \leq p_i. \qquad (7.29)$$

Rather than equating actual input prices p_i to the respective shadow prices $\beta \partial g / \partial z_i^-$, the firm equates artificial prices $\widetilde{p}_i$ which are too low to the shadow prices. Calculating inputs at too low prices, however, means too much input is used. The associated reduction in productivity pushes output prices upwards. This is exactly the result we expected from the explicit introduction of factor productivity in the price-cap regulation. If productivity increases are deducted from RPI when calculating the maximum increases of output prices, the firm is punished for productivity increases. Consequently the firm will keep the productivity increases lower and maximize its profits by increasing output prices. The conclusion of this result is straightforward. X must remain an exogenously given constant to maintain the firm's incentives to efficient input policy.

7.2.4   Twice-Distorted Regulation

Twice-distorted regulation results from introducing into the price-cap constraint both revenue weights in PI_{mon} and a productivity index for X. The results simply are a combination of the revenue and productivity distortions mentioned in the preceding two subsections. Hence there is no need for an explicit detailed treatment of this case.

7.3   Conclusion

This chapter presents an analysis of a recently invented new form of price regulation. An index of prices of monopolistically supplied goods must never exceed the retail price index minus X. The main results of the chapter are as follows:

(i)   If the constant X is politically chosen, price-cap regulation does not distort factor inputs. Hence X should be specified *ex ante* and not be linked to actual productivity growth through the regulatory period. Otherwise the firm is punished for large productivity increases, which implies undesired efficiency losses.

(ii)   The ideal price-cap regulation has exogenous (= political) X and a price index of monopolistically supplied goods which is a subindex of the retail price index. It is shown that this regulation leads to pricing similar to Feldstein (1972a): the consumption of necessities is favored by relatively lower prices.

(iii)   In practice, sometimes the price index of monopolistically supplied goods is calculated on the basis of revenue weights. This leads to serious distortions of the pricing structure. However, as we show, a simple remedy for these distortions is the use of revenue weights which relate to the base period of the retail price index. Then, once again, Feldstein prices are obtained.

8 Partial Privatization

8.1 Introduction

A partially privatized firm is owned partly by private shareholders
and partly by the government. In that case there are two possible
scenarios which depict the role of the government. In the first the
government remains totally inactive, leaving the role of the principal to the private shareholders. The government accepts that the
firm maximizes profit (or the value of the firm). As a sort of silent
partner, the government confines itself to receiving the dividends
from its shares. This scenario holds in particular if the partial
privatization is perceived as a transitory state, which can happen
quite easily if capital market constraints make it impossible to sell
the privatized firm in one step. This would induce the existence
of a partially privatized firm between the first and the last step
of privatization. The government is interested in receiving a good
price from selling its remaining shares in the firm in the further
steps of privatization. Consequently, it wants the firm to realize a
high profit, which implies a high value of the firm, which, in turn,
is the basis of a high share offer price in forthcoming privatization
steps. Another explanation of this scenario pertains to firms in a
competitive market, for example automobile firms. If the market
were perfectly competitive, profit maximization would mean welfare maximization, in which case the interests of private and public
owners would simply coincide. If competition is very intense, although not perfect, profit maximization might be perceived by the
government as a good approximation of welfare maximization.

In an alternative scenario of a partially privatized firm the government retains shares of the firm in order to maintain an influence
in the firm.[1] The government chooses an 'internal regulation' of
the firm, sending its representatives to the board of the firm where
they advocate welfare interests and make compromises with representatives of the private shareholders who advocate profit interests.
The present chapter deals with this second scenario.

We assume that compromising between public and private
owners occurs only at the board level.[2] Here representatives of

---

[1] Note that the so-called 'golden share' is not a share of the usual type,
but a veto against particular decisions of the privatized firm.

[2] In contrast to Bös and Peters (1988a) where such a compromise is also
attained at the level of the technological management. See pp. 48–9 above.

public and private owners coordinate their special interests in a bargaining process. The result is a compromise between welfare and profit, depending on the bargaining power of each group of owners as determined by the degree of privatization. We define the degree of privatization by the percentage of shares which are owned by private shareholders: $\Theta = 0$ characterizes a fully public firm; partial privatization is given if $0 < \Theta < 1$.

In this chapter we shall deal with a particularly simple model of the partially privatized firm. More sophisticated modelling will be postponed to the normative part of the book (Section 12.3.2). In our simple model we assume that the firm's board consists of Θ percent representatives of the private owners and $(1 - \Theta)$ percent representatives of the government. Hence Θ percent propose to maximize profits and $(1 - \Theta)$ percent to maximize welfare. Let the representatives arrive at a compromise leading to a mixed objective function where both profit and welfare win the percentage weight of their respective supporters on the board. Welfare, in this context, may be measured by a social benefit–cost difference, the sum of consumer and producer surpluses. We consider a one-product monopoly which sells its output z at price p. The objective of the privatized firm, therefore, is

$$\Phi = (1 - \Theta)[S(p) + \Pi] + \Theta\Pi, \tag{8.1}$$

where $S(p)$ is consumer surplus, $\partial S/\partial p = -z(p)$, and Π is the profit of the firm. This formulation implies that in the present simple model we exclude all income effects and assume that the firm meets all demand, whence z denotes both demand and supply.

The objective function (8.1) assumes a linear continuous move from welfare to profit maximization as the degree of privatization moves from 0 to 100 percent. The fully public firm maximizes welfare; the fully privatized firm maximizes profit. Note that a small percentage of shares gives a group of owners a minority right in the firm, which forces us to consider the special interests of this group. If the number of shares held by one of the groups is increased, then the influence of this group is increased: the group wins more influence in the shareholders' meetings, the representatives can more successfully engage in public relations. This means that the board of the firm cannot be considered as a simple majority rule committee where the group which owns more than 50 percent dictates everything. Admittedly, however, objective function (8.1) over-exaggerates the continuity of the increase in power which results from an increase in shares. To model this paradigm more realistically, a logistic form of an increase in the bargaining power might be adequate (see Figure 4). In the present chapter, for didactical purposes we use the simple linear combination of welfare and profit; a more realistic model will be chosen in the normative theory part of the book. The qualitative results to be achieved in this chapter do not depend on this special assumption.

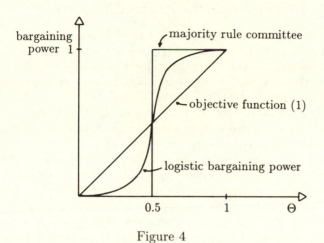

Figure 4

The concept of partial privatization, as presented in the preceding paragraphs, considers the board of the firm as an institution of compromise. On the board, representatives of various groups meet and bargain about the firm's policy. The West German codetermination, which sends representatives of labor into the firms' decision bodies, follows precisely this line of thinking.

The concept of the board of a firm as a place of compromise is in sharp contrast to that of an entrepreneur who singlehandedly decides on everything in the firm. Such a figure is more a maverick than a decision body of a modern enterprise. When Schumpeter wrote about his entrepreneur, he was thinking of this maverick type. However, this concept of an entrepreneur is outdated.[3] His was the entrepreneur of unbridled capitalism, without the limits and restrictions which have been imposed on today's entrepreneurs to reconcile entrepreneurial spirit and socially desirable outcomes. If somebody today speaks of a Schumpeterian entrepreneur, he does not mean that person which Schumpeter himself dealt with

[3] For a detailed reasoning see Albach (1979).

in the twenties and thirties: typically, the reference to Schumpeter is only a catchphrase, a sort of general reference to innovative behavior, and is not meant to imply that the Schumpeterian spirit must be absent from the boards where members of various groups compromise on the firm's policy.

8.2   Internal versus External Regulation

Until now the question has been left open as to whether it is better to partially privatize a firm or to fully privatize it and apply a regulatory constraint. Both policies address the same problem: how to cope with the undesired consequences of the profit maximization which is expected from a fully privatized firm. In the preceding chapters, partial privatization did not occur: rather, we compared totally privatized and totally public firms. If full privatization led to socially undesired results, we suggested 'capping' the prices of the privatized firm. In the normative theory part of this book partial privatization will be dealt with as a means to cope with the trade-off between allocative and production efficiency.

Partial privatization, as described in Section 8.1 above, implies an *internal regulation of the firm*. The government's representatives use all the rights they have in the firm to promote the government's interest, i.e. welfare maximization. Thus regulation is internal, coming from within the firm. On the other hand, price caps for a private firm constitute an *external regulation*. The firm operates as a profit maximizer; the welfare interest in low prices is imposed from outside the firm. Partial privatization without a price constraint can be considered as an alternative to full privatization with a price constraint.

The recent UK privatizations of public utilities favored the policy of full privatization under some sort of regulatory constraint. In many other countries, like Austria, West Germany, Portugal, and Spain, the concept of partial privatization finds strong support. Recall the example of a member of West Germany's conservative party who suggested that the percentage of Lufthansa's shares which is held by public owners should be reduced to 26 percent (not 51 percent as one might have expected).

Partial privatization, moreover, is a concept of particular interest for Eastern Europe as recently stressed by Lipton and Sachs (1990: 129):

Because the capacity of the government to sell a large number of enterprises may be limited, and because direct transfers of shares may be limited for budgetary or other reasons, the partial approach may allow for a greater number of firms to enter the process.

In the following we shall investigate the pros and cons of partial privatization versus regulated private ownership.

8.3 Government's Information Status

Partial privatization implies government representatives on the board of the firm. These representatives have the same inside knowledge as the representatives of the private owners. This is an advantage of partial privatization as compared with full privatization plus regulation. In the latter case the regulator lacks inside knowledge and has to regulate under incomplete information. When designing the $RPI - X$ constraint, the UK government tried to minimize the informational requirements of regulation. However, as shall be shown in what follows, they cannot be fully eliminated.

Let us compare two simple principal–agent models of a partially privatized firm and a fully privatized regulated firm. In both cases we assume that the government's decision on privatization has taken place at some earlier time. Hence in the case of partial privatization $0 < \Theta < 1$ is exogenously given; and so is $\Theta = 1$ for the price-regulated firm. In the normative theory part of the book we shall explicitly show the consequences which result from confining the government to regulated full private ownership as compared with the government's possibility to choose intermediate degrees of privatization.[4] In the present section, however, we compare the performance of already existing privatized firms. We shall deal with simple models of the type applied in Chapter 6 on efficiency and privatization.

In both models to be considered there are three economic actors: the technological management, the firm's board of directors, and the government. In models of partial privatization, these actors operate in a two-tier setting: tier one is the management, tier two is the board of directors. The government as an actor is integrated into tier two because it places its representatives on the board and there is no further government activity with respect to the firm. In models of fully privatized regulated firms, there is a three-tier setting: tier one is the management; tier two is the board; and tier three is the regulating government.

---

[4] See Sect. 13.2.3 below.

Let us begin with two heroic assumptions. *First*, at the moment of contracting with the board, the management is fully informed about any possible source of uncertainty. It knows the actual value of ϑ, which is an exogenous variable influencing costs. It also knows the actual value of ϕ, which is an exogenous variable influencing demand. *Second*, the board of the firm is fully informed about everything which is known to the management. It should be mentioned that later on these two assumptions will be relinquished. Table 4 summarizes the precise setting of the principal–agent relations treated in this section.

Table 4   Privatization with Perfectly Informed Board

Partial privatization	Full privatization plus price-cap regulation
Management knows ϑ and ϕ at the moment of contracting. Is fully monitored with respect to effort. Income I set by the board.	Management knows ϑ and ϕ at the moment of contracting. Is fully monitored with respect to effort. Income I set by the board.
Board (includes government) knows ϑ and ϕ at the moment of contracting. $\max_{e,I,p}[(1-\Theta)S+\Pi]$ s.t. $V(I,e) \geq \overline{V}, \Pi \geq 0.$	Board knows ϑ and ϕ at the moment of contracting. $\max_{e,I,p} \Pi$ s.t. $V(I,e) \geq \overline{V}, p \leq \overline{p}.$
	Government knows $f(\vartheta)$ and $g(\phi)$; learns ϑ and ϕ only ex *post*. $\max_{\overline{p}} E_{\vartheta,\phi}(S+\Pi)$ s.t. $\min_{\vartheta,\phi} \Pi \geq 0.$

Since in the *partially privatized firm* the management and the board are the only two actors involved, the above assumptions lead to a full-information setting, comparable to our benchmark models on private and public firms treated in the chapter on efficiency and privatization. The management wants to maximize utility $V(I,e)$ with respect to e, adjusting effort e to its income I. Since the board is completely informed, it can fully monitor the management and instruct it to choose that combination of effort and income which maximizes the board's objective function (equation (8.1) above). The board aims at maximizing this objective with respect to effort e, income I, and price p. It has to take account of the management's participation constraint: if the management's utility falls below the reservation utility $\overline{V}$, the management quits the job and the firm cannot operate any longer. Moreover, we assume that the firm must be run profitably.

For ease of explanation we assume that effort and incomes of the board of the firm can be neglected. The following analysis would become much more difficult if the behavior of the members of the board were modelled completely analogous to the behavior of the technological managers.

The board faces the following optimization problem:

$$\max_{e,I,p} (1 - \Theta)S + \Pi$$

$$\text{subject to } V(I,e) \geq \overline{V} \qquad (\beta)$$

$$\Pi \geq 0 \qquad (\gamma), \qquad (8.2)$$

where β and γ are Lagrangean multipliers associated with the constraints. We know that in full-information models of this type the manager's utility never exceeds his reservation utility $\overline{V}$ and the participation constraint is binding.

The board formulates the relevant Lagrangean function as

$$\mathcal{L} = (1 - \Theta)S(p) + pz(p) - C(z(p), e) - I$$
$$- \beta[V(I,e) - \overline{V}] - \gamma[pz(p) - C(z(p), e) - I]. \qquad (8.3)$$

X-efficiency is always guaranteed because we obtain the following two marginal conditions:

$$-C_e(1 - \gamma) - \beta V_e = 0, \qquad (8.4)$$

$$-(1 - \gamma) - \beta V_I = 0, \qquad (8.5)$$

which can be combined to achieve

$$V_e/V_I = C_e. \qquad (8.6)$$

The reader may recall that in our treatment of privatization and efficiency we characterized this as the condition of X-efficiency.

Allocative efficiency is not reached if the firm is partially privatized, because the price is set according to

$$(p - C_z)z_p = -\frac{\Theta - \gamma}{1 - \gamma}z. \qquad (8.7)$$

The worst price distortion is achieved if the firm is fully privatized because $\Theta = 1$ implies monopoly prices.

Let us now deal with a *fully privatized regulated firm*, once again under the assumption that the board is completely informed about everything which is known to the management. Notice that this assumption does not imply that the regulating government is completely informed about everything which is known to the board and to the management: we assume that the government does not know the actual values of ϑ and ϕ, but only the distributions $f(\vartheta)$ and $g(\phi)$ at the moment of regulation.

Since the board has complete information, it can fully monitor the effort of the management and choose an income I so as to achieve the profit-maximizing effort–income combination. This combination must comply with the management's participation constraint. Moreover, the firm faces a price-cap regulation as set by the government. Accordingly, the board deals with the following optimization problem:

$$\max_{e,I,p} \Pi$$

$$\text{subject to } V(I,e) \geq \overline{V} \qquad (\beta)$$
$$p \leq \overline{p} \qquad (\chi), \qquad (8.8)$$

where β and χ are Lagrangean multipliers, $\beta, \chi \leq 0$. The participation constraint once again will be binding. Since the price limit $\overline{p}$ of a public utility typically implies low price elasticities of demand, we can assume that the price-cap constraint is also binding.

The board maximizes the Lagrangean function:

$$\mathcal{L} = pz(p) - C(z(p),e) - I$$
$$- \beta(V(I,e) - \overline{V}) - \chi(\overline{p} - p). \qquad (8.9)$$

This implies X-efficiency,

$$V_e/V_I = C_e. \qquad (8.10)$$

Allocative efficiency can result only if the government requires the firm to set the marginal-cost price, i.e. if $\overline{p} = C_z(z(\overline{p}),e)$. Otherwise there are price distortions, the worst distortion arising when there is a non-binding price constraint, where the monopoly price is charged by the firm.

Until now there has been no inherent reason to prefer partial privatization to full privatization with price capping. Both lead to

X-efficiency but allocative inefficiency. However, we have not yet dealt with the government. Since the government is incompletely informed, it has to start from demand as depending on ϕ and from costs as depending on ϑ. Moreover, since the firm has found the optimal effort, manager income, and price for some given values of ϑ and ϕ, the government has to consider the dependence of the firm's instruments on the exogenous variables ϑ and ϕ. More formally, the government takes account of the binding price-cap constraint, $p = \overline{p}$, and of the board's optimization which leads to $e(\overline{p}, \vartheta, \phi)$ and $I(\overline{p}, \vartheta, \phi)$. In its optimization approach the government considers expected values, where the expectation operator E is taken over both ϑ and ϕ.

We exclude the possibility that a deficit of the firm could be financed by tax revenues. The participation constraint of the board, therefore, is a profitability constraint which has to be included in the government's optimization approach.[5]

Two possible formulations of the profitability constraint are possible.[6] First, the government can postulate non-negative expected profits:

$$E\Pi \geq 0. \tag{8.11}$$

Second, it can postulate that profits are non-negative for all possible realizations of the exogenous variables ϑ and ϕ, whence the firm never can go bankrupt:

$$\Pi \geq 0 \qquad \forall \, \vartheta, \phi. \tag{8.12}$$

Since in the present model the board is fully informed about ϑ and ϕ, only the second constraint makes sense. It can be rewritten as a non-negative worst-case constraint,

$$\Pi^{min} := \min_{\vartheta,\phi} \Pi \geq 0. \tag{8.13}$$

Price capping implies that the profit-maximizing price is not desirable and therefore the government intervenes. Hence the government is supposed to maximize welfare.

The government's optimization problem is then as follows:

$$\max_{\overline{p}} \ E(S + \Pi)$$

$$\text{subject to } \Pi^{min} \geq 0. \tag{8.14}$$

---

[5] The participation constraint of the technological management has been fully taken care of by the board when choosing e, I, and p.
[6] Compare Schmalensee (1989: 422).

The details of this optimization are spared the reader since they are not crucial for understanding our point, namely, that full privatization under price regulation faces severe problems of incomplete information which are avoided in the case of partial privatization. This implies an edge for partial privatization.

8.4 Management Incentives

In this section we introduce an additional informational asymmetry, that between the management and the board of directors. Since the informational asymmetry between the government and the firm is retained, an informational advantage of partial privatization still prevails. However, we now pose the question as to whether or not partial privatization leads to correct incentive structures within the firm.

Table 5   Privatization with Imperfectly Informed Board*

Partial privatization	Full privatization plus price-cap regulation
Management	Management
knows ϕ and $f(\vartheta)$ at the moment of contracting; learns ϑ before setting effort. $I = k + a\mathcal{D}$ $\max_e V(I, e).$	knows ϕ and $f(\vartheta)$ at the moment of contracting; learns ϑ before setting effort. $I = k + a\mathcal{D}$ $\max_e V(I, e).$
Board (includes government)	Board
knows ϕ and $f(\vartheta)$; learns ϑ only *ex post*. $\max_{a,k,p} E_\vartheta[(1 - \Theta)S + \Pi]$ s.t. $E_\vartheta V \geq \overline{V}$ $E_\vartheta \Pi \geq 0.$	knows ϕ and $f(\vartheta)$; learns ϑ only *ex post*. $\max_{a,k,p} E_\vartheta \Pi$ s.t. $E_\vartheta V \geq \overline{V}$ $p \leq \overline{p}.$
	Government
	knows $g(\phi)$ and $f(\vartheta)$; learns ϕ and ϑ only *ex post*. $\max_{\overline{p}} E_{\vartheta,\phi}(S + \Pi)$ s.t. $\min_{\vartheta,\phi} \Pi \geq 0.$

* Since ϕ is known to both management and board, we do not explicitly mention the functional dependency on ϕ whenever management and board are considered.

We assume that management and board are asymmetrically informed about costs, i.e. about ϑ. The firm and the government are asymmetrically informed about demand, i.e. about ϕ, unless the government has inside information from its representatives on the board. Table 5 aids our understanding of the principal–agent setting in this section. We abandon the two heroic assumptions employed in the preceding section. When stipulating the contract of employment of the manager, neither the manager nor the board knows the precise value of ϑ. After entering the employment, the manager observes the actual value of ϑ and chooses his level of effort so as to maximize his utility. This implies an informational advantage of the agent who is informed about ϑ when choosing the effort level. As in the chapter on privatization and efficiency, the board applies a linear incentive scheme to entice the management into acting in the interest of the board.

The asymmetric information of the management and of the board makes it necessary to deal with the incentive compatibility of the management's decision: when maximizing, the board must take account of the management's decision on effort as a constraint of its (the board's) optimization. By choosing a linear incentive-pay schedule, we avoid a complicated control-theoretical setting.

Let us first deal with the *partially privatized firm*, $0 < \Theta < 1$. Ideally, the board would like to apply the incentive pay schedule

$$I = k + a[(1 - \Theta)S + \Pi], \qquad (8.15)$$

which would induce X-efficient behavior of the management.[7] However, as mentioned in our treatment of welfare-oriented incentive schemes on pp. 114–16, linking managerial incomes to consumer surplus is not likely to work in economic practice. Hence we assume that the board of the partially privatized firm chooses another incentive pay schedule which can be applied in practice; i.e., it links pay to profits:

$$I = k + a\mathcal{D}, \qquad (8.16)$$

where $\mathcal{D} := R - C$.[8] However, in that case the board will typically give wrong incentives to the management. This can be shown as follows.

The management maximizes utility, given the linear incentive scheme,

$$\max_{e} \ V(k + a\mathcal{D}, e). \qquad (8.17)$$

---

[7] See Sect. 2.6 above.
[8] Recall n. 13 in Ch. 6.

Therefore, managerial effort is characterized by

$$V_e/V_I = aC_e. \qquad (8.18)$$

X-efficiency would require $a = 1$. Typically, however, this will not be the result of the board's optimization:

$$\max_{a,k,p} \ E[(1 - \Theta)S + \Pi]$$

$$\text{subject to } EV \geq \overline{V}$$

$$E\Pi \geq 0. \qquad (8.19)$$

The expectation operator refers to ϑ. The board explicitly takes account of the management's optimization which led to $e(a, k, p, \vartheta)$. This guarantees the incentive compatibility of the management's decision.

Why is $a = 1$ unlikely to occur?[9] Recall that $a = 1$ implies that the board gives total profits to the management after deducting a lump sum k. In that case the management would maximize its utility by trading off profit and effort. However, the board is not interested in maximizing only profit: rather, it is interested in maximizing a weighted sum of profit and consumer surplus. Hence from the board's point of view, $a = 1$ would over-accentuate the board's interest in profit and $a \neq 1$ typically is chosen. Only if the linear incentive pay were made dependent on the objective of the board would $a = 1$ be considered the best way to reach perfect coordination between the board's and the management's interests.

Let the above plausible explanation of distorted X-efficiency suffice for the moment. I do not want to delve into the tedious analytical details of determining and transforming the necessary optimum conditions. The reader may be referred to the explicit treatment of the relevant problems in Chapter 6 on privatization and efficiency. The argument here is exactly the same as presented in Section 6.4.5 above, where we dealt with a welfare-interested government which gives an incentive pay depending on profit.

The result $a \neq 1$ is quite important for the evaluation of partial privatization. Moreover, the result is puzzling. A neutral observer, not familiar with the principal–agent setting, certainly would have thought that there could be no better way to achieve X-efficiency than by tying managerial salaries to the firm's profit. However,

---

[9] The following arguments assume a risk-neutral management. See p. 103 above.

X-efficiency would result only if the *total* profit were given to the management after deducting a lump sum k. Since the board is not interested in only maximizing profit, it has no incentive to pay total profit to the management. Hence the management will not work X-efficiently. The distorted X-efficiency is a major disadvantage of partial privatization.

Let us next consider a *fully privatized regulated firm*. The board is interested in maximizing profit and therefore quite naturally chooses an incentive pay schedule which depends on profit, namely

$$I = k + a\mathcal{D}. \tag{8.20}$$

The management's optimization,

$$\max_e V(I, e), \tag{8.21}$$

once again leads to the usual condition for X-efficiency,

$$V_e/V_I = aC_e. \tag{8.22}$$

The board maximizes expected profit, taking account of the management's participation constraint and of the management's choice of $e = e(a, k, p, \vartheta)$. Moreover, the board faces price-cap regulation; therefore, we have the following optimization approach:

$$\max_{a,k,p} E\Pi$$
$$\text{subject to } EV \geq \overline{V}$$
$$p \leq \overline{p}, \tag{8.23}$$

where the expectation operator refers to ϑ.

Once again we should ask whether $a = 1$ is likely to occur. The answer is yes. Both management and firm are interested in profits. Therefore the best the board can do is to pay total profit to the management after deducting the lump sum k.[10] The resulting X-efficient production is a major advantage of full privatization with price-cap regulation.

However, we still have to consider the third tier in the regulatory setting, i.e. the government's choice of the price limit $\overline{p}$.

---

[10] For a formal treatment of the problem the reader is referred to Sect. 6.3. The inclusion of the price-cap constraint does not change the marginal conditions which are obtained by differentiating the respective Lagrangean function with respect to a and k.

The government is incompletely informed about both ϑ and ϕ. It takes account of the management's and the board's optimization by substituting into the relevant functions

   (i)   the binding price cap $p = \overline{p}$,

  (ii) the technological managers' incentive-compatible choice of effort $e(a, k, \overline{p}, \vartheta, \phi)$,

 (iii) the board's incentive-compatible choice of the manager's income, $a(\overline{p}, \vartheta, \phi)$ and $k(\overline{p}, \vartheta, \phi)$.

After these substitutions, the government proceeds according to an optimization problem,

$$\max_{\overline{p}} \ E(S + \Pi)$$

$$\text{subject to } \Pi^{min} \geq 0, \tag{8.24}$$

where the expectation operator refers to both ϑ and ϕ.

Once again I shall not go into mathematical details. The point is clear: the severe problems of the government's incomplete information have not vanished.

8.5   Conclusion

As could be expected, there is no general answer to the question whether or not partial privatization is preferable to full privatization plus price-cap regulation.

Partial privatization provides the superior arrangement of the interaction between government and firm. It also gives the government informational advantages because the government has its representatives on the board and these representatives are as well informed as the private representatives on the board. In contrast, the regulating government outside the firm faces information problems which cause serious trouble.

Partial privatization, however, provides for inferior interaction between the management and the board within the firm. Since incentive pay schedules will never be linked to consumer surplus, the board which is partially interested in consumer surplus will give wrong incentives to the management. Full privatization provides the better solution: both management and board share the same interest in profit. This leads to X-efficient production.

Which effect is more important cannot generally be determined. Only numerical calculations for specified functions could reveal when it is preferable to choose partial privatization and when full privatization plus price-cap regulation is the better policy. In any case, neither policy can be excluded *ex ante* as unreasonable.

9 Government versus Trade Unions

In this chapter the government is perceived as an institution which wants to draw some money from selling its property and so willingly cooperates with private shareholders who also are interested in the value of the firm. For an explanation we can assume that the government is interested in reducing the tax pressure, increasing particular public expenditures, reducing the public debt, or 'taking the nationalised industries out of the public sector borrowing requirement' (Brittan, 1986). In short: the government is interested in money.

Let us assume that a representative trade union acts as antagonist to the government in this setting. We exclude the possibility that several trade unions representing various groups of the firm's employees each follow different objectives and have to coordinate their different interests in a complex system of hierarchical order. The representative trade union is interested in the firm preserving jobs, even if this leads to more inefficiency in production and less profit. It is, however, willing to agree to at least some firing of employees if the remaining employees receive some share of the increased profits and if there is some sort of 'social safety net' for the dismissed.

Therefore, when deciding on privatization, the government enters into negotiations with the trade union about some plan of employee shares and some financial compensation for the dismissed.

In the course of the negotiations the players have to anticipate how the firm will adjust to the compromise the government and the trade union have made. This adjustment can be described as a cooperative game between the (private and public) shareholders and the representatives of the trade union in the firm. The decision-making in the firm as a two-person cooperative game is modelled similarly to Aoki (1980, 1982).

9.1 The Model

9.1.1 The Firm

This chapter deals with a one-product monopolistic firm, selling output z at price p. We assume that the firm faces the market demand

$$z = z(p); \quad z_p < 0, \qquad (9.1)$$

where z_p denotes the first derivative. We assume a price elasticity of demand $z_p p/z < -1$ for $p > \mathcal{P}$ where $\mathcal{P}$ is an arbitrarily chosen high price level. For prices $p > \mathcal{P}$ revenue decreases with increasing price.[1]

The output is produced by labor and capital inputs according to a production function

$$z = f(N, K); \quad f_N, f_K > 0, \tag{9.2}$$

where N is labor input and K capital input.

The firm covers all demand for its output,

$$z(p) = f(N, K). \tag{9.3}$$

Producing outputs and selling them to the market leads to a profit

$$\Pi := pz - p_N N - p_K K, \tag{9.4}$$

where p_N is the wage rate and p_K is the interest rate. For the time being we assume that wage and interest rate are exogenously given. In Section 9.5.3 below the wage rate is treated as an endogenous variable.

We deal with a static model. The profit Π accrues within the period for which the model holds. This period is a long one, longer than a year. Hence the reader should think of Π as if it were the discounted sum of all future dividends. This interpretation will also be chosen in the normative theory part of this book.

9.1.2 Sharing the Profit

When sharing the profit, the firm has to consider two different forms of entitlements.

First, $1 - \Psi$ percent[2] of the profit, $0 \leq \Psi \leq 1$, will be claimed by the employees. The basis of their claim is employee shares. The employees do not have to pay for the shares; on the other hand, they have no voting rights in the shareholders' meeting. Hence the employee shares are the basis of some percentage of profits

---

[1] This assumption is necessary to guarantee the existence of the Nash equilibrium in this chapter.

[2] It is convenient to speak of Ψ percent and of Θ percent although Ψ and Θ are figures between zero and one. Purists may prefer always to multiply Ψ and Θ by 100.

transferred to employees. They do not influence the firm's decision process in any direct way. (Indirectly, of course, it matters
for the firm's decisions how much of the profit remains with the
government and with the private shareholders.)

Second, the remaining profit, $\Psi\Pi$, is divided between the government and private shareholders, depending on the degree of privatization. This degree of privatization is measured by Θ, where
$0 \leq \Theta \leq 1$. If $\Theta = 0$, we have a public firm, no private shareholders can claim any dividends, and the remaining profit $\Psi\Pi$ goes to
the government. On the other hand, if $\Theta = 1$, the firm is fully
privatized and 100 percent of $\Psi\Pi$ goes to the private shareholders.
Partial privatization is not excluded from our model. The government may find it appropriate to retain some part of the shares. It
may, for example, believe that its objectives can be met better if
it still has some representatives in the firm. In the case of partial
privatization, the remaining profit $\Psi\Pi$ is split: Θ percent goes to
the private shareholders, $(1 - \Theta)$ percent goes to the government.
Summarizing, the profit is shared as follows:

$$(1 - \Psi)\Pi \quad \text{employees}$$

$$\Theta\Psi\Pi \quad \text{private shareholders}$$

$$(1 - \Theta)\Psi\Pi \quad \text{government.}$$

The *employees'* share in the profit is evenly spread over the working
force which was active when the privatization started, N^o. All
employees who worked in the firm prior to privatization are given
shares. This implies a sort of 'social safety plan' for those who are
dismissed in the course of privatization, $N^o - N$. For the other
employees it is a simple transfer. Hence the employees' share in
the profit is spread according to[3]

$$\frac{(1 - \Psi)\Pi}{N^o}. \tag{9.5}$$

The *private shareholders'* share constitutes the dividend payments
they receive. Let the shares be indexed by h and assume that a
share represents an ownership of θ_h percent of the firm, $0 \leq \theta_h \leq 1$,
$\sum \theta_h = \Theta$. The ownership right θ_h entitles shareholder h to claim
dividend payments of $\theta_h \Psi\Pi$. Consequently, a potential purchaser

---

[3] It is easy to think of alternative specifications where only the actually
employed people N get employee shares.

of an ownership right in θ_h percent of the firm is willing to pay up to $\theta_h \Psi \Pi$. We denote the purchaser's payment by $\theta_h s \Pi$, where $s \geq 0$, and

$$0 \leq s \leq \Psi. \tag{9.6}$$

We assume that the private shareholders buy the shares even if $s = \Psi$.[4] The payment $\theta_h s \Pi$ is defined as a share of the profit. However, after solving the model, the government requires payment of $\theta_h s \Pi$. Hence it is convenient to speak of $s\Pi$ as the issue price of the shares.[5]

The *government* is interested in earning at least a minimal revenue. It has to trade off the revenues from its remaining shares, $(1 - \Theta)\Psi \Pi$, and the revenue from selling shares, $s\Theta\Pi$. The government enters the privatization game only if its revenues do not fall below some threshold R^o:

$$(1 - \Theta)\Psi \Pi + s\Theta\Pi \geq R^o; \qquad R^o > 0. \tag{9.7}$$

In the simple partial model of this chapter we do not explicitly explain how R^o came about, but take it as exogenously given.[6]

The government revenue constraint has some interesting implications. First, the positive revenue requirement implies that only profitable firms will be privatized. (Given our assumptions on s, Θ, and Ψ, positive R^o requires positive Π.) Second, the government revenue requirement excludes $\Psi = 0$. In this case the government would neither receive money from its remaining shares ($\Psi = 0$) nor receive money from selling shares. ($s = 0$ is implied by $\Psi = 0$, otherwise private shareholders would not be willing to accept the shares.) Hence R^o could not be positive and the government would not play the game. This result sounds reasonable. We would not expect a privatization campaign to lead to such an intensive participation of employees that they are awarded all the profits. Note, by the way, that $s = 0$ is not *a priori* excluded by the government revenue requirement.

---

[4] Alternatively we could think of a constraint $0 \leq s \leq \Psi - \epsilon$ for some small positive ϵ. Then the private shareholders always obtain at least some minimal profit.

[5] The symbol s has been chosen to remind the reader that the issue price is defined as a share of the profit. We intentionally avoided the symbol P, which in the normative theory part of the book denotes the issue price.

[6] How revenue from privatization can be used for public expenditures, or for a reduction of the overall tax pressure, will be treated in the normative theory part of this book, where we apply a general equilibrium model. See Ch. 15 below.

9.1.3 The Goals of the Trade Union, the Government, and the Private Shareholders

The *trade union* is interested in the employees' part in the profit, i.e. in setting up a system of employee shares. However, it is also interested in keeping jobs at the firm. Hence we impute to the trade union an objective function

$$U = U\left(\frac{(1 - \Psi)\Pi}{N^o}, N\right); \qquad U_1, U_2 > 0. \tag{9.8}$$

This function captures the conflict of interests inherent in the trade union. On the one hand, the union is interested in high profits, because the dividends from employee shares are higher, the more profitable the firm. On the other hand, the union is interested in jobs, even if this reduces profits.

The (conservative) *government* and the *private shareholders* in our model are interested in the same goals. There is a permanent coalition between the government and the private shareholders. The government is not interested in a welfare objective, which would most probably be challenged by the private shareholders: rather, the government is interested in profit, and so are the private shareholders. Taking together their shares in the profit of the firm, the government and the private shareholders calculate the non-employee share of profit as $\Psi\Pi$.

The government interest in the value of the firm goes back to some basic insight which can be attributed to a conservative government. Higher profits, i.e. a higher value of the firm, is thought of as leading to a long-run improvement of the private economy, in contrast to short-run Keynesian policies. A high value of the firm may also imply higher government revenues when selling some further shares during later privatization activities.

Moreover, the (conservative) government has an ideological interest in privatization and this interest is fully shared by the (conservative) private shareholders. Hence we obtain an objective function

$$V = V(\Psi\Pi, \Theta); \qquad V_1, V_2 > 0. \tag{9.9}$$

9.2 The Two-Tier Optimization Approach

We are interested in a two-tier decision problem. Tier one is the *privatization game*. It is a two-person game, played by the government and the trade union. In this game the players compromise over (i) how many shares should be given to employees and (ii) how many shares should be sold to private shareholders and at which price they should be sold. Therefore, the instruments which are set in this game are Ψ, Θ, and s.

The cooperative solution of the game is of the Nash type, as formulated by Zeuthen (1930) and Harsanyi (1956, 1977). Both players have concave von Neumann–Morgenstern utility functions, $U(\cdot)$ for the trade union and $V(\cdot)$ for the government. If cooperation fails, the worst that can happen are utility levels $\overline{U}$ and $\overline{V}$ which we treat as given in the model. We assume the utilities which result from cooperation exceed these reservation levels: $U^* > \overline{U}$, $V^* > \overline{V}$. As in Aoki (1980), this implies that both players have appropriate threat potential so that the utilities of the cooperative solution exceed the utilities of open conflict. The threat potential of the union is rooted in its ability to paralyze the firm by a long-standing strike. The threat potential of the government can be based on the following threat strategies:[7]

(i) political staying power against the strike, which implies that the trade union loses money and influence;

(ii) diversification by splitting up the firm, which reduces the trade-union power by exposing the negative consequences of trade-union policy. This strategy is of particular interest for public transportation or telecommunications enterprises;

(iii) increase of the profit requirement which has to be paid to the government;

(iv) increase of particular 'social obligations' of the firm without government compensation payments. This strategy is of interest because trade unions like to oppose privatization by hinting at the social obligations of the firm and therefore cannot easily oppose this threat strategy of the government. The obligation to work at 'overcapacity' is a special example of such a strategy;

(v) a threat to close the firm. Trade unions 'have demonstrated their ultimate pragmatism by at times accepting denationalisation as the lesser of two evils, when the alternative was complete closure of an enterprise or plant' (Thomas, 1984: 66 with concrete examples).

The government's threat potential may be restricted by the short-run political pressure of the next election. However, this does not leave the government without any threat potential against the trade unions, as British experiences in the 1980s clearly illustrated.

***

[7] I gratefully acknowledge helpful comments by Jürgen Backhaus.

It is well known that the Nash solution can be represented as the result of an optimization approach, maximizing

$$[\log (U - \overline{U}) + \log (V - \overline{V})] \qquad (9.10)$$

subject to the relevant constraints.

When solving that optimization approach, the government and the trade union must take account of the firm's behavior. For any given Ψ, Θ, and s, the firm will choose particular inputs and a particular price. How far privatization and employee shares are desirable will depend on this adjustment of the firm. This adjustment is captured by the tier-two game.

The second tier of the game situation we model here is also a two-person game; this time, however, the game deals with efficiency and pricing. Player 1 is the group of trade-union representatives in the firm, player 2 represents the shareholders. Private and public shareholders have entered a permanent coalition, as both are interested in the value of the firm and both favor privatization. So their interest is described by the utility function $V(\cdot)$. The representatives of the trade union are interested in the employee shares and in keeping up the number of jobs in the firm. So their interest is described by the utility function $U(\cdot)$.

The two players compromise over

(i)   how many employees should work in the firm,
(ii) how much should be invested,
(iii) at what price the output should be sold.

Therefore, the instruments which are set in this game are N, K, and p.

The two players apply a cooperative Nash solution, hence the description of the firm bears some resemblance to Aoki's (1980, 1982) theory of the firm as a cooperative game. Once again, the Nash solution can be represented as the result of an optimization approach with $U(\cdot)$ and $V(\cdot)$ as the objectives of the two players. We assume the security levels $\overline{U}$ and $\overline{V}$ are identical in the two games. This amounts to assuming that the cooperation in the tier-one game is cancelled if the trade union and the shareholders fail to reach cooperation at the firm level. Therefore, the tier-one and the tier-two games can be described by the same optimization approach if the constraints are identical. Only the choice of instruments is different in the two games.

Let us present all relevant constraints, adding in brackets the associated Lagrangean parameters. We have:

$$z(p) = f(N, K), \qquad (\lambda) \qquad (9.11a)$$

$$s \leq \Psi, \qquad (\nu) \qquad\qquad (9.11b)$$
$$R^o \leq (1 - \Theta)\Psi\Pi + s\Theta\Pi, \qquad (\rho) \qquad\qquad (9.11c)$$
$$\Theta \leq 1, \qquad (\sigma) \qquad\qquad (9.11d)$$
$$\Psi \leq 1. \qquad (\tau) \qquad\qquad (9.11e)$$

The non-negativity of s and Θ is not introduced as explicit structural constraints, but is taken care of in the necessary optimum conditions.[8]

It is evident that all the above constraints are relevant for the tier-one game. This is immediately clear for the government revenue requirement and for the constraints on s, Θ, and Ψ. However, we assumed that the players of the tier-one game anticipate the firm's adjustment. Doing so, the tier-one players must also take account of the market equilibrium and of the input policy of the firm.

Which constraints are relevant for the tier-two game? It is evident that the constraints on the market equilibrium and the input policy are relevant. The particular constraints on s, Θ, and Ψ can be added to the firm's optimization problem without doing harm, as s, Θ, and Ψ are exogenously given in the tier-two game and no firm instruments enter these three constraints. However, what about the government revenue requirement? We assume that the government has the threat potential to ensure that its revenue constraint is accepted by the firm. The private shareholders and the trade union's representatives in the firm know that privatization and employee shares are worthwhile for the government only if its revenue requirements are met. If the firm does not accept this constraint, the government will reverse its policy which would be detrimental to the private shareholders and the trade union.

Given the formal identity of the tier-one and the tier-two games, the *strategic connection of the two games* is as follows.

In the tier-one game, the adjustment of the firm is anticipated. Accordingly, the results of the tier-two game are taken into account. Hence in the tier-one game the optimization problem is solved with respect to *all* unknown variables. Calculating the optimal values of s, Θ, and Ψ is the basis of setting these instruments by the government. Calculating the optimal values of N, K, and p means the anticipation of the firm's adjustment to the tier-one game. These variables are only *calculated* in the tier-one game, but are *not set* on the basis of this game. The players of the tier-one

[8] See Panik (1976: 297).

game take the role of a Stackelberg leader, fully exploiting their knowledge of the adjustment of the firm.[9]

The firm always plays second and therefore can only take the role of a Stackelberg follower. The two players of the tier-two game do not exist prior to the government's setting of s, Θ, and Ψ. Hence they cannot strategically anticipate the adjustment of the privatization policy to the firm's behavior. The best they can do is to find the optimal firm policy given some extent of privatization, and of employee shares. Therefore, in the tier-two game the optimal values of N, K, and p are calculated as the basis of setting these instruments by the firm.

The tier-one and tier-two games are described by the same optimization approach. Hence incentive compatibility is ensured. The firm, in the tier-two game, will choose those values of labor, capital, and price which the government and the trade union had anticipated in the tier-one game.

9.3 The Tier-One Game: Privatization and Employee Shares

We solve the optimization approach of the tier-one game, taking account of the relevant constraints and the relevant choice of variables to be set and calculated, respectively: the instruments s, Θ, and Ψ are set on the basis of the tier-one game, the variables N, K, and p are only calculated to anticipate the results of the tier-two game. The details of the optimization and all proofs can be found in the appendix to this chapter. It should be possible to understand the results of the model without necessarily reading the proofs. However, before dealing with economic results, some additional terminology is needed.

We apply the following abbreviations:

$$b_{Ui} = \frac{U_i}{U - \overline{U}}, \quad b_{Vi} = \frac{V_i}{V - \overline{V}}; \quad i = 1, 2. \tag{9.12}$$

The measures b_{Ui} and b_{Vi} represent the bargaining power of the two players[10] with respect to the various arguments in the utility functions; $b_{Ui}, b_{Vi} > 0$ results from our assumptions.

The relation between the government's and the trade union's bargaining power can be used to distinguish three different types of firms:

---

[9] For a similar informational setting see Bös and Peters (1988a,b).
[10] See Aoki (1980: 605).

(i)   the conservative firm with a positive value of firm power F,

$$F := \left[b_{V1} - \frac{b_{U1}}{N^o} - \rho(1 - \Theta) \right], \qquad (9.13)$$

(ii)   the trade-union-dominated firm with $F < 0$,

(iii)   the neutral firm with $F = 0$.

If the firm is fully privatized, the sign of F depends only on the comparison between the government bargaining power b_{V1} and the trade union bargaining power b_{U1}/N^o, where both bargaining powers are related to the respective shares in profit. If parts or all of the firm remain in public ownership, the trade union has to trade off its interest in profit and its interest in jobs, where the latter is measured by ρ, the Lagrangean parameter associated with the government budget constraint. ρ is associated with the trade union because it is the only player in the game whose interest in jobs may imply an interest in lower profits and hence in a binding government revenue requirement. The government itself is interested in a high value of the firm. Its revenue requirement is a minimum constraint and it is quite happy if the constraint is not binding because the firm is very profitable. Therefore, the government has no particular interest in the revenue constraint being binding.

In the tier-one game we are particularly interested in

• the issue price at which the shares are sold to private shareholders,

• the degree of privatization,

• the extent of employee shares.

The results are summarized in the following propositions.

Proposition 1 (degree of privatization)

(i)   Partial privatization never happens. Either the firm remains in public ownership or it is fully privatized.

(ii)   A trade-union-dominated firm always is fully privatized.

(iii)   There are two cases of total privatization. In the first case the profit is only high enough to meet the government revenue requirement and the private shareholders get nothing. In the second case any combination of binding and not-binding revenue constraint and issue price constraint is possible.

(iv)   It is possible that the firm remains in full public ownership. Then the government gets its revenue requirement only.

Economic Interpretation 1

For the interpretation let us consider the marginal condition $\mathcal{L}_\Theta$, which results from differentiating the Lagrangean function of the optimization approach $\mathcal{L}$ with respect to the degree of privatization Θ. We obtain

$$\mathcal{L}_\Theta = b_{V2} + \rho(\Psi - s)\Pi + \sigma \le 0 \qquad (9.14)$$

where the Lagrangean parameter ρ refers to the government budget constraint (9.11c) and σ refers to the 'Θ never exceeds 1' constraint (9.11d). Hence $\rho < 0$ means the government budget constraint is binding and $\sigma < 0$ implies total privatization.

Total privatization results from two main reasons: first from trade-union dominance in the firm; second from the government's ideological interest in privatization.

Trade-union dominance leads to equating issue price and dividend incomes because the trade union wants to minimize the private shareholders' net returns from their investment in shares, $(\Psi - s)\Pi$. Hence trade-union dominance leads to total privatization because

$$\mathcal{L}_\Theta = b_{V2} + \sigma \le 0 \qquad (9.14')$$

implies $\sigma < 0$. We realize that the result also depends on $b_{V2} > 0$. There must be some ideological interest of the government, but it is of no importance how large b_{V2} is, i.e. how much the government accentuates its ideological interest. Hence we can argue that the government's interest is intensified by the trade union's policy of appropriating financial means and jobs to its members.

In the *conservative or neutral firm* the issue price may fall below the dividends. Then we have a basic trade-off which is responsible for the results. This trade-off is the comparison

$$b_{V2} + \rho(\Psi - s)\Pi \gtrless 0. \qquad (9.14'')$$

Those factors which are traded-off are

(i) the government's ideological interest in privatization, measured by b_{V2},

(ii) the union's interest in jobs, transferred into the interest in a binding government revenue constraint and measured by ρ,

(iii) the interest of private shareholders, measured by $(\Psi - s)$,

(iv) the interest in profit Π, which is shared by all.

Let us now interpret proposition 1 in light of the trade-off we have presented in the preceding paragraphs. *Total privatization* is achieved if the ideological interest in privatization exceeds the product of the other interests. This happens if either the trade union or the private shareholders fail to promote their interests. The trade union's promotion of jobs is achieved if $\rho < 0$ because then the government revenue requirement is binding. Otherwise there may be excess profit which could have been used to create jobs. Of course the trade union's interest in the employees' share in the profit might fully be satisfied, and if the trade union is not very much interested in jobs, it might be content. However, the profit interest has overcompensated the job interest; therefore it is fair to say that not achieving $\rho < 0$ means failing to promote the interest in jobs. The private shareholders fail to promote their interest if $\Psi = s$, because in that case they do not earn anything. We should not be too surprised if the private shareholders' interest is not promoted in the tier-one game. After all, they are not even players in that game.

Note that it is impossible to simultaneously promote the job interest of the trade union and the earning interest of the private shareholders. As is shown in proof 1(iii) in the appendix to this chapter, $\rho < 0$ and $\Psi > s$ cannot hold simultaneously if at least one share is sold. This excludes *partial privatization*, which would require a precise balancing of the ideological interest in privatization and the product of the other three interests to obtain $b_{V2} + \rho(\Psi - s)\Pi = 0$. However $b_{V2} > 0$ and $\rho(\Psi - s)\Pi = 0$ if at least one share is sold.

On the other hand, $\rho < 0$ and $\Psi > s$ can be fulfilled simultaneously if *no privatization* takes place. Economically, in that case, private shareholders have failed to promote their own interests. $s < \Psi$ does not mean anything to them if $\Theta = 0$. They do not earn anything from such a formal fixing of s. Thus it is possible that the firm remains in full public ownership. Employee shares may have been issued in that case.

It is a little paradoxical that trade-union dominance always implies full privatization whereas the conservative firm might fully remain in public ownership. Note, however, that we defined a conservative firm with respect to its interest in the value of the firm (b_{V1}), not with respect to its ideological interest in privatization (b_{V2}). Therefore, the government may reject privatization if its ideological interest is not too pronounced and its interest in profit cannot be satisfied in negotiations with the trade union. In the trade-union-dominated firm there is no comparable trade-off between profit interest and ideological interest. The trade union's interest reinforces the government's ideological interest; in other words, the trade union takes advantage of the government's position, and reduces as far as possible both shareholders' and government's revenues.

Of course, our result crucially depends on the assumption that the trade union retains its influence in the privatized firm. Hence the union is willing to accept a form of privatization which excludes financial gains of non-employee shareholders, depresses the government to its reservation level of revenues from privatization, but implies guaranteed jobs and high wages plus transfers to the employees by means of employee shares.

Proposition 2 (issue price of shares)

  (i) Private shareholders never get shares free of charge.

  (ii) If the issue price is equated to the dividend, $s = \Psi$, then the firm never remains in public ownership but is always fully privatized.

Economic Interpretation 2

In our model the government wants to earn at least a minimal revenue $R^o > 0$. Revenues from retaining shares in the firm are traded off against revenues from selling shares. Now recall that partial privatization is excluded in our model. The government, therefore, has two options to meet the revenue requirement: first, it can leave the firm in full public ownership and enjoy the dividend income; second, it can fully privatize the firm and forgo any dividend income. In the latter case the revenue requirement $R^o > 0$ can be met only if the private shareholders pay a (positive) price for the shares. Giving away the shares free of charge would leave the government with no revenues at all.

Let us next deal with the second part of proposition 2. If the issue price is equated to the dividend, the private shareholders are excluded from sharing in earnings.[11] This makes the privatization particularly attractive for both the government and the trade union. Hence the firm always is fully privatized and never left in public ownership. Note that the issue price s is the only variable set in the tier-one game which does not enter the objective function that characterizes the Nash solution. Hence s can easily be increased if necessary because there is no countervailing trade-off in the objective function. As we shall see in the following, it depends on the relative bargaining power of the trade union and the

---

[11] If we choose $s \leq \Psi - \epsilon$, there is always some minimal gain for the private shareholders.

government who gains most from excluding the private shareholders from earning anything. If the trade union is more powerful, its interest in high labor inputs (b_{U2}) and its willingness to accept the ensuing profit reductions will lead to a binding government revenue requirement, withdrawing the money from the government. If the government is more powerful, the revenue requirement may be not binding, withdrawing the money from the creation of further jobs.

An issue price below the dividend is chosen if the profit is high, and therefore the government can share some of its revenues with the private shareholders by setting $\Psi > s$. We shall see in proposition 3, however, that this cannot happen in a trade-union-dominated firm. The low issue price of shares must never lead to giving shares to private investors free of charge.

Proposition 3 (employee shares)

(i)   A conservative firm never issues employee shares.

(ii) If the firm is trade-union-dominated, the private shareholders earn nothing; the shares are always sold at a price equal to the dividends. The government revenue constraint is binding. Any amount of Ψ which is compatible with the government revenue requirement can be obtained as the result of the tier-one game.

(iii) In the neutral firm any combination of private shareholders' earnings and employee shares can occur.

Economic Interpretation 3
If conservative interests dominate, the value of the firm $\Psi\Pi$ is maximized by maximizing Ψ. This excludes employee shares. On the other hand, if trade-union interests dominate, the issue price of the shares is increased because then the government revenue requirement can be met by higher revenues from selling shares and lower dividends from the remaining shares. Hence the trade-union-dominated policy consists of equating s to Ψ and reducing Ψ until the government revenue requirement is binding. The trade union makes use of the substitutive relation of Ψ and s along a binding government revenue constraint.

In summary, we can say that there are many different results in this chapter. It is an important result that private shareholders never get shares free of charge. And it is an equally important result that partial privatization never happens in our positive theory. Either the firm remains in full public ownership or it is fully privatized.

As can be expected in such a cooperative game, other results depend on the relative power of the trade union and the government. Two scenarios are particularly characteristic.

First, where the trade union dominates, the union precludes the private shareholders from any net incomes from dividends and confines the government to that minimum revenue requirement which is necessary to get the government to privatize. All profit which exceeds the government minimum revenue requirement goes to the employees by a plan of employee shares or is used to keep inefficient jobs in the firm.

Second, where the conservative interests of the government dominate, the government is not willing to share any part of the profit with the employees: there are no employee shares. However, it is willing to share part of the profit with private shareholders.

9.4   The Tier-Two Game: The Decision on Efficiency and Price

Let us now solve the optimization approach of the tier-two game. The privatization game is over, hence the ownership situation is decided upon and so is the sharing of the profit. The firm chooses optimal inputs and an optimal price. The results on efficiency and price are summarized in the following two propositions.

Proposition 4 (efficiency)
The firm employs more workers than is efficient.

Economic Interpretation 4
The trade union's interest in high employment leads to a distortion in the labor–capital inputs. For any two inputs, cost minimization requires an equalization of the ratio of marginal productivities and the ratio of factor prices, in our case

$$f_N/f_K = p_N/p_K. \tag{9.15}$$

In the privatized firm, however, the ratio of marginal productivities falls below the factor prices,

$$f_N/f_K < p_N/p_K. \tag{9.16}$$

If we interpret f_N and f_K as firm-internal shadow prices, the shadow price of labor f_N is too low compared with the market price of labor p_N. Consequently, the privatized firm employs more workers than is efficient.

Proposition 5 (pricing)
The firm sets the price like a profit-maximizing monopolist. The
price formula is

$$\left(p - \frac{p_K}{f_K}\right) z_p = -z. \tag{9.17}$$

Economic Interpretation 5
The price formula (9.17) can directly be compared with the usual
monopoly price formula

$$(p - C_z)z_p = -z. \tag{9.18}$$

This comparison shows that p_K/f_K can be treated as the marginal
costs of producing z. The firm behaves like a profit-maximizing
monopolist who specifies the marginal costs as p_K/f_K. Note that
p_K/f_K depends on the bargaining power of both players, including
the trade union's accentuation of jobs, b_{U2}.[12] Hence the 'marginal
costs' p_K/f_K take account of the particular interests of the government and the trade union, and therefore the price p typically
will be different from the price set by a pure profit maximizer.

However, we still expect a high price as a result of our model
unless the trade union's interest in jobs is predominant. Such a
high price may be undesirable. Hence let us assume that the government introduces an $RPI - X$ constraint.[13]

If there is one price only, $RPI - X$ can be transformed into
the following simple price constraint:[14]

$$p \le a_0 - a_1 X. \tag{9.19}$$

---

[12] This can directly be seen from the conditions $\mathcal{L}_N \le 0$ and $\mathcal{L}_K \le 0$ in the
appendix of this chapter.
[13] For details the reader is referred to our treatment of price-cap regulation
in Sect. 4.1.2 and in Ch. 3 above.
[14] We start from the price constraint
$$\frac{p}{p^o} - 1 \le \frac{\Sigma_i \zeta_i^o \pi_i + z^o p}{\Sigma_i \zeta_i^o \pi_i^o + z^o p^o} - 1 - X,$$
where π_i^o and ζ_i^o are base period prices and quantities of all goods in the
price index except the good of the privatized firm whose base period price
and quantity are denoted by p^o and z^o. Solving explicitly for p, we obtain
inequality (9.19) where a_0 and a_1 are positive constants which depend on
exogenous variables only, namely on prices and quantities of the base period
and on present prices of the other goods. We have
$$a_0 = [\frac{\Sigma_i \zeta_i^o \pi_i}{\Sigma_i \zeta_i^o \pi_i^o + z^o p^o}]/[\frac{1}{p^o} - \frac{z^o}{\Sigma_i \zeta_i^o \pi_i^o + z^o p^o}],$$
$$a_1 = 1/[\frac{1}{p^o} - \frac{z^o}{\Sigma_i \zeta_i^o \pi_i^o + z^o p^o}].$$

If this constraint is added to our optimization approach, the price formula changes into

$$\left(p - \frac{p_K}{f_K}\right) z_p = -\left(z - \frac{\chi}{\lambda}\frac{p_K}{f_K}\right) \qquad (9.20)$$

where χ is the Lagrangean parameter of the price constraint. The firm behaves like a profit-maximizing monopolist who has marginal costs p_K/f_K and overestimates[15] the price elasticity of demand by $1/(1 - \frac{\chi}{\lambda}\frac{p_K}{z f_K})$. A firm which overestimates the price elasticity reacts more carefully than a monopolist would, which implies a lower price. The extent of overestimation falls if the conceded profit increases, as expressed by χ.

9.5   Extensions of the Cooperative Game

9.5.1   *Degree of Privatization in a Bilateral Ideological Monopoly*

One of the most challenging results of our basic model is the impossibility of partial privatization. Although the dichotomization between only fully public and fully private firms fits nicely into the thinking of many public enterprise economists, it is not a *priori* clear why such a result is brought about in our model. We shall see in Part Three of the book that welfare-optimal privatization can very well be partial privatization. Hence why is partial privatization excluded in our positive theory?

Obviously the government's ideological interest in privatization is the driving force for achieving full privatization. In the present formulation of the model, there are no effective countervailing elements which, at the optimum, can offset the government's ideological interest. Let us therefore think of some alternative specification which might allow for partial privatization. For this purpose it seems straightforward to give up the ideological neutrality of the trade union. Hence we specify the trade union's utility according to

$$U = U\left(\frac{(1 - \Psi)\Pi}{N^0},\ N,\ -\Theta\right), \qquad U_1, U_2, U_3 > 0. \qquad (9.8')$$

The third component shows that the trade union has an ideological interest in nationalized firms and opposes privatization for ideological reasons. Therefore, we have a bilateral ideological monopoly.

---

[15] $\lambda < 0$ results from equation (9.36) as can be seen in the appendix to this chapter.

There is a mixture of common and conflicting interests of the two players. The interest in profit is shared by both players. The ideological interest in privatization of any player is opposed by the other player. The rest of the basic model remains unchanged. The abbreviation b_{U3} has the obvious meaning and the obvious positive sign.

We have to replace propositions 1 and 2 with the following propositions 1A and 2A.

Proposition 1A (degree of privatization in a bilateral ideological monopoly of government and trade union)

(i) Partial privatization is possible.

(ii) If $s > 0$, the following special results can be deduced:

• In the case of partial privatization the government's bargaining power in favor of privatization b_{V2} must be exactly offset by the trade union's bargaining power against privatization b_{U3}.

• In the case of total privatization the government's bargaining power b_{V2} is never lower than the trade union's bargaining power b_{U3}.

• There are two cases of no privatization: first, the 'low profit case', where the firm remains public regardless of the bargaining powers of the two players; second, the 'ideology case', where the government's bargaining power b_{V2} weakly falls short of the trade union's bargaining power b_{U3}.

Proposition 2A (issue price of shares)

(i) A zero issue price of shares is possible unless the firm is trade-union-dominated.

(ii) Even if the issue price is equated to the dividend, $s = \Psi$, partial privatization is possible.

Economic Interpretation 1A and 2A
As expected, the trade-off in bargaining powers makes it possible to attain partial privatization. The government's ideological interest which had dominated proposition 1 is outweighed by the opposite ideological interest of the trade union. Since partial privatization is possible, the government revenue requirement $R^o > 0$ can be met by dividends from government shares in the firm even if the shares are given away free of charge. Trade-union dominance, however, always leads to a positive issue price because the trade union is

interested in reducing the private shareholders' net return from buying the shares.

Let us now concentrate on that case which is more relevant for economic practice, namely the case of a positive issue price. At the optimum of partial privatization the ideological interests of the government and the trade union are of exactly the same size. To what extent is this exact balancing a good description of economic reality? One could of course think of political processes which lead to higher opposition to public enterprises the more the trade union favors the public enterprise. Then partial privatization seems to be a probable outcome of such a situation. On the other hand, one can expect total privatization if the government's ideology is very strong and exceeds the opposition of the trade union, both measured in terms of bargaining powers. It is interesting to see that there is still the 'low profit case' where no privatization occurs regardless of which bargaining power exceeds the other.

It should be noted that the $\mathcal{L}_\Theta$-condition is only used in the proofs of propositions 1, 2, and 3(ii), second sentence. Hence all other qualitative results of the basic model hold regardless of whether the trade union is ideologically neutral or involved.

9.5.2 Employee Shares as a Wedge between Trade Union and Employees

In our basic model, the trade union is favorable to employee shares only because on the basis of these shares the employees are given more money. However, it is a well-known fact that trade unions are not always so much in favor of employee shares because these shares may drive a wedge between the trade unions and the employees by reducing the employees' willingness to strike and increasing their willingness to cooperate with the management. That property of employee shares can be integrated into our model by assuming that the trade union's security level $\overline{U}$ is increasing in Ψ: lower $\underline{\Psi}$ implies higher employee shares which reduces the security level $\overline{U}$. We denote

$$b_{\overline{U}} = \frac{\overline{U}_\Psi}{U - \overline{U}} > 0. \tag{9.12'}$$

The trade union faces a dilemma: it is in favor of employee shares because they entitle the employees to claim part of the profit of the firm ($b_{U1} > 0$). On the other hand, it is against employee shares because they reduce the trade union's influence on the employees

$(b_{\overline{U}} > 0)$. The rest of the model remains unchanged. Proposition 3 has to be replaced with the following proposition 3A.

Proposition 3A (employee shares driving a wedge between trade union and employees)

   (i)   Even a conservative firm may issue employee shares.

  (ii)   Same as in proposition 3, except second sentence.

 (iii)   Same as in proposition 3.

Economic Interpretation 3A

If the reduction of the trade union's security level is important enough, the government may be willing to issue employee shares although this reduces the share of the dividends which is accrued to the government and to private shareholders. It helps for the interpretation to consider the marginal condition $\mathcal{L}_\Psi$ which results from differentiating the Lagrangean function of the optimization approach $\mathcal{L}$ with respect to the non-employee share in profit Ψ. We obtain

$$\mathcal{L}_\Psi = F\Pi - b_{\overline{U}} - \nu + \tau = 0. \tag{9.21'}$$

Since $\tau \leq 0$, this condition implies

$$F\Pi \geq b_{\overline{U}} + \nu. \tag{9.21''}$$

If employee shares are issued, we have $(1 - \Psi) < 0$ whence $\tau = 0$ and the above formula (9.21″) holds as an equality. Hence there is no issuing of employee shares if the conservative firm's bargaining power is very high, and the trade union's security level cannot be influenced very much by issuing employee shares.

    It should be mentioned that the $\mathcal{L}_\Psi$-condition also is used in the proof of proposition 1(ii). However, the result remains unchanged. Therefore, we can conclude that all qualitative results of the basic model hold regardless of whether or not the employee shares drive a wedge between trade union and employees.

9.5.3 *The Trade Union's Interest in Higher Wages*

Until now we have assumed the wage rate to be exogenously given, say by the market, or by firm-internal negotiations. The exogeneity of the wage rate means that wages are not negotiated at the same time as privatization and employee shares. This is a little superficial. The employees of public firms often have higher wage rates than employees in comparable private industry positions. Therefore employees' participation in equity profits could be perceived as a compensation for an adjustment of higher pre-privatization wages to lower after-privatization wages. Hence it seems worthwhile to consider the setting of wages as a further variable in the second-tier game.

Let us assume that the trade union is interested both in a share of the profit and in maintaining a high level of wages. We redefine the trade union's utility as follows:

$$U = U\left(\frac{(1-\Psi)\Pi}{N^o}, N, p_N - p_N^*\right); \qquad U_1, U_2, U_3 > 0. \quad (9.8'')$$

Here $p_N^* > 0$ is the market wage rate. The actual wage rate in the firm will never fall below the market wage, otherwise all employees would leave the firm. Therefore, we have to consider one more constraint:

$$p_N \geq p_N^* \qquad (\varphi). \qquad (9.11f)$$

The rest of the model remains unchanged.

We obtain the following result:

Proposition 6 (wages in a privatized firm)
Even in the presence of employee shares, there is no guarantee that overly high wages in the firm are brought down to the market wage rates.

Economic Interpretation 6
Proposition 6 is very plausible. We would not have expected the trade union to forgo all interest in higher wages because of the introduction of employee shares. This result would be even more plausible if we had explicitly considered that employee shares might draw a wedge between trade union and employees.

Unfortunately, the interpretation of the marginal conditions does not yield insight into the quantitative changes of variables. Hence we can only argue that employee shares need not lead to bringing down overly high wages to market wages. We cannot show whether overly high wages are reduced to an important extent if the employees earn a noteworthy income from equity profits. Only by numerical simulation analyses we could give examples where the hypothesis of the preceding sentence holds. Therefore, in spite of its plausibility, proposition 6 leaves the economic reader a little unsatisfied.

As in the previous extensions, the inclusion of negotiated wage rates does not change the other results of the basic game.

9.6   Appendix

9.6.1   *The Optimization Approach*

The optimization approach consists of maximizing the objective function
(9.10) with respect to s, Θ, Ψ, N, K, and p, given the constraints (9.11).
The corresponding Lagrangean function equals

$$\mathcal{L} = \log \left[U \left(\frac{(1 - \Psi)\Pi}{N_o}, N \right) - \overline{U} \right] + \log \left[V(\Psi\Pi, \Theta) - \overline{V} \right]$$
$$- \lambda[f(N, K) - z(p)] - \nu(\Psi - s)$$
$$- \rho[(1 - \Theta)\Psi\Pi + s\Theta\Pi - R^o] - \sigma(1 - \Theta) - \tau(1 - \Psi). \quad (9.22)$$

Differentiation leads to the following marginal conditions:

$$\mathcal{L}_s \leq 0; \quad \mathcal{L}_s s = 0; \quad \nu(\Psi - s) = 0; \quad \nu \leq 0; \quad 0 \leq s \leq \Psi, \quad (9.23)$$
$$\mathcal{L}_\Theta \leq 0; \quad \mathcal{L}_\Theta \Theta = 0; \quad \sigma(1 - \Theta) = 0; \quad \sigma \leq 0; \quad 0 \leq \Theta \leq 1, \quad (9.24)$$

$$\mathcal{L}_\Psi = 0;^{16} \qquad \tau(1 - \Psi) = 0; \quad \tau \leq 0; \quad 0 < \Psi \leq 1, \qquad (9.25)$$

$$\mathcal{L}_N = 0; \quad \mathcal{L}_K = 0; \quad \mathcal{L}_p = 0, \qquad (9.26)$$

$$z = f(N, K), \qquad (9.27)$$

$$[(1 - \Theta)\Psi + s\Theta]\Pi \geq R^o; \quad \rho\{[(1 - \Theta)\Psi + s\Theta]\Pi - R^o\} = 0;$$
$$\rho \leq 0. \qquad (9.28)$$

9.6.2   *The Tier-One Game*

The instruments s, Θ, and Ψ are determined on the basis of the tier-
one game. Hence propositions 1–3 are based on the interpretation of
(9.23)–(9.25) where

$$\mathcal{L}_s = \nu - \rho\Theta\Pi, \qquad (9.29)$$

$$\mathcal{L}_\Theta = b_{V2} + \rho(\Psi - s)\Pi + \sigma, \qquad (9.30)$$

$$\mathcal{L}_\Psi = \left(b_{V1} - \frac{b_{U1}}{N^o} - \rho(1 - \Theta) \right) \Pi - \nu + \tau. \qquad (9.31)$$

The bargaining power is denoted by

$$b_{Vi} = \frac{U_i}{U - \overline{U}}; \quad b_{Vi} = \frac{V_i}{V - \overline{V}}, \quad i = 1, 2. \qquad (9.12)$$

---

[16] Remember $\Psi > 0$ because of the government revenue requirement.

Proposition 1 (degree of privatization)

(i) Partial privatization never happens. Either the firm remains in public ownership or it is fully privatized.

(ii) A trade-union-dominated firm always is fully privatized.

(iii) There are two cases of total privatization. In the first case the profit is only high enough to meet the government revenue requirement and the private shareholders get nothing ($\nu < 0$ and $\rho < 0$). In the second case any combination of binding and not-binding revenue constraint and issue price constraint is possible ($\nu = 0$ and $\rho = 0$).

(iv) It is possible that the firm remains in full public ownership. In that case the government gets its revenue requirement only. We have $\rho < 0$ and $\nu = 0$.

Proof 1

Preliminary: $s > 0$

Assume $s = 0$. Then $\Psi > s$, because $\Psi = 0$ is excluded by the government revenue requirement. Therefore the issue price constraint is not binding and $\nu = 0$. Then we must have $0 \leq \rho\Theta\Pi$. Exclude $\Theta = 0$, because it is of no economic interest which value of s is chosen in that case. Then $0 \leq \rho\Theta\Pi$ requires $\rho = 0$. For $s = 0$ we have $(1 - \Theta)\Psi\Pi \geq R^o > 0$. As $\Psi, \Pi > 0$, this implies $1 - \Theta > 0$ which, in turn, implies $\sigma = 0$. Therefore $\mathcal{L}_\Theta$ reduces to $b_{V2} \leq 0$. This contradicts the requirement $b_{V2} > 0$. Therefore s cannot be zero, as soon as shares are given to private shareholders ($\Theta \neq 0$).

Let us now turn to the proof of proposition 1.

(i) For $0 < \Theta < 1$ we have $\sigma = 0$ and therefore $b_{V2} + \rho(\Psi - s)\Pi = 0$. Recall $b_{V2} > 0$. Hence $\rho(\Psi - s)\Pi < 0$. This is possible only if $\rho < 0$ and at the same time $\Psi > s$. However, $\Psi > s$ implies $\nu = 0$. As $s > 0$, we have $\mathcal{L}_s = 0$, implying $\nu = \rho\Theta\Pi = 0$. This cannot hold if $\rho < 0$, and $0 < \Theta < 1$. Hence partial privatization is impossible.

(ii) If $F < 0$, we have $\nu < 0$. The proof is by contradiction. Assume $\nu = 0$. Then we must have $F\Pi + \tau = 0$ which is impossible because of $F\Pi < 0$ and $\tau \leq 0$. Hence $\nu < 0$. Next we prove $\Theta \neq 0$. Since $s > 0$, we have $\mathcal{L}_s = 0$ and therefore $\nu = \rho\Theta\Pi$. If $\Theta = 0$, this is a contradiction to $\nu < 0$. So $\Theta = 0$ is impossible. Partial privatization was excluded by the proof 1(i) above. So $F < 0$ implies $\Theta = 1$.

(iii) Since $s > 0$ we have $\mathcal{L}_s = 0$ or, equivalently $\nu = \rho\Theta\Pi$. Hence $\nu < 0$ and $\rho = 0$ cannot hold at the same time. On the other hand, $\nu = 0$ and $\rho < 0$ can hold only for $\Theta = 0$. Hence we are left with the combinations ($\nu = 0$, $\rho = 0$) and ($\nu < 0$, $\rho < 0$). Both lead to $\rho(\Psi - s)\Pi = 0$. Partial privatization is excluded by proposition 1(i). The case of no privatization can be eliminated because it would require $\sigma = 0$ and $\mathcal{L}_\Theta$ would reduce to $b_{V2} \leq 0$ which is in contrast to our assumptions. Hence the firm must be fully privatized. We have $b_{V2} + \sigma = 0$ with $b_{V2} > 0$ and $\sigma < 0$.

(iv)   As shown in the proof 1(iii), only the the combination ($\nu = 0, \rho < 0$) can occur at $\Theta = 0$. In this optimum we always have $b_{V2} + \rho(\Psi - s)\Pi \leq 0$.

Proposition 2 (issue price of shares)

(i)   Private shareholders never get shares free of charge.

(ii)   If the issue price is equated to the dividend, $s = \Psi$, then the firm never remains in public ownership but is always fully privatized.

Proof 2

(i) $s > 0$ has been proved as a preliminary to proof 1.

(ii)   If $s = \Psi$, we obtain $\mathcal{L}_\Theta = b_{V2} + \sigma \leq 0$ and therefore $\sigma < 0$. Therefore $\Theta = 1$.[17]

Proposition 3 (employee shares)

(i)   A conservative firm never issues employee shares.

(ii)   If the firm is trade-union-dominated, the private shareholders earn nothing; the shares are always sold at a price equal to the dividends. The government revenue constraint is binding. Any amount of Ψ which is compatible with the government revenue requirement can be obtained as the result of the tier-one game.

(iii) In the neutral firm any combination of private shareholders' earnings and employee shares can occur ($\Psi \leq 1$ and $s \leq \Psi$).

Proof 3

(i) $F\Pi - \nu + \tau = 0$ holds only if $\tau < 0$ because $F\Pi > 0$ and $\nu \leq 0$. Hence the optimal Ψ is unity, which means we have no employee shares. Note that this holds for both $\nu = 0$ and $\nu < 0$.

---

[17] It is interesting to consider the government budget constraint. Let us distinguish two cases: (i) If $s=\Psi$, we have $\nu \leq 0$ and, given $s>0$ and assuming $\Theta>0$, we cannot exclude $\rho=0$. The government revenue constraint can be binding or not-binding. (ii) $s<\Psi$ implies $\nu=0$. Since $s>0$, we have $0=\rho\Theta\Pi$. Once again, the case of $\Theta=0$ is of no economic interest. Therefore, let us assume $\Theta>0$. Hence we must have $\rho=0$. The government revenue constraint is not necessarily binding, $[(1-\Theta)\Psi+s\Theta]\Pi \geq R^o$.

(ii) *First sentence* (issue price equated to dividends): we know from proof 1(ii) that in the trade-union-dominated firm $\nu < 0$. But $\nu < 0$ implies $s = \Psi$. *Second sentence* (binding government revenue requirement): as $s > 0$, we have $\mathcal{L}_s = 0$ whence $\nu = \rho\Theta\Pi$. This implies $\rho < 0$ because of $\nu < 0$, $\Pi > 0$ and $\Theta = 1$.[18] The revenue constraint is binding. The *third sentence* ($\Psi \leq 1$) results trivially from $F\Pi - \nu + \tau = 0$.

(iii) L_Ψ is reduced to $-\nu + \tau = 0$ which can be fulfilled for (a) $\nu = 0$ and $\tau = 0$, i. e. $s \leq \Psi$ and $\Psi \leq 1$ or for (b) $\nu < 0$ and $\tau < 0$, i. e. $s = \Psi$ and $\Psi = 1$.

9.6.3 The Tier-Two Game

The instruments N, K, and p are determined on the basis of the tier-two game. Hence propositions 4 and 5 are based on the interpretation of the following marginal conditions:

$$\mathcal{L}_N = -\frac{b_{U1}}{N^o}p_N(1 - \Psi) + b_{U2} - b_{V1}p_N\Psi - \lambda f_N$$
$$+ \rho p_N[(1 - \Theta)\Psi + s\Theta] = 0, \tag{9.32}$$

$$\mathcal{L}_K = -\frac{b_{U1}}{N^o}p_K(1 - \Psi) - b_{V1}p_K\Psi - \lambda f_K$$
$$+ \rho p_K[(1 - \Theta)\Psi + s\Theta] = 0, \tag{9.33}$$

$$\mathcal{L}_p = (z + pz_p)\left(\frac{b_{U1}}{N^o}(1 - \Psi) + b_{V1}\Psi - \rho[(1 - \Theta)\Psi + s\Theta]\right)$$
$$+ \lambda z_p = 0, \tag{9.34}$$

$$z = f(N, K), \tag{9.27}$$

$$[(1-\Theta)\Psi + s\Theta]\Pi \geq R^o; \quad \rho\{[(1-\Theta)\Psi + s\Theta]\Pi - R^o\} = 0; \quad \rho \leq 0. \tag{9.28}$$

Proposition 4 (efficiency)
The firm employs more workers than is efficient.

Proof 4
Simple algebraic manipulation of $\mathcal{L}_N = 0$ and $\mathcal{L}_K = 0$ yields

$$-\frac{b_{U1}}{N^o}(1 - \Psi) - b_{V1}\Psi + \rho[(1 - \Theta)\Psi + s\Theta] = \frac{\lambda f_N}{p_N} - \frac{b_{U2}}{p_N}, \tag{9.35}$$

$$-\frac{b_{U1}}{N^o}(1 - \Psi) - b_{V1}\Psi + \rho[(1 - \Theta)\Psi + s\Theta] = \frac{\lambda f_K}{p_K}. \tag{9.36}$$

---

[18] Recall proposition 1(ii).

We note in passing that (9.36) implies $\lambda < 0$. Subtracting (9.36) from (9.35) leads to

$$\lambda \left(\frac{f_N}{p_N} - \frac{f_K}{p_K} \right) = \frac{b_{U2}}{p_N}. \qquad (9.37)$$

Since $\lambda < 0$, $b_{U2} > 0$, $p_N > 0$, condition (9.37) requires

$$\frac{f_N}{f_K} < \frac{p_N}{p_K}, \qquad \begin{matrix} (9.38) \\ (= 9.16) \end{matrix}$$

which means too high labor inputs.

Proposition 5 (pricing)
The firm sets the price like a profit-maximizing monopolist. The price formula is

$$\left(p - \frac{p_K}{f_K} \right) z_p = -z. \qquad (9.17)$$

Proof 5
Substitute (9.36) into (9.34) and transform to obtain (9.17).

9.6.4   Extensions

Bilateral Ideological Monopoly   All earlier derivations (9.23)–(9.31) hold once again. The only exception is the derivative with respect to Θ. Here we obtain

$$\mathcal{L}_\Theta = b_{V2} - b_{U3} + \rho(\Psi - s)\Pi + \sigma, \qquad (9.30')$$

where $b_{U3} > 0$.

Proposition 1A (degree of privatization in bilateral ideological monopoly of government and trade union)

(i)   Partial privatization is possible.

(ii)   If $s > 0$, the following special results can be deduced:

- In the case of partial privatization the government's bargaining power in favor of privatization b_{V2} must be exactly offset by the trade union's bargaining power against privatization b_{U3}.

- In the case of total privatization the government's bargaining power b_{V2} is never lower than the trade union's power b_{U3}.

- There are two cases of no privatization: first, the 'low profit case' ($\nu = 0$, $\rho < 0$), where the firm remains public regardless of the bargaining powers of the two players; second, the 'ideology case' ($\nu < 0$, $\rho < 0$), where the government's bargaining power b_{V2} weakly falls short of the trade union's bargaining power b_{U3}.

Proof 1A

(i) The proof by contradiction, which was given for proposition 1(i), does not hold because of the interaction between b_{V2} and b_{U3} and because $s = 0$ is possible.

(ii) If $s > 0$, we have $\mathcal{L}_s = 0$ or, equivalently $\nu = \rho\Theta\Pi$. Hence $\nu < 0$ and $\rho = 0$ cannot hold at the same time. $\nu = 0$ and $\rho < 0$ can hold only for $\Theta = 0$. For partial and total privatization we are left with the combinations ($\nu = 0$, $\rho = 0$) and ($\nu < 0$, $\rho < 0$). They both imply $\rho(\Psi - s)\Pi = 0$. For $0 < \Theta \leq 1$ we have $\mathcal{L}_\Theta = 0$, which after substituting $\rho(\Psi - s)\Pi = 0$ yields $b_{V2} - b_{U3} + \sigma = 0$. For partial privatization $\sigma = 0$ and therefore we have $b_{V2} - b_{U3} = 0$. For total privatization $\sigma \leq 0$ whence $b_{V2} - b_{U3} \geq 0$. If no privatization is performed, we have $\mathcal{L}_\Theta \leq 0$ and $\sigma = 0$. We distinguish two cases. (a) For $\nu = 0$, $\rho < 0$ we have $b_{V2} - b_{U3} + \rho(\Psi - s)\Pi \leq 0$. Since $\rho(\Psi - s)\Pi \leq 0$, the inequality holds for $b_{V2} - b_{U3} \underset{<}{\geq} 0$. (b) For ($\nu = 0$, $\rho = 0$) and ($\nu < 0$, $\rho < 0$) we have $b_{V2} - b_{U3} \leq 0$.

Proposition 2A (issue price of shares)

(i) A zero issue price of shares is possible unless the firm is trade-union-dominated.

(ii) Even if the issue price is equated to the dividend, $s = \Psi$, partial privatization is possible.

Proof 2A

The proof by contradiction, which was given as a preliminary to proof 1, does not hold because of the interaction between b_{V2} and b_{U3}. If $s = 0$, $\mathcal{L}_\Theta$ reduces to $b_{V2} - b_{U3} \leq 0$, which is no contradiction. However, for the trade-union-dominated firm we can prove $s > 0$ by contradiction. Assume $s = 0$. Then $\nu = 0$ follows as in the preliminary to proof 1. $\mathcal{L}_\Psi = 0$ in that case requires that $F\Pi + \tau = 0$, which cannot hold if $F < 0$.

Employee Shares as a Wedge between Trade Union and Employees
All earlier derivations, namely (9.23)–(9.29) and (9.30) or (9.30') hold

once again. However, given the new specification of the trade union's security level, the first-order condition $\mathcal{L}_\Psi$ changes into

$$\mathcal{L}_\Psi = F\Pi - b_{\overline{U}} - \nu + \tau = 0. \tag{9.31'}$$

Proposition 3A (employee shares driving a wedge between trade union and employees)

    (i)   Even a conservative firm may issue employee shares.

    (ii)   Same as in proposition 3, except second sentence.

    (iii) Same as in proposition 3.

Proof 3A

    (i) $F\Pi - b_{\overline{U}} - \nu + \tau = 0$ holds for $\tau \leq 0$. Hence $(1 - \Psi) \leq 0$ and there may be employee shares.

    (ii)   Similar to proof 3.

    (iii) Similar to proof 3.

    The proof of proposition 1(ii) remains unchanged because for the trade-union-dominated firm both $F\Pi < 0$ and $F\Pi - b_{\overline{U}} < 0$.

Endogenous Wages   All earlier derivations, namely (9.23)–(9.29), (9.30) or (9.30') and (9.31) or (9.31') hold once again. However, we have to add one more set of Kuhn–Tucker conditions:[19]

$$\mathcal{L}_{p_N} = 0; \qquad \varphi(p_N - p_N^*) = 0; \qquad \varphi \leq 0; \qquad p_N^* \leq p_N, \tag{9.39}$$

where

$$\mathcal{L}_{p_N} = -\frac{b_{U1}}{N^o} N(1 - \Psi) + b_{U3} - b_{v1} N\Psi + \rho[(1 - \Theta)\Psi + s\Theta]N - \varphi. \tag{9.40}$$

Proposition 6 (wages in a privatized firm)
Even in the presence of employee shares, there is no guarantee that overly high wages in the firm are brought down to the market wage rates.

Proof 6
Substituting into (9.40) the $\mathcal{L}_K$-condition (9.36) yields

$$\lambda f_K \frac{N}{p_K} = \varphi - b_{U3} \tag{9.41}$$

whence $\varphi = 0$ is well possible. (Recall $\lambda < 0$ from (9.36).)

---

[19] Recall $p_N^* > 0$. Hence we have $p_N > 0$, too, and therefore $\mathcal{L}_{p_N} = 0$.

10   Privatization and Market Entry

Consider a public utility, like gas, electricity, or telecommunications, which is going to be privatized. The government does not want the utility to exploit its monopolistic market position and therefore makes two provisions: it regulates the firm with respect to its prices, and it encourages market entry to promote competition and lower prices. Such a combination of fiscal policy provisions has been applied to privatized firms. A recent UK example is British Telecom.

In this chapter we present a model of entry into a regulated market. We restrict ourselves to dealing with a duopolistic market structure where we have one incumbent and one potential entrant. The two best-known models of duopoly are attributed to Cournot and Bertrand. In a Cournot duopoly the producers simultaneously and independently set the quantity of goods produced which will be offered for sale on the market. An auctioneer then sets the market-clearing price. By contrast, in a Bertrand duopoly the producers simultaneously and independently set prices. The producer who supplies at the lower price covers all demand. If two duopolists choose the same price, some rule must be found to allocate demand between the two producers.

Bertrand competition is fiercer than Cournot competition. For example, when considering one-product enterprises, the equilibrium of a Bertrand duopoly is characterized by prices equal to average costs and zero profits if average costs are constant and if capacity constraints are non-binding. The equilibrium of a Cournot duopoly, on the other hand, allows positive profits. Consequently, if a privatized incumbent and a private market entrant operate in a Bertrand duopoly, there is no need for a profit regulation of the privatized firm. Market entry and subsequent price competition lead to those zero profits which the government desires. This is different if after market entry a Cournot duopoly arises. Here regulation makes sense even after market entry occurred.

The statements of the preceding paragraph hold only if there are no *capacity constraints*. In dealing with privatization and market entry, however, capacity constraints are of major importance. Public firms are often characterized by excess capacity which has

---

This chapter is a slightly extended reproduction of Bös and Nett (1990).

been accumulated as a result of assorted government intervention. For example, public railways run many branch lines which are not cost-efficient, public telecommunications enterprises have many phone booths in rural areas which a profit maximizer would immediately close down, etc. Therefore, a privatized incumbent chooses a desired capacity by reducing the existing capacity which was acquired during its public enterprise past. The only capacity costs which the privatized incumbent faces are the costs of maintenance of the reduced capacity. A market entrant, on the other hand, would have to build up new capacity from scratch. Thus the costs of the installation of new capacity *and* maintenance costs would have to be financed. Market entry with a privatized incumbent is hence characterized by *asymmetric costs* with respect to incumbent and entrant.

If each duopolist can only produce output up to a previously chosen capacity, we speak of a capacity-constrained duopoly. In a recent paper, Kreps and Scheinkman (1983) presented a model in which Bertrand competition under capacity constraints yields Cournot outcomes which imply positive profits. In such a case profit regulation of the duopoly makes sense although the firms set prices à *la* Bertrand.

Dealing with profit regulation in a capacity-constrained Bertrand duopoly quite naturally allows us to deal with *regulation by means of price capping*. Since the firms compete by setting prices, the consequences of capping these prices can be treated directly in the model.

In the following we first present the multistage structure of the game between a privatized incumbent and a potential market entrant (Section 10.2). Then we deal with the subgame-perfect equilibrium of the game without price regulation (Section 10.3). Finally, we turn to the consequences of a price-cap regulation in a capacity-constrained duopoly (Section 10.4).

10.2   The Model

We consider a market for one homogeneous good. There is a privatized incumbent (firm 1), and a potential market entrant (firm 2). Both firms are interested in maximizing profits. The strategic variables of the game are the prices p_j and the capacities $q_j, j = 1, 2$. A capacity of q_j means that firm j subsequently can produce up to q_j units of output. Decisions on prices and capacities are chosen in two stages. In a first stage, the firms decide on capacities; then, in a second stage, they decide on prices. The sequence in which these decisions are made is quite realistic, as capacities cannot be changed as quickly as prices. Hence choosing capacity is a long-run decision, whereas choosing output (via prices) is a short-run decision which takes place within the framework of a given capacity. Moreover, the capacity decision of firm 2 is a decision about entry ($q_2 > 0$) or non-entry ($q_2 = 0$). Clearly, the incumbent makes his decision on price only after he knows whether he has a competitor or not. On the other hand, the potential entrant must first make a decision on market participation and only thereafter on price.

In our model the incumbent moves first, both in capacity and price.[1] We have a game structure with perfect information as shown in Figure 5.

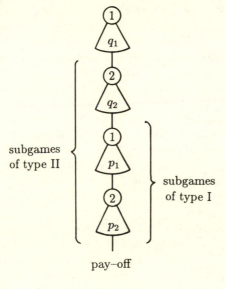

Figure 5

The sequence of capacity decisions results from the simple fact that the incumbent's capacity already exists, whereas the capacity of the potential entrant must be built up. The sequence of price

---

[1] Kreps and Scheinkman (1983) deal with two identical firms which compete in a market. Hence, in their model, there are no institutional reasons why any of the firms should move first. Consequently, Kreps and Scheinkman assume that capacities are set simultaneously at stage one and prices are set simultaneously at stage two of the game.

decisions is primarily caused by institutional reasons. We assume
that the former public firm still faces institutional obligations to
publish prices at particular points of time. The entrant is more
flexible and waits until the incumbent has announced p_1.[2]

Perfect information implies that the entrant (firm 2) knows
the capacity of the incumbent (firm 1) when choosing the amount
of capacity q_2. Moreover, the entrant knows q_1, q_2, and p_1 when
he sets p_2. The rules of the game are common knowledge.[3]

The game proceeds as follows: First, the two agents decide on
capacity. The incumbent has inherited a high capacity from his
public past, acquired when the firm was a publicly owned monopoly. Privatization makes market entry possible. We assume, however, that there is only one potential entrant.[4] Knowing this, the
privatized incumbent chooses his capacity q_1: he decides to reduce the inherited capacity because we implicitly assume that the
given capacity at the time of privatization is so high that a reduction is profitable, regardless of the behavior of the potential
entrant. Given the capacity of the incumbent, the entrant decides
on whether or not to enter. If the firm enters, then q_2 is greater
than zero; if it stays out of the market, q_2 is equal to zero. We assume that both firms have the same constant-capacity maintenance
costs per unit of capacity, m. While the reduction of capacity is
assumed to be costless, the installation of capacity induces costs
equal to i per unit of capacity. Hence we have an asymmetric cost
situation because a capacity q induces the costs $(m + i)q$ to the
entrant and mq to the incumbent. It is natural to assume $i > m$.
To simplify the model we assume that output $z_j(\leq q_j), j = 1, 2$ is
produced at zero cost.

Knowing the capacity of each other, the firms engage in *price
competition*. When setting prices, the two firms have to consider
the demand they face at the market. If there is only one firm which
sets the price p, then it faces the following demand:

$$D(p) = 1 - p. \qquad (10.1)$$

In this one-firm case the maximum saleable output at a price p
simply is $1 - p$. In our model, however, there are two compet-
ing firms and therefore possible capacity constraints and various

---

[2] A classic paper about capacity-restricted price competition is Levitan
and Shubik (1972). However, in their paper capacities are exogenously given.

[3] See Aumann (1976).

[4] Recall the example of Mercury and British Telecom.

forms of price-setting lead to a complicated scheme of the maximum saleable output z_j. For the incumbent this so-called efficient rationing scheme is presented in the following:[5]

$$z_1(p_1,p_2) = \begin{cases} \min(q_1; 1-p_1) & \text{if } p_1 < p_2, \\ \min\left[q_1; \max\left(\dfrac{1-p_1}{2}; 1-q_2-p_1\right)\right] & \text{if } p_1 = p_2, \\ \min[q_1; \max(0; 1-q_2-p_1)] & \text{if } p_1 > p_2. \end{cases}$$

$$(10.2)$$

$z_1(p_1,p_2)$ is the output the incumbent will sell at prices p_1 and p_2, because at any given price profit is maximized by selling as much output as possible. Output z_1 may be constrained by capacity q_1. This explains the 'min' function in (10.2): more than the capacity can never be supplied. Alternatively, z_1 may be constrained by the market demand. Here we distinguish three cases:

(i)   even if $p_1 < p_2$, the incumbent can never sell more than the total quantity demanded at price p_1, which is $1-p_1$.

(ii)   if $p_1 > p_2$, the incumbent faces the demand which is left after the entrant has sold his output $z_2 = q_2$. This residual demand may be zero if, at price p_2, the entrant has satisfied all market demand. However, the entrant may have set capacity too low to cover all demand at price p_2, which leaves to the incumbent a residual demand of $1-q_2-p_1$.

(iii)   if $p_1 = p_2$, we follow Kreps and Scheinkman (1983: 328) in assuming either that demand is divided evenly between incumbent and new entrant or that the incumbent can serve more than half of the market if the entrant has chosen a capacity lower than half of the market demand at the respective price.

Since we assume that both firms maximize profits, their payoff functions Π_i equal

$$\Pi_1 = z_1 p_1 - m q_1, \qquad (10.3)$$

$$\Pi_2 = z_2 p_2 - (m+i) q_2. \qquad (10.4)$$

10.3   The Game without Price Regulation

As usual in games with perfect information, individually rational behavior requires that players always anticipate what will happen

---

[5] Although we do not provide details here, an analogous formula holds for the entrant.

in subsequent stages of the game. Hence an analysis of a multistage game has to employ backward induction. Therefore, our analysis begins with subgames dealing with the setting of prices, given the capacities. From here we deduce the strategies in those subgames where firm 2 decides on whether to enter or not and, in the case of entry, which capacity to choose. The potential entrant takes account of the given capacity of the incumbent and anticipates which prices and profits will be induced by his choice of capacity. Finally, the argument is followed back to the first decision node which deals with the incumbent's capacity choice, where the equilibrium of all proper subgames is correctly anticipated by the incumbent.

10.3.1   Choosing Prices for Given Capacities (Subgames I) [6]

The price competition subgames start at decision node 3 of Figure 5 where the capacities q_1 and q_2 are given. The subgame-perfect equilibrium is characterized by the condition that the incumbent chooses his profit-maximizing price knowing the capacities of both firms and anticipating the entrant's response. This response consists in an entrant's price, which maximizes the entrant's profit given the capacities of the incumbent and the entrant, and the incumbent's price. Since capacities are given at this stage, costs do not influence the decisions made in subgames I. Therefore in the treatment of these subgames the words 'profit' and 'revenue' are used as synonyms. We assume that a firm which is indifferent between setting a price a or b selects the lower of the two.

The prices chosen depend on the specific values of the capacities. Four cases have to be distinguished as illustrated in Figure 6. We denote a capacity q_j as 'low' if it falls short of a hypothetical Cournot capacity $r(q_k)$; otherwise it is denoted as 'high'.

The hypothetical Cournot capacity of the incumbent is the result of the following optimization approach:[7]

$$\max_{q_1}(1 - q_2 - q_1)q_1. \tag{10.5}$$

The resulting first-order condition yields

$$q_1^* = r(q_2) = \frac{1 - q_2}{2}. \tag{10.6}$$

---

[6] For the analysis of these subgames see Deneckere and Kovenock (1988).
[7] An analogous approach holds for the entrant.

The capacity $r(q_2)$ is the optimal response of the incumbent if the entrant has chosen capacity q_2 and subsequently has sold q_2 units of output to the consumers. This is a hypothetical capacity because it is not guaranteed that the entrant actually will succeed in selling q_2 units of output. In the traditional model of a Cournot duopoly there are no capacity constraints and $z_j = q_j$. Then $r(q_j)$ is the usual reaction curve of one of the duopolists; therefore, we see that $r(q_j)$ represents a hypothetical Cournot capacity.

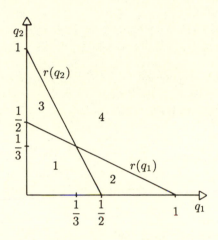

Figure 6

In the following, it will often be convenient to denote prices by the inverse demand function, for instance

$$p_1 = p_2 = p(q_1 + q_2) := 1 - (q_1 + q_2) \qquad (10.7)$$

or

$$p_2 = p(q_1 + r(q_1)) := 1 - (q_1 + r(q_1))$$
$$= 1 - q_1 - \frac{1 - q_1}{2} = \frac{1 - q_1}{2}. \qquad (10.8)$$

The first price is market-clearing. If both agents choose this price, they sell an output equal to their capacity. In the second case, the incumbent has set a lower price than the entrant and accordingly sells all his capacity q_1. The entrant optimally adjusts to the incumbent's capacity by choosing capacity $q_2 = r(q_1)$ and selling at price p_2 as denoted in (10.8).

In case 1 of Figure 6 both firms choose a low capacity and, as we shall see shortly, both succeed in selling an output quantity equal to the capacity. In fact, case 1 leads to a Cournot result in the sense that both firms sell an amount of output equal to capacity, and at the market-clearing price $p(q_1 + q_2)$. In cases 2–4 at least one firm chooses a high capacity and, as will be shown, at least one firm fails to utilize its full capacity.

Let us now successively examine these four cases. In the interest of the reader who wants to concentrate on the economic meaning of the model, the following text only presents the propositions and their economic interpretation. Readers who are interested in technical details of the model will find the explicit proofs in the appendix to this chapter. It should be possible to understand the results of the model without necessarily reading the proofs.

Proposition 1 (low capacities – region 1 in Figure 6)
In case of $q_1 \leq r(q_2)$ and $q_2 \leq r(q_1)$, the equilibrium of the price-competition subgames is characterized by $p_1 = p_2 = p(q_1 + q_2)$ and $z_j = q_j, j = 1, 2$.

Proposition 2 (high-incumbent capacity – region 2 of Figure 6)
If $q_1 > r(q_2)$ and $q_2 \leq r(q_1)$, the equilibrium is characterized by $p_1 = p(q_2 + r(q_2)), p_2 = p(q_2 + r(q_2)) - \epsilon, z_1 = r(q_2)$, and $z_2 = q_2$ where $\epsilon > 0$ is small.

Proposition 3 (high-entrant capacity – region 3 of Figure 6)
If $q_1 \leq r(q_2)$ and $q_2 > r(q_1)$, the equilibrium is characterized by $p_1 = \hat{p}$, $p_2 = p(q_1 + r(q_1)), z_1 = q_1$, and $z_2 = r(q_1)$, where $\hat{p}$ is defined as

$$\hat{p} = \frac{(1 - q_1)^2}{4z_2}, \tag{10.9}$$

and where $z_2 = \min(q_2, 1 - \hat{p})$.

Proposition 4 (high capacities – region 4 of Figure 6)
If $q_1 > r(q_2)$ and $q_2 > r(q_1)$, the equilibrium is characterized by either $p_1 = \hat{p}$ or $p_1 = p(q_2 + r(q_2))$.

  (i) $p_1 = \hat{p}$ is chosen if $p(q_2 + r(q_2))r(q_2) \leq [(1 - q_1)^2/4q_2]q_1$. In this case $p_2 = p(q_1 + r(q_1)), z_1 = q_1$, and $z_2 = r(q_1)$.

  (ii) Otherwise $p_1 = p(q_2 + r(q_2))$ is chosen, in which case $p_2 = p_1 - \epsilon; z_1 = r(q_2)$, and $z_2 = q_2$.

Economic Interpretation of Propositions 1–4
The subgames of type I deal with price competition when the capacities of both incumbent and entrant are given. Using existing

capacity, either agent can produce at zero cost. The agent who underbids the other faces the entire market demand at the price he has chosen.[8] The agent who is underbid faces only the residual demand (which might be zero). Assume for the moment that it is the incumbent who is underbid. As illustrated in Figure 7, he then faces residual demand $RD = 1 - q_2 - p_1$. In this case the incumbent is monopolist with respect to the residual demand.

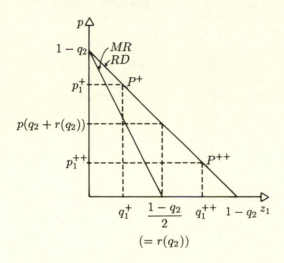

Figure 7

His maximum profit, therefore, occurs when marginal revenue MR is equal to marginal cost (which is equal to zero in subgames I). Maximum profit is given at a quantity $(1 - q_2)/2$, which is exactly the best response $r(q_2)$ to the entrant's capacity. The incumbent will try to produce the quantity $(1 - q_2)/2$ or at least come as close as possible, i.e. as far as his chosen capacity allows. Hence if he has a low capacity, for instance q_1^+ in Figure 7, he has no incentive to set a price higher than p_1^+. If he has a high capacity, for instance q_1^{++} in the figure, he has no incentive to choose a lower price than p_1^{++}. In the low-capacity case q_1^+, the incumbent also has no incentive to set a price lower than p_1^+, because he can sell q_1^+ at price p_1^+ and hence loses money only if he sells q_1^+ at a price lower than p_1^+. In the high-capacity case q_1^{++}, however, the incumbent has an incentive to set a price higher than p_1^{++} and

---

[8] Note that $q_1 > 1$ is never chosen because 1 is the maximum demand at zero prices, and therefore no quantity in excess of 1 will ever be sold.

not to use part of his capacity because his profit is increased if p_1 increases up to the profit-maximizing price. However, this price increase is a best strategy only if the incumbent is underbid. If the entrant sets a higher price than the incumbent, then the high-capacity incumbent will sell q_1^{++} and the entrant will choose an optimal response (which could be illustrated in a figure analogous to Figure 7).

The pricing strategies of subgames I differ with respect to the capacities chosen by the two economic agents. We have four different capacity constellations, as illustrated in Figure 6.

Case one is the situation in which both incumbent and entrant have chosen low production capacities; i.e., both have capacities below the best response $r(q_j)$. Both agents are in a position indicated by point P^+ in Figure 7. The agents share the market. They choose a price $p(q_1 + q_2)$ and both utilize their full capacity. No agent has an interest in raising or reducing the price of his product for reasons mentioned earlier. The low capacities prevent intense price competition. No agent faces the danger of being under- or overbid.

In the second case, the incumbent has a high capacity and the entrant a low capacity. This seems to be a very plausible situation for a large privatized incumbent who faces potential entry from smaller competitors. If the incumbent is underbid, he faces a situation similar to P^{++} in Figure 7. Hence he has an incentive to increase his price up to $p_1 = p(q_2 + r(q_2))$. The entrant has an incentive to underbid while tracking the increased price of the incumbent as closely as possible. This enables him to sell all his capacity at the highest possible price, which is $p_1 - \epsilon$. Since the incumbent moves first, he sets his optimal price, anticipating the underbidding by the entrant. The entrant, moving second, chooses a price slightly below the incumbent's. Note that the high-capacity agent does not utilize all his capacity.

In the third case, a low-capacity incumbent has to face a high-capacity potential entrant. The high-capacity entrant could calculate his position in the same way as the high-capacity incumbent in the second case; however, the entrant has the second – not the first – move. Hence he cannot set a price and anticipate that the incumbent will follow with a similar but slightly lower price. The incumbent has the first move and must, therefore, set the price first. What will happen if he acts in a similar manner to the second case? This would imply that the incument sets a price $p(q_1 + r(q_1)) - \epsilon$, expecting to be slightly overbid by the entrant. However, facing the price $p_1 = p(q_1 + r(q_1)) - \epsilon$, the entrant has an incentive to *underbid* by ϵ' in order to sell output equal to his capacity q_2. In fact, since ϵ and ϵ' are very small, this underbidding would allow him to sell q_2 at a price which is practically identical to $p(q_1 + r(q_1))$. This is obviously better than selling only $r(q_1) < q_2$ at price $p(q_1 + r(q_1))$; therefore, the incumbent would not set such a high price. He must continually reduce his price in search of a price which is low enough to induce the entrant to overbid and thereby maximize profits. This is the price $\hat{p}$, as defined in proposition 3. The price competition in the third case is therefore fiercer than in the second case. In the second case the incumbent sets a price and anticipates being slightly underbid by the entrant. In the third case the incumbent sets a price and anticipates being significantly overbid by the entrant. Note once again that the high-capacity agent does not utilize all his capacity.

The fourth case is a mixture of the second and third cases. Accordingly, the incumbent has two options and chooses that which leads to higher profit. Option one is the second-case option: set price $p(q_2 + r(q_2))$ and allow the entrant to underbid by a very small amount. Option two is the third-case option: set price $\hat{p}$ and let the entrant overbid by a significant amount. Which option leads to the highest profits depends on the relative proportions of the two capacities. The higher q_2 is compared with q_1, the higher the probability that $\hat{p}$ is the best strategy of the incumbent. Note that the agent who sets the higher price does not utilize all his capacity; however, the other agent does.

10.3.2 The Entrant's Capacity Decision (Subgames II)

In subgames of type II the entrant decides on the best reply strategy with respect to capacity q_2, given the capacity q_1 and anticipating the price competition which will be induced by his decision.[9] This price competition is specified by the subgame-perfect solutions of subgames I which we analyzed in the previous subsection. In the subgames of type II (Figure 5) the capacity costs are variable and, consequently, are taken into account by the entrant.

Any strategy of the entrant consists in choosing a capacity q_2. The set of all strategies can be partitioned into the following three subsets:

---

[9] We assume that an entrant who is indifferent between capacity a or b selects the lower one.

(i)   strategies which induce equilibrium prices $p_1 > p_2$. As an abbreviation we speak of U strategies (U stands for 'underbidding' by the entrant). The set of all U strategies is denoted as U;

(ii) strategies which induce equilibrium prices $p_1 < p_2$, for short O strategies. They constitute the set O;

(iii) strategies which induce identical equilibrium prices, $p_1 = p_2$. We denote these as 'Cournot' strategies, abbreviated C strategies.[10] They are contained in set C.

Note that we define these subsets according to the prices induced, and not according to particular properties of capacity q_2 with respect to the given capacity q_1. A U strategy lies either in area 2 or 4 of Figure 6; an O strategy lies either in area 3 or 4; a C strategy always lies in area 1. A U strategy implies that capacity q_2 is fully utilized, an amount of output q_2 is sold, and the incumbent chooses $z_1 = r(q_2)$ and price $p_1 = p(q_2 + r(q_2))$. An O strategy implies that capacity q_1 is fully utilized, an amount of output q_1 is sold, and the entrant chooses $z_2 = r(q_1)$ and price $p_2 = p(q_1 + r(q_1))$. A C strategy leads to $p_1 = p_2$, whereby both agents sell an output equal to their capacity at the market-clearing price $p(q_1 + q_2)$.

For the following three propositions, we have to distinguish various cases according to the size of the incumbent's capacity. If $q_1 \leq 1/3$, then the entrant chooses a C strategy. If $q_1 > 1/2$, the entrant chooses a U strategy. If $1/3 < q_1 \leq 1/2$, the entrant will choose either a C strategy or a U strategy, depending on the capacity costs.

For a better understanding of the following propositions, consider two special capacity choices of the entrant. First, there is a C or an O strategy where the entrant maximizes profit given the residual demand $(1 - q_1 - z_2)$ subject to $z_2 = q_2$, because any overcapacity only costs money without contributing to profit. The optimization $\max_{q_2}(1 - q_1 - q_2)q_2 - (m + i)q_2$ yields a first-order condition,

$$q_2^* = \frac{1 - q_1 - (m + i)}{2}. \tag{10.10}$$

Second, consider the following special case of a U strategy which implies a constant capacity of the entrant: if q_2 is element

---

[10] Since identical prices occur only if the price is equal to the market-clearing price with respect to the aggregate capacity.

of U, this leads to a price $p_1 = p(q_2 + r(q_2))$. Let the entrant chose $p_2 = p_1 - \epsilon$. In this case the entrant's profit can be approximated[11] by $p(q_2 + r(q_2))q_2 - (m + i)q_2 = [(1 - q_2)/2]q_2 - (m + i)q_2$. The capacity which maximizes this profit is

$$q_2^* = 1/2 - (m + i). \tag{10.11}$$

Let us now turn to the presentation of propositions 5–7.

Proposition 5
If $q_1 \leq 1/3$, the subgame-perfect equilibrium of a subgame II is characterized by $q_2 = \max\{[1 - q_1 - (m+i)]/2; 0\}, z_1 = q_1, z_2 = q_2$, and $p_1 = p_2 = p(q_1 + q_2)$.

Proposition 6
If $1/3 < q_1 \leq 1/2$, then

$$q_2 = \begin{cases} \min[q_1 - \epsilon; 1/2 - (m + i)] & \text{if } (m + i) \leq 1/6, \\ [1 - q_1 - (m + i)]/2 & \text{if } 1/6 < (m + i) < 1/2 \\ & \quad \text{and } 1/3 < q_1 \leq \hat{q}_1, \\ 1/2 - (m + i) & \text{if } 1/6 < (m + i) < 1/2 \\ & \quad \text{and } \hat{q}_1 < q_1 < 1/2, \\ \max\{[1 - q_1 - (m + i)]/2; 0\} & \text{if } (m + i) \geq 1/2, \end{cases}$$

where $\hat{q}_1 = (\sqrt{2} - 1)[1/\sqrt{2} + (m + i)]$.

Proposition 7
If $1/2 \leq q_1 \leq 1$, then $q_2 = \max[1/2 - (m + i); 0]; z_2 = q_2, z_1 = r(q_2); p_1 = p[q_2 + r(q_2)], p_2 = p_1 - \epsilon$.

Economic Interpretation of Propositions 5–7
The equilibrium of each subgame II can be illustrated in three figures (Figure 8a–c), depending on the capacity costs $m+i$. There is always an incentive to market entry unless the capacity costs are very high ($m + i \geq 1/2$). Only when this is the case can the incumbent set capacity q_1 at a level which deters entry. In the following section we shall see that the incumbent's decision crucially depends on the relative size of m and i.

---

[11] We neglect ϵ.

If the entrant's capacity costs are not very high, the incumbent cannot deter entry. This leaves the entrant with two possible alternative responses, once again, contingent on the capacity choice of the incumbent:

(i) If the incumbent chooses a low capacity ($q_1 < 1/3$), the entrant will respond with a C strategy, where both agents sell all their capacity at the market-clearing price $p = p_1 = p_2$. The entrant's capacity in that case is a decreasing linear function of the incumbent's capacity $q_2 = [1 - q_1 - (m + i)]/2$. Concretely, this means that the more capacity the incumbent holds, the less capacity is held by the entrant, and the two capacities add up to market demand.

(ii) If the incumbent chooses a high capacity ($q_1 > 1/2$), the entrant will always find a capacity which later on induces underbidding so that $p_1 > p_2$. In that case the entrant chooses a constant capacity $q_2 = 1/2 - (m + i)$, regardless of the extent of the incumbent's capacity.

Switching from a 'Cournot strategy' to a strategy which induces $p_1 > p_2$ is a tricky transition problem. For small-capacity costs $(m+i \leq 1/6)$ there may even be an interval where the entrant matches the incumbent's capacity and sells at a price $p_2 = p_1 - \epsilon$.

10.3.3   The Incumbent's Capacity Decision

At decision node 1 the incumbent decides on the capacity q_1, well aware of the responses of the entrant, which are illustrated in Figures 8a–c. The incumbent also anticipates the price competition and his profit, while taking into account his capacity costs.

Proposition 8
If $(m + i) \leq 1/6$, then $q_1 = 1/3$. There is market entry and $q_2 = 1/3 - (m + i)/2$.

Proposition 9
If $1/6 < (m + i) < 1/2$, then $q_1 = \hat{q}_1$ where $\hat{q}_1 = (\sqrt{2} - 1)[1/\sqrt{2} + (m + i)]$. There is market entry and $q_2 = [1 - \hat{q}_1 - (m + i)]/2$.

Proposition 10
If $(m + i) \geq 1/2$, then $q_1 = \max[(1 - m)/2; 1 - (m + i)]$. There is no market entry.

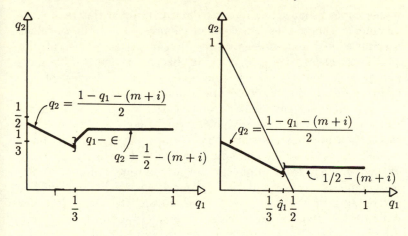

Figure 8a $(m + i \leq 1/6)$ Figure 8b $(1/6 < m + i < 1/2)$

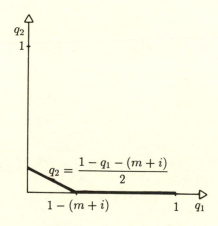

Figure 8c $(m + i \geq 1/2)$

Economic Interpretation of Propositions 8–10
Market entry can be deterred only when there are very high capacity costs. In this respect, capacity installation and capacity maintenance costs have the same influence: only if $(m + i) \geq 1/2$ is entry deterrence possible. However, if capacity installation costs are relatively high compared with maintenance costs, the incumbent is able to realize his monopoly profit. If capacity installation costs are low, the monopoly capacity is not sustainable. Instead, a

higher capacity must be chosen to deter entry. For this reason the incumbent chooses the 'Stackelberg capacity' $1 - (m + i)$, which maximizes his profit given the 'reaction function' of the entrant, $q_2 = \max\{[1 - q_1 - (m + i)]/2; 0\}$. In this case the 'Stackelberg capacity' is the lowest capacity which deters entry in the case of low-capacity installation costs and high-capacity maintenance costs.

For medium- and small-capacity costs, $m + i < 1/2$, the incumbent can never choose a capacity which deters entry, even if the capacity installation costs are very high compared with the maintenance costs. If the incumbent chooses a high capacity, $q_1 > 1/3$ or $q_1 > \hat{q}_1$, then the entrant can always guarantee himself a minimal profit by setting capacity q_2 at a level which would induce overbidding by the incumbent. The entrant then chooses a low but positive capacity. Since capacity is low, the incumbent earns a higher profit if he accepts that the entrant sells all his capacity and leaves 'only' the residual capacity to the incumbent. It is interesting to note that the equilibrium capacities of the incumbent are lower than the 'Stackelberg capacities' $(1 - m + i)/2$.

10.4   Price Regulation of the Incumbent

We assume that the incumbent faces a price constraint,

$$p_1 \le \bar{p}. \tag{10.12}$$

This 'price cap' is well known from the recent UK and US discussions, as already mentioned in Sections 4.1.2 and 7.1 above. Hence a price constraint of type (10.12) is appropriate to model regulation according to the most recent trends in the practice of privatized and regulated utilities.

We assume that only the incumbent faces the price constraint: the entrant is free to choose a higher price. However, in an indirect way he too will be affected because the price regulation imposes low-price competition on the market.

10.4.1   *Choosing Prices for Given Capacities (Subgames I)*

As in the previous section, we must first analyze the effect of price regulation in a subgame I. Once again, we have to distinguish four cases, as illustrated in Figure 6.

Proposition 11

Case 1:

If $q_1 \leq r(q_2)$ and $q_2 \leq r(q_1)$, then $p_1 = \min[\bar{p}; p(q_1 + q_2)]$, $p_2 = p(q_1 + q_2)$.

Case 2:

If $q_1 > r(q_2)$ and $q_2 \leq r(q_1)$, then $p_1 = \min[\bar{p}; p(q_2 + r(q_2))]$, $p_2 = \max[p_1 - \epsilon; p(q_1 + q_2)]$.

Case 3:

If $q_1 \leq r(q_2)$ and $q_2 > r(q_1)$, then $p_1 = \min(\bar{p}; \hat{p})$, $p_2 = p(q_1 + r(q_1))$.

Case 4:

If $q_1 > r(q_2)$ and $q_2 > r(q_1)$, then

(i) $p_1 = \min[\bar{p}; p(q_2 + r(q_2))]$, $p_2 = p_1 - \epsilon$, for $\hat{p}q_1 < (1 - q_2 - p_1)p_1$, and $\hat{p} < \bar{p}$;

(ii) $p_1 = \min(\bar{p}; \hat{p})$, $p_2 = p(q_1 + r(q_1))$ otherwise.

Corollary

If $q_1 + q_2 < 1 - \bar{p}$, then $p_1 = \bar{p} < p(q_1 + q_2)$.

Economic Interpretation of Proposition 11

If price competition is strong enough, the price-cap constraint may fail to be binding, in which case all the results of the non-regulated market are possible. In economic practice, British Telecom's price-cap constraint was not always binding, since Telecom, in particular, cut prices where competition from Mercury was present.[12]

Let us now turn to the more interesting case where the price constraint is binding. The incumbent always faces a revenue loss (given capacities q_1 and q_2). As can be seen in proposition 11, however, the entrant's revenue is unaffected by the regulatory constraint on the incumbent if we have the same situation as in case 1 or 3 of Figure 6. In the absence of price regulation, these cases were characterized by $p_1 \leq p_2$, i.e. by a sort of Cournot behavior or by overbidding by the entrant. The price cap reduces p_1 without inducing any change in p_2. It is easy to grasp that $p_1 \leq p_2$ can be realized at lower values of p_1 and that the entrant has no reason to change his price behavior. In case 1, the incumbent sells q_1 at a price lower than $p(q_1 + q_2)$, which allows the entrant to sell his capacity q_2 at the highest possible price, namely $p(q_1 + q_2)$.

---

[12] For details see Vickers and Yarrow (1988a: 223–5).

In case 3, the entrant is not concerned with how low the price is at which the incumbent sells q_1: since the incumbent never sells more than q_1, whatever the price, the entrant adjusts by setting $p_2 = p(q_1 + r(q_1))$.

Matters are more complicated in those parts of cases 2 and 4 where, in the absence of price regulation, $p_1 > p_2$, i.e. where the entrant underbids the incumbent. Since p_1 is subject to price capping, $\overline{p}$ may prohibit the underbidding by the entrant. Case 2 offers a good example where p_2 may switch from

(i) $p(q_2 + r(q_2)) - \epsilon$: underbidding by the entrant in the absence of price regulation (proposition 2)

to

(ii) $p(q_1 + q_2)$: overbidding by the entrant in the presence of price-cap regulation (proposition 11).

10.4.2 The Influence of Price Regulation on the Entrant's Capacity Choice (Subgames II)

Proposition 12

Given $q_1 \leq 1/3$, price regulation has no influence on q_2.

Proposition 13A

For $q_1 > 1/3$ and $(m + i) \leq 1/6$, we have four possible cases:

(i) $\overline{p} \geq 1/3$ has no influence on q_2. The capacity q_2 is chosen as in propositions 6 and 7, $q_2 = \min[q_1 - \epsilon; 1/2 - (m + i)]$.

(ii) If $1/3 > \overline{p} \geq p\{1/2 - (m + i) + r[1/2 - (m + i)]\}$, then

$$q_2 = \begin{cases} [1 - q_1 - (m + i)]/2 & \text{if } q_1 \leq \overline{q}_1 \\ (1 - \overline{p})/2 + (1/2)\sqrt{\cdot} - \epsilon & \text{if } \overline{q}_1 < q_1 \leq 1 - 2\overline{p} \\ \min[q_1 - \epsilon; 1/2 - (m + i)] & \text{if } q_1 > 1 - 2\overline{p}, \end{cases}$$

where $\sqrt{\cdot} := \sqrt{(1 - \overline{p})^2 - (1 - q_1)^2 (q_1/\overline{p})}$

and $\overline{q}_1 := 1 - \overline{p}/2 - \sqrt{\overline{p}[1 - (3/4)\overline{p}]}$.

(iii) If $p\{1/2 - (m + i) + r[1/2 - (m + i)]\} > \overline{p} > (m + i)$, then

$$q_2 = \begin{cases} [1 - q_1 - (m + i)]/2 & \text{if } q_1 \leq \overline{q}_1 \\ (1 - \overline{p})/2 + (1/2)\sqrt{\cdot} - \epsilon & \text{if } \overline{q}_1 < q_1 \leq 1 - 2\overline{p} \\ 1 - 2\overline{p} & \text{if } q_1 > 1 - 2\overline{p}. \end{cases}$$

(iv) If $\bar{p} \leq (m+i)$, then $q_2 = \max\{[1 - q_1 - (m+i)]/2; 0\}$.

Proposition 13B
For $q_1 > 1/3$ and $1/6 < (m+i) \leq 1/2$, we have three possible cases:

(i) $\bar{p} \geq p\{1/2 - (m+i) + r[1/2 - (m+i)]\}$ has no influence on q_2. The capacity q_2 is chosen as in propositions 6 and 7.

(ii) If $(m+i) < \bar{p} < p\{1/2 - (m+i) + r[1/2 - (m+i)]\}$, then

$$q_2 = \begin{cases} [1 - q_1 - (m+i)]/2 & \text{if } q_1 \leq \bar{\bar{q}}_1 \\ 1 - 2\bar{p} & \text{if } q_1 > \bar{\bar{q}}_1 \end{cases}$$

where $\bar{\bar{q}}_1 = [1-(m+i)]-2\sqrt{(\bar{p}-(m+i))(1-2\bar{p})}$, $\bar{\bar{q}}_1 > \hat{q}_1$.

(iii) If $\bar{p} \leq (m+i)$, then $q_2 = \max\{[1 - q_1 - (m+i)]/2; 0\}$.

Proposition 13C
If $q_1 > 1/3$ and $(m+i) > 1/2$, price regulation has no influence on q_2.

Economic Interpretation of Propositions 12–13
Any binding price constraint has an influence on the sets O, U, and C and on the best element of the respective sets. The set U is reduced if the price constraint is binding because the incumbent may not be allowed to set a price such that it is best for the entrant to respond with a lower price. This is illustrated in Figure 9.

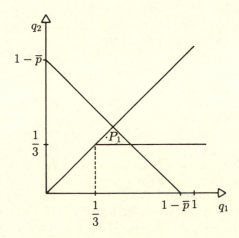

Figure 9

The strategy q_2, which corresponds to point P_1, is a U strategy if there is no price constraint. Now let us introduce a binding price constraint, as illustrated by the straight line $1 - \overline{p}$. All points to the left of $1 - \overline{p}$ are characterized by $q_1 + q_2 < 1 - \overline{p}$ and therefore $p(q_1 + q_2) > \overline{p}$: the highest possible incumbent's price $\overline{p}$ is lower than the market-clearing price $p(q_1 + q_2)$ and we already know that, in this case, the entrant responds with $p_2 > p_1 = \overline{p}$. Hence the strategy q_2 at point P_1 has become an O strategy.

For similar arguments, the set C is reduced if a binding price constraint is imposed. Since O, U, and C constitute a partition, O increases if the incumbent faces a binding price constraint.

Any O or C strategy implies that the incumbent sells an output equal to the capacity. If $q_2 = [1 - q_1 - (m + i)]/2$ is contained in either O or C, it is always the best element of the union of the two sets. Consequently, the entrant's capacity choice remains unchanged if a C strategy was his best response in the game without a price constraint. Therefore, the entrant's response in the high-cost case $(m + i) \geq 1/2$ can once again be seen in Figure 8c. In the same way, in the lower-cost cases we can apply Figures 8a and 8b up to $q_1 = 1/3$ and $q_1 = \hat{q}_1$, respectively.

If q_1 is greater than $1/3$ and $\hat{q}_1$, respectively, a binding price constraint influences the entrant's U capacity choice. The binding price constraint lowers the price set by the incumbent, as well as the price set by the entrant, because a U strategy now implies that $p_2 < \overline{p}$. Accordingly, the lower $\overline{p}$, the higher the entrant's best U capacity q_2. Since the incumbent can no longer set the price $p_1 = p\{1/2 - (m+i) + r[1/2 - (m+i)]\}$, the optimal capacity is determined by $p(q_2 + r(q_2)) = \overline{p}$, which is $q_2 = 1 - 2\overline{p}$. The entrant's profit, which can be achieved by the best U strategy, decreases because of the price reduction $p_2 < \overline{p}$. On the other hand, the set O increases; in particular, $q_2 = [1 - q_1 - (m + i)]/2$ is the profit-maximizing O strategy for larger values of q_1 than in the absence of price regulation.

Hence the capacity choice of the entrant changes in the following way: the O interval, where he sets $q_2 = [1 - q_1 - (m+i)]/2$, increases; and in the U interval he sets capacity higher than in the absence of the price constraint. Of course, a U strategy can never be optimal if the maximal price the incumbent can set is lower than the entrant's per-unit capacity costs.

Let us finally deal with the incumbent's capacity choice in the game with price regulation. As in propositions 8–10, we shall have to distinguish three different cases depending on the maintenance and installation costs.

10.4.3   The Regulated Incumbent's Capacity Decision

Proposition 14

(i) If $(m+i) \leq 1/6$, then

$$q_1 = \begin{cases} 1/3 & \text{if } \bar{p} > 1/3 \\ \bar{q}_1 & \text{if } (m+i) < \bar{p} \leq 1/3 \\ 1-\bar{p} & \text{if } m < \bar{p} \leq (m+i) \\ 0 & \text{if } \bar{p} \leq m. \end{cases}$$

(ii) If $1/6 < (m+i) < 1/2$, then

$$q_1 = \begin{cases} \hat{q}_1 & \text{if } \bar{p} \geq p\{1/2 - (m+i) + r[1/2 - (m+i)]\} \\ \bar{\bar{q}}_1 & \text{if } (m+i) < \bar{p} < p\{1/2 - (m+i) + r[1/2 - (m+i)]\} \\ 1-\bar{p} & \text{if } m < \bar{p} \leq (m+i) \\ 0 & \text{if } \bar{p} \leq m. \end{cases}$$

(iii) If $(m+i) \geq 1/2$, then

$$q_1 = \begin{cases} \max\{(1-\bar{p}); (1-m)/2; [1-(m+i)]\} & \text{if } \bar{p} > m \\ 0 & \text{if } \bar{p} \leq m. \end{cases}$$

Economic Interpretation of Proposition 14
In the high-cost case, $(m+i) \geq 1/2$, the binding price constraint plays the same role as in a monopolistic situation. The incumbent always deters entry, as he did in the situation without price regulation.

Let us now turn to the medium- and low-cost cases. If a binding price $\bar{p}$ is reduced, then the *incumbent* increases his capacity and, subsequently, his output. The reason for this is twofold: first, a lower price gives an incentive to sell a higher quantity; second, since the interval of the entrant's O strategies increases, selling such a higher quantity is feasible. Trivially, the incumbent leaves the market if the regulated price does not cover the capacity maintenance costs per unit of capacity.

Market entry occurs at the equilibrium as long as the price $\bar{p} > (m+i)$. Hence entry deterrence at low and medium costs is

caused by the regulator and not by the incumbent. At an equilibrium, in the presence of market entry, the lower the regulated
price, the lower the capacity and output of the entrant. This implies a reduction of the entrant's market share because aggregate
capacity and output increase if $\bar{p}$ decreases.

However, in two exceptional cases it is possible that a binding price constraint has no influence on the incumbent's capacity
choice. We call this phenomenon the *capacity trap*. The two exceptional cases occur over the following intervals:

(i) in the low-cost case, over the interval $\{p[2/3 - (m + i)/2];$
     $p(2/3)\}$;
(ii) in the medium-cost case, over the interval $\langle p\{\hat{q}_1 + [1 - \hat{q}_1 - (m + i)]/2\}; p\{1/2 - (m + i) + r[1/2 - (m + i)]\}\rangle$.

In these cases, the price constraint has no influence on the response
of the entrant because, without a price constraint, any best U
strategy in the U interval leads to an equilibrium price $p_1 < \bar{p}$.
With respect to the O interval, the price constraint is binding.
The incumbent chooses the O strategy with the highest capacity
q_1 because this leads to a higher profit than any capacity in the
U interval where the incumbent would sell a lower output at a
lower price. Hence the incumbent chooses a point where the price
constraint is binding. A change of $\bar{p}$ in the respective intervals will
not lead to any change in the incumbent's capacity choice.

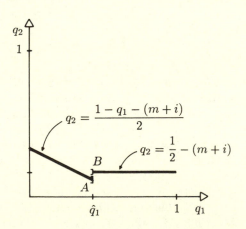

Figure 10 $(1/6 < m + i < 1/2)$

'Capacity trap':
$p_1(A) \geq \bar{p} \geq p_1(B)$, where $p_1(A) = p\{\hat{q}_1 + [1 - \hat{q}_1 - (m + i)]/2\}$,
$p_1(B) = p\{1/2 - (m + i) + r[1/2 - (m + i)]\}$, $p_1(A) > p_1(B)$.

For the convenience of the reader, I would like to add the following plausible explanation of the 'capacity trap'. We consider the medium-cost case where in the absence of price regulation the entrant's capacity choice is discontinuous, as illustrated in Figure 10 above. Up to capacity $\hat{q}_1$, the two agents set the market-clearing price and sell output equal to their capacity. If the incumbent chooses a capacity in excess of $\hat{q}_1$, at the induced equilibrium he is underbid and does not utilize his full capacity. The incumbent's equilibrium price, as induced by the capacity decisions, is monotonically falling in capacity q_1. In particular, the incumbent's price in A is higher than in B, $p_1(A) > p_1(B)$. Hence there exist price constraints which are binding in A but not in B. If they are not binding in B, they have no influence on the entrant's response in B. For the incumbent it is optimal to choose the maximum capacity he can fully utilize, i.e. $\hat{q}_1$. Therefore, he will choose this capacity for all price constraints which are binding in A but not in B. This is the interval of price constraints which fall into the 'capacity trap'.

Before concluding this subsection, let me mention another interesting result of the model. We observe that the entrant sets a higher price than the incumbent if the price constraint is binding and market entry occurred. As we have seen in the corollary to proposition 11, the price $\bar{p}$ is lower than the price at which the aggregate capacity can be sold, $p(q_1 + q_2)$. Consequently, the incumbent chooses $p_1 = \bar{p}$ and the entrant sells at the higher price $p_2 = p(q_1 + q_2)$. This is a good description of economic reality. The phenomenon cannot adequately be modelled in a Cournot or Bertrand framework without capacity choices.

10.5 Conclusion

In this chapter we have dealt with a privatized firm facing potential market entry. The firm has inherited excess capacity from its public past. Hence, in contrast to all other market entry models, the incumbent will not build up capacity, but rather will reduce it. Consequently, we have a game with asymmetric costs. The incumbent has zero capacity installation costs since we assume that capacity reduction is costless. The entrant, on the other hand, must install new capacity and, therefore, incurs positive capacity installation costs.

We consider the subgame-perfect equilibria in a four-stage game. The incumbent and the entrant decide first on capacities and subsequently on prices. In both cases the incumbent moves first. The game we analyze is one with perfect foresight; therefore the strategic setting and the demand, supply, and cost functions are common knowledge.

We are particularly interested in the influence on entry which is caused by price regulation of the incumbent. As a first step in such an analysis we consider the pure market entry game in the absence of a price constraint. The results of this game are different for high-, medium-, and low-capacity costs of the entrant. In the case in which the entrant faces high-capacity costs the incumbent is able to deter market entry. In cases in which the entrant faces medium- and low-capacity costs, market entry always occurs because a high-capacity incumbent faces an entrant who is able to set a capacity which induces the incumbent to set a higher price than the entrant. Consequently the entrant enjoys a positive profit and the incumbent faces a lower profit the higher his capacity.

We do not know of any other recent paper in which these results have been derived. Kreps and Scheinkman (1983) implicitly proposed that there is almost no difference between the results of the classical Cournot-duopoly model and their model, in which capacities and prices are chosen subsequently. In their paper they consider a two-stage game with two identical firms. In the first stage both firms simultaneously build up their capacities, in the second stage both firms simultaneously set prices. By contrast, in our model the incumbent has a first-mover advantage. Therefore, one would expect that the outcome of our model should be equivalent to the outcome of the classical Stackelberg-duopoly model. However, this is not always the case. For medium- and small-capacity costs of the entrant, the results of our model differ from those of a Stackelberg duopoly with the incumbent as the leading firm. We believe that this is an important result for the theoretical literature on entry in duopolistic markets.

In the second main part of this chapter we imposed a price constraint on the incumbent. We saw that the incumbent chooses higher capacity and output the lower the binding price. Market entry can be prevented by the regulator even in the case of low- and medium-capacity costs if the incumbent has to choose a regulated price which is lower than the entrant's capacity costs per unit. Two special results of the game with price regulation deserve attention.

(i)   If the price constraint is binding and market entry occurs, the entrant sells at a higher price than the incumbent. This is an empirically realistic result which cannot be derived from Cournot- or Bertrand-duopoly models on market entry.

(ii)   A binding price constraint does not necessarily lead to an increase in capacity and output. In the case of low- and medium-capacity costs we observed particular intervals of prices where a tighter price constraint only induces a lower price of the incumbent, but leaves the supply unchanged. This 'capacity trap' does not occur in any other model on price regulation.

10.6   Appendix

Proposition 1 (low capacities – region 1 of Figure 6)
If $q_1 \leq r(q_2)$ and $q_2 \leq r(q_1)$, the equilibrium of the price-competition subgames is characterized by $p_1 = p_2 = p(q_1 + q_2)$ and $z_j = q_j, j = 1, 2$.

Proof 1
As in all the proofs of propositions 1–4, we first ask how the entrant responds to the incumbent's price. Second, we determine the incumbent's optimal price, which takes account of the entrant's response.

Let us define the following reference price: assume that both firms want to sell at the same price $p(q_1 + q_2) := 1 - (q_1 + q_2)$. According to (10.2), at this price both firms sell an output which is equal to their capacity, and market demand is covered; $z_1 = q_1, z_2 = q_2$.

Assume *first* that the incumbent chooses the reference price $p_1 = p(q_1 + q_2)$.

(i)   If the entrant sets $p_2 \leq p(q_1 + q_2)$, he faces a demand equal to $1 - p_2$, which is greater than q_2. Hence the entrant's revenue is $p_2 q_2$. Consequently, the entrant will never set a price which falls below $p(q_1 + q_2)$, where he sells $z_2 = q_2$.

(ii)   If the entrant sets a higher price than the incumbent, then he faces the residual demand $1 - q_1 - p_2 < q_2$. If there were no capacity constraint, maximum profit would be $\max_{z_2}(1 - q_1 - z_2)z_2$. Hence the entrant would like to have $z_2^* = (1 - q_1)/2$ and $p_2^* = (1 - q_1)/2$. However, in case 1 we have $q_2 \leq r(q_1) = (1 - q_1)/2$ and therefore $z_2^* \geq q_2$. The capacity constraint is $z_2 \leq q_2$ and therefore the entrant has to set $p_2 = p(q_1 + q_2)$ which induces $z_2 = q_2$.

Second, assume $p_1 < p(q_1 + q_2)$. Similar arguments as in the preceding paragraph lead to the entrant's response $p_2 = p(q_1 + q_2); z_2 = q_2$. Consequently, the incumbent will never choose $p_1 < p(q_1 + q_2)$ because, given the response of the entrant, he can guarantee himself a higher profit at $p_1 = p(q_1 + q_2)$.

Third, assume $p_1 > p(q_1 + q_2)$. Recall that the entrant would not set a higher price than p_1 if $p_1 = p(q_1 + q_2)$. Hence it is immediately clear that he will neither do so in the case where $p_1 > p(q_1 + q_2)$. Therefore we know that the entrant will set a price such that he utilizes his full capacity. There is no need to elaborate upon the specific extent of underbidding.

Let us now turn to the incumbent. What is his maximal profit? Knowing that he will be underbid, he calculates his demand according to $1 - q_2 - p_1$. If there were no capacity constraint, maximum profit would be $\max_{z_1}(1 - q_2 - z_1)z_1$. Hence the incumbent would like to have $z_1^* = (1 - q_2)/2$ and $p_1^* = (1 - q_2)/2$. However, in case 1 we have $q_1 \leq r(q_2) = (1 - q_2)/2$ and therefore $z_1^* \geq q_1$. The capacity constraint is $z_1 \leq q_1$; therefore, the incumbent prefers $p_1 = p(q_1 + q_2)$ and will never choose $p_1 > p(q_1 + q_2)$.

Proposition 2 (high-incumbent capacity – region 2 of Figure 6)
If $q_1 > r(q_2)$ and $q_2 \leq r(q_1)$, the equilibrium is characterized by $p_1 = p(q_2 + r(q_2))$, $p_2 = p(q_2 + r(q_2)) - \epsilon$, $z_1 = r(q_2)$, and $z_2 = q_2$ where $\epsilon > 0$ is small.

Proof 2
Since the entrant is in the same low-capacity position as in proposition 1, his response to any price p_1 is the same as described in proof 1. For the same reasons as in proposition 1, p_1 is never lower than $p(q_1 + q_2)$. If the incumbent sets a price $p_1 \geq p(q_1 + q_2)$, the entrant will respond with a price at which he can sell $z_2 = q_2$ because $q_2 \leq 1/2$ (see Figure 6). Hence the incumbent faces demand $1 - q_2 - p_1$. He wants to achieve maximum profit, $\max_{z_1}(1 - q_2 - z_1)z_1$, which implies $z_1^* = (1 - q_2)/2 = r(q_2)$. Since $z_1^* < q_1$, he can actually choose z_1^*. This implies $p_1 = p(q_2 + r(q_2)) > p(q_1 + q_2)$. As described in the third part of proof 1, the entrant will underbid this price. If underbidding implies setting a price which is lower than $1/2$, then the best underbidding strategy consists in setting the highest possible price, because the profit $\min(1 - p, q)p$ is monotonically increasing in p up to $p = 1/2$, regardless of the amount of capacity q. Therefore the entrant sets $p_2 = p_1 - \epsilon$ because $p(q_j + r(q_j)) = (1 - q_j)/2 \leq 1/2$.

Proposition 3 (high-entrant capacity – region 3 of Figure 6)
If $q_1 \leq r(q_2)$ and $q_2 > r(q_1)$, the equilibrium is characterized by $p_1 = \hat{p}$, $p_2 = p(q_1 + r(q_1))$, $z_1 = q_1$, and $z_2 = r(q_1)$, where $\hat{p}$ is defined as

$$\hat{p} = \frac{(1 - q_1)^2}{4z_2}, \qquad \text{where } z_2 = \min(q_2, 1 - \hat{p}). \qquad (10.9)$$

Proof 3

Consider first the case $p_1 \leq p(q_1 + q_2)$. The entrant will never underbid (see the reasoning in proofs 1 and 2). Hence $p_2 \geq p_1$, the incumbent sells $z_1 = q_1$, and the entrant faces residual demand $1 - q_1 - p_2$. Profit maximization, $\max_{z_2}(1-q_1-z_2)z_2$, leads to $z_2^* = (1-q_1)/2 = r(q_1) < q_2$. Hence the entrant chooses price $p_2 = p(q_1+r(q_1)) > p(q_1+q_2)$. Knowing this response of the entrant, the incumbent realizes that he always sells q_1 if $p_1 \leq p(q_1 + q_2)$. Therefore, he prefers the highest possible price in this range which is $p_1 = p(q_1 + q_2)$.

Consider next the case $p_1 > p(q_1 + q_2)$. The incumbent looks for the highest price he can set where the entrant is indifferent between overbidding and underbidding.

(i)   Assume first that $p_1 < p(q_1 + r(q_1))$. In this case the best overbidding strategy of the entrant leads to $z_2^* = (1 - q_1)/2$ and $p_2^* = (1 - q_1)/2 = p(q_1 + r(q_1))$. This implies a profit $\Pi_2^* = (1 - q_1)^2/4$. The best underbidding strategy of the entrant is $p_2 = p_1 - \epsilon$, which leads to $z_2 = \min(q_2, 1 - p_2)$ according to (10.2). If, starting from $p(q_1 + q_2)$, the incumbent successively increases his price, at first overbidding leads to higher entrant's profit than underbidding; after some threshold price $\hat{p}+\epsilon$, however, underbidding is more profitable. At price $\hat{p}+\epsilon$ the entrant is indifferent. $\hat{p}$ is determined by[13]

$$\frac{(1 - q_1)^2}{4} = z_2\hat{p}, \qquad \text{where } z_2 = \min(q_2, 1 - \hat{p}). \qquad (10.13)$$

The left-hand side reflects the maximum profit induced by an overbidding strategy, the right-hand side the maximum profit of an underbidding strategy as long as $p_1 < p(q_1+r(q_1))$. The threshold price $\hat{p}$ is lower than $p(q_1 + r(q_1))$. Consider first $z_2 = q_2$ and rewrite $\hat{p} = \alpha(1 - q_1)/2$ where $\alpha = (1 - q_1)/2q_2$. Since $q_2 > r(q_1) = (1 - q_1)/2$, we have $\alpha < 1$. Recall $(1 - q_1)/2 = p(q_1 + r(q_1))$. Hence $\hat{p} < p(q_1 + r(q_1))$. Consider next $z_2 = 1-\hat{p}$. In that case $\hat{p}$ is also lower than $p(q_1+r(q_1))$. This can be shown by contradiction. Assume $\hat{p} = p(q_1 + r(q_1))$ and $q_2 > 1 - \hat{p}$. It can immediately be seen that in such a case the right-hand side of equation (10.13) is greater than the left-hand side. Since $\hat{p}$ is lower than $p(q_1+r(q_1))$, so that the best overbidding strategy is constant up to this price p_1, while the profit of the best underbidding strategy increases, we furthermore have uniqueness of $\hat{p}$.

How will the incumbent set price p_1 if he anticipates the entrant's response? As long as $p_1 \leq \hat{p}$, he will be overbid and therefore he will always sell $z_1 = q_1$. Hence he will increase his price until $p_1 = \hat{p}$. On

---

[13] An underbidding entrant faces profit of $z_2p_2=z_2(p_1-\epsilon)$. Indifference is given at $\hat{p}+\epsilon$ where profit is $z_2\hat{p}$. This explains the right-hand side of (10.13).

the other hand, if $p_1 > \hat{p}$ the incumbent knows that he will be underbid. He will never choose such a price for reasons given in proof 2. Therefore the incumbent chooses $p_1 = \hat{p}$. The entrant at $\hat{p}$ will then overbid. His best overbidding leads to a price $p_2 = p(q_1 + r(q_1))$.

(ii)   Now assume that $p_1 \geq p(q_1 + r(q_1))$. Here underbidding is always the best response of the entrant and consequently the incumbent will never choose such a price.

Proposition 4 (high capacities – region 4 of Figure 6)
If $q_1 > r(q_2)$ and $q_2 > r(q_1)$, the equilibrium is characterized by either $p_1 = \hat{p}$ or $p_1 = p(q_2 + r(q_2))$.

(i) $p_1 = \hat{p}$ is chosen if $p(q_2 + r(q_2))r(q_2) \leq [(1 - q_1)^2/4q_2]q_1$. In this case $p_2 = p(q_1 + r(q_1)), z_1 = q_1$, and $z_2 = r(q_1)$.

(ii)   Otherwise $p_1 = p(q_2 + r(q_2))$ is chosen, in which case $p_2 = p_1 - \epsilon$, $z_1 = r(q_2)$, and $z_2 = q_2$.

Proof 4
Since the entrant is in the same high-capacity position as in proposition 3, his response to any price p_1 is the same as described in proof 3. Recall $\hat{p} < p(q_1 + r(q_1)) = p[(1 + q_1)/2]$. If, therefore, $q_2 \leq (1 + q_1)/2$ at price $\hat{p}$, the entrant sells q_2 at $\hat{p} = (1 - q_1)^2/4q_2$. In proof 5 we shall show that the case when $q_2 > (1 + q_1)/2$ is irrelevant[14] because the entrant will never set a capacity in this way.

The incumbent will never choose a price $p_1 < \hat{p}$. At any price between 0 and $\hat{p}$, he sells $z_1 = q_1$ because he is overbid by the entrant. Hence profit is increasing in price up to $\hat{p}$. For prices $p_1 \geq \hat{p}$ we have to distinguish two cases:

(i)   If $p(q_2 + r(q_2)) \leq \hat{p}$, then $p_1^* = \hat{p}$. A price $p_1 > \hat{p}$ is never chosen because $\hat{p}q_1 \geq p(q_2 + r(q_2))q_1 > p(q_2 + r(q_2))r(q_2)$ since $q_1 > r(q_2)$. However, $p(q_2 + r(q_2))r(q_2)$ is greater than the maximal profit which the incumbent could achieve by setting $p_1 > \hat{p}$.

(ii)   If $p(q_2 + r(q_2)) > \hat{p}$, then either $p(q_2 + r(q_2))$ or $\hat{p}$ is chosen, whichever yields the higher profit. These profits are $p(q_2 + r(q_2))r(q_2) = (1 - q_2)^2/4$ and $\hat{p}q_1 = [(1 - q_1)^2/4q_2]q_1$.

Proposition 5
If $q_1 \leq 1/3$, the subgame-perfect equilibrium of a subgame II is characterized by $q_2 = \max\{[1 - q_1 - (m + i)]/2; 0\}, z_1 = q_1, z_2 = q_2$, and $p_1 = p_2 = p(q_1 + q_2)$.

---

[14] Although it is possible to characterize the equilibria for $q_2 > (1+q_1)/2$, we skip this characterization to avoid clumsy presentation which would not lead to further insight because it does not change the results of this chapter.

Proof 5

Assume first that the entrant responds with a capacity $q_2 \le 1 - 2q_1$, hence we are in case 1 or 3 of Figure 6.[15] As shown in proofs 1 and 3, at equilibrium the incumbent utilizes all of his capacity and sells an output equal to his capacity. Hence the entrant maximizes profit, given the residual demand $(1 - q_1 - z_2)$, subject to $z_2 = q_2$ because overcapacity only induces costs without contributing to profit. $\max_{q_2}(1 - q_1 - q_2)q_2 - (m + i)q_2$ yields a first-order condition

$$q_2^* = \frac{1 - q_1 - (m + i)}{2}. \tag{10.10}$$

If q_2^* is negative, then $q_2 = 0$ is chosen. In any case $q_2 < r(q_1)$, hence the equilibrium price is $p(q_1 + q_2)$, as shown in proposition 1.

Second, assume that the entrant responds with $1 \ge q_2 > 1 - 2q_1$ (case 4 in Figure 6). We then have the following possible situations:

(i) If $q_2 \le (1 + q_1)/2$, then the U set is empty; the incumbent will always choose $\hat{p}$. The proof is as follows. As shown in proposition 4, the incumbent would choose a higher price than the entrant if this implied higher profit,[16]

$$\frac{(1 - q_1)^2}{4q_2}q_1 < \frac{(1 - q_2)^2}{4} \tag{10.14}$$

or, equivalently,

$$(1 - q_1)^2 q_1 < (1 - q_2)^2 q_2. \tag{10.15}$$

Let us now define

$$f(q) := (1 - q)^2 q. \tag{10.16}$$

This function is illustrated in Figure 11 on the overleaf page. It reaches a maximum at $q = 1/3$ and two local minima where the value of the function is zero at $q = 0$ and $q = 1$. $f(q)$ is strictly monotonically increasing over the interval $[0, 1/3]$, and over the interval $[1/3, 1]$ it is strictly monotonically decreasing. We know that $q_1 \le 1/3$ and $1/3 \le q_2 \le 1$. Hence $f(q_2)$ reaches a maximum at the lowest possible level of q_2. Since we are in case 4, this lowest level is approximately $q_2 = 1 - 2q_1$.[17] At this level, $f(q_2) \le f(q_1)$, because

$$
\begin{aligned}
f(1 - 2q_1) \le f(q_1) &\iff 4q_1^2(1 - 2q_1) \le (1 - q_1)^2 q_1 \\
&\iff 4q_1 - 8q_1^2 \le (1 - q_1)^2 \\
&\iff 0 \le 1 - 6q_1 + 9q_1^2 \\
&\iff 0 \le (1 - 3q_1)^2. \tag{10.17}
\end{aligned}
$$

---

[15] In case 1 and 3 $q_1 \le r(q_2) = (1 - q_2)/2$.

[16] $\hat{p} = (1 - q_1)/4q_2$ because $q_2 \le (1 + q_1)/2$.

[17] For purists: q_2 is infinitesimally above $1 - 2q_1$.

The incumbent therefore always chooses $\hat{p}$. Consequently the entrant realizes profits equal to $p(q_1 + r(q_1))r(q_1) - (m + i)q_2$. However, this profit is lower than $\Pi_2(q_2^*)$ where q_2^* is defined as in (10.10).[18]

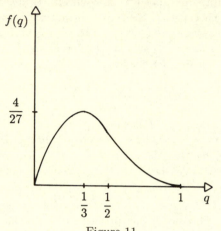

Figure 11

(ii)   The case $q_2 > (1 + q_1)/2$ never occurs. The entrant's maximum profit in this area is achieved if the incumbent sets a price $p_1 > p_2$ and therefore $\widetilde{\Pi}_2 = [p(q_2 + r(q_2)) - \epsilon]q_2 - (m + i)q_2$. It can be shown that this profit is lower than the profit which he obtains if he sets $q_2 = [1 - q_1 - (m + i)]/2$, viz.

$$\frac{[1 - q_1 - (m + i)]^2}{4} > \frac{1 - q_2}{2}q_2 - (m + i)q_2, \qquad (10.18)$$

where q_2 on the right-hand side can be replaced by $(1 + q_1)/2$ since the profit $\widetilde{\Pi}_2$ is decreasing in q_2.

Proposition 6
If $1/3 < q_1 \leq 1/2$, then

$$
q_2 = \begin{cases}
\min[q_1 - \epsilon; 1/2 - (m + i)] & \text{if } (m + i) \leq 1/6, \\
[1 - q_1 - (m + i)]/2 & \text{if } 1/6 < (m + i) < 1/2 \\
& \text{and } 1/3 < q_1 \leq \hat{q}_1, \\
1/2 - (m + i) & \text{if } 1/6 < (m + i) < 1/2 \\
& \text{and } \hat{q}_1 < q_1 < 1/2, \\
\max\{[1 - q_1 - (m + i)]/2; 0\} & \text{if } (m + i) \geq 1/2,
\end{cases}
$$

[18] Recall $q_2 > r(q_1)$.

where $\hat{q}_1 = (\sqrt{2} - 1)[1/\sqrt{2} + (m + i)]$.

Proof 6

Let us first consider the case of $(m + i) \leq 1/6$.

(i)   On the basis of proposition 4 we can calculate that any $q_2 \in (1/3, q_1 - \epsilon)$ is element of the set U. Furthermore, recall the U strategy $\mathrm{argmax}_{q_2}[p(q_2 + r(q_2))q_2 - (m+i)q_2] = 1/2 - (m+i)$. Since $(m+i) \leq 1/6$, we obtain $1/2 - (m+i) \geq 1/3$. Hence the best U strategy of the entrant is $q_2 = \min[q_1 - \epsilon; 1/2 - (m + i)]$ because he wants to set capacity as close to $1/2 - (m + i)$ as possible.

(ii)   An O or C strategy can never lead to a profit higher than $[1 - q_1 - (m+i)]^2/4$; however, the minimal profit of the best U strategy is higher than the above maximal profit of a C or an O strategy. Hence the entrant chooses the best U strategy.

Let us next consider the case of $1/6 < (m + i) < 1/2$. The upper bold line in Figure 12 illustrates the best U strategy which is given by $q_2 = \max[1 - 2q_1 + \epsilon; 1/2 - (m+i)]$. The lower bold line, $q_2 = [1 - q_1 - (m + i)]/2$, is element of C up to P_2. Note that it dominates any O strategy. Considering the intersections of the respective straight lines in Figure 12, it is easy to see that $q_1(P_1) < q_1(P_2)$, where $q_1(P_1) = 1/4 + (m+i)/2$ and $q_1(P_2) = [1 + (m + i)]/3$.

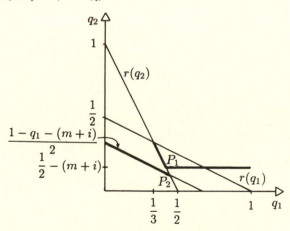

Figure 12

Let us now distinguish the following three cases:

(i) $q_1 < q_1(P_1)$. Here the entrant employs the best C strategy. This is because the maximum profit which could result from a U strategy is equal to $[1/2 - (m + i)]^2/2$. This profit, however, is lower than the minimal profit which is implied by the capacity choice $q_2 = [1 - q_1 - (m + i)]/2$, which minimal profit is achieved at $q_1 = 1/4 + (m + i)/2$.

Therefore, we have

$$\frac{[1/2 - (m+i)]^2}{2} < \frac{[1 - (\frac{1}{4} + \frac{m+i}{2}) - (m+i)]^2}{4}. \qquad (10.19)$$

(ii) $q_1 \geq q_1(P_2)$. Here the entrant sets a U capacity. The best U strategy is $q_2 = 1/2 - (m+i)$. The corresponding profit is $[1/2 - (m+i)]^2/2$, which is higher than the maximum perceivable profit which could have been achieved otherwise, namely at $q_1(P_2)$. We have

$$\frac{[1/2 - (m+i)]^2}{2} > \frac{[1 - (\frac{1+(m+i)}{3}) - (m+i)]^2}{4}. \qquad (10.20)$$

(iii) $q_1(P_1) \leq q_1 < q_1(P_2)$. In this interval $q_2 = [1 - q_1 - (m+i)]/2$ is an element of C and also $q_2 = 1/2 - (m+i)$ is an element of U. Up to $\hat{q}_1$ the best C strategy leads to a higher profit; from $\hat{q}_1$ onwards the best U strategy leads to a higher profit, where

$$\hat{q}_1 = (\sqrt{2} - 1)[1/\sqrt{2} + (m+i)]. \qquad (10.21)$$

$\hat{q}_1$ is the solution of equating the maximum profit which results from the best C and U strategies, respectively:

$$\frac{[1/2 - (m+i)]^2}{2} = \frac{[1 - q_1 - (m+i)]^2}{4}. \qquad (10.22)$$

Third, we deal with the case of $(m+i) \geq 1/2$. Here it is never optimal to set $q_2 \in U$, because any U profit $[(1-q_2)/2]q_2 - (m+i)q_2$ is positive only if $1 - 2(m+i) > 0$, which does not hold if $(m+i) \geq 1/2$. On the other hand, $q_2 = [1 - q_1 - (m+i)]/2$ is element of C and, therefore, $q_2 = \max\{[1 - q_1 - (m+i)]/2; 0\}$ is the best strategy.

Proposition 7
If $1/2 \leq q_1 \leq 1$, then $q_2 = \max[1/2 - (m+i); 0]; z_2 = q_2, z_1 = r(q_2); p_1 = p(q_2 + r(q_2)), p_2 = p_1 - \epsilon$.

Proof 7
If q_2 is an element of U, it induces an incumbent's price $p_1 = p(q_2+r(q_2))$ and an entrant's price $p_2 = p_1 - \epsilon$. In this case the entrant's profit can be approximated[19] by $p(q_2+r(q_2))q_2 - (m+i)q_2 = [(1-q_2)/2]q_2 - (m+i)q_2$. The capacity which maximizes this profit is $q_2^* = 1/2 - (m+i)$. If this quantity is negative, then $q_2 = 0$ is chosen. This capacity leads to

---

[19] We neglect ϵ.

an underbidding by the entrant as is shown in what follows. Assume that the entrant sets a capacity $q_2^* = 1/2 - (m + i)$. Now we have two possibilities:

(i)   If $0 < (m + i) < 1/4$, we have the same situation as in case 2 of Figure 6.[20] Here $q_2 \in (1/4, 1/2)$. If $q_2 \in (1/3, 1/2)$, then $f(q_2) > f(q_1)$ because $q_1 > 1/2$ (see Figure 11). If $q_2 \in (1/4, 1/3)$, then $\min_{q_2} f(q_2) = f(1/4) > f(1/2) = \max_{q_1} f(q_1)$. Hence q_2^* is a U strategy.

(ii)   If $1/4 \leq (m + i) < 1/2$, we have the same situation as in either case 2 or case 4 of Figure 6. If we are in case 2, underbidding by the entrant directly follows from proposition 2. If we are in case 4, $q_1 > 2(m + i)$ and underbidding by the entrant follows if $f(1/2 - (m + i)) > f(2(m + i))$, which can easily be shown to hold.

Next we show that an O capacity[21] cannot be optimal because it implies a lower profit than the profit which results from $q_2^* = 1/2 - (m + i)$. At q_2^* we have $\Pi_2(q_2^*) = [1/2 - (m+i)]^2/2$. The O profit, which must be compared with $\Pi_2(q_2^*)$, is always lower than $\Pi_2 = [1 - q_1 - (m+i)]^2/4$. If $q_1 > 1/2$, it can easily be shown that $\Pi_2(q_2^*)$ is higher than the O profit.

Proposition 8
If $(m + i) \leq 1/6$, then $q_1 = 1/3$. There is market entry and $q_2 = 1/3 - (m + i)/2$.

Proof 8
Consider Figure 8a. If $q_1 \leq 1/3$, then the incumbent's profit is increasing in capacity since

$$\left(1 - q_1 - \frac{1 - (m + i) - q_1}{2}\right) q_1 - m q_1 \qquad (10.23)$$

increases in q_1 up to $q_1 = (1 - m + i)/2 > 1/3$. Hence the best capacity choice in this interval is $q_1 = 1/3$.

If $q_1 > 1/3$, the incumbent's profit is decreasing in capacity q_1. It is easy to show that the profit at $q_1 = 1/3 + \epsilon$ is lower than the profit at $q_1 = 1/3$, because $q_1 = 1/3 + \epsilon$ induces the incumbent to set a price lower than the equilibrium price if $q_1 = 1/3$. At this lower price he sells less than $1/3$. Hence the incumbent sets $q_1 = 1/3$.

Proposition 9
If $1/6 < (m+i) < 1/2$, then $q_1 = \hat{q}_1$ where $\hat{q}_1 = (\sqrt{2}-1)[1/\sqrt{2}+(m+i)]$. There is market entry and $q_2 = [1 - \hat{q}_1 - (m + i)]/2$.

---

[20] Substitute $q_2 = 1/2 - (m+i)$ into $r(q_1) = (1 - q_1)/2$.
[21] As can be seen in Fig. 6, C is empty if $q_1 > 1/2$.

Proof 9

Consider Figure 8b. If $q_1 \leq \hat{q}_1$, then the incumbent's profit is increasing in capacity q_1, because $\Pi_1 = \{1 - q_1 - [1 - (m + i) - q_1]/2\}q_1 - mq_1$ monotonically increases up to $(1 - m + i)/2$ and $(1 - m + i)/2 > \hat{q}_1$. This follows from the inequality

$$(\sqrt{2} - 1)[1/\sqrt{2} + (m + i)] < (1 - m + i)/2, \qquad (10.24)$$

which is equivalent to

$$[2(m + i) - 1](\sqrt{2} - 1) < i - m. \qquad (10.25)$$

Inequality (10.24) holds because $i > m$ by assumption. Therefore, the best capacity choice in the interval $(0, \hat{q}_1]$ is $q_1 = \hat{q}_1$.

If $q_1 > \hat{q}_1$, the maximum profit which could be realized is lower than $\langle\{1 - [1/2 - (m + i)]\}/2\rangle\hat{q}_1 - m\hat{q}_1$. However, this profit is lower than the profit which would be earned at $q_1 = \hat{q}_1$,

$$\frac{1 - \hat{q}_1 + (m + i)}{2}\hat{q}_1 - m\hat{q}_1 > \frac{1 - [1/2 - (m + i)]}{2}\hat{q}_1 - m\hat{q}_1, \qquad (10.26)$$

which is equivalent to

$$1/2 > \hat{q}_1. \qquad (10.27)$$

Therefore $q_1 > \hat{q}_1$ is never chosen by the incumbent.

Proposition 10

If $(m + i) \geq 1/2$, then $q_1 = \max[(1 - m)/2; 1 - (m + i)]$. There is no market entry.

Proof 10

The lowest capacity q_1 which deters entry is given by $q_1 = 1 - (m + i)$, as illustrated in Figure 8c. Given the reaction function of the potential entrant, it can be shown that the incumbent's profit is increasing in capacity q_1 up to $q_1 = 1 - (m + i)$. This follows from the following optimization problem (recall $i > m$):

$$\max_{q_1} \left(1 - q_1 - \frac{1 - (m + i) - q_1}{2}\right) q_1 - mq_1. \qquad (10.28)$$

Hence the incumbent never chooses a capacity lower than $q_1 = 1 - (m + i)$. Since he is a monopolist, he chooses the monopoly capacity $(1 - m)/2$, if this capacity exceeds $1 - (m + i)$. This is the case if $(m + i) > (1 + m)/2$, which holds for a high i and a low m. Otherwise, he chooses the minimum entry-deterring capacity, $1 - (m + i)$.

Proposition 11
Case 1:
If $q_1 \leq r(q_2)$ and $q_2 \leq r(q_1)$, then $p_1 = \min[\overline{p}; p(q_1+q_2)]$, $p_2 = p(q_1+q_2)$.

Case 2:
If $q_1 > r(q_2)$ and $q_2 \leq r(q_1)$, then $p_1 = \min[\overline{p}; p(q_2 + r(q_2))]$, $p_2 = \max[p_1 - \epsilon; p(q_1 + q_2)]$.

Case 3:
If $q_1 \leq r(q_2)$ and $q_2 > r(q_1)$, then $p_1 = \min(\overline{p}; \hat{p})$, $p_2 = p(q_1 + r(q_1))$.

Case 4:
If $q_1 > r(q_2)$ and $q_2 > r(q_1)$, then

(i) $p_1 = \min[\overline{p}; p(q_2 + r(q_2))], p_2 = p_1 - \epsilon$, for $\hat{p}q_1 < (1 - q_2 - p_1)p_1$
     and $\hat{p} < \overline{p}$;
(ii) $p_1 = \min(\overline{p}; \hat{p})$, $p_2 = p(q_1 + r(q_1))$ otherwise.

Proof 11
This follows directly from the analysis of propositions 1–4.

Proposition 12
Given $q_1 \leq 1/3$, price regulation has no influence on q_2.

Proof 12
The best strategies which are elements of O or C are not influenced by price regulation, because $q_2 = [1 - q_1 - (m+i)]/2$ lies in area 1 of Figure 6 and we know from proposition 11, case 1, that the profit of the entrant is independent of the price constraint. From proposition 5 we know that U is an empty set for $q_1 \leq 1/3$.

Proposition 13A
For $q_1 > 1/3$ and $(m + i) \leq 1/6$, we have four possible cases:

(i) $\overline{p} \geq 1/3$ has no influence on q_2. The capacity q_2 is chosen as in propositions 6 and 7, $q_2 = \min[q_1 - \epsilon; 1/2 - (m + i)]$.

(ii) If $1/3 > \overline{p} \geq p\{1/2 - (m + i) + r[1/2 - (m + i)]\}$, then

$$q_2 = \begin{cases} [1 - q_1 - (m + i)]/2 & \text{if } q_1 \leq \overline{q}_1 \\ (1 - \overline{p})/2 + (1/2)\sqrt{\cdot} - \epsilon & \text{if } \overline{q}_1 < q_1 \leq 1 - 2\overline{p} \\ \min[q_1 - \epsilon; 1/2 - (m + i)] & \text{if } q_1 > 1 - 2\overline{p}, \end{cases}$$

where $\sqrt{\cdot} := \sqrt{(1 - \overline{p})^2 - (1 - q_1)^2(q_1/\overline{p})}$

and $\overline{q}_1 := 1 - \overline{p}/2 - \sqrt{\overline{p}[1 - (3/4)\overline{p}]}$.

(iii)   If $p\{1/2 - (m + i) + r[1/2 - (m + i)]\} > \bar{p} > (m + i)$, then

$$q_2 = \begin{cases} [1 - q_1 - (m + i)]/2 & \text{if } q_1 \leq \bar{q}_1 \\ (1 - \bar{p})/2 + (1/2)\sqrt{\cdot} - \epsilon & \text{if } \bar{q}_1 < q_1 \leq 1 - 2\bar{p} \\ 1 - 2\bar{p} & \text{if } q_1 > 1 - 2\bar{p}, \end{cases}$$

(iv)   If $\bar{p} \leq (m + i)$, then $q_2 = \max\{[1 - q_1 - (m + i)]/2; 0\}$.

Proof 13A
(i)   The best U strategy is not affected; hence the arguments of propositions 6 and 7 can be applied directly.
(ii) and (iii)   If $q_1 \leq 1 - 2\bar{p}$, a strategy $q_2 \geq 1 - 2\bar{p}$ cannot be an element of U because $f(q_2) \leq f(q_1)$. Hence an overbidden incumbent sets price $p_1 = \bar{p}$ because $q_2 \leq 1 - 2\bar{p}$. (Note that $p(q_2 + r(q_2)) \leq \bar{p}$.)
Next, we determine the capacity q_2 which would give the incumbent the highest incentive to choose $p_1 > p_2$. This occurs if

$$\frac{(1 - q_1)^2}{4q_2}q_1 < \bar{p}(1 - \bar{p} - q_2), \tag{10.29}$$

which is equivalent to

$$(1 - q_1)^2 q_1 < 4\bar{p}q_2(1 - \bar{p} - q_2). \tag{10.30}$$

The right-hand side reaches a maximum if $q_2 = (1 - \bar{p})/2$. This is the capacity q_2 which gives the highest incentive to set $p_1 > p_2$. Hence there exists no $q_2 \in U$ up to $\bar{q}_1 = 1 - \bar{p}/2 - \sqrt{\bar{p}[1 - (3/4)\bar{p}]}$, where $\bar{q}_1$ is determined by the equation[22]

$$(1 - q_1)^2 q_1 = (1 - \bar{p})^2 \bar{p}. \tag{10.31}$$

Hence the entrant chooses $q_2 = [1 - q_1 - (m + i)]/2$ which is the best element of C or O.
If $q_1 > \bar{q}_1$, then the best U strategy is the largest value of q_2 which fulfills inequality (10.30), namely

$$q_2 = (1 - \bar{p})/2 + (1/2)\sqrt{(1 - \bar{p})^2 - (1 - q_1)^2(q_1/\bar{p})} - \epsilon. \tag{10.32}$$

It is easy to show that this U strategy leads to a higher profit than any O or C strategy.

[22] The right-side of (10.31) results from substituting $q_2 = (1 - \bar{p})/2$ into the right-side of (10.30).

Finally, if $q_1 > 1 - 2\bar{p}$, then we have to distinguish between (ii) and (iii):

(ii) if $\bar{p} \geq p\{1/2 - (m+i) + r[1/2 - (m+i)]\}$, then it is feasible and optimal to choose the best U strategy which would have been chosen if there had been no price regulation.

(iii) If $(m+i) < \bar{p} < p\{1/2 - (m+i) + r[1/2 - (m+i)]\}$, then $q_2 = 1 - 2\bar{p}$ is the best U strategy. Since the incumbent can no longer set the price $p_1 = p\{1/2 - (m+i) + r[1/2 - (m+i)]\}$, the optimal capacity is determined by $p(q_2 + r(q_2)) = \bar{p}$, which is $q_2 = 1 - 2\bar{p}$. If the entrant chooses a U capacity which is smaller than $1 - 2\bar{p}$, then the incumbent sets $p_1 = \bar{p}$. The entrant's profit is reduced because he sells less at the same price $\bar{p} - \epsilon$. If, on the other hand, the entrant chooses a U capacity which is greater than $1 - 2\bar{p}$, then the price constraint is not binding and the entrant's profit is reduced because $1 - 2\bar{p} > 1/2 - (m+i)$. It is easy to show that the U strategy $q_2 = 1 - 2\bar{p}$ leads to a higher profit than any O or C strategy.

(iv) Obvious.

Proposition 13B

For $q_1 > 1/3$ and $1/6 < (m+i) \leq 1/2$, we have three possible cases:

(i) $\bar{p} \geq p\{1/2 - (m+i) + r[1/2 - (m+i)]\}$ has no influence on q_2. The capacity q_2 is chosen as in propositions 6 and 7.

(ii) If $(m+i) < \bar{p} < p\{1/2 - (m+i) + r[1/2 - (m+i)]\}$, then

$$q_2 = \begin{cases} [1 - q_1 - (m+i)]/2 & \text{if } q_1 \leq \bar{\bar{q}}_1 \\ 1 - 2\bar{p} & \text{if } q_1 > \bar{\bar{q}}_1 \end{cases}$$

where $\bar{\bar{q}}_1 = [1 - (m+i)] - 2\sqrt{[\bar{p} - (m+i)](1 - 2\bar{p})}$, $\bar{\bar{q}}_1 > \hat{q}_1$.

(iii) If $\bar{p} \leq (m+i)$, then $q_2 = \max\{[1 - q_1 - (m+i)]/2; 0\}$.

Proof 13B

(i) As argued in proof 12, the strategy of the entrant does not change if, in the absence of a price constraint, the best strategy is an element of O or C, i.e. $p_1 \leq p_2$. Hence, up to $\hat{q}_1$ nothing changes. If $\bar{p} > p\{[1/2 - (m+i)] + r[1/2 - (m+i)]\}$, then for $q_1 > \hat{q}_1$ the best U strategy does not change. The best U strategy is optimal; see proposition 6, in particular equation (10.22).

(ii) If $q_2 = [1 - q_1 - (m+i)]/2$ is an element of C or O, then it is the best strategy contained in these sets.
Consider next the set U: $q_2 = 1 - 2\bar{p}$ is the best capacity, if it is an element of this set. Since the incumbent can no longer set the price

$p_1 = p\{1/2-(m+i)+r[1/2-(m+i)]\}$, the optimal capacity is determined by $p(q_2 + r(q_2)) = \bar{p}$, which is $q_2 = 1 - 2\bar{p}$. If the entrant chooses a U capacity which is smaller than $1 - 2\bar{p}$, then the incumbent sets $p_1 = \bar{p}$. The entrant's profit is reduced because he sells less at the same price $\bar{p}-\epsilon$. If, on the other hand, the entrant chooses a capacity which induces $p_1 > p_2$ and is greater than $1-2\bar{p}$, then the price constraint is not binding and the entrant's profit is reduced because $1 - 2\bar{p} > 1/2 - (m + i)$.

Over the interval $(0, \bar{\bar{q}}_1]$,

$$\frac{[1 - q_1 - (m + i)]^2}{4} \geq [\bar{p} - (m + i)](1 - 2\bar{p}) \qquad (10.33)$$

and $q_2 = [1 - q_1 - (m + i)]/2$ is element of C or O.[23]
For $q_1 > \bar{\bar{q}}_1$,

$$\frac{[1 - q_1 - (m + i)]^2}{4} < [\bar{p} - (m + i)](1 - 2\bar{p}) \qquad (10.34)$$

in which case $q_2 = 1-2\bar{p}$ is an element of U, because $(\bar{\bar{q}}_1+1-2\bar{p}) > 1-\bar{p}$.

(iii)   If $\bar{p} \leq (m+i)$, it is obvious that the entrant will never choose a U strategy because he could only choose a price which would not cover his costs. Hence the best capacity choice is $\max\{[1 - q_1 - (m+i)]/2; 0\}$. If the entrant chooses this capacity his response to any price $p_1 \in [0, \bar{p}]$ will be $p_2 = p(q_1 + q_2)$. Consequently, the best capacity is not element of the set U because $\bar{p} < p(q_1 + q_2)$.

Proposition 13C
If $q_1 > 1/3$ and $(m + i) > 1/2$, price regulation has no influence on q_2.

Proof 13C
Obvious.

Proposition 14
(i) If $(m + i) \leq 1/6$, then

$$q_1 = \begin{cases} 1/3 & \text{if } \bar{p} > 1/3 \\ \bar{q}_1 & \text{if } (m + i) < \bar{p} \leq 1/3 \\ 1 - \bar{p} & \text{if } m < \bar{p} \leq (m + i) \\ 0 & \text{if } \bar{p} \leq m. \end{cases}$$

---

[23] $\bar{p} < p(q_1+q_2)$ if $q_1 \leq \bar{\bar{q}}_1$ and $q_2 = [1-q_1-(m+i)]/2$.

(ii) If $1/6 < (m + i) < 1/2$, then

$$q_1 = \begin{cases} \hat{q}_1 & \text{if } \bar{p} \geq p\{1/2 - (m + i) + r[1/2 - (m + i)]\} \\ \bar{\bar{q}}_1 & \text{if } (m + i) < \bar{p} < p\{1/2 - (m + i) + r[1/2 - (m + i)]\} \\ 1 - \bar{p} & \text{if } m < \bar{p} \leq (m + i) \\ 0 & \text{if } \bar{p} \leq m. \end{cases}$$

(iii) If $(m + i) \geq 1/2$, then

$$q_1 = \begin{cases} \max\{(1 - \bar{p}); (1 - m)/2; [1 - (m + i)]\} & \text{if } \bar{p} > m \\ 0 & \text{if } \bar{p} \leq m. \end{cases}$$

Proof 14

(i) If $\bar{p} > p\{1/3 + [1 - (m + i) - 1/3]/2\}$, the price constraint is not binding in equilibrium and proposition 8 holds as is. If $1/3 < \bar{p} \leq p\{1/3 + [1 - (m + i) - 1/3]/2\}$, then $\bar{p}$ is binding for $q_1 \leq 1/3$; however, since the incumbent's profit increases until $q_1 = 1/3$, this capacity is chosen. The profit at $q_1 = 1/3$ is greater than the profit for any $q_1 > 1/3$.

(ii) If $\bar{p} \geq p\{1/2 - (m+i) + r[1/2 - (m+i)]\}$, then the price constraint is not binding and proposition 9 holds unchanged. If, however, $(m+i) < \bar{p} < p\{1/2 - (m+i) + r[1/2 - (m+i)]\}$, then $q_2 = [1 - q_1 - (m+i)]/2$ up to $\bar{\bar{q}}_1$. Since $p\{\bar{\bar{q}}_1 + [1 - \bar{\bar{q}}_1 - (m + i)]/2\} > \bar{p}$, the incumbent's profit is $\bar{p}q_1 - mq_1$ which is increasing in q_1 up to $\bar{\bar{q}}_1$. Obviously the incumbent's profit is lower if he chooses a capacity higher than $\bar{\bar{q}}_1$ because the entrant chooses a U strategy. This forces the incumbent to set $p_1 = \bar{p}$, at which price he sells an output lower than $\bar{\bar{q}}_1$. The rest of the proof is trivial.

(iii) If $\bar{p} \geq \min\{p[(1 - m)/2]; p[1 - (m + i)]\}$, then proposition 10 holds and $q_1 = \max\{(1 - m)/2; [1 - (m + i)]\}$. Otherwise $\bar{p}$ is binding and it is optimal to choose capacity $1 - \bar{p}$, which is greater than both $(1 - m)/2$ and $1 - (m + i)$.

Part Three
Normative Theory

11 What is Normative Theory?

A *'normative' theory of privatization* shows the composition of private and public ownership which maximizes welfare in an economy. Consequently, the respective rules on privatization can be justified by some higher-order value judgments as formally expressed by social welfare functions. It should be noted that the results of normative theory have empirical content: in principle they are empirically applicable.

If privatization is performed by selling shares, any mix of public and private ownership is possible which is desirable for the achievement of the government's objectives. There is no necessity for a 0–1 decision between a totally public and a totally private firm, but a continuum of ownership relations is possible (*partial privatization*). In this case the board of the privatized firm consists of both representatives of the government and of the private shareholders. The government's influence on the board can, for instance, be set so as to obtain an optimal mix between monopolistic prices and higher efficiency. In the case of partial privatization the government applies a sort of *regulation from within the enterprise* instead of the usual regulation from outside the enterprise. There are many empirical examples of partial privatization, but often the government has not fully been aware of how to use its influence as a shareholder as a sort of regulation from within the enterprise. Many of those partially privatized firms are run like private profit maximizers, and government representatives on the board do not try to change that. In this book we argue that the government should fully exert its influence on the board. Partial privatization then turns out to be the main instrument to cope with the trade-off between efficiency gains and monopoly pricing.

The preceding paragraphs make clear that this part of the book deals with a *normative approach to privatization*. We look for the degree of privatization the government should choose which is welfare-optimal, given a board of the firm where government representatives plead for welfare and representatives of the private owners plead for profit. As an instrument to maximize welfare, the government applies the composition of the board of the firm, where profit-oriented members are necessary to increase efficiency and welfare-oriented members are necessary to keep price increases low.

When deciding on the optimum degree of privatization, the government has not only to anticipate how the board of the firm will set prices given a particular degree of privatization: it is also expected to consider all feedbacks from privatization on individual incomes and on the government budget. A consumer who earns high dividend incomes from his shares in the privatized firm may be willing to accept the higher prices of that firm because these prices are the basis of the high profit of the firm which, in turn, leads to the high dividend incomes. Moreover, it is not only the consumers who earn from privatization. In the case of partial privatization, the government is a shareholder too and therefore entitled to receive dividends. And, of course, the government earns money by selling shares to the consumers. Government revenues from privatization could be spent on public expenditures, used for a reduction of the public debt, or used to reduce the overall tax pressure in the economy.

The normative theory model presented below emerges from the Boiteux tradition of public enterprise economics.[1] However, I introduce shifts in ownership from the public to the private sector. Shifting ownership changes the production possibilities of the privatized firm and changes the objective of the firm from welfare to profit maximization. The government earns dividend income from the shares it still owns as well as receiving revenue from selling the shares and from taxing the dividend incomes of the private shareholders of the privatized firm. Fortunately, in our model the government budget constraint is always fulfilled by Walras's law because all markets clear. This makes it possible to investigate in a fairly general way all the far-reaching feedbacks of privatization mentioned in the preceding paragraph.

This introduction to the normative theory of privatization is a good place to briefly elucidate the historical development of what I call the 'models of the Boiteux tradition'.[2] There have been substantial conceptual changes in these models over time. The general equilibrium model of Arrow and Debreu (1954) concentrates on the decentralization of a Pareto-optimal allocation in a fully competitive economy without government intervention. All prices and incomes of the economic agents are endogenous. Among the many restrictive assumptions which are needed to prove the existence of a Pareto-optimal equilibrium is one which often fails to hold in the

---

[1] See Boiteux (1956, 1971), Drèze (1964, 1984), Drèze and Marchand (1976), Hagen (1979), Marchand, Pestieau, and Weymark (1982), Bös (1985, 1986a), and Sheshinski (1986).

[2] The following 3 pages are based on an unpublished paper by W. Peters and myself.

public sector: the assumption of non-increasing returns to scale. As is well known, this is closely related to the assumption of a competitive economy, i.e. that exploitation of increasing returns leads to monopolistic market structures. In those cases, Boiteux (1956, 1971) suggests that a decentralization by markets is impossible and government regulation is encouraged.

In his model the private firms only operate in that part of the economy where a competitive environment exists. These private firms are price-takers which produce under non-increasing returns to scale. The rest of the economy consists of one or more public enterprises. They are price-setting firms. They do not maximize profits, but are subject to exogenously given budget constraints.[3] The introduction of these constraints makes this a second-best model. Moreover, it signals the decisive point of departure from Arrow–Debreu. In their model all economic variables are endogenously determined (with the sole exception of the consumers' initial endowments). In the Boiteux model the public sector deficit (or profit) is exogenously fixed and the economy adjusts to that exogenous determination.

Boiteux is not primarily interested in the existence of equilibria in his model:[4] rather, he wants to determine the optimal inputs and outputs in the public sector and to design prices which optimize the planner's objective function and allow the decentralization of decisions in the private sector. To achieve the optimal quantities and prices, the planner can also set the consumer's nonlabor incomes by choosing an appropriate lump-sum redistribution. It is only this redistribution which leads to prices of the Ramsey type.[5]

The Boiteux model is a planning model. The decentralization of the economy is not its main intention: rather, a central planner sets all prices in the economy, buys and sells all outputs and inputs in order to achieve market-clearing, and chooses an optimal lump-sum redistribution to guarantee the feasibility of the chosen prices and quantities. The spirit of the French economic planning seems

---

[3] Alternatively, the case of a single budgetary condition for the entire nationalized sector is treated in Boiteux (1956, 1971).

[4] This question recently has been addressed in some interesting papers which deal with the existence of marginal-cost pricing equilibria and of equilibria in the presence of Ramsey prices. See for instance Beato (1982), Cornet (1982), and Bonnisseau and Cornet (1987) on the marginal-cost pricing problem, and Dierker, Guesnerie, and Neuefeind (1985) and Bonnisseau (1987) on general pricing rules which include Ramsey pricing.

[5] See Bös (1986a: 102–5, 187).

to be present in the Boiteux model, which comes as no surprise for a model stemming from the mid-1950s.

The Boiteux model is not a general equilibrium model of the Arrow–Debreu type, since the public sector budget is exogenously fixed. On the other hand, it is an equilibrium model because the planner sets his instruments in such a way that all markets are in equilibrium.

The French economic planning model is not appropriate for the economies of the eighties and the nineties. Hence some of the basic assumptions of the Boiteux model have to be relinquished. In this book, we do not consider a central planner, but rather the board of a public or privatized firm. This board will not be able to set all prices in the economy. Hence, we have to follow Hagen (1979), who assumed that the public sector sets only a sub-set of prices. The other prices are exogenously determined by the monopolistic private firms. Moreover, the board of a firm will not be able to redistribute all incomes by lump-sum transfers and taxes. Accordingly, Bös (1986a: 93–103; 212–24) assumes that non-labor incomes are exogenously given. However, both Hagen and Bös re-tain the far-reaching Boiteux assumption that the public sector sets outputs and inputs in order to guarantee market-clearing in each and any market of the economy.[6]

The model, which is presented in this part of the book, is articulated in the Hagen–Bös way. Some prices as well as the per-centages of ownership in private firms, which are the basis for part of the consumers' non-labor incomes, are exogenous. Given exoge-nous prices and ownership rights in private firms, we distinctly face a partial model, even if all markets clear. The model is therefore less general, but more realistic.

Sometimes readers wonder whether it is possible to solve such a model. It is solvable, but we must, of course, exclude patholog-ical cases. No solution is possible, for instance, if the public or privatized[7] firm is only allowed to set one price, which refers to a good which is not supplied or demanded by any private firm and where all inputs and outputs of private firms do not depend on

---

[6] In models of the Boiteux tradition this assumption is given up by Drèze (1984) who deals with the government's adjustment to rationed labor markets. See also Bös (1986a: 241–57, 261–74) who deals with rationing of labor and transportation and with rationing in the peak-load case.

[7] We speak of a 'public or privatized' firm because the normative models in this part of the book always allow for the possibility that the firm remains in full public ownership. Moreover, all arguments of this chapter also refer to my models on public enterprises in Bös (1986a).

this price. However, in the original Boiteux model it is also necessary to exclude particular pathological cases, as mentioned in Bös
(1986a: 96, n. 10).

Any reader who believes that, given the exogenous variables,
the equilibrium in all markets cannot be achieved should be referred to three arguments:

(i)   The supply of and demand for all goods produced by private firms depends on all prices, including the prices which are set
by the public or privatized firm. This leaves ample scope to secure
market equilibria. Public and privatized firms often supply close
substitutes and complements to private firms' products; therefore
the cross-price elasticities are non-negligible.

(ii)   The public or privatized firm is instructed to buy and sell
quantities *of all goods in the economy* in order to guarantee that
all markets clear. Hence the firm has very many instruments at
its disposal. One could even argue that in the original Boiteux
model the planner had too many instruments: if a planner can
set all quantities, prices, and non-labor incomes, why doesn't he
achieve the first-best instead of accepting exogenous public-sector
budget constraints? Our setting is more realistic. The acceptance
of a budget constraint becomes more plausible if the firm has fewer
instruments, i.e. if it is less powerful.

(iii)   When facing exogenous prices and non-labor incomes, the
public or privatized firm adjusts to monopolistic structures of the
private economy. Likewise, the private economy adjusts to the
prices of the public or privatized firm. In the models of Hagen and
Bös, only one part of this double adjustment is treated. However,
the other part of the adjustment also helps to achieve the market
equilibria.

This chapter concludes with a brief sketch of the contents of
this part of this book.[8] Chapter 12 presents the participants in the
market, namely the consumers, the private firms, and the privatized firm. Here we also deal with decision-making on the board of

---

[8]   As already mentioned in the preface, for this part of the book several
papers have been compiled into one coherent text. These papers are Bös
(1986b, 1987, 1988b) and Bös and Peters (1988a,b). Since two of these papers
are joint work with Peters, it may be of interest to note that the following
passages reproduce text from these joint papers: pp. 230–5 are based on
Bös and Peters (1988b); pp. 235–6 are taken from Bös and Peters (1988a);
pp. 243–6 and 247–9 are taken from Bös and Peters (1988b); pp. 257–60
reproduce text from Bös and Peters (1988b), and pp. 281–4 are taken from
Bös and Peters (1988a).

the privatized firm, which is based on bargaining between government representatives and representatives of the private shareholders. Chapter 13 deals with the basic features of welfare-optimal privatization. Here we ignore income effects and concentrate on the trade-off between unwanted profit increases and desired productivity increases. In Chapter 14 we introduce dividend income effects and consider how the optimal issue price is set and how shares should be optimally distributed among the population. The trade-off between profit and productivity increases is replaced by a trade-off between allocative and distributional effects. Chapter 15 includes fiscal policy measures, showing the feedback on privatization if the government's revenues from privatization are used either to finance public expenditures or to reduce the pressure of the income tax.

12 The Economy

12.1 Economic Background

Private goods are indexed with $i = 1, \ldots, n$. Their prices are $(p_1, \ldots, p_n) =: p$. Good n is labor, so p_n is the wage rate. There is one *public good* whose quantity $G \geq 0$ is determined by the government. The public good serves as the numeraire. Hence G denotes both the quantity of the public good and the corresponding amount of public expenditures. We define an extended price vector $(p, 1) =: p^G$.

Private firms are indexed with $j = 1, \ldots, J$. They sell or buy netputs of private goods, $(y_{1j}, \ldots, y_{nj})$, where positive quantities are outputs and negative quantities are inputs. Moreover, they sell quantities $y_{n+1j} \geq 0$ which are bought by the government and made available to consumers as the public good $G = \sum_j y_{n+1j}$. Consequently, the public good is perfectly divisible in production, although there is no rivalry in consumption. The total netput of any single good is $y_i := \sum_j y_{ij}$, $i = 1, \ldots, n+1$. Furthermore, we define a vector of total netputs as $y := (y_1, \ldots, y_{n+1})$.

There is one price-setting *privatized firm*; Θ percent of its shares are owned by consumers, $(1-\Theta)$ percent are publicly owned, and $0 \leq \Theta \leq 1$.[1] The firm will be called 'privatized' regardless of whether its shares are owned publicly and privately or wholly privately. The privatized firm of our model can be interpreted as a single firm, as a group of related enterprises, or as the total enterprise sector which was publicly owned before the privatization process started.[2] The firm sells or buys netputs $(z_1, \ldots, z_n) = z$, where positive quantities are outputs and negative quantities are inputs. The profit of the privatized firm is $\Pi := pz$.

Consumers are indexed as $h = 1, \ldots, H$. They buy or sell netputs of private goods, $(x_{1h}, \ldots, x_{nh})$, where positive quantities denote consumption and negative quantities supply. (Note in particular that the labor supply $x_{nh} < 0$.) Moreover, they consume the quantity G of the public good which is made available by the government free of charge. Total consumer net demand or net supply of any single good is $x_i := \sum_h x_{ih}$, $i = 1, \ldots, n$. Furthermore, we define a vector of total netputs as $x := (x_1, \ldots, x_n)$.

---

[1] Once again, it is convenient to speak of Θ percent although Θ is a figure between zero and one.
[2] See Bös (1986a: 23–4).

The consumers maximize utility $u_h(x_{1h}, \ldots, x_{nh}, G)$ given the budget constraint. The utility function is concave, twice continuously differentiable, and increasing. The indirect utility function $v_h(\cdot)$ depends on all prices, on the quantity of the public good, and on the capital income net of income tax. The capital income consists of dividends accruing on the basis of ownership rights in the privatized and private firms.

Markets are assumed to clear for every good. Neglecting for the moment all functional dependencies, we obtain

$$x_i - z_i - y_i = 0, \qquad i = 1, \ldots, n \qquad (12.1)$$

$$G - y_{n+1} = 0. \qquad (12.2)$$

The market equilibria imply the financial equilibrium of the economy. Multiplying every market-clearing condition in (12.1) and (12.2) by its respective price and adding up yields

$$px + G - pz - p^G y = 0. \qquad (12.3)$$

At (financial) equilibrium the profits of the privatized firm and the private firms, $pz + p^G y$, are equal to the sum of consumers' non-labor incomes px and the public good expenditures, which are equal to G because the public good serves as the numeraire. A detailed analysis of this financial equilibrium follows in Section 12.4.

12.2 The Private Firms

The technology of *private firms* is not explicitly modelled. We assume, however, that the government and the board of the privatized firm have information on the net supply functions $y_{ij}(p^G)$ of private firms. This does not imply any particular knowledge of the decision rules used by private firms. In our model the private sector is exogenous and the other components of the economic model must adjust to it, as is usual in a 'second best' approach. We always assume that private supply functions $y_{ij}(p^G)$ exist even if the private firms are monopolies. The profit of any private firm j is $\Pi_j := \sum_{i=1}^{n+1} p_i y_{ij}$. Since we deal with a static model,[3] we assume that this model holds for a long period and think of profits Π_j as if they were the discounted sum of dividend payments.

In the general formulation of our model the private firms are owned by the consumers. $\theta_{hj} \geq 0$ is the percentage of firm j which

---

[3] Compare p. 150 above.

is owned by consumer h; $\sum_h \theta_{hj} = 1$ for all j. The percentages θ_{hj} are exogenously given. The ownership rights may have been bought in some earlier periods or may have been inherited. Hence consumer h must pay nothing for his ownership right θ_{hj} but is entitled to claim the amount of $\theta_{hj}\Pi_j$ as part of his non-labor income. The exogenous ownership rights θ_{hj} imply that shares of the privatized firm are not acquired by portfolio substitution.

For expositional clarity it will sometimes be convenient to exclude income effects from dividend payments. When this is the case, we set $\theta_{hj} = 0$ for all consumers.

12.3 The Privatized Firm

Θ percent of the privatized firm is owned by the consumers. Consumer h owns $0 \le \theta_h \le 1$ percent of the shares of the privatized firm and $\sum_h \theta_h = \Theta$. For his shares he must pay $\theta_h P$, where P is the issue price. The ownership right θ_h entitles consumer h to claim dividend payments of $\theta_h \Pi$. Hence a net return of $\theta_h(\Pi - P)$ is added to his non-labor income.

12.3.1 *Privatization and the Efficiency of the Firm*

The transition to profit maximization will change the efficiency of the firm. Profit maximization, in practice, provides a better incentive towards efficiency than welfare maximization.

Models in the Boiteux tradition define the technology of a public firm as

$$Q(z) \le 0 \tag{12.4}$$

where X-inefficiency is given if $Q(z) < 0$. In our model X-inefficiency is assumed to depend on the degree of privatization. A first, intuitive approach would assume that changing Θ, i.e. changing the percentage of shares held by consumers, *shifts* the production function $Q(z)$, as expressed by the production possibility frontier

$$Q(z) + IN(\Theta) = 0. \tag{12.5}$$

The inefficiency function $IN(\Theta) \ge 0$ is decreasing in Θ if a higher degree of privatization leads to more efficient production.

By assuming an additive structure of the production function, the first intuitive approach treats increasing efficiency as equivalent to decreasing the fixed costs of production. However, changes in the degree of privatization will also influence the variable costs of production. The marginal productivities $\partial Q/\partial z_i$ will also depend on Θ! The management of the firm may, for instance, concentrate on improving the efficiency of those parts of production in which the relative extent of inefficiency is highest. Hence we choose a more general approach. For any given extent of privatization we define a production possibility frontier[4]

$$g(z, \Theta) = 0. \tag{12.6}$$

We define $g_i := \partial g/\partial z_i$ and $g_\Theta := \partial g/\partial \Theta$. If $g_\Theta < 0$, efficiency increases in Θ because the production possibility frontier is shifted in such a way that a given set of inputs is used to produce more outputs. If $g_\Theta > 0$, the opposite situation occurs; i.e., for a given set of inputs, fewer outputs are produced. The empirical studies comparing private and public firms suggest that $g_\Theta < 0$ is the more probable situation.

The strict equality characterizes the production as *technically efficient*,[5] given the extent of privatization. Technical efficiency is a necessary condition not only for maximum profit, but also for maximum welfare and maximum output, and for many other conceivable objectives of the management and government representatives on the board of the privatized firm.

The production function $g(z, \Theta) = 0$ always is technically efficient. However, the technically efficient frontier is shifted depending on Θ: there is a different set of technology $g(z, \Theta) \leq 0$ for every degree of privatization.[6] The outputs and inputs which are optimal for Θ_1 may well be located *within* the technology set $g(z, \Theta_2) \leq 0$. The overall production possibilities of the firm are fully described only if we consider *all* technology sets which the firm faces if Θ takes all feasible values between zero and one. The overall production possibilities, therefore, can be described by the union of the technology sets for all feasible degrees of privatization Θ and by the envelope of the technology sets. This envelope is the *overall* production possibility frontier of the firm:

$$\Gamma(z) = 0. \tag{12.7}$$

In a two-output diagram we typically expect the production possibility frontier to move away from the origin with increasing privatization. This is illustrated in Figure 13a. This neat picture can,

[4] Increasing returns to scale are not excluded from our analysis.

[5] For the terminology see Marchand, Pestieau, and Tulkens (1984: 27–8).

[6] Once again, we solve Leibenstein's (1976, 1978) X-inefficiency problem in the Stigler (1976) fashion. See above pp. 47–8 and 96.

of course, be blurred if production possibility frontiers for various degrees of privatization intersect, as illustrated in Figure 13*b*.

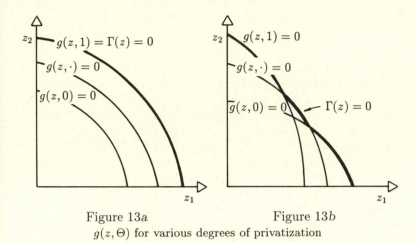

Figure 13*a*   Figure 13*b*

$g(z, \Theta)$ for various degrees of privatization

The envelope $\Gamma(z)$ is that frontier where no further productivity increases can be gained from changing the degree of privatization, typically from increasing it. In Figures 13*a* and 13*b* the bold frontiers present the envelopes. It can clearly be seen that the envelope may coincide with the production function of a fully privatized firm (as in Figure 13*a*), but this is not necessarily so. (Figure 13*b* presents a counterexample.) Input–output combinations on the envelope are only attainable for particular Θs. It is plausible, for instance, that input–output combinations on the envelope can be attained only by high degrees of privatization.

If the firm produces on the envelope, we call the production *privatization-efficient*. Privatization efficiency implies that any arbitrarily chosen netput is maximized with respect to Θ, given all other netputs. Recall that maximization of a netput means either the maximization of an output or the minimization of an input. Hence, privatization efficiency can be described in the following optimization approach:

$$\max_{z_i, \Theta} z_i \qquad i = 1, \ldots, n$$

subject to $g(z, \Theta) = 0$

$$\Theta \leq 1. \qquad (12.8)$$

Such an optimization approach can be formulated for each z_i when all other z_k, $k \neq i$, are held constant. In any case, the Kuhn–Tucker conditions yield the following properties of privatization efficiency:[7]

$$
\begin{aligned}
g_\Theta &\geq 0 && \text{for } \Theta^* = 0 \\
g_\Theta &= 0 && \text{for } 0 < \Theta^* < 1 \\
g_\Theta &\leq 0 && \text{for } \Theta^* = 1.
\end{aligned}
\tag{12.9}
$$

For the economic interpretation of privatization efficiency let us begin with a firm which is fully owned by the government. If efficiency is reduced or remains the same after the sale of the very first share, then it is privatization-efficient to leave the firm in public ownership ($g_\Theta \geq 0$ at $\Theta = 0$). Typically, however, we expect some increase in efficiency if shares are sold. We may thereafter reach a point where neither selling more nor selling fewer shares increases efficiency. In that case it is privatization-efficient to stop the sale of shares, leading to a firm with mixed public and private ownership ($g_\Theta = 0$ at $0 < \Theta < 1$). It is possible that a further sale of shares continues to improve efficiency until all shares are sold. At that point further sales are impossible even if hypothetically the efficiency could be improved by selling more than 100 percent of the shares. Such a situation is also privatization-efficient ($g_\Theta \leq 0$ at $\Theta = 1$).

Before concluding this subsection on technology, it should be noted that the $g(z, \Theta)$ approach can well be criticized for its *ad hoc* character. It does not give an explicit explanation as to why the behavior of the management changes because of changes in ownership. To overcome this criticism, in a recent paper Bös and Peters (1988a) presented a more sophisticated model of privatization-related changes in the firm's technology. This approach has been dealt with in our survey on incentives and efficiency (see Section 3.1.3 above). The reader who finds $g(z, \Theta)$ in the normative part of the book could think of that model as a detailed explanation of $g(z, \Theta)$.

12.3.2   The Board of the Privatized Firm

If a public firm is partially privatized, on the board of the firm there are two different groups of owners who follow different objectives. On the one hand there are representatives of the private owners

[7] Starred variables are optimal ones.

whose main interest is in profits. On the other hand there are government representatives who want to maximize welfare, as measured by a Bergson welfare function $W(v)$, where $v := (v_1, \ldots, v_H)$. In the following we shall describe how the two groups of representatives reach a compromise between profit and welfare.

Let the privatized firm be restricted to prices and netputs which are market-clearing and technically efficient, as described by the following feasibility set:

$$f(\Theta) = \{(p^G, z) \mid x_i(\cdot) - z_i - y_i(\cdot) = 0; \; G - y_{n+1} = 0; \; g(z, \Theta) = 0\}.$$
(12.10)

f depends on the extent of privatization because the production function changes in Θ which influences the technically efficient netputs z. This, in turn, influences the market equilibria.

Each feasible vector (p^G, z) implies a particular combination of profit and welfare which can be obtained by the two groups of representatives on the board of the privatized firm. These combinations of profit and welfare constitute the set of feasible outcomes

$$F(\Theta) = \{(\Pi, W) \mid (p^G, z) \in f(\Theta)\}.$$
(12.11)

If there are feasible price–quantity combinations, there exists a non-empty subset of F which denotes the combinations of profit and welfare where no participant in the bargaining process is able to improve his objective except at the expense of the other. They are denoted by the profit–welfare frontier $\mathcal{F}$:

$$\mathcal{F}(\Theta) = \{(\Pi, W) \in F(\Theta) \mid \not\exists (\Pi', W') \in F(\Theta) \text{ such that}$$
$$(\Pi', W') \geq (\Pi, W), (\Pi', W') \neq (\Pi, W)\}.$$
(12.12)

For expositional clarity we assume the frontier to be connected. There are jumps in neither profit nor welfare. Since $\mathcal{F}(\Theta)$ is not necessarily convex, this assumption guarantees continuity and reduces the mathematical apparatus in the following subsections without loss of economic plausibility. Hence, both profit and welfare change continuously.

It can easily be seen that the set of feasible outcomes F depends on the degree of privatization Θ. Consequently the frontier $\mathcal{F}$, which is a subset of F, also depends on Θ. Note that the bargaining within the privatized firm determines prices and netputs, whereas the degree of privatization is exogenously given to the firm. Therefore pricing possibilities of the two opponent groups of owners depend on the degree of privatization.

Each element of the frontier $\mathcal{F}(\Theta)$ can be described by the maximal value of the government's objective given a particular profit level, or by the maximal value of the private shareholders' objective given a particular welfare level. Therefore, the profit–welfare frontier can be represented by the solution of a maximization problem.

Let the board of the firm choose all netputs z and a subset of all prices, denoted by p_e, where $e \in \mathcal{E} \subset \mathcal{I}, \mathcal{I} = \{1, \ldots, n\}$. Non-regulated prices for goods which are supplied or demanded by the privatized firm may also exist. In those cases, the privatized firm has to accept prices which are set by private enterprises or by government agencies outside our model. We exclude regulation of wages, p_n. All uncontrolled prices $p_i, i \notin \mathcal{E}$, are exogenously given.

From the government representatives' point of view, the instruments should be set so as to maximize welfare W. Hence, we get the following optimization approach:

$$\max_{p_e,z} \ W(v)$$

$$\text{subject to} \quad pz = \Pi^o \quad \text{and} \quad (p_e, z) \in f(\Theta). \qquad (12.13)$$

The welfare maximization is constrained by an arbitrary profit level which is due to the profit–welfare frontier, for short denoted Π^o. Additionally, the prices and quantities should be feasible, which explains the second constraint. The optimization in (12.13) is formally identical with the usual approach of the regulation of a public enterprise given a revenue-cost constraint.

The profit–welfare frontier can be deduced by yet another optimization approach. This approach considers the private shareholders' point of view and is the dual to the optimization approach of the government's representatives, as expressed in (12.13). We obtain

$$\max_{p_e,z} \ \Pi = pz$$

$$\text{subject to} \quad W(v) = W^o \quad \text{and} \quad (p_e, z) \in f(\Theta). \qquad (12.14)$$

The profit maximization is constrained by an arbitrary welfare level of the profit–welfare frontier, for short W^o.

The maximization approaches of the government and of the private shareholders are equivalent and can be used as alternative descriptions of the privatized firm's policy. The profit–welfare combinations can be deduced from any of the two optimization approaches.

For any degree of privatization, there is a corresponding element in the profit–welfare frontier. This is determined through a bargaining process between the private and public shareholders on the firm's board. The choice of this profit–welfare combination depends on the bargaining power of both groups. The bargaining power of the private shareholders guarantees some profit level $\Pi(\Theta)$ which must be conceded by the public representatives. The bargaining power of the government shareholders guarantees some welfare level $W(\Theta)$ which must be conceded by the private shareholders. $\Pi(\Theta)$ and $W(\Theta)$ are chosen in such a way that both agents agree to the compromise.

We assume that the bargaining power of any group of representatives depends on the degree of privatization. Private shareholders have no bargaining power in a public firm and government representatives have no bargaining power in a fully privatized firm. For situations which fall between these two extremes, the bargaining power of private shareholders increases and that of the government decreases as further shares are sold by the government. The intensity of such an increase and decrease will be different, depending on how many shares have already been sold. If 10 percent of the shares are privately owned, selling a further share will increase the bargaining power of private shareholders only slowly. If 40 percent of the shares are sold to consumers, selling further shares will increase the bargaining power much more rapidly, particularly if a share majority comes into reach. If, on the other hand, 80 percent of the shares are privately owned, selling a further share will not add very much to the bargaining power of the private shareholders. If there are discontinuities in the bargaining power at particular percentages, for instance at 50 percent, we can apply continuous differentiable approximations to the actual bargaining power. Therefore we do not assume that the bargaining power of the private shareholders is zero until the 50 percent private ownership level is reached and thereafter simply jumps to its maximum. We assume instead a continuous (differentiable) increase in private bargaining power if shares are sold.[8] Selling more shares extends minority rights to a greater number of private individuals or increases the influence of those already holding shares. It also allows for more influence in the different decision bodies of the firm, more representatives on the board, more influence in shareholders' meetings, and hence more coverage in the mass media.

For the mathematical presentation of the bargaining process

---

[8] Compare Fig. 4 in Sect. 8.1 above.

234   *Normative Theory*

we concentrate on the determination of the profit level $\Pi(\Theta)$. Duality guarantees that there is a unique $W(\Theta)$ which is associated with $\Pi(\Theta)$. Therefore there is no need for an explicit treatment of $W(\Theta)$.

Since the profit–welfare frontier is compact and connected, there exists an interval of the profit level function which contains the bargaining solutions for any given degree of privatization. We obtain

$$\Pi(\Theta) \in \left[\Pi^{\min}(\Theta), \Pi^{\max}(\Theta)\right]. \qquad (12.15)$$

$\Pi^{\min}$ is the profit which is attained if welfare is maximized without considering a profit constraint; $\Pi^{\max}$ is obtained, on the other hand, if the firm applies monopolistic pricing. The limits of Π are determined for any Θ. They are different for different Θ because the production possibilities change with the degree of privatization. Needless to say, there are analogous upper and lower bounds for $W(\Theta)$.

The outcome of the bargaining process depends on the bargaining power of both groups. Once again, it suffices to concentrate on the private shareholders. We denote their bargaining power by $B(\Theta)$. Then the profit level which results from bargaining can be written as follows:

$$\Pi(\Theta) = B(\Theta)\left[\Pi^{\max}(\Theta) - \Pi^{\min}(\Theta)\right] + \Pi^{\min}(\Theta), \qquad (12.16)$$

where the function $B(\Theta)$ has the following properties:
P1: $B_\Theta(\Theta) \geq 0$, i.e. increasing private bargaining power;
P2: $1 \geq B(\Theta) \geq 0, B(0) = 0$, and $B(1) = 1$, as a normalization.

It is interesting to analyze how the profit constraint varies if the extent of privatization increases, viz., $\Pi_\Theta(\Theta)$. Profits will rise if privatization increases efficiency. This can be shown by

$$\Pi_\Theta(\Theta) = B_\Theta(\Theta)\left[\Pi^{\max}(\Theta) - \Pi^{\min}(\Theta)\right] + B(\Theta)\Pi_\Theta^{\max}(\Theta)$$
$$+ \left[1 - B(\Theta)\right]\Pi_\Theta^{\min}(\Theta). \qquad (12.17)$$

The bargaining power of the private shareholders is an increasing function of the degree of privatization. Hence the first term on the right-hand side is positive. Additionally, the maximum and minimum profits increase because production wastes decrease with further privatization and therefore costs decline.[9] Hence the profit

[9] Applying the envelope theorem to $\Pi^{\max}$ and $\Pi^{\min}$ shows that $\Pi_\Theta^{\max}$ and $\Pi_\Theta^{\min}$ are positive for $g_\Theta < 0$.

of the privatized firm increases continuously from the marginal-cost price profit up to the monopolistic one.

Applying the Bös–Peters approach, the pricing decisions at the board of the firm are derived from the maximization of a Bergson welfare function subject to the profit constraint set by the bargaining power of the private shareholders.[10] As mentioned above, this description of the firm's decision on prices is equivalent to the derivation of prices from the maximization of profit given a welfare constraint.

12.4 The Government

12.4.1 The Government Privatization Body

If a public enterprise is privatized, the group of private shareholders enforces profits of the firm at least within that scope which is due to the bargaining process. This also implies a change in the welfare level. However, possible welfare losses resulting from the reduction in government power may be offset by welfare gains resulting from efficiency gains. Therefore welfare may increase or decrease with privatization. This effect gives us further economic insight into the desirability of privatization. For some given degree of privatization Θ it may be possible to improve welfare by selling more shares, whereas for some other Θ the reverse may be true.

Hence an astonishing phenomenon occurs. A reduction in government ownership may increase the welfare level, at least for some range of Θ. The economic rationale of this phenomenon is as follows. The efficiency gains make it possible to increase both welfare and profit. The government will therefore be willing to accept profit increases, as long as they are matched by welfare improvements. Efficiency gains mean that outputs can be produced at lower cost. These lower costs could then be passed on to consumers in the form of lower prices in such a way that both profit and welfare are improved. However, the more power the private shareholders attain, the more weight will be given to the profit motive in the firm. If the private shareholders are given substantial economic power in the firm, they will enforce profit increases in excess of the cost savings which result from the efficiency gains. In such a situation, profit increases at the expense of welfare.

---

[10] Taking into account technological feasibility and market-clearing constraints.

12.4.2   The Strategic Setting

We assume there is a particular government body which decides
on the sale of shares.[11] This body has been instructed to apply
the Bergson welfare function $W(v)$. Hence the government privatization body applies the same welfare function as the government
representatives on the board of the firm. When selling shares, the
privatization body is restricted to the feasibility set $f(\Theta)$ whence it
has to consider the market equilibria and the production function
of the firm. Moreover, the privatization body knows that the firm
adjusts prices and netputs to any degree of privatization, depending on the bargaining power of the various representatives on the
board.

The strategic setting in this normative model is as follows.
We consider the government privatization body as the Stackelberg leader and the board of the privatized firm as the Stackelberg
follower. When selling shares, the government explicitly takes account of the board's adjustment. The board, on the other hand,
takes the degree of privatization as given and optimally adjusts
its prices and quantities. It does not strategically take account of
the government's adjusting the privatization policy to the expected
prices and quantities. This strategic setting results from the fact
that the government has the first move. It starts from the situation of a public firm. Hence in the opening position there is no
board of the firm where representatives of the public and private
shareholders meet and bargain about prices and quantities. The
government can dictate everything. In doing so it will anticipate
the future policy of the board. This means that the government
privatization body acts as a Stackelberg leader. When the board
of the privatized firm first enters the stage, the degree of privatization has already been fixed. Therefore, the best the board can do
is to adjust to the given degree of privatization. This means that
the board acts as a Stackelberg follower.

12.4.3   The Instruments

The government is given the right to sell shares of public firms to
the consumers. In doing so it sets as instruments

  * the maximum percentages of shares, $\overline{\theta}_h$, any consumer is
    allowed to buy,

---

[11] Regardless of whether in some country it is the parliament, the government, or a particular minister who is responsible for privatization.

- the issue price of shares P.

Moreover, the government considers the feedback of its privatization policy on tax revenues and on public expenditures. It chooses as instruments

- the parameters of a linear tax on labor and capital incomes, τ_0 and τ_n,
- the expenditures for some public good, G.

Let us now turn to a more detailed analysis of the instruments. We begin with the *direct instruments of the privatization policy*. In our full-information model a consumer will buy a percentage θ_h of the shares of the privatized firm only if the net return is positive or equal to zero,

$$\Pi - P \geq 0. \qquad (12.18)$$

If the issue price exceeds the dividends, the consumer will not buy the shares. If the net return is zero, we assume that some transaction motive is sufficient to guarantee the clearing of the shares market. A positive net return implies a present from the government and hence the consumer will buy as many shares as possible within the limit $\overline{\theta}_h$ given by the government. Hence for a positive net return, the consumer always chooses

$$\theta_h = \overline{\theta}_h. \qquad (12.19)$$

Given the adjustment of θ_h to the government instruments $\overline{\theta}_h$, we can omit the bar in the following and denote both the limit and the actual percentage of ownership by θ_h.

Note that, by determining the allocation of the individual ownership rights, the government also chooses the degree of privatization

$$\overline{\theta}_h = \theta_h \quad \Longrightarrow \quad \sum_h \overline{\theta}_h = \sum_h \theta_h = \Theta. \qquad (12.20)$$

Setting Θ in a welfare-optimal way means making a decision on the profit of the firm and on its efficiency. A profit increase is acceptable for the government if the implied efficiency gains allow both profit and welfare to be increased. A welfare gain which can be achieved is twofold: first, through the lower prices which are due to efficiency gains; and second, through the consumers' higher non-labor incomes. Here the issue price as an instrument of the government becomes important as well. Non-labor incomes in the economy can be increased by increasing Θ and by reducing the issue price P. However, the policy-maker faces a political constraint when reducing the issue price. He would be exposed to harsh

criticism by both the opposition and the media if the decision were
made to subsidize the acquisition of shares of public firms. Hence a
negative issue price cannot be chosen for political reasons even if it
might be the correct policy for privatizing public firms which run
a permanent deficit. Typically, the policy-maker will also avoid
giving the shares away free of charge. Therefore, there exists some
political threshold which must be taken care of,

$$P \geq \overline{P}, \tag{12.21}$$

where the threshold $\overline{P}$ is non-negative. The actual issue price will
be somewhere between $\Pi(\Theta)$ and $\overline{P}$. It must not exceed profits,
as mentioned in (12.18), otherwise no one would buy the shares.
And it must not fall below a threshold $\overline{P}$, otherwise the political
opposition to privatization would be too great.

Public firms running a deficit are not privatized. Hence we
assume $\Pi(0) > \overline{P}$, which implies $\Pi(\Theta) > \overline{P}$ because $\Pi_\Theta > 0$. Thus
we have three regimes of an issue price:

(i) high issue price if $\Pi(\Theta) = P > \overline{P}$
(ii) medium issue price if $\Pi(\Theta) > P > \overline{P}$
(iii) low issue price if $\Pi(\Theta) > P = \overline{P}$.

Net incomes from dividends increase from case (i) to (ii) and (iii)
successively.

Let us now turn to the *government budget*. Government revenues consist of the revenues from selling shares, ΘP, and of that
part of the profit which the government earns as the owner of
$(1 - \Theta)$ percent of the shares, namely $(1 - \Theta)\Pi(\Theta)$. Let us, for
the moment, interpret $\Pi(\Theta)$ as a discounted stream of future dividends. Then a non-myopic government will perform a cost–benefit
analysis to guarantee that

$$(1 - \Theta)\Pi(\Theta) + \Theta P > \Pi(0), \tag{12.22}$$

where $\Pi(0)$ are the forgone dividend streams which would accrue
to the government if it retained its ownership of the firm. To
avoid clumsiness, we refrain from adding (12.22) as a constraint to
the various optimization problems of the following chapters. We
assume that the government considers privatization only when the
above inequality holds.

Let us next characterize the fiscal policy. The government
imposes a linear income tax

$$t_h = \tau_n[-p_n x_{nh} + \theta_h(\Pi(\Theta) - P) + \sum_j \theta_{hj}\Pi_j] - \tau_0. \tag{12.23'}$$

The government taxes the labor income and the net returns from the consumer's shares in the privatized and in the private firms. Recall that $\theta_h \Pi$ can be interpreted as the discounted stream of future dividends, i.e. the market value of the ownership right. Assume the shareholder h realizes this value and, as a sort of capital gains tax, has to pay for the difference between market value and issue price. This capital gains tax is part of the income tax.[12] There is no differentiation of the tax rates on income and capital gains although such a differentiation could be introduced into the model without great complication.

Alternatively, one could think of an income tax which does not allow for the deduction of the costs of acquiring the shares, $\theta_h P$. In that case, the tax would amount to

$$t_h = \tau_n(-p_n x_{nh} + \theta_h \Pi(\Theta) + \sum_j \theta_{hj} \Pi_j) - \tau_0. \qquad (12.23'')$$

Both forms of taxation, however, lead to exactly the same qualitative results; therefore it is convenient to deal with one form only. In this book I have chosen the capital gains tax specification.

Both τ_0 and τ_n can be used as government instruments. The marginal tax rate τ_n is always a typical instrument of government revenues, whereas the lump sum τ_0 can be either an instrument of revenues, $\tau_0 < 0$, or an instrument of government expenditures, $\tau_0 > 0$. If there were no further public expenditures, then τ_0 would be a subsidy to the consumers, because τ_0 would be the only way the government could spend its revenues from privatization and from taxation. However, if there are further government expenditures included in the model, τ_0 may also become another means of taxation.

For a more general analysis of the government budget, it is adequate to introduce government expenditures which are devoted to the provision of a public good. Taking that public good as the numeraire, G measures both the quantity and the corresponding expenditures.

In models of the Boiteux tradition the government budget is always balanced according to Walras's law. Remember our assumption that all markets clear, which yields a financial equilibrium in the economy,

$$px + G - pz - p^G y = 0. \qquad (12.3)$$

---

[12] This is the West German regulation. It holds unless the shares are retained for more than half a year.

Now consider the individual budget equations,

$$\sum_{i=1}^{n-1} p_i x_{ih} = (1 - \tau_n)[-p_n x_{nh} + \theta_h(\Pi(\Theta) - P) + \sum_j \theta_{hj}\Pi_j] + \tau_0.$$
(12.24)

We sum these over all individuals and substitute this into the equation for a financial equilibrium (12.3). Moreover, we substitute the definition of the firms' profits. After some algebraic manipulation, the financial equilibrium can be expressed as

$$(1-\Theta)\Pi+\Theta P+\tau_n\sum_h[-p_n x_{nh}+\theta_h(\Pi-P)+\sum_j \theta_{hj}\Pi_j] = H\tau_0+G.$$
(12.25)

This financial equilibrium is a balanced-budget equation for the government. $(1 - \Theta)\Pi$ is the government dividend income and ΘP is the revenue from selling shares. Together they constitute the government revenues from privatization. These revenues and the revenues from direct taxation are spent on subsidies $H\tau_0 > 0$ and used to finance public good expenditures G. If $H\tau_0$ is negative, it is another instrument of government revenues.

12.5   The Consumers

The budget constraint (12.24) depends on all available privatization and tax policy instruments. Hence the consumer's net demand and supply depend on the net wage rate $(1-\tau_n)p_n$ and on the capital income net of tax. In the following we denote the capital income by

$$\kappa_h := \theta_h(\Pi(\Theta) - P) + \sum_j \theta_{hj}\Pi_j. \qquad (12.26)$$

Therefore, we can write

$$x_{ih} = x_{ih}[p_1, p_2, \ldots, (1 - \tau_n)p_n, (1 - \tau_n)\kappa_h + \tau_0, G]. \qquad (12.27)$$

This can be substituted into the utility function $u_h(x_{1h}, \ldots, x_{nh}, G)$ to obtain

$$v_h = v_h[p_1, p_2, \ldots, (1 - \tau_n)p_n, (1 - \tau_n)\kappa_h + \tau_0, G]. \qquad (12.28)$$

On the basis of the individual utility functions, the government defines its welfare function as

$$W(v_1, \ldots, v_H) \quad \text{with} \quad W_h := \partial W/\partial v_h > 0. \qquad (12.29)$$

This specification of a welfare function is fairly general. It allows us to describe a utilitarian government whose welfare is the sum of individual utilities. It also allows us to deal with inequality-averse governments $(\partial^2 W/\partial v_h^2 < 0)$.

13 The Allocative Basic Features of Welfare-Optimal Privatization

13.1 The Optimization Approach

For explanatory clearness, in this chapter we exclude income taxation from our analysis and assume that the government expenditures are exogenously fixed at some positive level $\overline{G} > 0$. This implies

$$\tau_0 = 0; \qquad \tau_n = 0; \qquad G = \overline{G}. \tag{13.1}$$

Moreover, income effects are excluded by assuming

$$\theta_{hj} = 0; \qquad \Pi(\Theta) = P. \tag{13.2}$$

The exclusion of endogenous fiscal policy and of any income effects allows us to concentrate on the 'pure' consequences of choosing a welfare-optimal degree of privatization Θ. The distribution of the shares is irrelevant because there are no income effects. The issue price of the shares is always equated to the profit of the firm, which is distributed as dividend payments.

The financial equilibrium of the economy is guaranteed by Walras's law. We proceed in the same way as in Chapter 12 above but take account of the exclusion of endogenous fiscal policy and income effects, as presented in assumptions (13.1) and (13.2).[1] As a consequence, the following equation must always hold:[2]

$$\Pi + \sum_j \Pi_j = \overline{G}. \tag{13.3}$$

If the profit of the privatized firm increases because of higher productive efficiency and profit interests, then a reduction in private

---

[1] It would be tempting not to go through the whole calculation of the financial equilibrium, but simply to substitute equations (13.1) and (13.2) into the equilibrium (12.25) of Ch.12. However, this would be incorrect. Since in the present chapter $\theta_{hj}=0$, the profits of private firms are not shifted to the private households in the financial equilibrium. Hence the sum total of private profits does not cancel as in (12.25) where only the amount of tax on capital incomes from private profits remains to be included in the equation which describes the financial equilibrium. Accordingly, $\Sigma\Pi_j$ appears in equation (13.3).

[2] Equation (13.3) and the assumptions $\Pi=P\geq\overline{P}\geq0$ restrict the government's possible choices of $\overline{G}$, depending on the sum of private profits at the optimum.

profits is required. We do not explicitly model the way in which the private profits are reduced; however, we need this assumption for the logical consistency of the simplest case which can be treated in our framework. The model without income effects aims at showing the basic allocative features of privatization. As soon as income effects are included in the analysis, the perfect negative correlation between public and private profits is eliminated. Therefore, the reader is requested to accept this consequence of our assumptions in order to take the first step in the normative analysis of privatization. We shall see that this first step accentuates the trade-off between efficiency increases and profit increases. The former tend to increase welfare, the latter tend to reduce it.

If we read the financial equilibrium (13.3) as a government budget constraint, it implies that private-sector profits are taxed away at a 100 percent rate to finance the public expenditures. In practical economic policy this would not work. However, for didactical reasons it might be accepted for the moment, in the same way as it is accepted in the usual Boiteux model where the sum total of all profits, private as well as public, is equal to the sum of lump-sum incomes of the consumers (see Bös, 1986a: 64).

Let us now proceed to the presentation of the optimization approach. We know that, directly and indirectly, three agents are involved in the decision on the degree of privatization. They are (i) the representatives of the private shareholders on the board of the firm, (ii) the representatives of the government on the board of the firm, and (iii) the privatization body.

As the maximization approaches of the government and the private shareholders are equivalent, we use welfare maximization as representative of the firm's objectives. The optimum prices and netputs have to be feasible and the profit level refers to the bargaining solution. The privatization body chooses the welfare-optimal amount of shares to be sold while taking the board's bargaining solution into account.

Hence both the decision of the board and that of the privatization body can be treated with one and only one approach, described by the Lagrangean

$$\mathcal{L} = W(v) - \sum_1^n \alpha_i [x_i(p, \overline{G}) - z_i - y_i(p^G)]$$
$$- \alpha_{n+1} [\overline{G} - y_{n+1}(p^G)] - \beta g(z, \Theta)$$
$$- \gamma [\Pi(\Theta) - pz] - \delta(1 - \Theta). \tag{13.4}$$

For any given degree of privatization, the firm's board sets the prices for particular goods, labelled $e \in \mathcal{E} \subset \mathcal{I}$, and chooses netputs, labelled $i \in \mathcal{I}$, $\mathcal{I} = \{1, \ldots, n\}$. The controlled prices and netputs follow the first-order conditions

$$\mathcal{L}_{p_e} = 0, \quad \mathcal{L}_{z_i} = 0; \qquad e \in \mathcal{E}, \ i \in \mathcal{I}. \tag{13.5}$$

The privatization body is informed about the decision rules (13.5) of the board. Hence it can use these rules as the basis of its decision on whether or not to sell shares. It chooses the degree of privatization which is given by[3]

$$\mathcal{L}_\Theta \leq 0; \quad \mathcal{L}_\Theta \Theta = 0; \quad \delta(1 - \Theta) = 0; \quad \delta \leq 0; \quad 0 \leq \Theta \leq 1. \tag{13.6}$$

In the mathematical formulation, the decision of the board and the decision of the privatization body are treated by the same Lagrangean function. However, the respective decisions are decentralized, the board choosing optimal prices and netputs, the government selling shares so as to maximize welfare. The government calculates p_e, z, and Θ according to (13.5) and (13.6), then it sets Θ. The board takes Θ as given and sets p_e and z according to (13.5). The setting is, therefore, incentive-compatible: the board chooses exactly those prices and netputs which the government has anticipated.

13.2 Efficiency Increases versus Profit Increases

The privatization body concentrates on the trade-off between gains in productive efficiency and increases in profit. This can be seen explicitly after differentiating $\mathcal{L}$ with respect to Θ. We obtain

$$\mathcal{L}_\Theta = -\beta g_\Theta - \gamma \Pi_\Theta + \delta, \tag{13.7}$$

where g_Θ measures an efficiency change and Π_Θ a profit change. Recall that $g_\Theta < 0$ means an efficiency gain and $g_\Theta > 0$ an efficiency loss. $\Pi_\Theta > 0$ results from the bargaining on the board. The efficiency changes and the profit increases are weighted by the Lagrangean multipliers $\beta > 0$ and $\gamma \geq 0$.[4] These multipliers measure the welfare valuation of relaxing the technology constraint and the

---

[3] See Panik (1976: 297). The non-negativity constraint on Θ is not treated as a structural constraint but appears explicitly in the necessary optimum conditions.

[4] The proof is as follows (see Drèze and Marchand, 1976: 67): (i) Differentiate the Lagrangean function $\mathcal{L}$ with respect to labor z_n. Recall $\partial g / \partial z_n > 0$

bargaining constraint on profit. Hence the efficiency–profit trade-off is measured in terms of welfare. The Lagrangean multipliers β and γ also depend on the decisions of the firm and reflect the feedback of pricing on privatization.[5] The multiplier δ is zero if the firm remains public or is only partially privatized.

13.2.1 The Degree of Privatization

There are three different policies which the privatization body can choose.

(i) No Privatization

Consider a public firm ($\Theta = 0$). Since the private shareholders have no bargaining power, the firm's profit is at its minimum and the board operates at a welfare optimum without a binding profit constraint. The Lagrangean parameter γ is equal to zero. Thus shares would be sold only if

$$\mathcal{L}_\Theta = -\beta g_\Theta > 0, \tag{13.8}$$

which is the case if there are efficiency increases from selling the first share. Otherwise, if there are no possible efficiency increases from selling any shares, the firm remains in public ownership. Note that the sale of the first share depends only on efficiency. The influence of the sale of the first share on the profit of the firm is irrelevant. If the productive efficiency of a public firm can be increased by selling the first share, it should be done. Full public ownership will be retained only if the sale of the first share leads to efficiency losses or leaves the efficiency unchanged.

(ii) Partial Privatization

Here the efficiency effect ($-\beta g_\Theta$) and the profit effect ($\gamma \Pi_\Theta$) have to be traded off. As long as efficiency gains have heavier weights

is a property of the production function. Then $\beta > 0$ follows from economic plausibility. (ii) For any given Θ the profit $\Pi(\Theta)$ is exogenously given for the optimization. Assume Π exceeds the unconstrained welfare-maximizing profit. Differentiate $\mathcal{L}$ with respect to Π. $\partial \mathcal{L}/\partial \Pi = -\gamma < 0$ follows from economic plausibility (and from the appropriate Kuhn–Tucker formulation of the problem). Therefore $\gamma > 0$. On the other hand, if $\Pi(\Theta)$ is equal to the unconstrained welfare-maximizing profit, we have $\gamma = 0$. Profits below the welfare-maximizing profit are excluded in our model.

[5] The firm's pricing rules can be solved explicitly for γ/β. Then, after dividing (13.7) by β, we can substitute the pricing rules into (13.7).

than profit increases, the government sells shares. It will stop selling shares at that degree of privatization where the efficiency effect and the profit effect are equal. This is a welfare optimum, at least locally. The firm is said to be partially privatized if, at such an optimum, publicly owned shares still exist. Thus we would have

$$-\beta g_\Theta = \gamma \Pi_\Theta \qquad \text{for } \Theta^* < 1. \tag{13.9}$$

(iii) Total Privatization

It is possible that for any feasible Θ the efficiency effect outweighs the profit effect, in which case all shares of the firm would be sold to the public; there are no government-owned shares in existence. In this case, government representatives on the board would have no bargaining power. Thus, the firm can only be described as a profit maximizer, without any constraint on welfare but with the condition that prices and quantities reflect feasible alternatives. Therefore the ratio of the Lagrangean multipliers $(\gamma/\beta) =: 1/\widetilde{\beta}$ where $\widetilde{\beta} > 0$ is the change in the maximum profit achieved by relaxing the technology constraint. We have

$$-g_\Theta \geq \frac{1}{\widetilde{\beta}}\Pi_\Theta \qquad \text{for } \Theta^* = 1. \tag{13.10}$$

Once again, an efficiency effect and a profit effect are traded off.

13.2.2 Privatization Efficiency

In the following we will investigate whether the properties of privatization efficiency, as found in conditions (12.9) of the previous chapter, are fulfilled if the privatization body chooses the welfare optimal degree of privatization according to (13.6).

(i) No Privatization

No shares are sold if there are no possible efficiency increases from privatization, as we have seen in the preceding subsection,

$$g_\Theta \geq 0 \qquad \text{for } \Theta^* = 0. \tag{13.11}$$

This condition for no privatization (13.11) is identical with the corresponding condition for privatization efficiency. Hence it is privatization-efficient to leave the firm in public ownership unless efficiency can be increased by selling the first share.

(ii) Partial Privatization

If, at the optimum, not all shares are sold to the public, condition
(13.9) implies that

$$g_\Theta = -(\gamma/\beta)\Pi_\Theta < 0 \qquad \text{for } \Theta^* < 1. \qquad (13.12)$$

Since the Lagrangean multipliers and Π_Θ are positive, the efficiency measure g_Θ must be negative. This means that it would
be possible to increase efficiency by selling further shares. Partial
privatization has led to an area of technology where, from the efficiency point of view, it would be better to privatize more. We
obtain an under-privatization: *the optimum partial privatization
is not privatization-efficient.* Possible efficiency increases are not
fully exhausted, because the government takes account of the unwanted profit increases.

(iii) Total Privatization

If all shares are sold, condition (13.10) implies

$$g_\Theta \leq -(1/\tilde{\beta})\Pi_\Theta < 0 \qquad \text{for } \Theta^* = 1. \qquad (13.13)$$

Hence the optimum total privatization is privatization-efficient.
The negative g_Θ follows from (13.13). Efficiency increases are exhausted as far as possible.

13.2.3 *Partial Privatization versus Regulated Private Ownership*

The recent British privatizations concentrated on full private ownership. If undesired monopolistic prices were to be feared, price-
cap regulation was chosen to cope with the problem. In Part Two
above we explicitly compared the internal decision structures of a
partially privatized firm and a price-regulated firm in full private
ownership.[6] The normative theory treatment of privatization gives
us another opportunity to deal with a comparison of partial privatization versus price-cap regulation as two alternative instruments
of government policy.

The model of partial privatization has been explicitly treated
in the preceding section. Full private ownership under price-cap
regulation can easily be modelled along the same lines. We assume
that the government privatization body as a political decision sets

---

[6] See Ch. 8 above.

$\Theta = 1$, regardless of any considerations about the trade-off between efficiency increases and profit increases which result from privatization. Optimization with respect to Θ is without interest for the privatization body. Hence the marginal condition with respect to Θ is neglected. Government policy concentrates on capping prices. Let us assume that it sets a special price cap for each and any controlled price, $p_e \leq \overline{p}_e$. Since the decision of the board and of the government can be treated by the same optimization approach, the prices p_e which the firm chooses are identical to the government's price caps $\overline{p}_e$. The marginal conditions with respect to prices p_e, therefore, determine both the government's price caps and the firm's prices which are chosen by the board.

Accordingly, in this setting a government which has the option of partial privatization will never achieve a state of the world that is welfare-inferior to that of a government which always chooses full privatization under price constraint. Partial privatization implies that the government has one more instrument and therefore can never be worse off.

13.2.4 Privatization and Market Structure

Models in the Boiteux tradition typically deal with a price-setting public firm. Economies of scale are not excluded from the analysis; the public firm may be a natural monopoly. However, private firms are assumed to exist. Their supply of, or demand for, netputs is described by $y_{ij}(p^G)$. Hence competition between private and public firms is not excluded.

However, perfect competition cannot be treated in the Boiteux model, because it deals with a firm which sets prices and is instructed to bring about the market equilibria in all markets. If the economy is perfectly competitive, prices and equilibria are determined by the market. The firm takes prices as given and adjusts quantities. It maximizes profit for any technology g; therefore, increasing returns to scale are typically excluded. In that case, profit maximization is welfare-maximizing and we obtain a first-best solution.

Let us now consider a model of the privatization of a perfectly competitive public firm which can be compared with the privatization model in the Boiteux framework. In that case the bargaining on the board is replaced by the operation of the market forces. For any degree of privatization, the profit–welfare frontier is reduced to one point which is both the welfare and the profit maximum.

Given the identity of welfare and profit maximization, we can describe the policy of the privatization body by the Lagrangean

$$\mathcal{L} = pz - \beta g(z, \Theta) - \delta(1 - \Theta). \tag{13.14}$$

The market-clearing conditions need not be considered explicitly. They hold because of the assumption of perfect competition. There is no need to introduce a welfare constraint because the profit–welfare frontier consists of only one point. All prices are given by the markets; therefore, the optimization approach is solved with respect to z and Θ. We obtain

$$\mathcal{L}_{z_i} = p_i - \beta g_i = 0; \tag{13.15}$$

$$\mathcal{L}_\Theta = -\beta g_\Theta + \delta \leq 0; \quad \mathcal{L}_\Theta \Theta = 0; \quad \delta(1 - \Theta) = 0; \quad \delta \leq 0; \quad 0 \leq \Theta \leq 1. \tag{13.16}$$

Equations (13.15) characterize the netput policy of the privatized firm. Inputs and outputs are chosen so as to equate the ratios of marginal productivities to the price ratios. All inputs, therefore, are chosen in a cost-minimizing way, and all outputs are chosen so as to guarantee the identity of prices and marginal costs: if all prices p_i are proportional or equal to the shadow price vector βg_i, this shadow price vector is identical to the marginal costs. The latter interpretation can be found explicitly in Boiteux (1956, 1971).[7]

The degree of privatization is characterized by (13.16). If for all Θ privatization increases efficiency, $g_\Theta < 0$, then $\mathcal{L}_\Theta \leq 0$ can hold only for $\delta < 0$, which implies total privatization. There is no trade-off between profit increases and efficiency increases, because the profit is suppressed by competition. Hence we obtain a very simple rule: competitive public firms should be privatized if efficiency gains can be expected.

Since the empirical studies on efficiency of private and public firms hint at the superiority of private firms, we can now draw our conclusions. Most probably, the total privatization of a perfectly competitive public firm will be welfare-optimal. No privatization or partial privatization is optimal if at some point the efficiency is reduced by selling further shares. Needless to say, privatization efficiency is always given.

The result of the preceding paragraph seems to corroborate the value judgments of many conservative policy-makers. However,

[7] For a detailed analysis see Peters (1988).

the reader should recall that the result holds only for perfectly competitive markets. If there is monopolistic competition in the economy, the trade-off between profit increases and efficiency increases becomes relevant. For the practice of privatization, however, situations involving natural monopolies and monopolistic competition seem to be of greater relevance. Even free market entry will not naturally bring about a state of *perfect* competition in many of the markets where privatization has been discussed.

13.3 Privatization and Pricing

When deciding on the optimal degree of privatization, the government has to anticipate how the firm will adjust to the government's policy. Most interesting is the question of how the firm's prices change if it is privatized. Recall that for the time being we have excluded any form of endogenous fiscal policy. Moreover, we have excluded all income effects from dividend payments. This makes it easy to analyze how prices adjust to a changing degree of privatization. Before continuing, however, let us briefly consider the properties of the optimal prices which the firm chooses for any exogenously given degree of privatization.

13.3.1 Optimal Prices

Recall the compromise between government representatives and private owners on the board of the privatized firm. The resulting prices and netputs can be described as welfare-maximizing, given the profit which must be conceded to the private owners. Moreover, prices and netputs must be technologically feasible and market-clearing. This optimization approach is described by the Lagrangean function (13.4) above. For any degree of privatization, the board of the firm chooses optimal prices and netputs according to

$$\mathcal{L}_{p_e} = 0, \ \mathcal{L}_{z_i} = 0; \qquad e \in \mathcal{E}, \ i \in \mathcal{I}. \tag{13.5}$$

In greater detail, these marginal conditions are[8]

$$\mathcal{L}_{z_i} = \alpha_i - \beta \frac{\partial g}{\partial z_i} + \gamma p_i = 0; \qquad i = 1, \dots, n. \tag{13.17}$$

---

[8] To simplify the following analysis, we assume that the cross-price effects of the public-good supply are negligible, $\partial y_{n+1}/\partial p_e = 0$.

$$\mathcal{L}_{p_e} = \sum\nolimits_h \frac{\partial W}{\partial v_h} \frac{\partial v_h}{\partial p_e}$$

$$- \sum\nolimits_1^n \alpha_i \left(\frac{\partial x_i}{\partial p_e} - \frac{\partial y_i}{\partial p_e} \right) + \gamma z_e = 0; \qquad e \in \mathcal{E}, \quad (13.18)$$

After some algebraic manipulation,[9] we obtain the following pricing structure:[10]

$$\sum\nolimits_{i=1}^n (p_i - c_i) \frac{\partial z_i}{\partial p_e} = -z_e + D_e x_e; \qquad e \in \mathcal{E}. \quad (13.19)$$

Let us now explain the new variables which have been used in the above formula. First, consider c_i. It represents the 'marginal costs' and is defined as

$$c_i := g_i / g_n. \quad (13.20)$$

More precisely, c_i is a shadow price which measures the marginal *labor* costs of publicly producing good i (for $z_i > 0$; otherwise it is a partial marginal rate of transformation).[11]

Second, we define the response of the 'demand for public supply' as

$$\frac{\partial z_i}{\partial p_e} := \frac{\partial x_i}{\partial p_e} - \frac{\partial y_i}{\partial p_e}; \qquad i = 1, \dots, n, \; e \in \mathcal{E}. \quad (13.21)$$

Note that $\partial z_i / \partial p_e$ is a normal, 'Marshallian' demand response and not a 'Hicksian' compensated one.

Third, we come to the 'distributional characteristics' D_e which are a distributionally weighted sum of consumption shares,

$$D_e := \sum\nolimits_h \frac{W_h}{\beta_n} \frac{\partial v_h}{\partial \kappa_h} \frac{x_{eh}}{x_e}, \quad (13.22)$$

where $\beta_n := \beta(\partial g / \partial z_n) > 0$.

The social valuation of changes in the individual capital incomes is a decreasing function of the individual labor[12] incomes, thereby bringing about the distributional weighting we mentioned

---

[9] See Bös (1986a: 96–103).

[10] We assume that prices are equal to marginal costs in the private firms.

[11] We already mentioned this definition on p. 128 above.

[12] Recall that in this chapter $\kappa_h = 0$. Therefore, $\partial v_h / \partial \kappa_h$ is evaluated at $\kappa_h = 0$ for each consumer.

above. See Feldstein (1972a,b,c), and Atkinson and Stiglitz (1980: 387, 469).

For *intermediate goods*, $x_{eh} = 0$.[13] Hence monopoly-type pricing applies because equation (13.19) reduces to

$$\sum_{i=1}^{n} (p_i - c_i)\frac{\partial z_i}{\partial p_e} = -z_e; \qquad e \in \mathcal{E}. \tag{13.23}$$

The lack of concern over the distributional effects of this type of pricing is surprising because these intermediate goods are used by other firms to produce consumption goods, and the distributional valuations in $W(\cdot)$ refer to consumers and hence to their consumption. The reason for this surprising result is the omission of explicit production functions for the private firms in our model; therefore, there is no feedback relating to the welfare significance of intermediate goods.

When selling *consumption goods*, however, the privatized firm explicitly considers distributional objectives in the pricing structure. Let us first consider consumption goods which are supplied only by the privatized firm. In that case $y_e = 0$[14] and $z_e = x_e$. Equation (13.19) reads as follows:

$$\sum_{i=1}^{n} (p_i - c_i)\frac{\partial z_i}{\partial p_e} = -(1 - D_e)z_e; \qquad e \in \mathcal{E}. \tag{13.24}$$

A general interpretation of the distributional price structure (13.24) can be given by comparing this price structure with that of a perfect monopolist.[15] The board of the privatized firm behaves as if it were a monopolist who inflates each price elasticity of demand by $1/(1 - D_e)$.[16] For details the reader is referred to Section 7.2.1 above.

If the privatized firm is not the only supplier of the consumption good e, equation (13.19) can be transformed into

$$\sum_{i} (p_i - c_i)\frac{\partial z_i}{\partial p_e} = -(1 - D_e)x_e + y_e; \qquad e \in \mathcal{E}. \tag{13.25}$$

---

[13] D_e is not well-defined in this case. However, it can easily be seen that the right-hand side of (13.19) reduces to $-z_e$ if $x_{eh}=0$ for all e and h.

[14] Where $e\epsilon\mathcal{E}$ is taken as the index of outputs sold by the privatized firm at price p_e. We exclude $y_e>0$ by the assumption of monopolistic supply z_e and we exclude $y_e<0$ by the assumption that e refers to consumption goods only.

[15] This sort of interpretation is due to Drèze and Marchand (1976).

[16] See Bös (1986a: 216–18).

This formula shows that prices are reduced not only for distributional reasons but also because of competition from other firms.
This trade-off can be seen directly by looking at equation (13.25).
Cheaper prices for the necessities of life are brought about by lower
$(1 - D_e)x_e$. The price of good e is also reduced if y_e increases, i.e.
if the consumption of items supplied by other firms is greater (for
outputs $y_{ej} > 0$).

The qualitative results of this subsection are identical to the
well-known Feldstein prices, although, of course, all variables and
functions in (13.19) depend on Θ. Changes in Θ imply a shift from
welfare to profit maximization. Hence increasing Θ reduces the distributional intentions which are inherent in the price structure. If
the firm is 100 percent privatized, then it applies profit-maximizing
prices. For a price-setting monopoly profit-maximizing prices ex-
hibit a Ramsey-price structure. In the next subsection we will deal
with the question of how prices respond to changes in the degree
of privatization.

13.3.2   Comparative-Static Analysis of Pricing in a Simple Model

In this subsection we deal with a one-product monopoly which
sells its output z to consumers at price p. Similar to Chapter 8
above, we assume that the representatives on the board of the
firm achieve a compromise leading to a mixed objective function
where both profit and welfare win the percentage weight of their
respective supporters on the board,

$$\Phi = (1 - \Theta)(S(p) + \Pi) + \Theta\Pi, \qquad (13.26)$$

where $S(p)$ is consumer surplus, $\partial S/\partial p = -z(p)$, and Π is the
profit of the firm. This formulation excludes all income effects and
assumes that the firm meets all demand, whence z denotes both
demand and supply.

For any given extent of privatization, the board of the firm
chooses that price which maximizes the objective function. The
resulting first-order and second-order conditions are[17]

$$\frac{\partial \Phi}{\partial p} = (p - C_z)z_p + \Theta z = 0. \qquad (13.27)$$

$$\frac{\partial^2 \Phi}{\partial p^2} = (1 + \Theta - C_{zz}z_p)z_p + (p - C_z)z_{pp} < 0. \qquad (13.28)$$

[17] We only deal with cases where the second-order condition (13.28) holds.

Here we apply a cost function $C(z, \Theta)$ and abbreviate its derivatives as

$$\frac{\partial C}{\partial z} =: C_z(z, \Theta) > 0; \qquad \frac{\partial^2 C}{\partial z^2} =: C_{zz}(z, \Theta) \gtreqless 0. \qquad (13.29)$$

A similar convention holds for the demand function $z(p)$, where we define

$$\frac{\partial z}{\partial p} =: z_p(p) < 0; \qquad \frac{\partial^2 z}{\partial p^2} =: z_{pp}(p). \qquad (13.30)$$

The marginal costs depend on both the quantity supplied and the extent of privatization. We allow for decreasing, constant, and increasing marginal costs. As we have no revenue-cost constraint, fixed costs do not influence the price p.

Let us now interpret the first-order condition (13.27). This condition can be transformed into[18]

$$\frac{(p - C_z)}{p} = -\frac{\Theta}{\epsilon} \qquad (13.31)$$

where $\epsilon := z_p p / z$ is the price elasticity of demand. For $\Theta = 0$ price is equal to marginal costs. For $\Theta = 1$ the monopoly price is obtained. Therefore, we have a low welfare-maximizing price for the public firm, but a high monopoly price for the fully privatized firm. In the case of partial privatization, the firm will be more anxious about losing customers the higher the price elasticity of demand. We can conclude that the privatized firm will always behave as if it were an unconstrained profit-maximizing monopolist who inflates the price elasticity of demand by a factor $1/\Theta \geq 1$.[19] The reader may simply define a new elasticity $\eta := \epsilon/\Theta$ and rewrite (13.31) as follows:

$$\frac{(p - C_z)}{p} = -\frac{1}{\eta}. \qquad (13.32)$$

This is the monopoly-pricing rule for a modified price elasticity η.

We expect a higher price, the higher the degree of privatization. However, we cannot conclude in general that the price will always increase if the degree of privatization increases. As the

---

[18] A positive price results if $|\epsilon| > \Theta$. $|\epsilon| = \Theta$ must be excluded from the analysis.

[19] For a similar interpretation of Ramsey prices see Bös (1986a: 189–91, 198–9), and Drèze and Marchand (1976).

degree of privatization affects the price p in a variety of different ways, only a comparative-static analysis allows statements on how the price varies as Θ changes.

First, we can consider changes in the degree of monopoly power $mon := (p - C_z)/p$. We obtain

$$mon_\Theta = -(1/\epsilon)(1 - EL), \qquad (13.33)$$

where EL is an elasticity, $EL := \epsilon_\Theta \Theta/\epsilon$. If we start selling shares, the elasticity EL must be smaller than or equal to one.[20] Moreover, it is plausible that EL is small in all other cases. This plausibility results from the following argumentation. If $\Theta > 0$, then the price–cost margin is positive according to (13.31). Now, if the degree of privatization increases, the accentuation of the profit motive increases. Greater accentuation of the profit motive will typically imply an increase in the price–cost margin. Therefore, mon_Θ typically will be positive, which requires small EL according to (13.33).

It is interesting to note that the maximum degree of monopoly power is not necessarily achieved by full privatization. The maximum will rather depend on the elasticities ϵ and EL, as can be easily shown. Consider the following optimization approach:

$$\max_\Theta \; mon \qquad \text{subject to } 0 \le \Theta \le 1, \qquad (13.34)$$

where mon equals $-\Theta/\epsilon$ according to (13.31). The maximum degree of monopoly power can be characterized by the following marginal conditions:

$$-\frac{1}{\epsilon}(1 - EL) \begin{cases} < 0 & \text{for } \Theta^* = 0 \\ = 0 & \text{for } 0 < \Theta^* < 1 \\ > 0 & \text{for } \Theta^* = 1. \end{cases} \qquad (13.35)$$

According to these marginal conditions, the maximum degree of monopoly power will occur at partial privatization if $EL = 1$. $EL < 1$ is necessary for maximum monopoly power of a fully privatized firm.

However, looking only at changes in the degree of monopoly means that we forgo a lot of insight into the way that privatization affects pricing. Hence we apply a comparative-static analysis,

[20] From (13.31) we obtain $mon=0$ for $\Theta=0$, $mon>0$ for $\Theta>0$. Hence for $\Theta=0$ we must have $mon_\Theta \ge 0$.

moving from one equilibrium price to the other by exogenously changing the degree of privatization. As $\partial\Phi/\partial p = 0$ must hold along such a path, we obtain[21]

$$\frac{\partial^2\Phi}{\partial p^2}\frac{\partial p}{\partial\Theta} + \frac{\partial^2\Phi}{\partial p\partial\Theta} = 0. \tag{13.36}$$

Explicitly solving for $\partial p/\partial\Theta =: p_\Theta$ and simplifying yields

$$p_\Theta = \frac{1}{2}\frac{C_{z\Theta} - z/z_p}{1 + \Theta - C_{zz}z_p - \Theta(ED/\epsilon)}, \tag{13.37}$$

where the denominator is positive because it equals $\partial^2\Phi/\partial p^2 < 0$ after division by $z_p < 0$. The variable $C_{z\Theta} := \partial C_z/\partial\Theta$ measures the marginal cost savings from privatization. ED is the price elasticity of the demand response.[22]

We realize that even in our simple example it is impossible to obtain a general result with respect to the sign of p_Θ. If the extent of privatization increases, the price p might increase or decrease. Whether the price increases or decreases, and how intensive the price changes are, depends on

(i) $C_{z\Theta} < 0$,   the marginal-cost savings from privatization,

(ii) $-z/z_p = -p/\epsilon > 0$,   the inverse price elasticity of demand ($z_p < 0$ follows from the theory of consumer surplus),

(iii) $-C_{zz}z_p \gtrless 0$,   the increasing, constant, or decreasing marginal costs (scale effect),

(iv) $-\Theta(ED/\epsilon) \gtrless 0$,   the change in the slope of the demand curve, which results from privatization.

However, there is an asymmetry in the influence of effects (i)–(iv). Whether price increases or decreases depends only on the

---

[21] For the comparative-static analysis we apply the specifications $z=z(p(\Theta))$; $z_p=z_p(p(\Theta))$; $C_z=C_z(z(p(\Theta)),\Theta)$. A simple presentation of the envelope theorem can be found in Varian (1984: 328).

[22] $ED=z_{pp}(p/z_p)$.

cost savings and on the inverse elasticity of demand. The scale effect and the second-order effect pertaining to the slope of the demand curve can change the quantitative importance of a price increase or a price decrease, but can never change an increasing price into a decreasing price or vice versa. This asymmetry results from the fact that the denominator is positive.

Hence a price increase results from further privatization if the *price elasticity of demand* is low and if the *cost savings* from privatization are not too large. On the other hand, a high price elasticity of demand coupled with large cost savings leads to a price reduction as a consequence of further privatization. The large cost savings make it possible to reduce the price even if the price–cost margin increases. The high price elasticity of demand makes it impossible to exploit the market position too much.

The importance of the *cost savings* is illustrated in Figure 14. If there are no cost savings, C_z remains unchanged and increasing Θ leads to a movement from A to B which increases p. If there are considerable cost savings, leading to the marginal costs $C_z(\Theta = 1)$, the monopoly optimum C is obtained at a lower price than the welfare optimum A.

Let us next consider the influence of the scale effect and of the change in the slope of demand on p_Θ. These two terms enter the denominator of (13.37) and never change the sign of p_Θ. However, they either intensify or dilute the quantitative importance of the price changes.

Decreasing marginal costs lead to more volatile pricing. Any price increase is intensified because the higher price leads to a lower quantity which implies higher marginal costs. These higher costs, in turn, push the price upwards. A price decrease is intensified because the lower price makes it possible to exploit the economies of scale. The story for increasing marginal costs is exactly the opposite; all price movements are mitigated.

The influence of scale effects on the transition from marginal-cost to monopoly pricing is illustrated in Figure 15 for the case of $C_{z\Theta} = 0$. It can easily be seen that price increases in the case of a transition from the welfare to the profit maximum ($A \to B$) tend to be larger for decreasing than for increasing marginal costs.

The consequence of changes in the *slope of demand* for $\partial p/\partial \Theta$ is similar to that of the scale effects. Price movements are intensified in the case of convex demand ($ED < 0$) and diminished in the case of concave demand ($ED > 0$). A price increase is intensified by convex demand because the higher price reduces the price response which, in turn, pushes the price further upward. A price decrease is intensified because the price responds more elastically which, in turn, reduces the price.

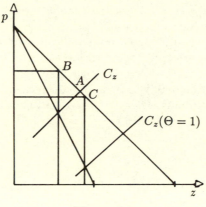

Figure 14

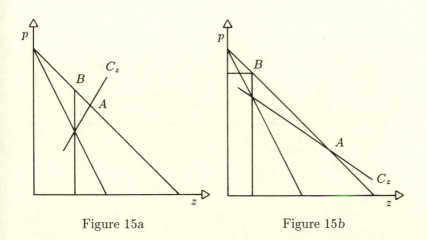

Figure 15a   Figure 15b

13.3.3   *Price Trajectories in a More Elaborated Model*

Even in the simple one-good economy of the preceding subsection we could not obtain clear-cut results on whether privatization leads to price increases or decreases. We can expect even less clear results in a more-good economy. A detailed comparative-static analysis

turns out to be very tedious and not worth the trouble. Hence
in the following, I shall present some simple thoughts on price
trajectories without any explicit analytical treatment.

As in all parts of this chapter, we exclude endogenous fiscal policy and assume that there are no capital incomes. Consequently, welfare $W(v(p,\overline{G}))$ increases only if privatization leads to
a decrease in at least one price. If privatization leads to increases
in all prices, the privatization body will not privatize at all. Figure 16a illustrates the price trajectory if the degree of privatization
changes from $\Theta = 0$ to $\Theta = 1$. The indifference curve W' leads
to the maximum welfare which can be attained by choosing any Θ
between zero and unity. Clearly the corner solution $\Theta = 0$ will be
chosen by the privatization body.

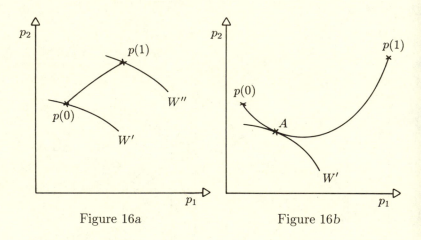

Figure 16a   Figure 16b

Efficiency increases, however, can imply falling prices, and
therefore partial or total privatization may be welfare-optimal. A
typical case is illustrated in Figure 16b. A price reduction as a
consequence of privatization can be expected if the price elasticity of demand for some good is high and if privatization leads to
considerable efficiency increases in the production of that good.
Of course, there is more incentive for price reductions if the welfare objective is still important to the firm. Hence in our example
we assume that p_2 falls from $p(0)$ to A and rises from A to $p(1)$
because in the second part of the price trajectory the profit motive is predominant. The price p_1 increases monotonically when

privatization proceeds. The maximum welfare is attained at some interior solution, point A. In Figure 16b the interaction of the privatization body and the firm is depicted. The changing prices $p(\Theta)$ describe the firm's response to the changing degree of privatization. At point A the privatization body achieves maximum welfare, given the price responses of the firm.

The price trajectory from $p(0)$ to $p(1)$ can be divided into two parts. The interval between $p(0)$ and A describes the effects of the government's privatization policy. The welfare optimum, however, could also be obtained by a government nationalization body. Then the trajectory interval between $p(1)$ and A could be used to describe the effects of a nationalization policy.

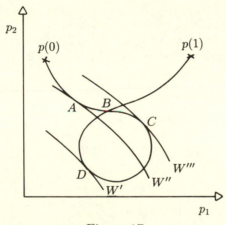

Figure 17

However, a looping, as illustrated in Figure 17, cannot be excluded from the analysis. p_2, in this figure, behaves as in Figure 16b: it falls in the welfare-dominated range of the price trajectory and rises in the profit-dominated range. p_1 follows with a delayed reaction. As soon as the privatization begins, p_1 increases. Afterwards, beginning at some medium level of privatization, price p_1 behaves like p_2. The most plausible explanation of such a situation is that the welfare function W is of the general Bergson type and includes all possible extents of inequality aversion, ranging from the utilitarian case to a very close approximation of the Rawls case. The distributional value judgments of the policy-maker are revealed in the relative structure of prices.

If good 1 is a necessity and good 2 is a luxury, then the welfare-maximizing prices $p(0)$ will imply a relatively low price of the necessity and a relatively high price of the luxury. If the welfare objective loses importance, p_1 will increase and p_2 will decrease. With increasing price p_1, the price elasticity of good 1 will also increase, which, coupled with cost-reducing efficiency gains, implies the falling price p_1 in the middle range of our figure. Only when the profit motive dominates will price p_1 again increase.

In that case, the privatization body must carefully examine the second-order conditions to avoid being stuck at a local maximum like A or, even worse, at a local minimum like C.

It is also interesting to note that Figure 17 illustrates the possibility of two different degrees of privatization leading to exactly the same prices. Point B reflects two different values, $\Theta_1 < \Theta_2$, each for one of the two curves which intersect at B. If privatization in such a case were to be performed in a series of steps, it would be a natural choice to sell Θ_1 percent of shares in the first step and then $\Theta_2 - \Theta_1$ percent in the second step, because such a sale would not disturb the market for goods 1 and 2.

14 Dividend Incomes and Optimal Privatization

14.1 The Optimization Approach

In this chapter we concentrate on the income effects from privatization. Hence we now assume that consumers own shares of the private firms and will buy shares of the privatized firm[1] at a price $P \leq \Pi$. Subsequently, they enjoy a capital income of

$$\kappa_h := \theta_h(\Pi(\Theta) - P) + \sum_j \theta_{hj}\Pi_j. \qquad (12.26)$$

The government's instruments are the issue price P and the shares θ_h. Therefore, for the first time in our normative analysis, capital income effects matter, because the issue price P may be low and thus lead to considerably large incomes for the owners of the privatized firm. Moreover, the distribution of shares is, of course, of central distributional concern.

For didactical reasons, in this chapter we once again exclude endogenous fiscal policy measures by assuming $\tau_0 = 0$, $\tau_n = 0$, and $G = \overline{G} > 0$.

The special assumptions of this chapter imply the following financial equilibrium for the economy:

$$(1 - \Theta)\Pi + \Theta P = \overline{G}; \qquad \overline{G} \geq \overline{P} \geq 0. \qquad (14.1)$$

This is a government budget constraint. Privatization leads to revenues from the sale of shares, ΘP, and to dividends on the basis of those shares which are retained in public ownership, $(1 - \Theta)\Pi$. The sum total of these government revenues from privatization must be equal to the predetermined public expenditures $\overline{G}$. The government budget constraint requires that the public expenditures $\overline{G}$ must always exceed the threshold issue price $\overline{P}$. Otherwise equation (14.1) would contradict the assumptions on the relations between profit and issue price, $\Pi \geq P \geq \overline{P} \geq 0$.

According to the government budget constraint, public expenditures $\overline{G}$ are a weighted average of profit and issue price. Hence $\Pi \geq \overline{G} \geq P$. This is intuitively plausible if we assume that $\overline{G}$ only refers to those public expenditures which are financed by the additional revenues which the government achieves from privatization.

---

[1] As mentioned in Ch. 12, $\theta_{hj} \geq 0$, $\Sigma_h \theta_{hj} = 1$, $\theta_h \geq 0$, $\Sigma_h \theta_h = \Theta$.

As in Chapter 13 above, both the decision of the privatization body and the decision of the board of the firm can be treated with the same optimization approach, described by the Lagrangean function

$$\mathcal{L} = W(v) - \sum_1^n \alpha_i[x_i(p,\overline{G},\kappa) - z_i - y_i(p^G)]$$
$$- \alpha_{n+1}[\overline{G} - y_{n+1}(p^G)] - \beta g(z,\Theta) - \gamma[\Pi(\Theta) - pz]$$
$$- \delta(1-\Theta) - \lambda(\Pi(\Theta) - P) - \mu(P - \overline{P}). \tag{14.2}$$

For any given issue price P and any given distribution of shares θ_h, the board of the firm chooses prices and netputs according to

$$\mathcal{L}_{p_e} = 0, \ \mathcal{L}_{z_i} = 0; \qquad e \in \mathcal{E}, \ i \in \mathcal{I}. \tag{14.3'}$$

The privatization body anticipates the resulting prices and quantities when choosing the optimum issue price and the optimal distribution of shares:

$$\mathcal{L}_P = 0, \ \mathcal{L}_{\theta_h} \le 0, \ \mathcal{L}_{\theta_h}\theta_h = 0; \qquad h = 1,\ldots,H. \tag{14.3''}$$

Any further constraints and conditions on Lagrangean parameters will always be explicitly stated when necessary for the analysis.

14.2   The Welfare-Optimal Issue Price

In this section we will concentrate on the welfare-optimal issue price P^*. Recall from Chapter 12 above that the issue price is bounded from above,

$$P \le \Pi, \tag{12.18}$$

and from below,

$$P \ge \overline{P}. \tag{12.21}$$

We speak of a high issue price if $\Pi = P > \overline{P}$, of a medium issue price if $\Pi > P > \overline{P}$, and of a low issue price if $\Pi > P = \overline{P}$.

For the economic interpretation of the optimal issue price, we use the following marginal conditions:

$$\mathcal{L}_P = -\sum_h \left(W_h \frac{\partial v_h}{\partial \kappa_h}\theta_h - \sum_1^n \alpha_i \frac{\partial x_{ih}}{\partial \kappa_h}\theta_h \right) + \lambda - \mu = 0, \tag{14.4}$$

$$\lambda(\Pi - P) = 0; \quad \lambda \le 0; \ P \le \Pi(\Theta), \tag{14.5}$$

$$\mu(P - \overline{P}) = 0; \quad \mu \le 0; \ \overline{P} \le P. \tag{14.6}$$

Abbreviating

$$A_h := W_h \frac{\partial v_h}{\partial \kappa_h} - \sum_1^n \alpha_i \frac{\partial x_{ih}}{\partial \kappa_h}; \qquad h = 1, \ldots, H, \qquad (14.7)$$

we write the $\mathcal{L}_P$-condition as follows:

$$\sum_h A_h \theta_h = \lambda - \mu. \qquad (14.8)$$

Let us now interpret this condition. We begin with the *left-hand side*. First, we exclude $\theta_h = 0$ for all h. If no shares are sold, questions concerning an issue price are irrelevant. There are no capital incomes regardless of any arbitrarily chosen issue price. It is of no importance whether the shares are denominated at $5 or $10 if no shares are sold. Hence we restrict the analysis to the case where at least one $\theta_h > 0$.

Next, we must interpret A_h. Fortunately, a nice economic meaning can be given to A_h: it measures the welfare effects of a change in the individual capital income of consumer h. This can most clearly be shown by dealing with the *hypothetical* case of an optimal distribution. Let the government set lump-sum transfers $\overline{\kappa}_h$ so as to maximize welfare on the basis of the Lagrangean function (14.2). Then the government applies the first-order conditions

$$W_h \frac{\partial v_h}{\partial \kappa_h} - \sum_i \alpha_i \frac{\partial x_{ih}}{\partial \kappa_h} = A_h = 0. \qquad (14.9)$$

Hence the welfare effects of an income change A_h would be equal to zero if the distribution of capital incomes were optimal. Admittedly, this theoretical limiting case is without great empirical relevance. Moreover, the lump-sum incomes $\overline{\kappa}_h$ are not chosen as instruments in our model.

However, the hypothetical case is a good basis of comparison. There are two terms which constitute A_h. First, we have the marginal social valuation of the individual capital income, $W_h(\partial v_h/\partial \kappa_h)$. This term is always positive. Second, we have the marginal social costs of issuing shares, $\sum_i \alpha_i(\partial x_{ih}/\partial \kappa_h)$. These marginal social costs refer to the influence which the spending of the individual capital income has on the objective function of the government. This is evident because the Lagrangean multiplier α_i corresponds to the marginal change of the optimum welfare W^* when the ith market-clearing condition is relaxed by a small change in income κ_h.

Therefore A_h is the difference between social marginal benefits and costs. It results from the twofold effect of an increase in an income κ_h on welfare. First, there is the direct effect: individual utility increases and so does welfare. Second, there is the indirect effect: the consumer's demand for outputs and supply of inputs will change. The indirect term can either be positive or negative. Without too much loss of generality, we could assume that demand always responds normally, implying $\partial x_{ih}/\partial \kappa_h > 0$ for both outputs and inputs.[2] However, the indirect term also depends on the Lagrangean multipliers α_i which have different signs. We know from the optimization that

$$\alpha_i = \beta g_i - \gamma p_i, \qquad (14.10)$$

where γp_i is a socially evaluated measure of the market price of good i, and βg_i is a shadow price which is related to our definition of marginal labor costs (equation (13.20)),

$$\beta g_i = c_i \beta g_n. \qquad (14.11)$$

Hence α_i is positive if the shadow price exceeds the social evaluation of the market price. Otherwise it is negative. It is impossible to conclude *a priori* which α_i is positive and which is negative. In particular, we cannot expect a positive α_i for inputs and a negative α_i for outputs.[3]

At the macro level, an aggregate effect of income changes matters, namely the weighted sum $\sum_h A_h \theta_h$. It is difficult to deduce when this sum will be positive and when it will be negative. We expect a positive A_h for poor consumers because the social marginal valuation of their capital incomes tends to be high. However, if they concentrate on demanding scarce goods, the marginal social costs may well compensate the valuation of their income leading to a negative A_h. Assuming a positive A_h for poor consumers, we obtain a positive $\sum_h A_h \theta_h$ if it is mainly the poor who receive shares of the privatized firm. However, as we will see in Section 14.3, there is no general tendency in our model to prefer the poor when deciding on the distribution of shares.

There is another way of interpreting $\sum_h A_h \theta_h$ which is more helpful. Recall that $A_h = 0$ for all consumers if the distribution of

---

[2] Recall $z_i < 0$ for inputs; therefore, increasing income will reduce the supply of inputs.

[3] In contrast to Bös (1988b).

capital incomes is optimal. Hence for a rather suboptimal distribution of incomes we expect many positive A_h. The 'better' the income distribution, the higher the probability of a negative A_h. Therefore a positive $\sum_h A_h \theta_h$ is more probable if, in spite of choosing an optimal θ_h^*, the capital-income distribution at the optimum is still far away from the lump-sum optimum where $A_h = 0$. The nearer the privatization optimum and the lump-sum optimum, the more probable is a negative $\sum_h A_h \theta_h$.

The considerations of the preceding paragraphs make clear that much depends on the distribution of capital incomes. If there is sufficient aversion to inequality intrinsic in the government's welfare function, in our model a positive $\sum A_h \theta_h$ is very probable.

We have now interpreted the left-hand side of (14.8) and are in the position to deal with the properties of the optimal issue price P. We distinguish three regimes.

(i) High Issue Price

The issue price is kept as high as possible and is set equal to the firm's profits,

$$\overline{P} < P = \Pi, \qquad \text{i.e. } \mu = 0, \ \lambda \leq 0. \qquad (14.12)$$

This case occurs if the aggregate welfare effect of capital-income changes is negative, i.e. $\sum A_h \theta_h \leq 0$. Because of the negative welfare effects, the policy-maker absorbs all dividends by choosing the high issue price $P = \Pi$. Therefore, the gains in productive efficiency which result from privatization can be exploited, but net incomes from dividends are excluded. However, as mentioned earlier, negative welfare effects of capital-income changes are not very probable.

(ii) Medium Issue Price

The issue price lies somewhere between the lower and the upper boundary,

$$\overline{P} < P < \Pi, \qquad \text{i.e. } \mu = 0, \ \lambda = 0. \qquad (14.13)$$

This holds if the aggregate welfare effect of capital-income changes is nil, i.e. $\sum A_h \theta_h = 0$. At the optimum, in this case, welfare cannot be increased by changing the dividend incomes.

(iii) Low Issue Price

The issue price is kept as low as possible; the firm's profit exceeds the issue price,

$$\overline{P} = P < \Pi, \qquad \text{i.e. } \mu \leq 0, \ \lambda = 0. \qquad (14.14)$$

This case can be given only if $\sum A_h \theta_h \geq 0$. The economic rationale is straightforward. If capital-income changes have a positive welfare effect, the net incomes from dividends should be set as high as possible. This can be achieved by setting the issue price as low as possible. Hence the low issue price $\overline{P}$ may well occur in our model. Therefore, the model gives a welfare-economic explanation of low issue prices in the case of privatization. Such an explanation is of interest because, in the practice of privatization, the issue price typically is set low and many policy-makers have been accused of throwing away national property because they set a low share issue price. Our model offers proof of the fact that such a low issue price can well be the result of a welfare-oriented policy.

14.3 People's Capitalism in a Welfare Context

In this section we deal with the optimal distribution of shares θ_h^*. We employ the same model as in the preceding section, described by the Lagrangean function (14.2); however, now we are interested only in those marginal conditions which determine the optimal θ_h,

$$\mathcal{L}_{\theta_h} = A_h \frac{\partial \kappa_h}{\partial \theta_h} - (\beta g_\Theta + \gamma \Pi_\Theta + \lambda \Pi_\Theta - \delta) \leq 0, \quad (14.15)$$

$$\mathcal{L}_{\theta_h} \theta_h = 0, \qquad\qquad h = 1, \ldots, H, \qquad\qquad (14.16)$$

$$(1 - \Theta) \geq 0, \qquad\qquad \delta(1 - \Theta) = 0, \qquad\qquad (14.17)$$

$$\delta \leq 0, \qquad\qquad\qquad \theta_h \geq 0. \qquad\qquad\qquad (14.18)$$

Recall that the term A_h describes the welfare effect of a change in capital income. It is the difference in the social marginal valuation of capital income and the social marginal costs of issuing shares,

$$A_h := W_h \frac{\partial v_h}{\partial \kappa_h} - \sum_i \alpha_i \frac{\partial x_{ih}}{\partial \kappa_h}. \qquad (14.7)$$

The income changes are brought about through the purchase of shares by the consumer,

$$\frac{\partial \kappa_h}{\partial \theta_h} = (\Pi(\Theta) - P) + \theta_h \Pi_\Theta. \qquad (14.19)$$

An infinitesimal change in the ownership of the privatized firm implies both a direct and an indirect capital-income effect. The direct effect consists of the dividends the consumer receives minus the issue price he has to pay for the shares. The indirect effect measures the feedback effect of increasing private ownership on the profit of the firm, and hence on the dividends. The indirect effect is higher, the more shares a person already holds, because the purchase of one more share also increases the dividend payments which are paid on the basis of all other shares held.

The most interesting question on the distribution of shares is whether the poor should be given more shares than the rich and, if this question is answered positively, how progressive the redistribution by shares should be. However, all marginal conditions in our model refer to the optimum state, i.e. to incomes after redistribution activities. An interpretation of the marginal conditions cannot lead to results which refer to the incomes before the redistribution unless there is some definite connection between the incomes before and after the redistribution. In fact, such a connection may well exist. Assume that the total amount of money which is redistributed, $\Theta(\Pi - P)$, is not too high as compared with the gross national product. This assumption is very realistic if practical privatization activities are considered. Then it can be assumed that even after privatization the poor are still poor and the rich are still rich. Let us, therefore, take the income positions after the redistribution as proxies for the income positions before the redistribution and consider whether the poor should be given more shares and, if so, how many.

The distributional consequences of privatization can be investigated by reference to a *lump-sum redistribution*. For a comparison which is meaningful from the distributional point of view, we postulate that the total amount of money which is distributed to the consumers is the same in both the privatization and the lump-sum redistribution. Hence we start from the amount of money $\sum^* := \Theta^*(\Pi^* - P^*)$ which results from adjusting θ_h and P to the distribution of private firm ownership θ_{hj}. This amount of money $\sum^*$ is taken as exogenous for the lump-sum approach and optimally redistributed by transfers $\rho_{oh} > 0$ or lump-sum taxes $\rho_{oh} < 0$. The shares θ_{hj} are exogenously given; in fact they are identical at the two optima compared.

The *lump-sum reference optimum* is achieved as follows:

$$\max_{\rho_{oh}, z_i} W(v_1, \ldots, v_H)$$

subject to

$$\sum_h x_{ih}(p, \overline{G}, \sum_j \theta_{hj} \Pi_j + \rho_{oh}) - z_i - \sum_j y_{ij}(p^G) = 0 \qquad (\tilde{\alpha}_i)$$

$$\overline{G} - \sum_j y_{n+1j}(p^G) = 0 \qquad (\tilde{\alpha}_{n+1})$$

$$g(z, \Theta) = 0 \qquad (\tilde{\beta})$$
$$\sum_h \rho_{oh} = \sum{}^* \qquad (\tilde{\gamma}). \tag{14.20}$$

The marginal conditions we are interested in are the following:

$$\widetilde{A}_h \frac{\partial \kappa_h}{\partial \rho_{oh}} = \tilde{\gamma} \qquad h = 1, \ldots, H. \tag{14.21}$$

The term $\widetilde{A}_h$ measures the social marginal benefit–cost difference which is brought about by a capital-income change, namely

$$\widetilde{A}_h = W_h \frac{\partial v_h}{\partial \kappa_h} - \sum_i \tilde{\alpha}_i \frac{\partial x_{ih}}{\partial \kappa_h}. \tag{14.22}$$

The capital-income changes which are brought about by the lump-sum transfers are equal to unity:

$$\frac{\partial \kappa_h}{\partial \rho_{oh}} = 1. \tag{14.23}$$

Hence we conclude on the basis of (14.21) that the difference between marginal social benefits and social costs at the lump-sum optimum is equated for all consumers.

At the *privatization optimum* the interpersonal relations are distorted. By defining a slack variable $SV_h \leq 0$, condition (14.15) can be rewritten as

$$A_h \frac{\partial \kappa_h}{\partial \theta_h} = \begin{cases} WEP & \text{for } \theta_h > 0 \\ WEP + SV_h & \text{for } \theta_h = 0 \end{cases} \tag{14.24}$$

where WEP is an abbreviation for the **w**elfare valuation of **e**fficiency and **p**rofit increases:

$$WEP := \beta g_\Theta + \gamma \Pi_\Theta + \lambda \Pi_\Theta - \delta. \tag{14.25}$$

Note that the slack variable SV_h is zero for consumers who are given shares and negative for consumers who are not.

There are great differences between the lump-sum optimum and the privatization optimum. At the lump-sum optimum it is directly the benefit–cost differences $\widetilde{A}_h$ which are equated. The effect of lump-sum transfers on income, $\partial \kappa_h/\partial \rho_{oh}$, is neutral, because it is equal to unity for each consumer. At the privatization optimum the effect on income of purchasing shares, $\partial \kappa_h/\partial \theta_h$, is

not neutral, but greater, the more shares owned.[4] Therefore, the
benefit–cost differences A_h are only equated among recipients who
own the same amount of shares at the optimum. There is no equating of A_h among recipients who own different amounts of shares.
Moreover, there is no equating of A_h with respect to non-recipients.

For a better understanding of the two optima, let us first deal
with the special case of marginal social costs $\sum_i \alpha_i (\partial x_{ih}/\partial \kappa_h)$ and
$\sum_i \tilde{\alpha}_i (\partial x_{ih}/\partial \kappa_h)$ which are equal for all consumers. Then, at the
lump-sum optimum, the marginal social valuations of capital in-
come are equated for all consumers. If, additionally, we assume
identical utility functions, the lump-sum transfers are chosen so as
to equate all capital incomes.

At the privatization optimum, under the same assumptions,
only the capital incomes of those recipients are equated who, at the
optimum, happen to own the same amount of shares. What about
the other consumers? Let us first deal with the recipients. The
greater the amount of shares owned by any consumer, the lower
the marginal social valuation of his capital income at the optimum. Hence, at the optimum, higher-income recipients own larger
amounts of shares. Let us next consider the non-recipients. Unfortunately, we cannot obtain any general conclusion as to whether
they are poor or rich consumers. For non-recipients in equation
(14.24) the left-hand side is reduced because $\partial \kappa_h/\partial \theta_h$ is lower than
for any recipient, but the right-hand side also is reduced, namely by
SV_h, and we do not know how the slack variable changes if capital
income changes. Consequently, we cannot conclude whether the
social marginal valuations of the capital incomes of non-recipients
are lower or higher than those of the recipients.

Moreover, even the result that richer recipients are allowed to
buy more shares is lost if the utility functions and the marginal
social costs vary among consumers. In particular, we do not know
whether the marginal social costs are increasing or decreasing in
capital income. They depend on the demand response $\partial x_{ih}/\partial \kappa_h$
and on the respective Lagrangean multipliers, α_i and $\tilde{\alpha}_i$. The
demand response usually is lower for necessities than for luxuries.
The Lagrangean multipliers, as indicators of the relative scarcity
of goods, can be low for necessities and high for luxuries or vice
versa. Hence we cannot conclude that the marginal social costs of
issuing shares are low for the poor and high for the rich. In any
case, the marginal social costs describe the allocational limits of
redistribution. The more a poor consumer demands scarce goods,

---

[4] See equation (14.19).

270

Normative Theory

the less will his income be increased upon receiving shares of the privatized firm.

Therefore, we conclude that it is not correct to argue that the poor should always be given more shares than the rich.

14.4 Allocation versus Distribution

Let us again return to our approach which excludes endogenous fiscal policy but includes the net effects from dividends. On the basis of the optimization approach (14.2), we have looked at the optimal issue price (Section 14.2) and at the optimal distribution of shares (Section 14.3). However, we have not yet combined the various optimum conditions to deal with the question of the optimum degree of privatization in the presence of capital incomes from dividends. This shall be done here.

Recall the trade-off between efficiency increases and profit increases which determined the degree of privatization in the absence of capital incomes. We shall see in the following how the trade-off in Chapter 13 must be replaced by a trade-off between allocative and distributional effects.

(i) The allocative effects depend on efficiency changes which result from privatization, g_Θ, and on the profit increases which must be conceded to the private shareholders if privatization proceeds, $\Pi_\Theta > 0$. From the allocative point of view, privatization is desirable if $-g_\Theta > \Pi_\Theta$. In such a case the efficiency gains in the production are high enough to allow an increase both in profit and in welfare. Therefore, the policy-maker is willing to accept the profit increases as the price which has to be paid for the efficiency gains which allow welfare to increase.

(ii) The distributional effects depend on how net incomes from dividends influence welfare. These effects are measured by A_h, as shown in the preceding section.

The trade-off between allocative and distributional effects basically means that higher profit increases will be accepted by the privatization body if the positive effects from efficiency increases are reinforced by positive effects from capital incomes. This trade-off between allocative and distributional effects depends decisively on the issue price of the shares.

To discuss the optimal degree of privatization for the various regimes of issue prices, we start from the marginal conditions which we derived by differentiating the Lagrangean function (14.2) with respect to P and θ_h:

$$\mathcal{L}_P = -\sum_h A_h \theta_h + \lambda - \mu = 0, \qquad (14.26)$$

$$\mathcal{L}_{\theta_h} = A_h[(\Pi - P) + \theta_h \Pi_\Theta]$$
$$- (\beta g_\Theta + \gamma \Pi_\Theta + \lambda \Pi_\Theta - \delta) \leq 0 \quad \forall h. \quad (14.27)$$

Taking the sum over all h of the inequalities (14.27) and substituting (14.26), we obtain[5]

$$\sum_h (A_h/H)(\Pi - P) - \lambda \Pi_\Theta - (\mu/H)\Pi_\Theta - \beta g_\Theta - \gamma \Pi_\Theta + \delta \leq 0. \quad (14.28)$$

This replaces the condition applied in the absence of capital incomes, namely

$$-\beta g_\Theta - \gamma \Pi_\Theta + \delta \leq 0. \qquad (13.7)$$

We are now in a position to discuss the optimal extent of privatization for the various regimes of issue prices.

(i) High Issue Price $(\overline{P} < P = \Pi)$

In this case there are no direct income effects from dividends because $\Pi - P = 0$. However, an infinitesimally small change in privatization also causes an indirect income effect, the welfare implications of which are measured by $\lambda \Pi_\Theta$. Note that $\lambda \Pi_\Theta \leq 0$ does not represent the unwanted profit increases as does $\gamma \Pi_\Theta > 0$. As the issue price exceeds its minimum threshold, $\mu = 0$ and condition (14.28) reduces to

$$-\lambda \Pi_\Theta - \beta g_\Theta - \gamma \Pi_\Theta + \delta \leq 0. \qquad (14.29)$$

For the economic interpretation, let us begin with the case of no privatization. Here, private shareholders have no bargaining power, therefore, profit is at its minimum $(\gamma = 0)$. Hence we obtain as a necessary condition for no privatization,[6]

$$-\beta g_\Theta \leq \lambda \Pi_\Theta \leq 0 \qquad \text{for } \Theta^* = 0. \qquad (14.30)$$

For the right-hand side inequality recall that $\lambda \leq 0$ and $\Pi_\Theta > 0$. Condition (14.30) can be fulfilled only for $g_\Theta \geq 0$. Once again we can conclude that, if no share has been sold, efficiency increases

---

[5] For explanatory clearness we have assumed there is a large number of consumers and therefore approximated $(1-1/H) \approx 1$. Purists may multiply $\lambda \Pi_\Theta$ times $(1-1/H)$.

[6] Recall $\delta = 0$ as well.

by selling the first share must have been impossible. However, an efficiency decrease from privatization is only a *necessary* condition for full public ownership – in contrast to Chapter 13, where it was a necessary and sufficient condition. Now it is possible that the privatization body begins selling shares although this activity reduces efficiency. However, if the efficiency losses are low compared with the indirect income effects, then the sale of shares may be worthwhile.

The trade-off between efficiency increases, profit increases, and indirect income effects can most clearly be seen in the case of partial privatization, where we obtain as a necessary condition

$$-\beta g_\Theta = (\gamma + \lambda)\Pi_\Theta \qquad \text{for } 0 < \Theta^* < 1. \tag{14.31}$$

The indirect income effects partially offset the effects of the unwanted profit increases when the sum of these effects is equal to the efficiency effect.

In the case of total privatization, we have[7]

$$-\beta g_\Theta \geq (\gamma + \lambda)\Pi_\Theta \qquad \text{for } \Theta^* = 1 \tag{14.32}$$

and the interpretation follows the same arguments as before, taking into account that no more than 100 percent of a firm can be sold.

(ii)   Medium Issue Price $(\overline{P} < P < \Pi)$

A medium issue price implies that $\mu = 0$ and $\lambda = 0$. Hence the indirect income effects $\lambda\Pi_\Theta$ are irrelevant for the determination of the optimum degree of privatization. Consequently we have a trade-off between efficiency increases, profit increases, and direct capital-income effects, with all effects measured in welfare terms.

Necessary for the case of no privatization is the condition[8]

$$-\beta g_\Theta \leq -\sum_h (A_h/H)(\Pi - P). \tag{14.33}$$

Here the efficiency effects and the direct income effects are traded off. If the capital-income effects are positive, $\sum_h A_h(\Pi - P) > 0$, then full public ownership is retained only in case of relatively large efficiency reductions $\beta g_\Theta \gg 0$ from selling the first share. Small

---

[7] We could have introduced $(\gamma/\beta)=1/\tilde{\beta}$ as we did in equation (13.10) above. Note $\delta \leq 0$ for $\Theta^*=1$.

[8] This condition results from (14.28) after substituting $\lambda=0$, $\mu=0$, $\delta=0$, and, moreover, $\gamma=0$ (non-binding profit constraint).

efficiency reductions may be overcome by the positive income effects. If, on the other hand, the capital-income effects are negative, $\sum_h A_h(\Pi - P) < 0$, then the government may refrain from selling the first share even if this sale would increase the efficiency of the firm.

In the cases of partial and total privatization, the basic trade-off between efficiency and profit increases is extended so as to include the direct capital-income effects. Therefore, if these income effects are positive, more shares are likely to be sold. The relevant necessary conditions are[9]

$$-\beta g_\Theta = \gamma \Pi_\Theta - \sum_h (A_h/H)(\Pi - P) \quad \text{for } 0 < \Theta^* < 1 \quad (14.34)$$
$$-\beta g_\Theta \geq \gamma \Pi_\Theta - \sum_h (A_h/H)(\Pi - P) \quad \text{for } \Theta^* = 1. \quad (14.35)$$

(iii)   Low Issue Price $(\overline{P} = P < \Pi)$

The interpretation of this case is similar to the medium issue price case except for the term $(\mu/H)\Pi_\Theta \leq 0$, which always occurs on the right-hand side of the necessary conditions:

$$-\beta g_\Theta \leq (\mu/H)\Pi_\Theta$$
$$- \sum_h (A_h/H)(\Pi - P), \quad \Theta^* = 0, \quad (14.36)$$
$$-\beta g_\Theta = \gamma \Pi_\Theta + (\mu/H)\Pi_\Theta$$
$$- \sum_h (A_h/H)(\Pi - P), \quad 0 < \Theta^* < 1, \quad (14.37)$$
$$-\beta g_\Theta \geq \gamma \Pi_\Theta + (\mu/H)\Pi_\Theta$$
$$- \sum_h (A_h/H)(\Pi - P), \quad \Theta^* = 1. \quad (14.38)$$

$(\mu/H)\Pi_\Theta$ is an indirect income effect, similar to $\lambda\Pi_\Theta$ mentioned earlier. Therefore, for a low issue price, both direct and indirect income effects are traded off for the efficiency and (unwanted) profit effects.

Last but not least, we must investigate whether or not *privatization efficiency* is achieved. If we compare the results of this section with the conditions for privatization efficiency, equations (12.9), we realize that partial privatization is never privatization-efficient. The same qualitative result was obtained in Chapter 13; however, we now have to trade off profit *and* income effects for

---

[9] For simplification once again we refrain from writing $(\gamma/\beta)=1/\tilde{\beta}$. Compare equation (13.10).

efficiency effects. In dealing with no privatization and with total privatization, even the qualitative results of Chapter 13 may break down. Whether or not we obtain privatization efficiency depends on the quantitative importance of the capital-income effects.

In order to analyze the properties of privatization inefficiency in more detail, we consider the case of a medium issue price.[10] We have seen that high negative capital-income effects may induce the policy-maker not to privatize at all and to forgo possible efficiency increases. With respect to efficiency, an under-privatization then results. If partial privatization is optimal, g_Θ may be negative or positive. Negative capital-income effects intensify the profit effect and g_Θ is negative at the optimum; consequently we have an under-privatization. However, positive capital-income effects which outweigh the profit effect may even imply a positive g_Θ. In that case, partial privatization has led into a region of technology where, from the efficiency point of view, it would be better to privatize less. With respect to efficiency, an over-privatization then occurs. Furthermore, a positive g_Θ can also occur if the firm is fully privatized.

[10] Equations (13.33)–(13.35) above.

15 Government Budget and Privatization

15.1 Public Expenditures

This is the first section in which fiscal policy measures are discussed. We assume there are public expenditures which are spent for the provision of a public good. This good is the numeraire, so G measures both quantity and expenditures. The public good is perfectly divisible in production and is produced by the private firms as their $(n+1)$th output. The government and the privatized firm know the supply function $y_{n+1}(p^G)$, where p^G is the extended price vector $(p, 1)$. We postpone the treatment of taxation to the next section, hence $\tau_0 = \tau_n = 0$.

Capital incomes are included in this section. The consumer demand for, and supply of, private goods depends on the prices p, on the consumer's capital incomes, and on the quantity of the public good. The netput functions are

$$x_{ih} = x_{ih}(p, \kappa_h, G). \tag{15.1}$$

Demand depends on p and not on the extended price vector p^G. The quantity of the public good is exogenously given for the consumer, so there is no price responsiveness on the part of the consumer with respect to the public good. Hence this price must not be included in the demand function, although all other prices are defined with reference to the price of the public good as numeraire. Substituting the netput functions into the consumer's utility function $u_h(x_{1h}, \ldots, x_{nh}, G)$, we obtain

$$v_h = v_h(p, \kappa_h, G). \tag{15.2}$$

As mentioned in Chapter 12 above, all markets in the economy are assumed to clear; i.e.,

$$x_i - z_i - y_i = 0 \qquad i = 1, \ldots, n \tag{12.1}$$

$$G - y_{n+1} = 0. \tag{12.2}$$

These $n + 1$ market equilibria imply a financial equilibrium,

$$px + G - pz - p^G y = 0, \tag{12.3}$$

which can be transformed into

$$(1 - \Theta)\Pi(\Theta) + \Theta P = G. \tag{15.3}$$

The latter equation is a special case of equation (12.25) above. The financing of the public good is automatically guaranteed by Walras's law. The public revenues from dividends and from selling the shares are spent for the public good.

Of the $n + 2$ equations which constitute the market equilibria and the financial equilibrium, only $n + 1$ are independent. Thus, in an optimization approach we need to include only $n + 1$ of these equations. We are able to choose from the following two alternatives, depending on the particular purpose of the analysis.

In the *first specification* the market equilibrium of the public good is explicitly modelled. The financial equilibrium holds implicitly, say as the $(n + 2)$th constraint.

The Lagrangean function is extended so as to include the market equilibrium of the public good. We have

$$\mathcal{L} = W(v) - \sum_1^n \alpha_i [x_i(p, \kappa, G) - z_i - y_i(p^G)]$$
$$- \alpha_{n+1}[G - y_{n+1}(p^G)] - \beta g(z, \Theta) - \gamma[\Pi(\Theta) - pz]$$
$$- \delta(1 - \Theta) - \lambda(\Pi(\Theta) - P) - \mu(P - \overline{P}). \tag{15.4}$$

The government instruments are the shares θ_h, $h = 1, \ldots, H$, the public good G, and the issue price P, $\overline{P} \leq P \leq \Pi(\Theta)$. Moreover, the government anticipates the privatized firm's choice of prices p_e and netputs z_i. Compared with Chapter 14, there is no qualitative change in the marginal conditions $\mathcal{L}_{\theta_h} \leq 0$ and $\mathcal{L}_P = 0$. All economic interpretations on the welfare-optimal issue price, on 'people's shares', and on the trade-off between allocative and distributional effects remain unchanged.[1] However, assuming an interior solution of G, we impose one more condition, namely $\mathcal{L}_G = 0$,

$$\sum_h W_h \frac{\partial v_h}{\partial G} - \sum_1^n \alpha_i \frac{\partial x_i}{\partial G} - \alpha_{n+1} = 0. \tag{15.5}$$

The optimum supply of any public good is, therefore, based on the comparison of marginal social benefits and marginal social costs,

---

[1] The conditions $\mathcal{L}_{p_e} = 0$ change because the price response of the supply of the public good $\alpha_{n+1}(\partial y_{n+1}/\partial p_e)$ is explicitly included. However, this does not influence the qualitative interpretation of pricing we have dealt with in Section 13.3 above.

taking account of the scarcity of the public good as measured by the parameter α_{n+1}. The disadvantage of this sort of modelling can be seen directly: we cannot show how public expenditures influence the extent of privatization, the issue price, and the distribution of shares. For this reason the following alternative specification is preferred.

In the *second specification* the financial equilibrium of the public good is explicitly modelled. The market equilibrium of the public good holds implicitly, say as the $(n+2)$th constraint.

The Lagrangean function is extended so as to include the financial equilibrium. The associated Lagrangean multiplier is denoted by B. We then have

$$\mathcal{L} = W(v) - \sum_1^n \alpha_i [x_i(p, \kappa, G) - z_i - y_i(p^G)]$$
$$- B[G - (1-\Theta)\Pi(\Theta) - \Theta P] - \beta g(z, \Theta) - \gamma[\Pi(\Theta) - pz]$$
$$- \delta(1-\Theta) - \lambda(\Pi(\Theta) - P) - \mu(P - \overline{P}). \tag{15.6}$$

On the basis of this optimization approach, the government chooses the optimal shares θ_h, issue price P, and public expenditures G. It also computes the prices p_e and netputs z_i which the firm will choose in adjusting to the government policy.[2]

We differentiate with respect to P, θ_h, and G, once again assuming an interior solution of G. We obtain

$$\mathcal{L}_P = -(\sum_h A_h \theta_h - B\Theta) + \lambda - \mu = 0, \tag{15.7}$$
$$\mathcal{L}_{\theta_h} = A_h[(\Pi - P) + \theta_h \Pi_\Theta] - B[(\Pi - P) + \Theta \Pi_\Theta]$$
$$- [\beta g_\Theta + (\gamma + \lambda - B)\Pi_\Theta - \delta] \leq 0, \tag{15.8}$$
$$\mathcal{L}_G = \sum_h W_h \frac{\partial v_h}{\partial G} - \sum_1^n \alpha_i \frac{\partial x_i}{\partial G} - B = 0. \tag{15.9}$$

As usual, we define

$$A_h := W_h \frac{\partial v_h}{\partial \kappa_h} - \sum_1^n \alpha_i \frac{\partial x_{ih}}{\partial \kappa_h}, \tag{15.10}$$

which is the welfare effect of changes in consumer h's capital income. For the determination of the issue price, A_h is weighted by the percentage of shares θ_h. It is convenient to denote $\sum_h A_h \theta_h$ as the private welfare effect.

---

[2] The p_e- and z_i-marginal conditions remain unchanged.

From equation (15.9) we learn that the amount supplied of a public good is based on the comparison of marginal social benefits and marginal social costs, taking into account the scarcity of this good, as measured by the Lagrangean parameter B. A straightforward transformation of equation (15.9) shows the similarity of A_h and B:

$$B = \sum_h W_h \frac{\partial v_h}{\partial G} - \sum_1^n \alpha_i \frac{\partial x_i}{\partial G}. \tag{15.11}$$

Therefore, B is the welfare effect of changes in government expenditures. We denote $B\Theta$ as the public welfare effect.

The economic interpretation of B is similar to A_h. An increase in G has a twofold effect on welfare. First, individual utilities increase and so does welfare. Second, both consumer demand for outputs and consumer supply of inputs change. Both consumption and input effects may be positive or negative, depending on whether the public good and the private netputs are complements or substitutes.

The *optimal issue price* can easily be classified on the basis of condition (15.7).[3] We obtain the following results:

(i) high issue price if $(\sum_h A_h \theta_h - B\Theta) \leq 0$,
(ii) medium issue price if $(\sum_h A_h \theta_h - B\Theta) = 0$,
(iii) low issue price if $(\sum_h A_h \theta_h - B\Theta) \geq 0$.

The result depends on the trade-off between the private welfare effect and the public welfare effect. The net welfare effect is decisive because any increase in the share price P takes from the consumers and gives to the government. This means that we have to trade off the welfare effects of reduced consumer incomes for the welfare effects of increased government expenditures.[4]

If at the optimum the public exceeds the private welfare effect, the government increases public expenditures to the possible maximum by setting the issue price equal to profit. Since $P = \Pi$, all the profit of the privatized firm is spent as public expenditures. If, on the other hand, at the optimum the private exceeds the public welfare effect, the consumers' monetary gains from buying shares, $\Pi - P$, are increased to the possible maximum. This is achieved by choosing the lowest feasible issue price $\overline{P}$. The public expenditures are reduced by that amount of money which the low-issue-price policy has shifted to the consumers: we therefore

---

[3] As in Section 14.2, we exclude the case of $\theta_h = 0$ for all h.

[4] Recall that we are interpreting equation (15.7). The above argument therefore holds for constant Θ.

obtain $G = \Pi - \Theta(\Pi - \overline{P})$ as a special case of equation (15.3). At a point of transition from one polar case to the other, the private and the public welfare effects cancel out, giving the government the option of choosing a medium issue price.

The reader will have realized the close similarity between the issue-price policy in the public expenditure case and in the no-expenditure case. In the public expenditure case the issue price depends on both the private and the public welfare effects. In the no-expenditure case the issue price depends only on the private welfare effect. Otherwise in both cases the decision on the share price follows the same pattern.

Let us now turn to the *optimal degree of privatization* which can be discussed on the basis of condition (15.8). We sum (15.8) for all consumers to obtain

$$\sum_h \{(A_h/H)[(\Pi - P) + \theta_h \Pi_\Theta]\} - B[(\Pi - P) + \Theta \Pi_\Theta]$$
$$- [\beta g_\Theta + (\gamma + \lambda - B)\Pi_\Theta - \delta] \leq 0. \qquad (15.12)$$

Substituting $\mathcal{L}_P = 0$ into (15.12), we obtain the basic necessary condition for the degree of privatization in the presence of public expenditures:[5]

$$[\sum_h (A_h/H) - B](\Pi - P) - [\lambda - B(1 - \Theta)]\Pi_\Theta - (\mu/H)\Pi_\Theta$$
$$- \beta g_\Theta - \gamma \Pi_\Theta + \delta \leq 0. \qquad (15.13)$$

This condition is a straightforward extension of the conditions we obtained for economies without public expenditures, namely

$$\sum_h (A_h/H)(\Pi - P) - \lambda \Pi_\Theta - (\mu/H)\Pi_\Theta$$
$$- \beta g_\Theta - \gamma \Pi_\Theta + \delta \leq 0, \qquad (14.28)$$

or, eliminating capital-income effects,

$$- \beta g_\Theta - \gamma \Pi_\Theta + \delta \leq 0. \qquad (13.7)$$

We refrain from explicitly dealing with the issue price and degree of privatization for every single case. We are able to simplify this discussion because the economic meaning of the result is clear: in addition to the efficiency effect and the capital-income effects, the public welfare effect speaks in favor of privatization. Hence higher profit increases are accepted the higher the welfare effects of the public expenditures.

---

[5] As in Ch. 14, we have approximated $(1 - 1/H) \approx 1$.

15.2   Income Taxation

In this section we explicitly include taxation of the labor income $-p_n x_{nh}$ and the capital income κ_h. As already mentioned on pp. 238–9 above, we choose a capital gains specification of the income tax, knowing that all qualitative results can also be obtained if the income tax does not allow for the deduction of the costs of acquiring the shares, $\theta_h P$. The tax schedule is assumed to be linear, so that there is a guaranteed basic income τ_0 and a constant marginal tax rate τ_n,

$$t_h = \tau_n(\kappa_h - p_n x_{nh}) - \tau_0; \qquad h = 1, \dots, H. \qquad (15.14)$$

A negative tax $(t_h < 0)$ occurs for $\tau_n(\kappa_h - p_n x_{nh}) < \tau_0$.

The properties of the linear income tax are known from the literature (Hellwig, 1986; Sheshinski, 1972). Individual utility maximization implies that only $\tau_n < 1$ can be implemented. Otherwise the consumers would work less than anticipated by the policy-maker. In our model the disincentive effects of taxation are explicitly considered by taking account of the change in netputs caused by changes in the net wage rate $(1 - \tau_n)p_n$. Of particular importance are the changes in the labor–leisure choice $\partial x_{nh}/\partial(1 - \tau_n)p_n$.

Typically we expect $\tau_0 > 0$, which implies that the tax is progressive. Then the basic incomes τ_0 can be interpreted as poll subsidies which are given to consumers. These subsidies are the only public expenditures we treat in this section. We exclude public good expenditures, $G = 0$, to avoid too complicated modelling. On the other hand, we include capital incomes as we have done in the previous analyses beginning in Chapter 14.

The consumer maximizes utility for any given capital income, income tax, and prices in the economy. Therefore, the indirect utility he attains is expressed by

$$v_h = v_h[p_1, p_2, \dots, (1 - \tau_n)p_n, (1 - \tau_n)\kappa_h + \tau_0]; \qquad h = 1, \dots, H. \qquad (15.15)$$

As in earlier passages of this book, the financial equilibrium in the economy is implied in the market equilibria of the private goods. We multiply every market equilibrium condition by the respective price, sum the results, and substitute the individual budget equations, namely

$$\sum_{i=1}^{n-1} p_i x_{ih} = (1 - \tau_n)(\kappa_h - p_n x_{nh}) + \tau_0. \qquad (15.16)$$

After some algebraic manipulation, the financial equilibrium in the economy can be written as

$$(1 - \Theta)\Pi(\Theta) + \Theta P + \tau_n \sum_h (\kappa_h - p_n x_{nh}) = H\tau_0. \qquad (15.17)$$

The public revenues from dividends, from selling shares, and from income taxation are spent as poll subsidies τ_0.

Given the specifications of the preceding paragraphs, we will investigate the way in which privatization influences the income tax pressure in the economy.

15.2.1 How Far Does Privatization Reduce the Tax Pressure?

The influence of privatization on tax pressure can be shown using the government's budget constraint (15.17). This financial equilibrium is a balanced-budget equation for the government. $(1 - \Theta)\Pi$ is the government's dividend income, ΘP is the revenue from selling shares. Together they constitute the government revenues from privatization. According to (15.17), these revenues are always expended via the (negative) income taxation. Hence for any increase in Θ, a marginal change in the government revenues from privatization is equal to a marginal change in the tax revenues of the same size. We call this change in revenues a change in the tax pressure. Note that in this subsection we perform a comparative-static analysis of an equilibrium constraint which holds for any Θ. This analysis has nothing whatsoever to do with optimization.

Measuring the marginal change of the tax pressure by the corresponding change in government revenues from privatization, we obtain the following results.

(i) The tax pressure may be increased or reduced by privatization:

$$\frac{\partial[\tau_n \sum_h (\kappa_h - p_n x_{nh}) - H\tau_0]}{\partial \Theta} = -\frac{\partial[(1 - \Theta)\Pi(\Theta) + \Theta P]}{\partial \Theta}$$

$$= [\Pi(\Theta) - P] - (1 - \Theta)\Pi_\Theta \underset{<}{\overset{\geq}{}} 0. \tag{15.18}$$

This result contrasts with the usual *a priori* assumption that increasing privatization always reduces the tax pressure. The reason for the surprising result is the low issue price P. If shares are sold at a price which equals the expected dividends, increasing privatization always leads to a reduction of the tax pressure. There is a simple trade-off between the issue price and the tax pressure. The higher the issue price, the more revenues from privatization will be obtained by the government and the higher the reduction of the tax pressure. This can be seen directly from (15.17).

(ii) For the usual case of $P < \Pi(1)$, the maximum reduction of tax pressure will never be achieved by total privatization. This can be shown as follows. We maximize the Lagrangean function

$$\mathcal{L} = (1 - \Theta)\Pi(\Theta) + \Theta P - \delta(1 - \Theta) \qquad (15.19)$$

and therefore

$$\mathcal{L}_\Theta = (1 - \Theta)\Pi_\Theta - \left[\Pi(\Theta) - P\right] + \delta \leq 0. \qquad (15.20)$$

Now assume $\Theta^* = 1$, whence $\delta \leq 0$ and $\mathcal{L}_\Theta = 0$. But then P must be at least equal to $\Pi(1)$, which is a contradiction to our assumption of $P < \Pi(1)$. Hence the maximum reduction of tax pressure is achieved at $\Theta^* < 1$.

(iii)   The marginal reduction of the tax pressure is always smaller than the marginal change of profit Π_Θ. This can be seen directly from (15.18). The marginal reduction of tax pressure consists of $\Pi_\Theta - (\Theta\Pi_\Theta + \Pi - P)$ where $(\Theta\Pi_\Theta + \Pi - P) > 0$. Therefore, a reduction of tax pressure might be an interesting side-effect of privatization, but privatization does not seem to be the most efficient instrument for redistribution.

15.2.2 *Optimal Privatization and Optimal Taxation*

In this section, the number of government policy options has been increased. The government can now apply the individual shares θ_h, the marginal tax rate τ_n, and the lump-sum transfer τ_0 as instruments. We assume that privatization and tax instruments are set simultaneously by the same institution.

The government budget constraint is always fulfilled as an implication of the financial equilibrium, hence it need not be explicitly included in the government optimization approach. This makes it once again possible to describe the optimization approach of the government (privatization body) and the optimization approach of the firm's board through only one approach, namely the maximization of welfare, given the feasibility constraints and the bargaining constraint on profit, as described by the Lagrangean

$$\begin{aligned}
\mathcal{L} = &\, W(v) - \sum_1^n \alpha_i \{ x_i[p_1, p_2, \ldots, (1 - \tau_n)p_n, (1 - \tau_n)\kappa + \tau_0] \\
&- z_i - y_i(p) \} - \beta g(z, \Theta) - \gamma[\Pi(\Theta) - pz] \\
&- \delta(1 - \Theta) - \lambda(\Pi(\Theta) - P) - \mu(P - \overline{P}).
\end{aligned} \qquad (15.21)$$

The strategic setting remains unchanged. Once again the government is the Stackelberg leader and the firm is the Stackelberg follower. For any set of $\theta_1, \ldots, \theta_H, P, \tau_0$, and τ_n, the board of the firm chooses prices and netputs according to

$$\mathcal{L}_{p_e} = 0, \quad \mathcal{L}_z = 0. \qquad (15.22)$$

The government is informed about the decision rules (15.22) of the board. Hence it can use these rules as the basis of its decision when choosing an optimal privatization level and optimal parameters of the tax function. The relevant marginal conditions are as follows:[6]

$$\mathcal{L}_{\theta_h} : A_h(1 - \tau_n)[(\Pi - P) + \theta_h \Pi_{\Theta}]$$
$$\leq \beta g_{\Theta} + \gamma \Pi_{\Theta} + \lambda \Pi_{\Theta} - \delta, \qquad h = 1, \dots, H^7 \qquad (15.23)$$

$$\mathcal{L}_{\tau_n} : \sum_h A_h \kappa_h =$$
$$- p_n \sum_h \left(W_h \frac{\partial v_h}{\partial (1 - \tau_n) p_n} - \sum_1^n \alpha_i \frac{\partial x_{ih}}{\partial (1 - \tau_n) p_n} \right), \qquad (15.24)$$

$$\mathcal{L}_{\tau_0} : \sum_h A_h = 0, \qquad (15.25)$$

$$\mathcal{L}_P : \sum_h A_h \theta_h = \lambda - \mu. \qquad (15.26)$$

Once again we have used the abbreviation

$$A_h := W_h \frac{\partial v_h}{\partial \kappa_h} - \sum_1^n \alpha_i \frac{\partial x_{ih}}{\partial \kappa_h} \qquad (15.10)$$

for the welfare effect of changes in consumer h's income.

For the economic interpretation of the marginal conditions we distinguish two cases.

(i)   The government uses θ_h, P, τ_0, and τ_n as instruments. Substituting (15.25) into the sum of equations (15.23) yields

$$\sum_h A_h \theta_h \frac{(1 - \tau_n)\Pi_{\Theta}}{H} \leq \beta g_{\Theta} + \gamma \Pi_{\Theta} + \lambda \Pi_{\Theta} - \delta. \qquad (15.27)$$

The direct capital-income effects in (15.23), $\sum_h A_h(\Pi - P)$, are optimally offset by the income effects of the lump-sum transfer τ_0. However, the indirect income effects[8] still are decisive for the optimal degree of privatization. As in Section 14.4, we can conclude that the higher the profit increases that will be accepted by the privatization body, the higher the efficiency effect and the positive effects from capital incomes.

---

[6] Plus the usual further Kuhn–Tucker conditions.

[7] where the equality holds for $\theta_h^* \neq 0$;

[8] In contrast to Sect. 14.4, the indirect income effects are not represented by a Lagrangean multiplier times Π_{Θ}, but by Π_{Θ} times $\sum_h A_h \theta_h (1 - \tau_n)/H$. Note, however, that this term implies the welfare evaluation of Π_{Θ} which is exactly what the Lagrangean multiplier in Sect. 14.4 did.

There is one special case which we must examine in detail. Consider interior solutions of both θ_h and P, hence $0 < \theta_h^* < 1$ and $\overline{P} < P < \Pi$. The restriction to interior solutions of P implies $\lambda = \mu = 0$ and, therefore, $\sum_h A_h \theta_h = 0$ from (15.26). Hence (15.27) reduces to

$$\beta g_\Theta + \gamma \Pi_\Theta - \delta \geq 0. \tag{15.28}$$

All the results we deduced in Section 13.2 are also valid in this special case.[9] Choosing a medium issue price sets the aggregate welfare evaluation of the indirect income effects equal to zero. Consequently no income effects are left, as choosing the optimal τ_0 has offset the direct capital-income effects.

(ii)   The government uses θ_h, P, and τ_n as instruments; τ_0 is exogenously given and deviates from the welfare-optimal τ_0^*.

For the interpretation of this case we assume that $\mathcal{L}_{\tau_0\tau_0} < 0$ on the whole domain of $\mathcal{L}$. Then $\mathcal{L}_{\tau_0} > 0$ results if τ_0 has been chosen too low and $\mathcal{L}_{\tau_0} < 0$ if τ_0 has been chosen too high.

A particularly simple interpretation can once again be given if shares are sold at a medium issue price and $\sum_h A_h \theta_h = 0$. Summing $\mathcal{L}_{\theta_h}$ over all consumers then leads to

$$\mathcal{L}_{\tau_0} = \sum_h A_h = \frac{H(\beta g_\Theta + \gamma \Pi_\Theta - \delta)}{(1 - \tau_n)(\Pi - P)}. \tag{15.29}$$

This implies

$$\text{sign } \mathcal{L}_{\tau_0} = \text{sign } (\beta g_\Theta + \gamma \Pi_\Theta - \delta). \tag{15.30}$$

Too low a transfer τ_0 is compensated by too high an extent of privatization and vice versa. If there has not been enough redistribution because of τ_0, the extent of privatization Θ is used as a compensatory instrument of redistribution, and privatization is extended into a region where higher profit increases than those in the welfare-optimal case are accepted.

---

[9]   Another special case is treated in Bös and Peters (1988a,b). If the privatization body decides a priori to give the same amount of shares to everybody, $\theta_h = \Theta/H$, then the extent of privatization also follows from an inequality of the type (15.28).

References

Albach, H. (1979), 'Zur Wiederentdeckung des Unternehmers in der wirtschaftspolitischen Diskussion', *Zeitschrift für die gesamte Staatswissenschaft*, 135: 533–52.

Allen, F., and **Faulhaber, G. R.** (1987), 'Signaling by Underpricing in the IPO Market', Working Paper, Wharton School, University of Pennsylvania.

Aoki, M. (1980), 'A Model of the Firm as a Stockholder–Employee Cooperative Game', *American Economic Review*, 70: 600–10.

— (1982), 'Equilibrium Growth of the Hierarchical Firm: Shareholder–Employee Cooperative Game Approach', *American Economic Review*, 72: 1097–110.

Arrow, K. J. (1986), 'Agency and the Market', in K. J. Arrow and M. D. Intriligator (eds.), *Handbook of Mathematical Economics, iii.* Amsterdam: North-Holland.

— and **Debreu, G.** (1954), 'Existence of an Equilibrium for a Competitive Economy', *Econometrica*, 22: 265–90.

Asquith, P. (1983), 'Merger Bids, Uncertainty, and Stockholder Returns', *Journal of Financial Economics*, 11: 51–83.

Atkinson, A. B., and **Stiglitz, J. E.** (1980), *Lectures on Public Economics.* Maidenhead: McGraw-Hill.

Atkinson, S. E., and **Halvorsen, R.** (1986), 'The Relative Efficiency of Public and Private Firms in a Regulated Environment: The Case of US Electric Utilities', *Journal of Public Economics*, 29: 281–94.

Attali, J. (1978), 'Towards Socialist Planning', in S. Holland (ed.), *Beyond Capitalist Planning.* Oxford: Basil Blackwell.

Aumann, R. (1976), 'Agreeing to Disagree', *Annals of Statistics*, 4: 1236–9.

Backhaus, J. (1979), *Ökonomik der partizipativen Unternehmung, i.* Tübingen: Mohr.

Baron, D. P. (1982), 'A Model of the Demand for Investment Banking Advising and Distribution Services for New Issues', *Journal of Finance*, 37: 955–76.

— and **Myerson, R. B.** (1982), 'Regulating a Monopolist with Unknown Costs', *Econometrica*, 50: 911–30.

Baumol, W. J. (1959), *Business Behavior, Value and Growth.* New York: Macmillan.

— (1977), 'On the Proper Cost Tests for Natural Monopoly in a Multiproduct Industry', *American Economic Review*, 67: 809–22.

— , **Bailey, E. E.,** and **Willig, R. D.** (1977), 'Weak Invisible Hand Theorems on the Sustainability of Multiproduct Natural Monopoly', *American Economic Review*, 67: 350–65.

— and **Bradford, D. F.** (1970), 'Optimal Departures from Marginal

Cost Pricing', *American Economic Review*, 60: 265–83.

Baumol, W. J., Panzar, J. C., and **Willig, R. D.** (1982), *Contestable Markets and the Theory of Industry Structure*, rev. edn. 1988. New York: Harcourt Brace Jovanovich.

Beato, P. (1982), 'The Existence of Marginal Cost Pricing Equilibria with Increasing Returns', *Quarterly Journal of Economics*, 97: 669–88.

— and **Mas-Colell, A.** (1984), 'The Marginal Cost Pricing as a Regulation Mechanism in Mixed Markets', in M. Marchand, P. Pestieau, and H. Tulkens (eds.), *The Performance of Public Enterprises*. Amsterdam: North-Holland.

Beesley, M. E. (1981), *Liberalisation of the Use of British Telecommunications Network: Report to the Secretary of State, Department of Industry*. London: HMSO.

— and **Littlechild, S. C.** (1989), 'The Regulation of Privatized Monopolies in the United Kingdom', *Rand Journal of Economics*, 20: 454–72.

Bennett, J. T., and **Johnson, M. H.** (1980), 'Tax Reduction without Sacrifice: Private Sector Production of Public Services', *Public Finance Quarterly*, 8: 363–96.

Berg, S. V., and **Tschirhart, J.** (1988), *Natural Monopoly Regulation*. Cambridge: Cambridge University Press.

Binmore, K., Rubinstein, A., and **Wolinsky, A.** (1986), 'The Nash Bargaining Solution in Economic Modelling', *Rand Journal of Economics*, 17: 176–88.

Bishop, M., and **Kay, J. A.** (1988), *Does Privatization Work? Lessons from the UK*. London: Centre for Business Strategy, London Business School.

Boardman, A. E., Eckel, C., and **Vining, A. R.** (1986), 'The Advantages and Disadvantages of Mixed Enterprises', *Research in International Business and International Relations*, 1: 221–44.

— , **Freedman, R.,** and **Eckel, C.** (1986), 'The Price of Government Ownership: A Study of the Domtar Takeover', *Journal of Public Economics*, 31: 269–85.

— and **Vining, A. R.** (1988), 'The Behavior of Mixed Enterprises', mimeo, University of British Columbia.

— — (1989), 'Ownership and Performance in Competitive Environments: A Comparison of the Performance of Private, Mixed and State-Owned Enterprises', *Journal of Law and Economics*, 32: 1–33.

Boiteux, M. (1956, 1971), 'Sur la gestion des monopoles publics astreints à l'equilibre budgétaire', *Econometrica*, 24: 22–40. (English edition: 'On the Management of Public Monopolies Subject to Budgetary Constraints', *Journal of Economic Theory*, 3: 219–40.)

Bonnisseau, J.-M. (1987), 'General Pricing Rules, Bounded Losses and Existence of Equilibrium in Economies with Increasing Returns',

Discussion Paper no. 8711, CORE, Louvain-la-Neuve.

Bonnisseau, J.-M., and **Cornet, B.** (1987), 'Existence of Marginal Cost Pricing Equilibrium in an Economy with Several Nonconvex Firms', Discussion Paper no. 8723, CORE, Louvain-la-Neuve.

Borcherding, T. E., **Pommerehne, W. W.**, and **Schneider, F.** (1982), 'Comparing the Efficiency of Private and Public Production: The Evidence from Five Countries', in D. Bös, R. A. Musgrave, and J. Wiseman (eds.), *Public Production*. Vienna: Springer. (Zeitschrift für Nationalökonomie/Journal of Economics, Supplement 2).

Bös, D. (1978a), 'Cost of Living Indices and Public Pricing', *Economica*, 45: 59–69.

— (1978b), 'Distributional Effects of Maximisation of Passenger Miles', *Journal of Transport Economics and Policy*, 12: 322–9.

— (1981), *Economic Theory of Public Enterprise*. Berlin: Springer.

— (1984), 'Income Taxation, Public Sector Pricing and Redistribution', *Scandinavian Journal of Economics*, 86: 166–83.

— (1985), 'Public Sector Pricing', in A. Auerbach and M. Feldstein (eds.), *Handbook of Public Economics, i.* Amsterdam: North-Holland.

— (1986a), *Public Enterprise Economics*, 2nd rev. edn. 1989. *(Advanced Textbooks in Economics, xxiii.)* Amsterdam: North-Holland.

— (1986b), 'A Theory of the Privatization of Public Enterprises', in D. Bös and C. Seidl (eds.), *Welfare Economics of the Second Best.* Vienna: Springer (*Journal of Economics/Zeitschrift für Nationalökonomie*, Supplement 5).

— (1987), 'Privatization of Public Enterprises', *European Economic Review*, 31: 352–60.

— (1988a), 'Recent Theories on Public Enterprise Economics', *European Economic Review*, 32: 409–14.

— (1988b), 'Welfare Effects of Privatizing Public Enterprises', in D. Bös, M. Rose, and C. Seidl (eds.), *Welfare and Efficiency in Public Economics*. Berlin: Springer.

— (1989a), 'Arguments on Privatization', in G. Fels and G. von Fürstenberg (eds.), *A Supply-Side Agenda for Germany*. Berlin: Springer.

— (1989b), 'Privatization of Public Firms: A Government-Trade Union-Private Shareholder Cooperative Game', in M. Neumann and K. W. Roskamp (eds.), *Public Finance and the Performance of Enterprises*. Detroit: Wayne State University Press.

— and **Nett, L.** (1989), 'Employee Share Ownership and Privatisation: A Comment', Discussion Paper A–263, University of Bonn, forthcoming in *Economic Journal*, 101 (1991).

— — (1990), 'Privatization, Price Regulation, and Market Entry: An Asymmetric Multistage Duopoly Model', *Journal of Economics/Zeitschrift für Nationalökonomie*, 51: 221–57.

— and **Peters, W.** (1988a), 'Privatization, Internal Control, and Internal Regulation', *Journal of Public Economics*, 36: 231–58.

288 References

Bös, D., and **Peters, W.** (1988*b*), 'Privatization, Efficiency and Market Structure', in B. Rudolph and J. Wilhelm (eds.), *Bankpolitik, finanzielle Unternehmensführung und die Theorie der Finanzmärkte. Festschrift for Krümmel.* Berlin: Duncker & Humblot.

— — (1990), 'A Principal–Agent Approach on Manager Effort and Control in Privatized and Public Firms', Discussion Paper A-252, University of Bonn, forthcoming in A. Ott and K. Hartley (eds.), *Privatization and Economic Efficiency.* Hants: E. Elgar (1991).

—, **Tillmann, G.**, and **Zimmermann, H.-G.** (1984), 'Bureaucratic Public Enterprises', in D. Bös, A. Bergson, and J. R. Meyer (eds.), *Entrepreneurship.* Vienna: Springer (*Zeitschrift für Nationalökonomie/Journal of Economics*, Supplement 4).

— and **Zimmermann, H.-G.** (1987), 'Maximizing Votes under Imperfect Information', *European Journal of Political Economy*, 3: 523–53.

Bös, J. (1956), 'Volksaktie als Versprechen, Hoffnung und Wirklichkeit', *Berichte und Informationen*, no. 520: 1–3.

Boyd, C. W. (1986), 'The Comparative Efficiency of State-Owned Enterprise', in A. R. Negandhi, H. Thomas, and K. L. K. Rao (eds.), *Multinational Corporations and State-Owned Enterprises: A New Challenge in International Business (Research in International Business and International Relations*, i. Greenwich, Conn.: JAI Press.

Bradley, I., and **Price, C.** (1988), 'The Economic Regulation of Private Industries by Price Constraints', *Journal of Industrial Economics*, 37: 99–106.

Braeutigam, R. R., and **Panzar, J. C.** (1989), 'Diversification Incentives Under "Price-based" and "Cost-based" Regulation', *Rand Journal of Economics*, 20: 373–91.

Brede, H. (ed.) (1988), *Privatisierung und die Zukunft der öffentlichen Wirtschaft.* Baden–Baden: Nomos Verlagsgesellschaft.

Brennan, T. J. (1989), 'Regulating by Capping Prices', *Journal of Regulatory Economics*, 1: 133–47.

Brittan, S. (1986), 'Privatisation: A Comment on Kay and Thompson', *Economic Journal*, 96: 33–8.

Buckland, R. (1987), 'The Costs and Returns of the Privatization of Nationalized Industries', *Public Administration*, 65: 241–57.

Cabral, L. M. B., and **Riordan, M. H.** (1989), 'Incentives for Cost Reduction under Price Cap Regulation', *Journal of Regulatory Economics*, 1: 93–102.

Caillaud, B. R., Guesnerie, R., Rey, P., and **Tirole, J.** (1988), 'Government Intervention in Production and Incentives Theory: A Review of Recent Contributions', *Rand Journal of Economics*, 19: 1–26.

Cave, M., and **Trotter, S.** (1990), 'The Regulation of Competition and Entry in Markets for UK Telecommunications Services', in D. Elixmann and K.-H. Neumann (eds.), *Communications Policy in*

Europe. Berlin: Springer.

Chaffai, M. E. (1989), 'Efficacité technique comparée des entreprises publiques et privées en Tunisie', *Annals of Public and Cooperative Economics*, 60: 451–62.

Chamley, C., Marchand, M., and **Pestieau, P.** (1989), 'Linear Incentive Schemes to Control Public Firms', *European Journal of Political Economy*, 5: 229–43.

Charzat, M. M. (1981), *Rapport no. 456, Assemblée Nationale 1981–1982, au nom de la Commission Spéciale Chargée d'Examiner le Projet de Loi de Nationalisation (no. 384), i: Présentation Génerale*. Paris: Imprimerie de l'Assemblee Nationale.

Cornet, B. (1982), 'Existence of Equilibria in Economies with Increasing Returns', Working Paper, University of California at Berkeley.

Côté, D. (1989), 'Firm Efficiency and Ownership Structure: The Case of US Electric Utilities using Panel Data', *Annals of Public and Cooperative Economics*, 60: 431–50.

Cowling, K. *et al.* (1980), *Mergers and Economic Performance*. Cambridge: Cambridge University Press.

Cremer, H., Marchand, M., and **Thisse, J. F.** (1989), 'The Public Firm as an Instrument for Regulating an Oligopolistic Market', *Oxford Economic Papers*, 41: 283–301.

De Alessi, L. (1980), 'The Economics of Property Rights: A Review of the Evidence', in R. O. Zerbe (ed.), *Research in Law and Economics*, ii. Greenwich, Conn.: JAI Press.

De Fraja, G. (1990a), 'Union and Wages in Public and Private Firms: A Theoretical Analysis', mimeo, University of Bristol.

— (1990b), 'Incentive Contracts for Public Firms', mimeo, University of Bristol.

— (1991), 'Inefficiency and Privatisation in Imperfectly Competitive Industries', *Journal of Industrial Economics*, 39: 311–21.

— and **Delbono, F.** (1989), 'Alternative Strategies of a Public Enterprise in Oligopoly', *Oxford Economic Papers*, 41: 302–11.

Delors, J. (1978), 'The Decline of French Planning', in S. Holland (ed.), *Beyond Capitalist Planning*. Oxford: Basil Blackwell.

Deneckere, C., and **Kovenock, D.** (1988), 'Price Leadership', Discussion Paper no. 773, Center for Mathematical Studies in Economics and Management Science, Northwestern University.

Dierker, E., Guesnerie, R., and **Neuefeind, W.** (1985), 'General Equilibrium when Some Firms Follow Special Pricing Rules', *Econometrica*, 53: 1369–93.

Dixit, A. (1980), 'The Role of Investment in Entry-Deterrence', *Economic Journal*, 90: 95–106.

Domberger, S. (1988), 'Franchising and Competitive Tendering', in S. Estrin and C. Whitehead (eds.), *Privatisation and the Nationalised Industries*. London: ST/ICERD, London School of Economics.

Drèze, J. H. (1964), 'Some Postwar Contributions of French Economists to Theory and Public Policy with Special Emphasis on Problems of Resource Allocation', *American Economic Review*, 54 (no. 4, part 2, supplement), 1–64.

— (1984), 'Second-Best Analysis with Markets in Disequilibrium: Public Sector Pricing in a Keynesian Regime', in M. Marchand, P. Pestieau, and H. Tulkens (eds.), *The Performance of Public Enterprises*. Amsterdam: North-Holland.

— and **Marchand, M.** (1976), 'Pricing, Spending, and Gambling Rules for Non-profit Organizations', in R. E. Grieson (ed.), *Public and Urban Economics. Essays in Honor of William S. Vickrey*. Lexington, Mass.: D. C. Heath.

Ebrill, L. P., and **Slutsky, S. M.** (1988), 'Joint Pricing Rules for Intermediate and Final-Good Regulated Industries', mimeo.

Eckel, C., and **Vining, A. R.** (1985), 'Elements of a Theory of Mixed Enterprise', *Scottish Journal of Political Economy*, 32: 82–93.

Estrin, S., and **de Meza, D.** (1988), 'Should the Post Office's Statutory Monopoly be Lifted?', mimeo, London School of Economics.

— , **Grout, P. A.**, and **Wadhwani, S.** (1987), 'Profit-Sharing and Employee Share Ownership', *Economic Policy*, 2(4), 13–52; 59–62.

— and **Whitehead, C. M. E.** (eds.) (1988), *Privatisation and the Nationalised Industries*. London: ST/ICERD, London School of Economics.

Färe, R. (1988), *Fundamentals of Production Theory*. Berlin: Springer.

— and **Grosskopf, S.** (1987), 'On Price Efficiency', Discussion Paper A–119, University of Bonn.

— , — , and **Logan, J.** (1985), 'The Relative Performance of Publicly-Owned and Privately-Owned Electric Utilities', *Journal of Public Economics*, 26: 89–106.

Federal Communications Commission (1987), 'Policy and Rules Concerning Rates for Dominant Carriers', CC Docket no. 87–263.

— (1988), 'Further Notice of Proposed Rulemaking', CC Docket no. 87–313.

Feigenbaum, S., and **Teeples, R.** (1983), 'Public vs. Private Water Delivery: A Hedonic Cost Approach', *Review of Economics and Statistics*, 65: 672–8.

Feldstein, M.S. (1972a), 'Distributional Equity and the Optimal Structure of Public Prices', *American Economic Review*, 62: 32–6. (Corrected version of p. 33, fn. 7: *American Economic Review*, 62: 763.)

— (1972b), 'Equity and Efficiency in Public Sector Pricing: The Optimal Two-Part Tariff', *Quarterly Journal of Economics*, 86: 175–87.

— (1972c), 'The Pricing of Public Intermediate Goods', *Journal of Public Economics*, 1: 45–72.

— (1974), 'Financing in the Evaluation of Public Expenditure', in W. L. Smith, and J. M. Culbertson (eds.), *Public Finance and Stabilization*

Policy: Essays in Honor of Richard A. Musgrave. Amsterdam: North-Holland.

Fershtman, C. (1990), 'The Interdependence between Ownership Status and Market Structure: The Case of Privatization', *Economica*, 57: 319–28.

Finsinger, J., and **Vogelsang, I.** (1981), 'Alternative Institutional Frameworks for Price Incentive Mechanisms', *Kyklos*, 34: 388–404.

Fiscal Studies (1984), 'A Symposium on Privatisation and After', contributions by D. Heald, T. Sharpe, P. Forsyth, E. Davis, D. Steel, and K. Hartley, *Fiscal Studies*, 5(1), 36–105.

— (1985), Contributions by B. Hammond, D. Helm, and D. Thompson; D. Starkie and D. Thompson; C. Mayer and S. Meadowcroft, *Fiscal Studies*, 6(4), 1–20, 30–56.

Foreman-Peck, J., and **Waterson, M.** (1985), 'The Comparative Efficiency of Public and Private Enterprise in Britain: Electricity Generation between the World Wars', *Economic Journal*, Supplement: 83–95.

Franks, J. R., and **Harris, R. S.** (1986a), 'Shareholder Wealth Effects of Corporate Takeovers: The UK Experience 1955–85', Working Paper, London Business School and University of North Carolina at Chapel Hill.

— — (1986b), 'The Role of the Mergers and Monopolies Commission in Merger Policy: Costs and Alternatives', *Oxford Review of Economic Policy*, 2(4), 58–76.

Freixas, X., and **Laffont, J.-J.** (1985), 'Average Cost Pricing versus Marginal Cost Pricing under Moral Hazard', *Journal of Public Economics*, 26: 135–46.

Frydman, R., and **Rapaczynski, A.** (1990), 'Markets and Institutions in Large Scale Privatizations: An Approach to Economic and Social Transformations in Eastern Europe', mimeo, C. V. Starr Center for Applied Economics, New York.

Glaister, S., and **Collings, J. J.** (1978), 'Maximisation of Passenger Miles in Theory and Practice', *Journal of Transport Economics and Policy*, 12: 304–21.

Graham, C., and **Prosser, T.** (1987), 'Privatising Nationalised Industries: Constitutional Issues and New Legal Techniques', *Modern Law Review*, 50: 16–51.

— — (1988), ' "Rolling Back the Frontiers"? The Privatisation of State Enterprises', in C. Graham and T. Prosser (eds.), *Waiving the Rules: The Constitution under Thatcherism*. Milton Keynes: Open University Press.

Gravelle, H. S. E. (1982), 'Incentives, Efficiency and Control in Public Firms', in D. Bös, R. A. Musgrave, and J. Wiseman (eds.), *Public Production*. Vienna: Springer. (*Zeitschrift für Nationalökonomie/Journal of Economics*, Supplement 2.)

Gravelle, H. S. E. (1984), 'Bargaining and Efficiency in Public and Private Sector Firms', in M. Marchand, P. Pestieau, and H. Tulkens (eds.), *The Performance of Public Enterprises*. Amsterdam: North-Holland.

Green, R. (1990), 'Reshaping the CEGB: Electricity Privatisation in the UK', Department of Applied Economics, Cambridge.

Grimstone, G. (1988), 'The Financial Processes of Privatisation', in V. V. Ramanadham (ed.), *Privatisation in the UK*. London: Routledge.

Grinblatt, M., and **Hwang, C. Y.** (1989), 'Signalling and the Pricing of New Issues', *Journal of Finance*, 44: 393–420.

Grossman, S. J., and **Hart, O. D.** (1983), 'An Analysis of the Principal–Agent Problem', *Econometrica*, 51: 7–45.

Grout, P. A. (1987), 'The Wider Share Ownership Programme', *Fiscal Studies*, 8(3), 59–74.

— (1988), 'Employee Share Ownership and Privatisation: Some Theoretical Issues', *Economic Journal*, 98, Supplement, 97–104.

Guesnerie, R., and **Laffont, J.-J.** (1984), 'A Complete Solution to a Class of Principal–Agent Problems with an Application to the Control of a Self-Managed Firm', *Journal of Public Economics*, 25: 329–69.

Guski, H.-G. (1988), *Privatisierung in Großbritannien, Frankreich und USA*. Beiträge zur Wirtschafts- und Sozialpolitik 159, Institut der deutschen Wirtschaft. Cologne: Deutscher Institutsverlag.

Hagen, K. P. (1979), 'Optimal Pricing in Public Firms in an Imperfect Market Economy', *Scandinavian Journal of Economics*, 81: 475–93.

Harsanyi, J. C. (1956), 'Approaches to the Bargaining Problem Before and After the Theory of Games: A Critical Discussion of Zeuthen's, Hicks', and Nash's Theories', *Econometrica*, 24: 144-57.

— (1977), *Rational Behavior and Bargaining Equilibrium in Games and Social Situations*. Cambridge: Cambridge University Press.

Hayek, F. von (1960), *The Constitution of Liberty*. London: Routledge & Kegan Paul.

Heald, D. (1988), 'The United Kingdom: Privatisation and its Political Context', *West European Politics*, 11(4), 31–48.

— and **Steel, D. R.** (1981), 'The Privatisation of UK Public Enterprises', *Annals of Public and Co-operative Economy*, 52: 351–67.

— — (eds.) (1984), *Privatizing Public Enterprises: Options and Dilemmas*. London: Royal Institute of Public Administration.

Hellwig, M. (1986), 'The Optimal Linear Income Tax Revisited', *Journal of Public Economics*, 31: 163–79.

Helm, D. R. (1988a), 'A Regulatory Rule: RPI Minus X', in C. M. E. Whitehead (ed.), *Reshaping Nationalised Industries*. Berks: Policy Journals, Heritage.

— (1988b), 'Regulating the Electricity Supply Industry', in S. Estrin, and C. M. E. Whitehead (eds.), *Privatisation and the Nationalised Industries*. London: ST/ICERD, London School of Economics.

Hinds, M. (1990), 'Issues in the Introduction of Market Forces in Eastern European Socialist Economies', Internal Discussion Paper, Washington: The World Bank.

Holland, S. (1975), *The Socialist Challenge.* London: Quartet Books.

—— (1978), 'Planning Disagreements', in S. Holland (ed.), *Beyond Capitalist Planning.* Oxford: Basil Blackwell.

Holler, M. J. (1985), 'Strict Proportional Power in Voting Bodies', *Theory and Decision*, 19: 249–58.

Holmstrom, B., and **Milgrom, P.** (1987), 'Aggregation and Linearity in the Provision of Intertemporal Incentives', *Econometrica*, 55: 303–28.

Hotelling, H. (1938), 'The General Welfare in Relation to Problems of Taxation and of Railway and Utility Rates', *Econometrica*, 6: 242–69.

Howell, D. (1981), *Freedom and Capital: Prospects for the Property-Owning Democracy.* Oxford: Basil Blackwell.

Hyman, H. J. (1988), 'Preparing for Privatisation: The Financial Aspects', in V. V. Ramanadham (ed.), *Privatisation in the UK.* London: Routledge.

Jarrell, G. A., **Brickley, J. A.**, and **Netter, J. M.** (1988), 'The Market for Corporate Control: The Empirical Evidence Since 1980', *Journal of Economic Perspectives*, 2: 49–68.

Jensen, M. C. (1988), 'Takeovers: Their Causes and Consequences', *Journal of Economic Perspectives*, 2: 21–48.

—— and **Ruback, R. S.** (1983), 'The Market for Corporate Control: The Scientific Evidence', *Journal of Financial Economics*, 11: 5–50.

Jones, L., **Tandon, P.**, and **Vogelsang, I.** (1990), *Selling Public Enterprises: A Cost–Benefit Methodology.* Cambridge, Mass.: MIT Press.

Kay, J. A., **Mayer, C. P.**, and **Thompson, D. J.** (1986), *Privatisation and Regulation: The UK Experience.* Oxford: Clarendon Press.

—— and **Thompson, D. J.** (1986), 'Privatisation: A Policy in Search of a Rationale', *Economic Journal*, 96: 18–32.

Knauss, F. (1988a), 'Der Verlauf der Privatisierungsdiskussion im politischen Raum in den 70er und 80er Jahren', in H. Brede (ed.), *Privatisierung und die Zukunft der öffentlichen Wirtschaft.* Baden–Baden: Nomos Verlagsgesellschaft.

—— (1988b), 'Die Entscheidungen der Bundesregierung zur Privatisierung: Ein Sachstandsbericht', in H. Brede (ed.), *Privatisierung und die Zukunft der öffentlichen Wirtschaft.* Baden–Baden: Nomos Verlagsgesellschaft.

Kornai, J. (1990), *The Road to a Free Economy, Shifting from a Socialist System: The Example of Hungary.* New York: W. W. Norton.

Kreps, D. M., and **Scheinkman, J. A.** (1983), 'Quantity Precommitment and Bertrand Competition Yield Cournot Outcomes', *Bell Journal of Economics*, 14: 326–37.

Labour Party (1973), *Labour's State Holding Company*. Opposition Green Paper. London: Labour Party.

Laffont, J.-J., and **Tirole, J.** (1986), 'Using Cost Observation to Regulate Firms', *Journal of Political Economy*, 94: 614–41.

— — (1990a), 'The Regulation of Multiproduct Firms. Part I: Theory', *Journal of Public Economics*, 43: 1–36; 'Part II: Applications to Competitive Environments and Policy Analysis', *Journal of Public Economics*, 43: 37–66.

— — (1990b), 'Privatization and Incentives', mimeo, MIT, Cambridge, Mass.

Langohr, H. M., and **Viallet, C. J.** (1986), 'Compensation and Wealth Transfers in the French Nationalizations 1981–1982', *Journal of Financial Economics*, 17: 273–312.

Lawarree, J. (1986), 'Une Comparaison empirique des performances des secteurs privé et public: le cas des collectes d'immondices en Belgique. *Cahiers Économiques de Bruxelles*. First Trimester 109: 3–31.

LeGrand, J., and **Robinson, R.** (eds.) (1984), *Privatisation and the Welfare State*. London: Allen & Unwin.

Leibenstein, H. (1969), 'Organizational or Frictional Equilibria, X-Efficiency, and the Rate of Innovation', *Quarterly Journal of Economics*, 83: 600–23.

— (1976), *Beyond Economic Man*. Cambridge, Mass.: Harvard University Press.

— (1978), 'X-Inefficiency Xists — Reply to an Xorcist', *American Economic Review*, 68: 203–11.

Leray, C. (1983), 'L'Appréhension de l'efficacité dans les entreprises publiques industrielles et commerciales', *Revue Économique*, 34: 612–54.

Letwin, O. (1988), *Privatising the World*. London: Cassell.

Levis, M. (1990), 'The Winner's Curse Problem, Interest Costs and the Underpricing of Initial Public Offerings', *Economic Journal*, 100: 76–89.

Levitan, R., and **Shubik, M.** (1972), 'Price Duopoly and Capacity Constraints', *International Economic Review*, 13: 111–22.

Lewis, T. R., and **Sappington, D. E. M.** (1988), 'Regulating a Monopolist with Unknown Demand', *American Economic Review*, 78: 986–98.

— — (1989), 'Regulatory Options and Price-Cap Regulation', *Rand Journal of Economics*, 20: 405–16.

Lipsey, R. G., and **Lancaster, K.** (1956/7), 'The General Theory of Second Best', *Review of Economic Studies*, 24: 11–32.

Lipton, D., and **Sachs, J.** (1990), 'Creating a Market Economy in Eastern Europe: The Case of Poland', *Brookings Papers on Economic Activity*, i: 75–133.

Littlechild, S. C. (1979), 'Controlling the Nationalised Industries: Quis Custodiet Ipsos Custodes?' Series B Discussion Paper no. 56, University of Birmingham.

— (1983), *Regulation of British Telecommunications' Profitability*. London: HMSO.

— (1986), *Economic Regulation of Privatised Water Authorities*. London: HMSO.

— (1988), 'Economic Regulation of Privatised Water Authorities and Some Further Reflections', *Oxford Review of Economic Policy*, 4(2), 40–68.

Loeb, M., and **Magat, W.** (1979), 'A Decentralized Method for Utility Regulation', *Journal of Law and Economics*, 22: 399–404.

Loesch, A. von (1983), *Privatisierung öffentlicher Unternehmen: Ein Überblick über die Argumente (Schriftenreihe der Gesellschaft für öffentliche Wirtschaft und Gemeinwirtschaft, xxiii)*. Baden–Baden: Nomos Verlagsgesellschaft.

McCain, R. A. (1980), 'A Theory of Codetermination', *Zeitschrift für Nationalökonomie/Journal of Economics*, 40: 65–90.

McGuire, R. A., and **Ohsfeldt, R.** (1986), 'Public versus Private Water Delivery: A Critical Analysis of a Hedonic Cost Approach', *Public Finance Quarterly*, 14: 339–50.

Magenheim, E., and **Mueller, D. C.** (1987), 'On Measuring the Effect of Mergers on Acquiring Firm Shareholders', in J. Coffee (ed.), *Knights, Raiders, and Targets*. New York: Oxford University Press.

Malatesta, P. H. (1983), 'The Wealth Effect of Merger Activity and the Objective Functions of Merging Firms', *Journal of Financial Economics*, 11: 155–81.

Mandelker, G. (1974), 'Risk and Return: The Case of Merging Firms', *Journal of Financial Economics*, 1: 303–35.

Marchand, M., Pestieau, P., and **Tulkens, H.** (1984), 'The Performance of Public Enterprises: Normative, Positive and Empirical Issues', in M. Marchand, P. Pestieau, and H. Tulkens (eds.), *The Performance of Public Enterprises*. Amsterdam: North-Holland.

—, —, and **Weymark, J. A.** (1982), 'Discount Rates for Public Enterprises in the Presence of Alternative Financial Constraints', in D. Bös, R. A. Musgrave, and J. Wiseman (eds.), *Public Production*. Vienna: Springer. (*Zeitschrift für Nationalökonomie/Journal of Economics*, Supplement 2.)

Mathios, A. D., and **Rogers, R. P.** (1989), 'The Impact of Alternative Forms of State Regulation of AT&T on Direct-Dial, Long-Distance Telephone Rates', *Rand Journal of Economics*, 20: 437–53.

Mayer, C. P., and **Meadowcroft, S. A.** (1985), 'Selling Public Assets: Techniques and Financial Implications', *Fiscal Studies*, 6(4), 42–56. (Reprinted in J. A. Kay, C. P. Mayer, and D. J. Thompson (eds.), *Privatisation and Regulation: The UK Experience*. Oxford:

Clarendon Press, 1986.)

Merrill, W. C., and **Schneider, N.** (1966), 'Government Firms in Oligopoly Industries: A Short-Run Analysis', *Quarterly Journal of Economics*, 80: 400–12.

Milgrom, P., and **Roberts, J.** (1982), 'Limit Pricing and Entry under Incomplete Information: An Equilibrium Analysis', *Econometrica*, 50: 443–59.

Millward, R. (1982), 'The Comparative Performance of Public and Private Ownership', in Lord E. Roll (ed.), *The Mixed Economy*. London: Macmillan; New York: Holmes and Meier. (Reprinted in J. A. Kay, C. P. Mayer, and D. J. Thompson (eds.), *Privatisation and Regulation*. Oxford: Clarendon Press, 1986.)

— and **Parker, D. M.** (1983), 'Public and Private Enterprise: Comparative Behaviour and Relative Efficiency', in R. Millward, D. M. Parker, L. Rosenthal, M. T. Sumner, and T. Topham (eds.), *Public Sector Economics*. London: Longman.

Ministère de l'Economie, des Finances et de la Privatisation (1988), *Les Bleues notes*, 25–31 Jan. 1988, pp. 31, 33.

Mintz, J. M. (1980), 'Public–Private Mixed Enterprises: The Canadian Example', *Discussion Paper no. 325*, Queen's University, Department of Economics.

— (1982), 'Mixed Enterprises and Risk-Sharing in Industrial Development', in L. P. Jones (ed.), *Public Enterprises in Less-Developed Countries*. Cambridge: Cambridge University Press.

Mirrlees, J. (1971), 'An Exploration in the Theory of Optimum Income Taxation', *Review of Economic Studies*, 38: 175–208.

Murphy, K. J. (1985), 'Corporate Performance and Managerial Remuneration: An Empirical Analysis', *Journal of Accounting and Economics*, 7: 11–42.

Myers, S. C., and **Majluf, N. S.** (1984), 'Corporate Financing and Investment Decisions when Firms Have Information that Investors Do Not Have', *Journal of Financial Economics*, 13: 187–221.

Neu, W. (1988), 'A Theoretical Look at Price Capping Mechanisms: Some Clarifications and One Recommendation', mimeo, (Wissenschaftliches Institut für Kommunikationsdienste der Deutschen Bundespost), Bad Honnef.

Neumann, K.-H., and **Wieland, B.** (1986), 'Competition and Social Objectives: The Case of West German Telecommunications', *Telecommunications Policy*, 10: 121–31.

Newbould, G. D. (1970), *Management and Merger Activity*. Liverpool: Guttistead.

Ng, Y.-K. (1984), 'Quasi-Pareto Social Improvements', *American Economic Review*, 74: 1033–50.

Niskanen, W. A. (1971), *Bureaucracy and Representative Government*. Chicago: Aldine.

Oftel (1986), *Review of British Telecom's Tariff Changes.* A Report Issued by the Director-General of Telecommunications.

Olsen, M. (1974), 'On the Priority of Public Problems', in R. Marris (ed.), *The Corporate Society.* London: Macmillan.

Panik, M. J. (1976), *Classical Optimization: Foundations and Extensions.* Amsterdam: North-Holland.

Parker, D. M. (1985), 'Is the Private Sector More Efficient? A Study in the Public v. Private Debate', *Public Administration Bulletin,* August: 2–23.

Perelman, S., and **Pestieau, P.** (1988), 'Technical Performance in Public Enterprises: A Comparative Study of Railways and Postal Services', *European Economic Review,* 32: 432–41.

— and **Thiry, B.** (1989), *Productivity Studies of Public Transport Companies.* Special issue of *Annals of Public and Cooperative Economics,* 60(1).

Perry, M. K. (1989), 'Vertical Integration: Determinants and Effects', in R. Schmalensee and R. D. Willig (eds.), *Handbook of Industrial Organization, i.* Amsterdam: North-Holland.

Peters, W. (1988), 'Cost Inefficiency and Second Best Pricing', *European Journal of Political Economy,* 4: 29–45.

Pint, E. M. (1990), 'Nationalization and Privatization: A Rational-Choice Perspective on Efficiency', *Journal of Public Policy,* 10: 267–98.

— (1991), 'Nationalization vs. Regulation of Monopolies: The Effects of Ownership on Efficiency', *Journal of Public Economics,* 44: 131–64.

Pryke, R. (1981), *The Nationalised Industries: Policies and Performance since 1968.* Oxford: Martin Robertson.

— (1982), 'The Comparative Performance of Public and Private Enterprise', *Fiscal Studies,* 3(2). (Reprinted in J. A. Kay, C. P. Mayer, and D. J. Thompson (eds.), *Privatisation and Regulation: The UK Experience.* Oxford: Clarendon Press, 1986.)

Reder, M. W. (1975), 'The Theory of Employment and Wages in the Public Sector', in D. S. Hamermesh (ed.), *Labor in the Public and Nonprofit Sectors.* Princeton, NJ: Princeton University Press.

Rees, R. (1984a), 'The Public Enterprise Game', *Economic Journal,* 94, Supplement, 109–23.

— (1984b), 'A Positive Theory of the Public Enterprise', in M. Marchand, P. Pestieau, and H. Tulkens (eds.), *The Performance of Public Enterprises.* Amsterdam: North-Holland.

— (1988), 'Inefficiency, Public Enterprise and Privatisation', *European Economic Review,* 32: 422-31.

Reid, G. L., and **Allen, K.** (1970), *Nationalized Industries.* Harmondsworth: Penguin.

Rock, K. (1986), 'Why New Issues are Underpriced', *Journal of Financial Economics,* 15: 187–212.

Roemer, J. E., and **Silvestre, J.** (1989), 'A Welfare Comparison of Private and Public Monopoly', Working Paper no. 340, University of California, Davis.

Roth, A. E. (1979), *Axiomatic Models of Bargaining*, (Lecture Notes in Economics and Mathematical Systems, no. 170.) Berlin: Springer.

Rothschild, M., and **Stiglitz, J. E.** (1970), 'Increasing Risk: I, A Definition', *Journal of Economic Theory*, 2: 225–43.

Rubinstein, A. (1982), 'Perfect Equilibrium in a Bargaining Model', *Econometrica*, 50: 97–109.

Sappington, D. E. M., and **Stiglitz, J. E.** (1987), 'Privatization, Information and Incentives', *Journal of Policy Analysis and Management*, 6: 567–82.

Scherer, F. M. (1988), 'Corporate Takeovers: The Efficiency Arguments', *Journal of Economic Perspectives*, 2: 69–82.

Schmalensee, R. (1989), 'Good Regulatory Regimes', *Rand Journal of Economics*, 20: 417–36.

Schmidt, K. M. (1990), 'The Costs and Benefits of Privatization', Discussion Paper A–287, University of Bonn.

Schumpeter, J. A. (1949), *The Theory of Economic Development*, 3rd edn. of Eng. trans. Cambridge, Mass.: Harvard University Press.

Selten, R. (1975), 'Re-examination of the Perfectness Concept for Equilibrium Points in Extensive Games', *International Journal of Game Theory*, 4: 25–55.

Shapiro, C., and **Willig, R. D.** (1990), 'Economic Rationales for the Scope of Privatization', in E. N. Suleiman and J. Waterbury (eds.), *The Political Economy of Public Sector Reform and Privatization.* Boulder, Colorado: Westview Press.

Sharkey, W. W. (1982), *The Theory of Natural Monopoly.* Cambridge: Cambridge University Press.

Sheshinski, E. (1972), 'The Optimal Linear Income Tax', *Review of Economic Studies*, 39: 297–302.

— (1986), 'Positive Second-Best Theory', in K. J. Arrow and M. D. Intriligator (eds.), *Handbook of Mathematical Economics, iii.* Amsterdam: North-Holland.

Shleifer, A. (1985), 'A Theory of Yardstick Competition', *Rand Journal of Economics*, 16: 319–27.

— and **Vishny, R. W.** (1988), 'Value Maximization and the Acquisition Process', *Journal of Economic Perspectives*, 2: 7–20.

Singh, A. (1971), *Takeovers: Their Relevance to the Stock Market and the Theory of the Firm.* Cambridge: Cambridge University Press.

— (1975), 'Takeovers, Economic Natural Selection and the Theory of the Firm', *Economic Journal*, 85: 497–515.

Spann, R. M. (1977), 'Public versus Private Provision of Governmental Services', in T. E. Borcherding (ed.), *Budgets and Bureaucrats/The Sources of Government Growth.* Durham, NC: Duke

University Press.
Spulber, D. F. (1989), *Regulation and Markets*. Cambridge, Mass.:
MIT Press.
— and **Sengupta, S.** (1989), 'Vertical Integration, Technological Links
and Economies of Sequence', mimeo, Northwestern University.
Stein, J. C. (1988), 'Takeover Threats and Managerial Myopia', *Journal of Political Economy*, 96: 61–80.
Stigler, G. J. (1976), 'The Xistence of X-Efficiency', *American Economic Review*, 66: 213–16.
Stiglitz, J. E. (1974), 'Incentives and Risk Sharing in Sharecropping',
Review of Economic Studies, 41: 219–55.
Thiemeyer, T. (1986), 'Privatization: On the Many Senses in which
this Word is Used in an International Discussion on Economic Theory', in T. Thiemeyer and G. Quaden (eds.), *The Privatization of
Public Enterprises: A European Debate*. Liège: CIRIEC (*Annals of
Public and Co-operative Economy*, Special Issue).
— and **Quaden, G.** (eds.) (1986), *The Privatization of Public Enterprises: A European Debate*. Liège: CIRIEC (*Annals of Public and
Co-operative Economy*, Special Issue).
Thomas, C. (1988), 'Contracting-Out: Managerial Strategy or Political Dogma?' in V. V. Ramanadham (ed.), *Privatisation in the UK*.
London: Routledge.
Thomas, D. (1984), 'The Union Response to Denationalisation', in
D. R. Steel and D. A. Heald (eds.), *Privatizing Public Enterprises*.
London: Royal Institute of Public Administration. (Reprinted in
J. A. Kay, C. P. Mayer, and D. J. Thompson (eds.), *Privatisation and
Regulation: The UK Experience*. Oxford: Clarendon Press, 1986.)
Tinbergen, J. (1967), *Economic Policy: Principles and Design*. 4th
edn. Amsterdam: North-Holland.
Tivey, L. (1966), *Nationalization in British Industry*. London: Jonathan Cape.
Tulkens, H. (1986a), 'The Performance Approach in Public Enterprise
Economics: An Introduction and an Example', *Annals of Public and
Co-operative Economy*, 74: 429–43.
— (1986b), 'La Performance productive d'un service public: définitions,
méthodes de mesure et application à la régie des postes en Belgique',
L'Actualité Économique, Revue d'Analyse Économique, 62: 306–35.
Varian, H. R. (1984), *Microeconomic Analysis*, 2nd edn. New York:
W. W. Norton.
— (1988), 'Symposium on Takeovers', *Journal of Economic Perspectives*, 2: 3–5.
Viallet, C. J. (1982), 'A Note on the Impact of Ownership Structure on
Risk and Return: The Case of Mixed Firms', Working Paper, Insead,
Paris.
Vickers, J., and **Yarrow, G.** (1985), *Privatization and the Natural*

Monopolies. London: Public Policy Centre.

Vickers, J., and **Yarrow, G.** (1988a), *Privatization – An Economic Analysis.* Cambridge, Mass.: MIT Press.

— — (1988b), 'Regulation of Privatised Firms in Britain', *European Economic Review*, 32: 465–72.

Vogelsang, I. (1988), 'Deregulation and Privatization in Germany', *Journal of Public Policy*, 8: 195–212.

— (1989), 'Price Cap Regulation of Telecommunications Services: A Long-Run Approach', in M. Crew (ed.), *Deregulation and Diversification of Utilities.* Boston: Kluwer.

— (1990), *Public Enterprise in Monopolistic and Oligopolistic Markets. (Fundamentals of Pure and Applied Economics*, xxxvi.) Chur, Switzerland: Harwood.

— and **Finsinger, J.** (1979), 'A Regulatory Adjustment Process for Optimal Pricing by Multiproduct Monopoly Firms', *Bell Journal of Economics*, 10: 157–71.

Walsh, A. H. (1978), *The Public's Business.* Cambridge, Mass.: MIT Press.

Ware, R. (1986), 'A Model of Public Enterprise with Entry', *Canadian Journal of Economics*, 19: 642–55.

Waterson, M. (1984), *Economic Theory of the Industry.* Cambridge: Cambridge University Press.

Welch, I. (1989), 'Seasoned Offerings, Imitation Costs, and the Underpricing of Initial Public Offerings', *Journal of Finance*, 44: 421–49.

Whitehead, C. M. E. (ed.) (1988), *Reshaping Nationalised Industries.* Berks: Policy Journals, Heritage.

White Paper (1991), *Competition and Choice: Telecommunications Policy for the 1990s.* Cm 1461. London: HMSO.

Williamson, O. E. (1975), *Markets and Hierarchies: Analysis and Antitrust Implications.* New York: Free Press.

Windisch, R. (1987), 'Privatisierung natürlicher Monopole: Theoretische Grundlagen und Kriterien', in R. Windisch (ed.), *Privatisierung natürlicher Monopole im Bereich von Bahn, Post und Telekommunikation.* Tübingen: Mohr.

Wright, M., Thompson, R. S., and **Robbie, K.** (1989), 'Privatisation via Management and Employee Buyouts: Analysis and UK Experience', *Annals of Public and Cooperative Economics*, 60: 399–429.

Yarrow, G. (1985), 'Strategic Issues in Industrial Policy', *Oxford Review of Economic Policy*, 1(3): 95–109.

— (1986), 'Privatization in Theory and Practice', *Economic Policy*, 1: 324–77.

Zeuthen, F. (1930), *Problems of Monopoly and Economic Warfare.* London: Routledge.

Author Index

Subject Index

230–5, 246–7, 252
of a monopoly 8–9, 34, 42–5,
   66–9, 85, 91, 124–34,
   135–48, 221, 246–7
of an oligopoly 76–8, 80–3,
   177, 178, 192–201, 211–15
price cap 8–9, 61, 66–9, 77,
   81, 85, 91, 124–34, 139–40,
   142–4, 147–8, 164–5, 174,
   177, 178, 192–201, 211–15,
   246–7
rate-of-return 8, 65–9, 85,
   124
yardstick 34, 62, 80–3
renationalization 4, 25
resale option 5
retail price index, *see* index
returns:
   on capital 8, 11, 32, 57, 65–9,
     85, 124, 160, 167
   to control 46, 49
   to cost reduction 34–5, 69,
     81–2
   to scale 8, 13, 20, 63, 68, 69,
     70, 71, 77, 80, 89, 118,
     121–2, 125, 221, 228, 247,
     253, 255–75
revenues (public)
   from dividends 15, 16, 30,
     135, 149–76, 220, 238–40,
     261–2, 275–6, 281–2
   from selling shares 15, 16, 30,
     53–4, 61, 135, 149–76, 220,
     238–40, 261–2, 275–6,
     281–2
   see also issue price,
     public debt, taxation
revenue-cost constraint 61, 63,
   71, 73, 91, 107, 108–14,
   118–22, 131, 149–76, 221–3,
   232, 234, 238–40, 242, 244,
   253, 262, 276, 280–2
revenue maximization 64, 108–9
Rolls Royce 24
RPI–X 9, 61, 66–9, 91,

124–34, 139, 164–5
reward, *see* income,
   principal–agent relationships
risk-averse agents 20, 23, 29, 98,
   103, 104, 115
risk-loving agents 103
risk-neutral agent 20, 27, 28, 97,
   103, 104, 115–16, 122, 123,
   146

sales maximization 109
Scandinavia 1
separation of production units
   79–85
shareholders 2, 11
   foreign 3
   institutional 4
   lower-income 4, 5, 11, 12,
     24–6, 266–70
   see also employee shares,
     issue price, objectives,
     people's capitalism
shares, *see* employee shares,
   issue price, market value of
   the firm, people's capitalism
signalling 79
Social Democrats 1, 5, 6, 13–14
socialists 3, 5, 6, 79
Soviet Union 7
Spain 138
stabilization 7, 14–15
Stackelberg 156–7, 236, 282
   capacity 192
   duopoly 72–3, 200
   solution 156–7
steel industry 14
St. Gobain 5
stock market 1, 4–5, 8, 11, 23,
   24, 26, 53–6
strategic behavior, *see* bidding,
   over- and underbidding
   (market entry)
subsidies:
   for the consumers 12, 221,
     238, 239–40, 263, 267–8, 280

subsidies (*cont.*):
  for the firm 7
substitutes 7, 63,
  77, 78, 223, 278
surplus, *see* consumer surplus,
  costs, revenue, revenue-cost
  constraint
sustainability 8–9, 69–70, 84,
  191–2, 197–8, 200
Sweden 1

takeover 3, 28, 58–60, 79
takeover threats 58–60
taxation:
  of capital gains 237, 238–40
  of capital income 31–2, 237,
    238–40
  of income 12–13, 100, 237,
    238–40, 280–4
  lump-sum 81, 221, 222, 237,
    238–40, 267–70
  pressure of 16, 149, 152, 220,
    224, 281–2
  of wage income 31–2, 238–40,
    280–4
technocrats 10, 33, 47, 48, 50
technology, *see* costs,
  efficiency, management
technological efficiency,
  see X-inefficiency
telecommunications 1, 4–5, 9,
  22, 24, 27, 29, 53, 66, 67, 68,
  78, 79, 83, 84, 124, 126, 127,
  154, 177, 178, 180, 193
Telesat Canada 52
tender offer 19, 22, 23–4, 54
trade union 2, 3, 11, 65, 74–5,
  79, 89, 91, 149–76
transfer, *see* income, subsidies
transition from public to private
  ownership 36–42, 42–5, 45–50,
  53–4, 56–7, 61–85, 91, 135
  see also privatization
transportation 10, 21, 52, 64, 70,
  79–80, 90, 109, 115, 154, 222

Treuhandanstalt (Germany)
  42
Trustee Savings Bank 4, 24

UK 1, 3, 4, 5, 6, 9, 10, 21, 22,
  23, 24, 25, 26, 27, 29, 30, 51,
  53, 57, 64, 66–9, 79, 80, 83,
  91, 105, 109, 117, 124, 126,
  127, 139, 154, 177, 180, 192,
  193, 246
underpricing 4, 11, 15, 23, 24–6,
  26–30, 54, 151–2, 158–62,
  163, 166, 171, 172–3, 237–8,
  265–6, 272–4, 278–9, 284
undersubscription 22, 23
underwriter 19, 23, 26–30, 54
unnatural monopoly 76
USA 9, 10, 51, 52, 57, 58, 60,
  66, 83, 192
utility:
  of the consumers 13, 63, 90,
    129, 226, 240, 242, 250,
    262–3, 266–70, 276–8,
    280, 282–3
  of the government 149–76
  of the management of the
    private firm 38–42, 45–50,
    94, 96–7, 99, 100–4
  of the management of the
    public firm 38–42, 45–50,
    94, 95–6, 99, 104–23
  of the trade union 149–76

value of the firm, *see*
  market value of the firm
VEBA 53
vertical integration 83–5
vertical separation 62, 83–5
viable-firm Ramsey solution 71
viable-industry Ramsey
  solution 71
VŒSt 7
Vogelsang–Finsinger mechanism 114
Volkswagen 6, 53, 57
voters 25, 64, 90–1, 115–16, 154

voting rights in shareholders'
  meetings 136, 150, 233

wage 3, 10–11, 30–2, 58, 73–4, 79,
  128, 150, 163, 168–9, 173–4,
  176, 225, 238–40, 280–4
welfare 16, 62, 90–1
  function 13, 63, 71, 90,
    129–31, 231, 240, 242,
    249–52, 262–3, 266–8,
    276–8, 282–3
  loss 12–13, 78, 81
  maximization 20, 34–5, 35–42,
    42–5, 63, 66–7, 71–8, 81,
    95–6, 98, 104–23, 135–48,
    217–84
  weights 13, 37, 40–1, 63,

  129–31, 240, 250–2, 266–70
  see also consumer surplus
West Germany 1, 3, 4, 5, 6, 42,
  53, 54, 57, 79, 104, 137, 138,
  239
winner's curse 28

X-inefficiency 1, 7, 8, 10,
  33–60, 62, 93–123, 135–48,
  154–5, 163, 173–4, 227–30
  definition 47, 95–6, 228

yardstick regulation 34, 62,
  80–3

zero profit constraint, *see*
  revenue-cost constraint